Policing and Crime Act 2017

CHAPTER 3

Explanatory Notes are available separately

GRAN*GIS* UK Publishing

Adapted and Published by GRANGIS (Grand Register Library).
Online: www.grangis.com.
E-mail: contact@grangis.com.

In this version:
ISBN: 979-8-88559-096-9

Note: Title, sub-title and version of this publication is as described. For the most recent information please visit www.gov.uk.

Policing and Crime Act 2017

CHAPTER 3

POLICING AND CRIME ACT 2017

PART 1

EMERGENCY SERVICES COLLABORATION

CHAPTER 1

COLLABORATION AGREEMENTS

CHAPTER 2

POLICE AND CRIME COMMISSIONERS ETC: FIRE AND RESCUE FUNCTIONS

CHAPTER 3

LONDON FIRE COMMISSIONER

CHAPTER 4

INSPECTION OF FIRE AND RESCUE SERVICES

PART 2

POLICE COMPLAINTS, DISCIPLINE AND INSPECTION

CHAPTER 1

POLICE COMPLAINTS

CHAPTER 2

POLICE SUPER-COMPLAINTS

CHAPTER 3

WHISTLE-BLOWING: POWER OF IPCC TO INVESTIGATE

CHAPTER 4

POLICE DISCIPLINE

CHAPTER 5

IPCC: RE-NAMING AND ORGANISATIONAL CHANGE

CHAPTER 6

INSPECTION

PART 3

POLICE WORKFORCE AND REPRESENTATIVE INSTITUTIONS

CHAPTER 1

POLICE WORKFORCE

Powers of police civilian staff and volunteers

Removal of powers of police to appoint traffic wardens

Police rank structure

CHAPTER 2

REPRESENTATIVE INSTITUTIONS

PART 4

POLICE POWERS

CHAPTER 1

PRE-CHARGE BAIL

Release without bail or on bail

Conditions of bail

Time limits on period of bail

Re-arrest of person released under provisions of PACE

Notification of decision not to prosecute

Breach of pre-charge bail conditions relating to travel

CHAPTER 2

RETENTION OF BIOMETRIC MATERIAL

CHAPTER 3

POWERS UNDER PACE: MISCELLANEOUS

CHAPTER 4

POWERS UNDER THE MENTAL HEALTH ACT 1983

CHAPTER 5

MARITIME ENFORCEMENT: ENGLISH AND WELSH OFFENCES

Application of maritime enforcement powers: general

Ships in Scotland waters: hot pursuit

The maritime enforcement powers

Supplementary provision

CHAPTER 8

CROSS-BORDER ENFORCEMENT

CHAPTER 9

MISCELLANEOUS

PART 5

POLICE AND CRIME COMMISSIONERS AND POLICE AREAS

Deputy PCCs etc: terms and eligibility

Names of police areas

PART 6

FIREARMS AND PYROTECHNIC ARTICLES

Firearms

Pyrotechnic articles

PART 7

ALCOHOL AND LATE NIGHT REFRESHMENT

Licensing

Police collaboration

NCA powers

Requirements to confirm nationality

Seizure etc of travel documents

Pardons for certain abolished offences etc

Forced marriage: anonymity for victims

Stalking

Protection of children and vulnerable adults

Coroners' investigations into deaths

Policing and Crime Act 2017

2017 CHAPTER 3

An Act to make provision for collaboration between the emergency services; to make provision about the handling of police complaints and other matters relating to police conduct and to make further provision about the Independent Police Complaints Commission; to make provision for super-complaints about policing; to make provision for the investigation of concerns about policing raised by whistle-blowers; to make provision about police discipline; to make provision about police inspection; to make provision about the powers of police civilian staff and police volunteers; to remove the powers of the police to appoint traffic wardens; to enable provision to be made to alter police ranks; to make provision about the Police Federation; to make provision in connection with the replacement of the Association of Chief Police Officers with the National Police Chiefs' Council; to make provision about the system for bail after arrest but before charge; to make provision about the retention of biometric material; to make provision to enable greater use of modern technology at police stations; to make other amendments to the Police and Criminal Evidence Act 1984; to amend the powers of the police under the Mental Health Act 1983; to extend the powers of the police in relation to maritime enforcement; to make provision for cross-border enforcement; to make provision about the powers of the police to require removal of disguises; to make provision about deputy police and crime commissioners and the Deputy Mayor for Policing and Crime; to make provision to enable changes to the names of police areas; to make provision about the regulation of firearms and pyrotechnic articles; to make provision about the licensing of alcohol; to make provision about the implementation and enforcement of financial sanctions; to amend the Police Act 1996 to make further provision about police collaboration; to make provision about the powers of the National Crime Agency; to make provision for requiring arrested persons to provide details of nationality; to make provision for requiring defendants in criminal proceedings to provide details of nationality and other information; to make provision about the seizure etc of invalid travel documents; to make provision for pardons for convictions etc for certain abolished offences; to make provision to protect the anonymity of victims of forced marriage; to increase the maximum sentences of imprisonment for certain offences of putting people in fear of violence etc; to make provision to combat the sexual exploitation of children and to protect children and vulnerable adults from harm; to make provision about coroners' duties in respect of deaths in state detention; to make provision about the powers of litter authorities in Scotland; and for connected purposes. [31st January 2017]

BE IT ENACTED by the Queen's most Excellent Majesty, by and with the advice and consent of the Lords Spiritual and Temporal, and Commons, in this present Parliament assembled, and by the authority of the same, as follows:—

PART 1

EMERGENCY SERVICES COLLABORATION

CHAPTER 1

COLLABORATION AGREEMENTS

1 Collaboration agreements

(1) A collaboration agreement may be made by—

(a) one or more persons within a paragraph of subsection (2), and

(b) one or more persons within another paragraph of that subsection.

(2) Those persons are—

(a) an ambulance trust in England,

(b) a fire and rescue body in England, and

(c) a police body in England.

(3) A collaboration agreement is an agreement in writing that sets out how the parties to the agreement will work together in discharging their functions.

(4) Subsection (1) does not prevent a person other than a person listed in subsection (2) from being a party to a collaboration agreement.

(5) This section is subject to section 3 (collaboration agreements: specific restrictions).

(6) Section 4 makes further provision about collaboration agreements.

2 Duties in relation to collaboration agreements

(1) A relevant emergency service in England ("the relevant service") must keep under consideration whether entering into a collaboration agreement with one or more other relevant emergency services in England could be in the interests of the efficiency or effectiveness of that service and those other services.

(2) If the relevant service considers that entering into a collaboration agreement with one or more other relevant emergency services in England could be in the interests of the efficiency or effectiveness of that service and those other services ("the proposed

collaboration"), the relevant service must notify those other services of the proposed collaboration.

(3) The relevant service and the other services ("the proposed parties") must consider whether the proposed collaboration would be in the interests of the efficiency or effectiveness of the proposed parties.

(4) Subsection (5) applies if—

(a) a proposed party is of the view that the proposed collaboration would be in the interests of its efficiency or effectiveness (if it were to give effect to the proposed collaboration, or to give effect to it so far as it relates to that party), and

(b) at least one other proposed party is of the view that the proposed collaboration would be in the interests of its efficiency or effectiveness (if it were to give effect to the proposed collaboration, or to give effect to it so far as it relates to that party).

(5) Each proposed party which is of that view must give effect to the proposed collaboration, or give effect to it so far as it relates to that party, by entering into a collaboration agreement (if the party has power to do so).

(6) In the application of this section to a local policing body, references to the efficiency or effectiveness of that body include the efficiency or effectiveness of the police force it is responsible for maintaining.

(7) This section is subject to section 3 (collaboration agreements: specific restrictions).

3 Collaboration agreements: specific restrictions

(1) Section 2 does not require a relevant emergency service in England to enter into a collaboration agreement if the service is of the view that the proposed collaboration would have an adverse effect on public safety or otherwise have an adverse effect on its efficiency or effectiveness.

(2) Section 2 does not require an ambulance trust in England to enter into a collaboration agreement that would in the view of that trust have an adverse effect on—

(a) its ability to exercise any of its functions other than its functions of providing an emergency ambulance service, or

(b) the health service in England (within the meaning of the National Health Service Act 2006).

(3) Section 2 applies to an ambulance trust in England only so far as it provides an emergency ambulance service.

(4) Subsection (5) applies where an ambulance trust in England is considering whether a proposed collaboration would be in the interests of the efficiency or effectiveness of the trust for the purposes of section 2.

(5) The ambulance trust must have particular regard to any effect that entering into a collaboration agreement pursuant to the proposed collaboration would have on—

(a) its ability to exercise any of its functions other than its functions of providing an emergency ambulance service, and

(b) the health service in England (within the meaning of the National Health Service Act 2006).

(6) The London Fire Commissioner must consult the Mayor of London before entering into a collaboration agreement (unless the Mayor is a party to the agreement).

(7) A combined authority that exercises the functions of a fire and rescue authority by virtue of section 105 or 105A of the Local Democracy, Economic Development and Construction Act 2009 may only enter into a collaboration agreement where the functions of the authority to which the agreement relates are functions of a fire and rescue authority that the combined authority is entitled to exercise.

(8) An elected mayor who exercises the functions of a fire and rescue authority by virtue of section 107D of the Local Democracy, Economic Development and Construction Act 2009 may only enter into a collaboration agreement where the functions of the mayor to which the agreement relates are functions of a fire and rescue authority that the mayor is entitled to exercise.

(9) An elected mayor who exercises the functions of a police and crime commissioner by virtue of section 107F of the Local Democracy, Economic Development and Construction Act 2009 may only enter into a collaboration agreement where the functions of the mayor to which the agreement relates are functions of a police and crime commissioner that the mayor is entitled to exercise.

(10) A chief officer of police of a police force may not enter into a collaboration agreement unless the local policing body responsible for maintaining that police force also enters into the agreement.

(11) A local policing body must consult the chief officer of police of the police force which the body is responsible for maintaining before entering into a collaboration agreement (unless that chief officer is a party to the agreement).

4 Collaboration agreements: supplementary

(1) A collaboration agreement may, in particular, make provision about the use, for the purposes of the agreement, of a power of a party to the agreement to—

(a) make arrangements for the exercise of the party's functions by another person, or

(b) exercise functions jointly with another person.

(2) A collaboration agreement may include provision for payments to be made by the parties to the agreement for the purposes of facilitating that agreement.

(3) A party to a collaboration agreement may do anything that is necessary or expedient for the purposes of facilitating the agreement.

(4) Subsection (3) is subject to any restriction imposed on a party by, or by virtue of, an enactment or rule of law.

(5) A collaboration agreement may not include provision for the delegation of a function where that function may not otherwise be delegated.

(6) The delegation of a function pursuant to a collaboration agreement does not affect the responsibility of any party to the agreement for the exercise of its functions.

(7) A collaboration agreement must make provision for a party to withdraw from the agreement where in the view of that party the agreement is no longer in the interests of its efficiency or effectiveness.

(8) A collaboration agreement may be—
(a) varied with the agreement of all of the parties to the agreement, or
(b) replaced by a subsequent collaboration agreement.

5 Collaboration agreements: definitions

(1) This section has effect for the purposes of this Chapter.

(2) "Collaboration agreement" has the meaning given by section 1(3).

(3) "Relevant emergency service in England" means—
(a) an ambulance trust in England,
(b) a fire and rescue body in England, or
(c) a police body in England.

(4) "Ambulance trust in England" means—
(a) an NHS trust all or most of whose hospitals, establishments and facilities are in England and which provides ambulance services, or
(b) an NHS foundation trust which provides such services.

(5) "Fire and rescue body in England" means—
(a) a fire and rescue authority in England,
(b) a combined authority that exercises the functions of a fire and rescue authority by virtue of section 105 or 105A of the Local Democracy, Economic Development and Construction Act 2009, or
(c) an elected mayor who exercises the functions of a fire and rescue authority by virtue of section 107D of that Act.

(6) "Fire and rescue authority in England" has the same meaning as in the Fire and Rescue Services Act 2004.

(7) "Police body in England" means—
(a) a police and crime commissioner for a police area in England,
(b) a chief constable of a police force for a police area in England (see Schedule 1 to the Police Act 1996),
(c) the Mayor's Office for Policing and Crime,
(d) the Commissioner of Police of the Metropolis,
(e) the Common Council of the City of London in its capacity as police authority for the City of London police area,
(f) the Commissioner of Police for the City of London, or
(g) an elected mayor who exercises the functions of a police and crime commissioner by virtue of section 107F of the Local Democracy, Economic Development and Construction Act 2009.

(8) "Chief officer" means—
(a) a chief constable of a police force for a police area in England (see Schedule 1 to the Police Act 1996),
(b) the Commissioner of Police of the Metropolis, or
(c) the Commissioner of Police for the City of London.

(9) "Local policing body" means—

(a) a police and crime commissioner for a police area in England,
(b) the Mayor's Office for Policing and Crime,
(c) the Common Council of the City of London in its capacity as police authority for the City of London police area, or
(d) an elected mayor who exercises the functions of a police and crime commissioner by virtue of section 107F of the Local Democracy, Economic Development and Construction Act 2009.

(10) "The City of London police area" means the City of London as defined for the purposes of the Acts relating to the City of London police force.

CHAPTER 2

POLICE AND CRIME COMMISSIONERS ETC: FIRE AND RESCUE FUNCTIONS

6 Provision for police and crime commissioner to be fire and rescue authority

Schedule 1 makes provision for a person who is the police and crime commissioner for an area to be the fire and rescue authority for that area.

7 Involvement of police and crime commissioner in fire and rescue authority

(1) The Local Government Act 1972 is amended in accordance with subsections (2) to (4).

(2) In section 102 (appointment of committees) after subsection (5) insert—

"(6) Subsection (7) applies in relation to—
(a) a committee or sub-committee appointed by a local authority in England wholly or partly for the purposes of discharging functions of a fire and rescue authority,
(b) a joint committee appointed by two or more local authorities in England wholly or partly for the purposes of discharging such functions, or
(c) a sub-committee appointed by any such committee or joint committee wholly or partly for the purposes of discharging such functions.

(7) A relevant police and crime commissioner may only be appointed to a committee or sub-committee to which this subsection applies in response to a request made by the commissioner to the appointing authority or authorities or, in the case of a sub-committee, to the appointing committee.

(8) If a request under subsection (7) is made to an appointing authority or authorities or an appointing committee, they must—
(a) consider the request,
(b) give reasons for their decision to agree to or refuse the request, and
(c) publish those reasons in such manner as they think appropriate.

(9) A relevant police and crime commissioner may attend, speak at and vote at a meeting of a committee to which the commissioner is appointed in accordance with this section only if and to the extent that the business of the meeting relates to the functions of a fire and rescue authority.

(10) Subsection (11) defines "relevant police and crime commissioner" for the purposes of this section in relation to—

(a) a committee or sub-committee appointed by a local authority,

(b) a joint committee appointed by two or more local authorities, or

(c) a sub-committee appointed by a committee of a local authority or a joint committee of two or more local authorities.

(11) For those purposes "relevant police and crime commissioner" means a police and crime commissioner—

(a) whose area is the same as, or contains all of, the area of that local authority or (as the case may be) one or more of those local authorities, or

(b) all or part of whose area falls within the area of that local authority or (as the case may be) one or more of those local authorities."

(3) In Part 1 of Schedule 12 (meetings and proceedings of principal councils) after paragraph 6 insert—

"6ZA (1) A relevant police and crime commissioner may attend, speak at and vote at a meeting of a principal council in England which is a fire and rescue authority.

(2) Sub-paragraph (1) applies—

(a) only if and to the extent that the business of the meeting relates to the functions of the principal council as a fire and rescue authority, and

(b) only if the council have consented to the participation of the relevant police and crime commissioner in such meetings in response to a request by the commissioner to do so.

(3) If a request under sub-paragraph (2)(b) is made to a principal council, the council must—

(a) consider the request,

(b) give reasons for their decision to agree to or refuse the request, and

(c) publish those reasons in such manner as they think appropriate.

(4) If the principal council agree to the request, the relevant police and crime commissioner is to be treated as a member of the council for the purposes of the following provisions of this Schedule in the case of a meeting which relates to the functions of the council as a fire and rescue authority—

(a) paragraph 3(2);

(b) paragraph 4(1A);

(c) paragraph 5(3);

(d) paragraph 6;

(e) paragraph 39;

(f) paragraph 40;

(g) paragraph 41(3);

(h) paragraph 43.

(5) In this paragraph "relevant police and crime commissioner", in relation to a principal council, means a police and crime commissioner—

(a) whose area is the same as, or contains all of, the area of the principal council, or

(b) all or part of whose area falls within the area of the principal council."

(4) In Part 1A of Schedule 12 (joint authorities etc) in paragraph 6B (application of Part 1) after "this Schedule" insert "other than paragraph 6ZA".

(5) The Local Government Act 1985 is amended in accordance with subsections (6) and (7).

(6) In section 26 (metropolitan county fire and rescue authorities)—

(a) in subsection (3) for "Each" substitute "Subject to subsection (5), each", and

(b) after subsection (4) insert—

"(5) A metropolitan county fire and rescue authority may appoint a relevant police and crime commissioner to be a member of the authority.

(6) An appointment under subsection (5) may only be made in response to a request by the relevant police and crime commissioner.

(7) If a request under subsection (6) is made to a metropolitan county fire and rescue authority, the authority must—

(a) consider the request,

(b) give reasons for their decision to agree to or refuse the request, and

(c) publish those reasons in such manner as they think appropriate.

(8) In this section "relevant police and crime commissioner", in relation to a metropolitan county fire and rescue authority, means a police and crime commissioner—

(a) whose area is the same as, or contains all of, the area of the authority, or

(b) all or part of whose area falls within the area of the authority."

(7) In section 34 (chairman, vice-chairman and clerk of metropolitan county fire and rescue authority) in subsection (7) for the "and" at the end of paragraph (b) substitute—

"(ba) if the chairman is a police and crime commissioner and the authority and the commissioner have agreed that the commissioner should cease to be a member of the authority, the date agreed by the authority and the commissioner as the date on which the commissioner's membership should cease; and".

(8) In section 13 of the Local Government and Housing Act 1989 (voting rights of members of certain committees) after subsection (5) insert—

"(5ZA) Nothing in this section shall prevent the appointment of a police and crime commissioner as a voting member of—

(a) any committee or sub-committee appointed by a local authority in England wholly or partly for the purposes of discharging functions of a fire and rescue authority,

(b) any joint committee appointed by two or more local authorities in England wholly or partly for the purposes of discharging such functions, or

(c) any sub-committee appointed by any such committee or joint committee wholly or partly for the purposes of discharging such functions.

(5ZB) In subsection (5ZA) "local authority" does not include—

(a) a fire and rescue authority constituted by a scheme under section 2 of the Fire and Rescue Services Act 2004 or a scheme to which section 4 of that Act applies,

(b) a joint authority which is a metropolitan county fire and rescue authority, or

(c) the London Fire Commissioner."

(9) In Schedule A1 to the Local Government Act 2000 (executive arrangements in England: further provisions) after paragraph 4 insert—

"4A Attendance of police and crime commissioner at meetings

4A (1) A relevant police and crime commissioner may attend, speak at and vote at—

(a) a meeting of an executive of a local authority which is a fire and rescue authority, or

(b) a meeting of a committee of such an executive.

(2) Sub-paragraph (1) applies—

(a) only if and to the extent that the business of the meeting relates to the functions of the authority as a fire and rescue authority, and

(b) only if the executive has consented to the participation of the relevant police and crime commissioner in such meetings in response to a request by the commissioner to do so.

(3) If a request under sub-paragraph (2)(b) is made to an executive of a local authority, the executive must—

(a) consider the request,

(b) give reasons for its decision to agree to or refuse the request, and

(c) publish those reasons in such manner as it thinks appropriate.

(4) In this paragraph "relevant police and crime commissioner" means a police and crime commissioner—

(a) whose area is the same as, or contains all of, the area of the local authority, or

(b) all or part of whose area falls within the area of the local authority."

(10) Section 3 of the Fire and Rescue Services Act 2004 (creation of combined fire and rescue authority: supplementary) is amended in accordance with subsections (11) and (12).

(11) In subsection (3)(a) for "or by the Secretary of State" substitute ", by the Secretary of State or, in the case of a combined authority for an area which is wholly within England, by the combined authority".

(12) After subsection (5) insert—

"(6) The following provisions apply if a scheme under section 2 provides for members of a combined authority to be appointed by the authority.

(7) The scheme must provide that a relevant police and crime commissioner may only be appointed as a member of the authority in response to a request by the commissioner.

(8) The scheme must provide that, if such a request is made to the authority, the authority must—

(a) consider the request,

(b) give reasons for its decision to agree to or refuse the request, and

(c) publish those reasons in such manner as it thinks appropriate.

(9) In this section "relevant police and crime commissioner", in relation to a combined authority, means a police and crime commissioner—

(a) whose area is the same as, or contains all of, the area of the authority, or

(b) all or part of whose area falls within the area of the authority."

(13) The Localism Act 2011 is amended in accordance with subsections (14) and (15).

(14) In section 27 (duty to promote and maintain high standards of conduct) after subsection (4) insert—

"(4A) In this Chapter "co-opted member" includes a police and crime commissioner who—

(a) is entitled to participate in meetings of a county or district council by virtue of paragraph 6ZA of Part 1 of Schedule 12 to the Local Government Act 1972, or

(b) is entitled to participate in meetings of an executive of a county or district council by virtue of paragraph 4A of Schedule A1 to the Local Government Act 2000."

(15) In section 28 (codes of conduct) after subsection (11) insert—

"(11A) Subsections (11B) to (11D) apply if a police and crime commissioner is a member or co-opted member of a relevant authority in the commissioner's capacity as such.

(11B) Arrangements put in place under subsection (6)(b) by the relevant authority must include provision for an allegation against the commissioner to be referred to the police and crime panel for the commissioner's police area.

(11C) If, in response to an allegation referred to it by virtue of subsection (11B), the police and crime panel makes a report or recommendation to the police and crime commissioner under section 28(6) of the Police Reform and Social Responsibility Act 2011, the panel may also make a report or recommendation on the allegation to the relevant authority.

(11D) The relevant authority must take any such report or recommendation into account in determining—

(a) whether the police and crime commissioner has failed to comply with the authority's code of conduct,

(b) whether to take action in relation to the commissioner, and
(c) what action to take.”

8 Combined authority mayors: exercise of fire and rescue functions

(1) The Local Democracy, Economic Development and Construction Act 2009 is amended in accordance with subsections (2) to (4).

(2) After section 107E insert—

“107EA Exercise of fire and rescue functions

(1) This section applies to a mayor for the area of a combined authority who—
(a) by virtue of section 107D(1), may exercise functions which are conferred on a fire and rescue authority in that name (“fire and rescue functions”), and
(b) by virtue of section 107F(1), may exercise functions of a police and crime commissioner.

(2) The Secretary of State may by order make provision—
(a) authorising the mayor to arrange for the chief constable of the police force for the police area which corresponds to the area of the combined authority to exercise fire and rescue functions exercisable by the mayor;
(b) authorising that chief constable to arrange for a person within subsection (4) to exercise the chief constable’s fire and rescue functions.

(3) An order under subsection (2) may provide that arrangements made under the order—
(a) may authorise the exercise of any functions mentioned in that subsection;
(b) may authorise the exercise of any functions mentioned in that subsection other than those specified or described in the order;
(c) may authorise the exercise of such of the functions mentioned in that subsection as are specified or described in the order.

(4) The persons mentioned in subsection (2)(b) are—
(a) members of the chief constable’s police force;
(b) the civilian staff of that police force, as defined by section 102(4) of the Police Reform and Social Responsibility Act 2011;
(c) members of staff transferred to the chief constable under a scheme made by virtue of section 107EC(1);
(d) members of staff appointed by the chief constable under section 107EC(2).

(5) Provision in an order under section 107D(1) for a function to be exercisable only by the mayor for the area of a combined authority is subject to provision made by virtue of subsection (2).

(6) This section is subject to—
(a) section 107EB (section 107EA orders: procedure), and

(b) section 37 of the Fire and Rescue Services Act 2004 (prohibition on employment of police in fire-fighting).

(7) In this section "fire and rescue functions", in relation to a chief constable, means—

(a) functions which are exercisable by the chief constable by virtue of provision made under subsection (2)(a), and

(b) functions relating to fire and rescue services which are conferred on the chief constable by or by virtue of any enactment.

107EB Section 107EA orders: procedure

(1) An order under section 107EA(2) may be made in relation to the mayor for the area of a combined authority only if the mayor has requested the Secretary of State to make the order.

(2) A request under subsection (1) must be accompanied by a report which contains—

(a) an assessment of why—

(i) it is in the interests of economy, efficiency and effectiveness for the order to be made, or

(ii) it is in the interests of public safety for the order to be made,

(b) a description of any public consultation which the mayor has carried out on the proposal for the order to be made,

(c) a summary of the responses to any such consultation, and

(d) a summary of the representations (if any) which the mayor has received about that proposal from the constituent members of the combined authority.

(3) Before making the request the mayor must publish, in such manner as the mayor thinks appropriate, the mayor's response to the representations made or views expressed in response to any consultations on the proposal.

(4) Subsections (5) to (7) apply if—

(a) the mayor for the area of a combined authority makes a request under subsection (1) for the Secretary of State to make an order under section 107EA(2), and

(b) at least two thirds of the constituent members of the combined authority have indicated that they disagree with the proposal for the order to be made.

(5) The mayor must, in providing the report under subsection (2), provide the Secretary of State with—

(a) copies of the representations (if any) made by the constituent members of the combined authority about that proposal, and

(b) the mayor's response to those representations and to the responses to any public consultation which the mayor has carried out on that proposal.

(6) The Secretary of State must—

(a) obtain an independent assessment of that proposal, and

(b) in deciding whether to make the order, have regard to that assessment and to the material provided under subsection (5) (as well as the material provided under subsection (2)).

(7) The Secretary of State must publish the independent assessment—

(a) as soon as is reasonably practicable after making a determination in response to the proposal, and

(b) in such manner as the Secretary of State thinks appropriate.

(8) An order under section 107EA(2) may be made only if it appears to the Secretary of State that—

(a) it is in the interests of economy, efficiency and effectiveness for the order to be made, or

(b) it is in the interests of public safety for the order to be made.

(9) The Secretary of State may not make an order under section 107EA(2) in a case within subsection (8)(a) of this section if the Secretary of State thinks that the order would have an adverse effect on public safety.

(10) The Secretary of State may, in making an order under section 107EA(2) in relation to the mayor for the area of a combined authority, give effect to the mayor's proposal for the order with such modifications as the Secretary of State thinks appropriate.

(11) Before making an order which gives effect to such a proposal with modifications, the Secretary of State must consult the mayor and the combined authority on the modifications.

(12) In this section—

"constituent council", in relation to a combined authority, means—

(a) a county council the whole or any part of whose area is within the area of the combined authority, or

(b) a district council whose area is within the area of the combined authority;

"constituent member", in relation to a combined authority, means a member of the authority appointed by a constituent council (but does not include the mayor for the area of the combined authority).

107EC Section 107EA orders: further provision

(1) An order under section 107EA(2) may make provision for the making of a scheme to transfer property, rights and liabilities (including criminal liabilities)—

(a) from a fire and rescue authority or the combined authority to the chief constable, or

(b) from the chief constable to the combined authority,

(including provision corresponding to any provision made by section 17(4) to (6) of the Localism Act 2011).

(2) A chief constable to whom an order under section 107EA(2) applies may appoint staff for the purpose of the exercise of the chief constable's fire and rescue functions.

(3) A chief constable to whom an order under section 107EA(2) applies may—

(a) pay remuneration, allowances and gratuities to members of the chief constable's fire and rescue staff;

(b) pay pensions to, or in respect of, persons who are or have been such members of staff;

(c) pay amounts for or towards the provision of pensions to, or in respect of, persons who are or have been such members of staff.

(4) In subsection (3) "allowances", in relation to a member of staff, means allowances in respect of expenses incurred by the member of staff in the course of employment as such a member of staff.

(5) Subject to subsections (6) to (8), a person who is employed pursuant to a transfer by virtue of subsection (1) or an appointment under subsection (2) may not at the same time be employed pursuant to an appointment by a chief constable of the police force for a police area under Schedule 2 to the Police Reform and Social Responsibility Act 2011.

(6) Where an order under section 107EA(2) is in force in relation to the chief constable of the police force for a police area, the person who is for the time being the police force's chief finance officer is to be responsible for the proper administration of financial affairs relating to the exercise of the chief constable's fire and rescue functions.

(7) Subsection (5) does not prevent a person who is employed as a finance officer for fire functions from being at the same time employed as a finance officer for police functions.

(8) In subsection (7)—

"finance officer for fire functions" means a member of a chief constable's fire and rescue staff who—

(a) is not a chief finance officer of the kind mentioned in subsection (6), and

(b) is employed to carry out duties relating to the proper administration of financial affairs relating to the exercise of the chief constable's fire and rescue functions;

"finance officer for police functions" means a member of a chief constable's civilian staff within the meaning of the Police Reform and Social Responsibility Act 2011 who—

(a) is not a chief finance officer of the kind mentioned in subsection (6), and

(b) is employed to carry out duties relating to the proper administration of a police force's financial affairs.

(9) Where an order under section 107EA(2) is in force, the combined authority to which the order applies must pay—

(a) any damages or costs awarded against the chief constable to whom the order applies in any proceedings brought against the chief constable in respect of the acts or omissions of a member of the chief constable's fire and rescue staff;

(b) any costs incurred by the chief constable in any such proceedings so far as not recovered by the chief constable in the proceedings;

(c) any sum required in connection with the settlement of any claim made against the chief constable in respect of the acts or omissions of a member of the chief constable's fire and rescue staff, if the settlement is approved by the authority.

(10) Where an order under section 107EA(2) is in force, the combined authority to which the order applies may, in such cases and to such extent as appears to the authority to be appropriate, pay—

(a) any damages or costs awarded against a member of the fire and rescue staff of the chief constable to whom the order applies in proceedings for any unlawful conduct of that member of staff;

(b) costs incurred and not recovered by such a member of staff in such proceedings;

(c) sums required in connection with the settlement of a claim that has or might have given rise to such proceedings.

(11) In this section—

"fire and rescue functions" has the same meaning as in section 107EA;

"fire and rescue staff", in relation to a chief constable to whom an order under section 107EA(2) applies, means—

(a) staff transferred to the chief constable under a scheme made by virtue of subsection (1);

(b) staff appointed by the chief constable under subsection (2).

107ED Section 107EA orders: exercise of fire and rescue functions

(1) This section applies if—

(a) an order under section 107EA(2) makes provision in relation to the area of a combined authority, and

(b) by virtue of the order, fire and rescue functions exercisable by the mayor for the area of the combined authority are exercisable by the chief constable of the police force for the police area which corresponds to that area.

(2) The chief constable must secure that good value for money is obtained in exercising—

(a) functions which are exercisable by the chief constable by virtue of the order, and

(b) functions relating to fire and rescue services which are conferred on the chief constable by or by virtue of any enactment.

(3) The chief constable must secure that other persons exercising functions by virtue of the order obtain good value for money in exercising those functions.

(4) The mayor must—

(a) secure the exercise of the duties which are exercisable by the chief constable or another person by virtue of the order,

(b) secure the exercise of the duties relating to fire and rescue services which are imposed on the chief constable by or by virtue of any enactment,

(c) secure that functions which are exercisable by the chief constable or another person by virtue of the order are exercised efficiently and effectively, and

(d) secure that functions relating to fire and rescue services which are conferred or imposed on the chief constable by or by virtue of any enactment are exercised efficiently and effectively.

(5) The mayor must hold the chief constable to account for the exercise of such functions.

107EE Section 107EA orders: complaints and conduct matters etc

(1) If an order is made under section 107EA(2) that enables arrangements to be made for the exercise of functions by members of a police force or the civilian staff of a police force, the Secretary of State may by order amend Part 2 of the Police Reform Act 2002 (persons serving with the police: complaints and conduct matters etc) in consequence of that provision.

(2) If an order is made under section 107EA(2) that enables arrangements to be made for the exercise of functions by members of staff transferred to a chief constable under a scheme made by virtue of section 107EC(1) or appointed by a chief constable under section 107EC(2), the Secretary of State may by order make provision of the type described in subsection (3) in relation to those members of staff.

(3) The provision referred to in subsection (2) is—

(a) provision corresponding or similar to any provision made by or under Part 2 of the Police Reform Act 2002;

(b) provision applying (with or without modifications) any provision made by or under Part 2 of that Act.

(4) The Secretary of State may by order, in consequence of any provision made under subsection (2), amend Part 2 of the Police Reform Act 2002.

(5) Before making an order under this section the Secretary of State must consult—

(a) the Police Advisory Board for England and Wales,

(b) the Independent Police Complaints Commission,

(c) such persons as appear to the Secretary of State to represent the views of police and crime commissioners,

(d) such persons as appear to the Secretary of State to represent the views of fire and rescue authorities, and

(e) such other persons as the Secretary of State considers appropriate.

107EF Section 107EA orders: application of fire and rescue provisions

(1) The Secretary of State may by order—

(a) apply (with or without modifications) any provision of a fire and rescue enactment in relation to a person within subsection (2);

(b) make, in relation to a person within subsection (2), provision corresponding or similar to any provision of a fire and rescue enactment.

(2) Those persons are—

(a) a chief constable of a police force for a police area to whom an order under section 107EA(2) applies,

(b) a member of staff transferred to such a chief constable under a scheme made by virtue of section 107EC(1),

(c) a member of staff appointed by such a chief constable under section 107EC(2),

(d) a member of such a chief constable's police force by whom functions are exercisable by virtue of section 107EA(2)(b), and

(e) a member of the civilian staff of such a police force (as defined by section 102(4) of the Police Reform and Social Responsibility Act 2011) by whom functions are exercisable by virtue of section 107EA(2)(b).

(3) The power conferred by subsection (1)(a) or (b) includes power to apply (with or without modifications) any provision made under a fire and rescue enactment or make provision corresponding or similar to any such provision.

(4) The Secretary of State may by order amend, revoke or repeal a provision of or made under an enactment in consequence of provision made by virtue of subsection (1).

(5) In this section "fire and rescue enactment" means an enactment relating to a fire and rescue authority (including, in particular, an enactment relating to an employee of such an authority or property of such an authority).

(6) References in this section to an enactment or to provision made under an enactment are to an enactment whenever passed or (as the case may be) to provision whenever the instrument containing it is made.

107EG Section 107EA orders: application of local policing provisions

(1) The Secretary of State may by order—

(a) apply (with or without modifications) any provision of a local policing enactment in relation to a person within subsection (2);

(b) make, in relation to such a person, provision corresponding or similar to any provision of a local policing enactment.

(2) Those persons are—

(a) a mayor for the area of a combined authority to whom an order under section 107EA(2) applies,

(b) a chief constable to whom such an order applies, and

(c) a panel established by virtue of an order under paragraph 4 of Schedule 5C for such an area.

(3) The power conferred by subsection (1)(a) or (b) includes power to apply (with or without modifications) any provision made by or under a local policing enactment or make provision corresponding or similar to any such provision.

(4) The Secretary of State may by order amend, revoke or repeal a provision of or made under an enactment in consequence of provision made by virtue of subsection (1).

(5) In this section "local policing enactment" means an enactment relating to a police and crime commissioner.

(6) References in this section to an enactment or to provision made under an enactment are to an enactment whenever passed or (as the case may be) to provision whenever the instrument containing it is made."

(3) In section 107D(6)(b) (general functions exercisable by the mayor for the area of a combined authority) after "section 107E" insert "or 107EA".

(4) In section 120 (interpretation) after the definition of "EPB" insert—

""fire and rescue authority" means a fire and rescue authority under the Fire and Rescue Services Act 2004;".

(5) In section 26 of the Fire Services Act 1947 (firefighters' pension scheme) (as continued in force by order under section 36 of the Fire and Rescue Services Act 2004) in subsection (5A) (as inserted by paragraph 14 of Schedule 1)—

(a) omit the "or" at the end of paragraph (a), and

(b) after paragraph (b) insert—

"(c) a transfer to the chief constable under a scheme made by virtue of section 107EC(1) of the Local Democracy, Economic Development and Construction Act 2009, or

(d) an appointment by the chief constable under section 107EC(2) of that Act."

(6) In section 63 of the Police Act 1996 (Police Advisory Board for England and Wales) in subsection (4) (as inserted by paragraph 76 of Schedule 1) for "also imposes a requirement" substitute "and section 107EE of the Local Democracy, Economic Development and Construction Act 2009 also impose requirements".

(7) In section 38 of the Police Reform Act 2002 (police powers for civilian staff) in subsection (11A) (as inserted by paragraph 82 of Schedule 1) after paragraph (b) insert—

"(c) any member of staff transferred to that chief constable under a scheme made by virtue of section 107EC(1) of the Local Democracy, Economic Development and Construction Act 2009 (transfer of property, rights and liabilities to chief constable to whom fire functions of combined authority may be delegated);

(d) any member of staff appointed by that chief constable under section 107EC(2) of that Act (appointment of staff by chief constable to whom fire functions of combined authority may be delegated)."

(8) In section 34 of the Fire and Rescue Services Act 2004 (pensions etc) in subsection (11) (as inserted by paragraph 11 of Schedule 1)—

(a) omit the "or" at the end of paragraph (a), and

(b) after paragraph (b) insert—

"(c) transferred to the chief constable under a scheme made by virtue of section 107EC(1) of the Local Democracy, Economic Development and Construction Act 2009, or

(d) appointed by the chief constable under section 107EC(2) of that Act."

(9) In section 37 of the Fire and Rescue Services Act 2004 (prohibition on employment of police in fire-fighting) (as substituted by paragraph 12 of Schedule 1) in subsection (3) —

(a) after "whom" insert "—(a)", and

(b) after paragraph (a) insert ", or

(b) functions of a fire and rescue authority which are exercisable by the mayor of a combined authority have been delegated under an order under section 107EA(2) of the Local Democracy, Economic Development and Construction Act 2009."

(10) In Schedule 8 to the Police Reform and Social Responsibility Act 2011 (appointment, suspension and removal of senior police officers) in paragraph 2 (no appointment until end of confirmation process) in sub-paragraph (1AA) (as inserted by paragraph 93 of Schedule 1) after "section 4H of the Fire and Rescue Services Act 2004" insert "or section 107EA(2) of the Local Democracy, Economic Development and Construction Act 2009".

(11) In Schedule 1 to the Public Service Pensions Act 2013 (persons in public service: definitions) in paragraph 6 (fire and rescue workers) in paragraph (aa) (as inserted by paragraph 95 of Schedule 1)—

(a) omit the "or" at the end of sub-paragraph (i), and

(b) for the "or" at the end of sub-paragraph (ii) substitute—

"(iii) transferred to the chief constable under a scheme made by virtue of section 107EC(1) of the Local Democracy, Economic Development and Construction Act 2009, or

(iv) appointed by the chief constable under section 107EC(2) of that Act, or".

CHAPTER 3

London Fire Commissioner

9 The London Fire Commissioner

(1) The London Fire and Emergency Planning Authority is abolished.

(2) The functions of the London Fire and Emergency Planning Authority are (subject to this Act) transferred to the London Fire Commissioner.

(3) Schedule 2—

(a) amends the Greater London Authority Act 1999 in consequence of the abolition of the London Fire and Emergency Planning Authority,

(b) amends that Act so as to make provision about the London Fire Commissioner, and

(c) makes consequential amendments to other Acts.

10 Transfer of property, rights and liabilities to the London Fire Commissioner

(1) The Secretary of State may make one or more schemes for the transfer of property, rights and liabilities of the London Fire and Emergency Planning Authority to the London Fire Commissioner.

(2) The things that may be transferred under a transfer scheme include—

(a) property, rights and liabilities that could not otherwise be transferred;

(b) property acquired, and rights and liabilities arising, after the making of the scheme;

(c) criminal liabilities.

(3) A transfer scheme may make consequential, supplementary, incidental or transitional provision and may in particular—

(a) create rights, or impose liabilities, in relation to property transferred;

(b) make provision about the continuing effect of things done by the transferor in respect of anything transferred;

(c) make provision about the continuation of things (including legal proceedings) in the process of being done by, on behalf of or in relation to the transferor, in respect of anything transferred;

(d) make provision for references to the transferor in an instrument or other document in respect of anything transferred to be treated as references to the transferee;

(e) if the TUPE regulations do not apply in relation to the transfer, make provision which is the same or similar.

(4) A transfer scheme may provide—

(a) for the scheme to be modified by agreement after it comes into effect;

(b) for any such modifications to have effect from the date when the original scheme came into effect.

(5) In this section—

(a) references to the transfer of property include the grant of a lease;

(b) references to rights and liabilities include rights and liabilities under a contract of employment;

(c) "TUPE regulations" means the Transfer of Undertakings (Protection of Employment) Regulations 2006 (SI 2006/246).

CHAPTER 4

INSPECTION OF FIRE AND RESCUE SERVICES

11 Inspection of fire and rescue services

(1) The Fire and Rescue Services Act 2004 is amended as follows.

(2) In section 28 (inspectors), before subsection (1) insert—

"(A1) Her Majesty may appoint such number of inspectors of fire and rescue authorities in England (the "English inspectors") as the Secretary of State may determine.

(A2) Of the persons appointed under subsection (A1) one is to be appointed as the chief fire and rescue inspector for England.

(A3) The English inspectors must inspect, and report on the efficiency and effectiveness of, fire and rescue authorities in England.

(A4) The English inspectors must carry out such other duties for the purpose of furthering the efficiency and effectiveness of fire and rescue authorities in England as the Secretary of State may from time to time direct.

(A5) The chief fire and rescue inspector for England may appoint assistant inspectors and other officers for the purpose of assisting the English inspectors.

(A6) When carrying out an inspection under subsection (A3) of a fire and rescue authority created by an order under section 4A, an English inspector must not review or scrutinise decisions made, or other action taken, by the fire and rescue authority in connection with the discharge of an excluded function.

(A7) For the purposes of subsection (A6), the following are excluded functions in relation to a fire and rescue authority—

(a) the function of preparing a fire and rescue plan and a fire and rescue statement (within the meaning of Schedule A2);

(b) the functions that the authority has in its capacity as a major precepting authority for the purposes of Part 1 of the Local Government Finance Act 1992;

(c) the function of appointing a chief finance officer under section 4D(4);

(d) where functions of the authority have been delegated to a chief constable under an order under section 4H, the functions conferred on the authority by section 4J(4) and (5);

(e) functions specified, or of a description specified, in relation to that authority in an order made by the Secretary of State.

(A8) The power under subsection (A7)(e) may be exercised in relation to—

(a) all fire and rescue authorities created by an order under section 4A,

(b) a particular fire and rescue authority created by an order under section 4A, or

(c) a particular description of fire and rescue authorities created by an order under section 4A.

(A9) Schedule A3 makes further provision in relation to the English inspectors."

(3) In section 28, in subsection (1)(a), after "fire and rescue authorities" insert "in Wales".

(4) After section 28 insert—

"28A Inspection programme and inspection framework etc: England

(1) The chief fire and rescue inspector for England must from time to time prepare—

(a) a document setting out what inspections of fire and rescue authorities in England the English inspectors propose to carry out under section 28(A3) (an "inspection programme");

(b) a document setting out the manner in which the English inspectors propose to carry out the function conferred on them by section 28(A3) (an "inspection framework").

(2) The chief fire and rescue inspector for England must obtain the approval of the Secretary of State to an inspection programme or inspection framework before the English inspectors act in accordance with it.

(3) The Secretary of State may at any time require the chief fire and rescue inspector for England to carry out, or arrange for another English inspector to carry out, an inspection under section 28(A3) of—

(a) a fire and rescue authority in England;

(b) all fire and rescue authorities in England;

(c) all fire and rescue authorities in England of a particular type.

(4) A requirement imposed under subsection (3) may limit the inspection to a particular matter.

(5) The chief fire and rescue inspector for England or, at the request of that inspector, any other English inspector may carry out an inspection under section 28(A3) of a fire and rescue authority in England that has not been set out in an inspection programme (and has not been required under subsection (3)).

(6) Before deciding to carry out, or to request another English inspector to carry out, an inspection of a fire and rescue authority in England that has not been set out in an inspection programme, the chief fire and rescue inspector for England must consult the Secretary of State.

(7) Nothing in an inspection programme or inspection framework is to be read as preventing an English inspector from making a visit without notice.

(8) In this section "English inspector" means an inspector appointed under section 28(A1)."

(5) After section 28A (as inserted by subsection (4)) insert—

"28B Publication of inspection reports etc: England

(1) The chief fire and rescue inspector for England must arrange for a report prepared under section 28(A3) to be published in such manner as appears to him or her to be appropriate.

(2) But the chief fire and rescue inspector for England must exclude from publication under subsection (1) anything that he or she considers—

(a) would be against the interests of national security, or

(b) might jeopardise the safety of any person.

(3) The chief fire and rescue inspector for England must—

(a) send a copy of the published report to the Secretary of State, and

(b) disclose to the Secretary of State anything excluded from publication by virtue of subsection (2).

(4) The chief fire and rescue inspector for England must in each year submit to the Secretary of State a report on the carrying out of inspections under section 28(A3) (during the period since the last report).

(5) A report under subsection (4) must include the chief fire and rescue inspector for England's assessment of the efficiency and effectiveness of fire and rescue authorities in England for the period in respect of which the report is prepared.

(6) The chief fire and rescue inspector for England must lay before Parliament a copy of a report submitted under subsection (4).

(7) In this section "English inspector" means an inspector appointed under section 28(A1)."

(6) In Schedule A2 (application of legislation relating to police and crime commissioners) (as inserted by Schedule 1 to this Act), in paragraph 8(2) (powers of police and crime panels: modifications of section 28 of the Police Reform and Social Responsibility Act 2011), after paragraph (d) insert—

"(da) the references in subsection (6) to the commissioner's functions were to the functions of the relevant fire and rescue authority that are excluded functions for the purposes of section 28(A6) of this Act (see section 28(A7)),".

(7) After Schedule A2 insert the new Schedule A3 set out in Schedule 3 to this Act.

(8) A person appointed, before the coming into force of this section, under section 28 of the Fire and Rescue Services Act 2004 for the purpose of obtaining information in relation to the functions of fire and rescue authorities in England (including a person taken to have been so appointed by virtue of subsection (3) of that section) is to be taken—

(a) if an inspector, to have been appointed under subsection (A1) of that section, and

(b) if an assistant inspector or other officer, to have been appointed under subsection (A5) of that section.

12 Fire safety inspections

(1) The Regulatory Reform (Fire Safety) Order 2005 (S.I. 2005/1541) is amended as follows.

(2) In article 2 (interpretation), in the definition of "fire inspector"—

(a) after "inspector"" insert ", in relation to Wales,";

(b) for "section 28" substitute "section 28(1)".

(3) In article 27 (powers of inspectors), after paragraph (4) insert—

"(5) This article applies to a person authorised by the Secretary of State under article 25(1)(e) in relation to premises in England as it applies to an inspector; and article 32(2)(d) to (f), with the necessary modifications, applies accordingly."

(4) In article 28 (exercise on behalf of fire inspectors etc of their powers by officers of fire brigades)—

(a) in paragraph (1)—

(i) omit ", or any other person authorised by the Secretary of State under article 25(e),";

(ii) for "and (3)" substitute "to (4)";

(b) after paragraph (1) insert—

"(1A) The powers conferred by article 27 on an authorised person (by virtue of paragraph (5) of that article) are also exercisable by an employee of a fire and rescue authority in England when authorised in writing by such an authorised person for the purpose of reporting to him or her on any matter falling within the authorised person's functions under this Order; and articles 27(2) to (4) and 32(2)(d) to (f), with the necessary modifications, apply accordingly.";

(c) in paragraph (2), for ", or other person authorised by the Secretary of State," substitute "or authorised person";

(d) after paragraph (2) insert—

"(3) In this article, "authorised person" means a person authorised by the Secretary of State under article 25(1)(e) in relation to premises in England."

PART 2

POLICE COMPLAINTS, DISCIPLINE AND INSPECTION

CHAPTER 1

POLICE COMPLAINTS

13 Local policing bodies: functions in relation to complaints

In Part 2 of the Police Reform Act 2002 (complaints and misconduct), after section 13 insert—

"13A Local policing bodies: functions in relation to complaints

(1) The local policing body that maintains a police force may give notice to the chief officer of the police force that it (rather than the chief officer) is to exercise the functions conferred on the chief officer by the provisions specified in subsection (2) or subsections (2) and (3).

(2) The provisions specified in this subsection are—

(a) paragraph 2(6) to (6D) of Schedule 3, and

(b) paragraph 2(9) and (10) of Schedule 3 in so far as relating to a determination made for the purposes of paragraph 2(6) to (6C) of that Schedule.

(3) The provisions specified in this subsection are—

(a) section 20, and

(b) section 21 in so far as that section relates to complaints.

(4) In relation to any complaint in respect of which the chief officer is the appropriate authority that is made on or after the day on which a notice under subsection (1) is given—

(a) the functions of the chief officer to which the notice relates become functions of the local policing body,

(b) references to the chief officer, including in the chief officer's capacity as an appropriate authority, in the provisions specified in subsection (2) or (as the case may be) subsections (2) and (3) are to be read as references to the local policing body, and

(c) for the purpose of paragraph 6(1) of Schedule 3, the complaint is to be treated as having been recorded by the chief officer.

(5) Where the notice under subsection (1) relates to the functions conferred on the chief officer by the provisions specified in subsections (2) and (3), subsection (4)(b) does not apply to the references to an appropriate authority in sections 20(2)(a) and (3A)(a) and 21(7)(a) and (8A)(a).

(6) The Secretary of State may by regulations make provision in connection with the giving of notices under subsection (1) and their withdrawal.

(7) Regulations under subsection (6) may (amongst other things) make provision about—

(a) the steps that a local policing body must take before giving a notice;

(b) the circumstances in which a notice may be withdrawn."

14 Definition of police complaint

(1) Section 12 of the Police Reform Act 2002 (complaints, matters and persons to which Part 2 of the Act applies) is amended as follows.

(2) For subsection (1) substitute—

"(1) In this Part references to a complaint are references (subject to the following provisions of this section) to any expression of dissatisfaction with a police force which is expressed (whether in writing or otherwise) by or on behalf of a member of the public.

(1A) But an expression of dissatisfaction is a complaint for the purposes of this Part—

(a) where it relates to conduct of a person serving with the police, only if the person in question is a person falling within subsection (1B);

(b) in any other case, only if the person in question has been adversely affected by the matter about which dissatisfaction is expressed.

(1B) In relation to an expression of dissatisfaction that relates to conduct of a person serving with the police, a person falls within this subsection if the person is—

(a) a person who claims to be the person in relation to whom the conduct took place;

(b) a person not falling within paragraph (a) who claims to have been adversely affected by the conduct; or

(c) a person who claims to have witnessed the conduct."

(3) In subsection (3)—

(a) for "subsection (1)(b)" substitute "subsection (1B)(b)";

(b) for "made by or on behalf of a person who" substitute "where the person in question".

(4) After subsection (4) insert—

"(4A) In this section, "the person in question" means the person expressing dissatisfaction or the person on whose behalf dissatisfaction is being expressed."

(5) In subsection (6), for the words before paragraph (a) substitute "For the purposes of this Part a person is not to be taken to have authorised another person to make a complaint on his behalf unless—".

(6) Schedule 4 makes amendments of the Police Reform Act 2002 in consequence of the amendments of section 12 of that Act made by this section.

15 Duty to keep complainant and other interested persons informed

(1) Part 2 of the Police Reform Act 2002 (complaints and misconduct) is amended as follows.

(2) In section 20 (duty to keep the complainant informed), after subsection (3) insert—

"(3A) In any case in which a complaint is being handled—

(a) in accordance with paragraph 6(2A) of Schedule 3 otherwise than by the appropriate authority making arrangements for the complaint to be investigated by the authority on its own behalf, or

(b) otherwise than in accordance with Schedule 3 (as to which see paragraph 2(6C) of that Schedule),

it shall be the duty of the appropriate authority to provide the complainant with all such information as will keep him properly informed, while the complaint is being handled and subsequently, of all the matters mentioned in subsection (4)."

(3) In section 20, for subsection (4) substitute—

"(4) The matters of which the complainant must be kept properly informed are—

(a) the progress of the handling of the complaint;

(b) the outcome of the handling of the complaint;

(c) any right to apply for a review conferred on the complainant by paragraph 6A or 25 of Schedule 3 (as the case may be);

(d) such other matters as may be specified in regulations made by the Secretary of State.

(4A) The generality of subsection (4)(a) and (b) is not affected by any requirement to notify the complainant that is imposed by any other provision of this Part."

(4) In section 20, after subsection (8) insert—

"(8A) In any case in which there is an investigation of a complaint, the Commission or the appropriate authority may comply with its duty under subsection (1) or (2) (as the case may be) so far as relating to the findings of a report submitted under provision made by virtue of paragraph 20A(4)(b) of Schedule 3, or a report of the investigation submitted under paragraph 22 of Schedule 3, by sending the complainant a copy of the report.

(8B) Subsection (8A) applies notwithstanding any obligation of secrecy imposed by any rule of law or otherwise but is subject to—

(a) regulations made under subsection (5), and

(b) section 21A."

(5) In section 20(9), after "under this Part" insert ", or who is otherwise involved in the handling of a complaint under this Part,".

(6) In section 21 (duty to provide information for other persons), after subsection (8) insert—

"(8A) In any case in which—

(a) the complaint is being handled in accordance with paragraph 6(2A) of Schedule 3 otherwise than by the appropriate authority making arrangements for the complaint to be investigated by the authority on its own behalf, or

(b) the recordable conduct matter or DSI matter is being handled in a manner determined by the appropriate authority in accordance with paragraph 10(4D), 11(3E), 14(2) or 14D(2) of Schedule 3 otherwise than by the appropriate authority making arrangements for the matter to be investigated by the authority on its own behalf,

it shall be the duty of the appropriate authority to provide the interested person with all such information as will keep him properly informed, while the complaint, recordable conduct matter or DSI matter is being handled and subsequently, of all the matters mentioned in subsection (9)."

(7) In section 21, for subsection (9) substitute—

"(9) The matters of which the interested person must be kept properly informed are—

(a) the progress of the handling of the complaint, recordable conduct matter or DSI matter;

(b) the outcome of the handling of the complaint, recordable conduct matter or DSI matter;

(c) such other matters as may be specified in regulations made by the Secretary of State.

(9A) The generality of subsection (9)(a) and (b) is not affected by any requirement to notify an interested person that is imposed by any other provision of this Part."

(8) In section 21, after subsection (11) insert—

"(11A) In any case in which there is an investigation of a complaint, recordable conduct matter or DSI matter, the Commission or the appropriate authority may comply with its duty under subsection (6) or (7) (as the case may be) so far as relating to the findings of a report submitted under provision made by virtue of paragraph 20A(4)(b) of Schedule 3, or a report of the investigation submitted under paragraph 22 or 24A of Schedule 3, by sending an interested person a copy of the report.

(11B) Subsection (11A) applies notwithstanding any obligation of secrecy imposed by any rule of law or otherwise but is subject to—
(a) regulations made under subsection (10), and
(b) section 21A."

(9) In Schedule 3—
(a) in paragraph 23 (action by the Commission in response to an investigation report under paragraph 22), omit sub-paragraphs (4) and (9) to (12);
(b) in paragraph 24 (action by the appropriate authority in response to an investigation report under paragraph 22), omit sub-paragraphs (4) and (7) to (10).

(10) In consequence of the repeal made by subsection (9)(b), Schedule 3 is further amended as follows—
(a) in paragraph 24, after sub-paragraph (6A) (as inserted by Schedule 5) insert—

"(6B) It shall be the duty of the appropriate authority—
(a) to take the action which it determines under sub-paragraph (6) that it is required to, or will in its discretion, take, and
(b) in a case where that action consists of or includes the bringing of disciplinary proceedings, to secure that those proceedings, once brought, are proceeded with to a proper conclusion.";

(b) in paragraph 27 (duties with respect to disciplinary proceedings etc)—
(i) in sub-paragraph (1), omit paragraph (a) (including the "or" at the end);
(ii) in sub-paragraph (2)(a), omit "which has been or is required to be notified or, as the case may be,".

(11) In consequence of the repeals made by subsection (9), omit the following—
(a) in the Criminal Justice and Immigration Act 2008, in Schedule 23, paragraph 14(7) and (8);
(b) in the Anti-social Behaviour, Crime and Policing Act 2014, in Part 3 of Schedule 11, paragraph 95(6).

16 Complaints, conduct matters and DSI matters: procedure

Schedule 5 amends Schedule 3 to the Police Reform Act 2002 (handling of complaints and conduct matters etc).

17 Initiation of investigations by IPCC

(1) Schedule 3 to the Police Reform Act 2002 (handling of complaints and conduct matters etc) is amended as follows.

(2) In paragraph 4 (reference of complaints to the Commission), in sub-paragraph (7), in the words before paragraph (a), after "occasion" insert ", or that has been treated as having been so referred by virtue of paragraph 4A".

(3) After paragraph 4 insert—

"4A Power of Commission to treat complaint as having been referred

4A (1) The Commission may treat a complaint that comes to its attention otherwise than by having been referred to it under paragraph 4 as having been so referred.

(2) Where the Commission treats a complaint as having been referred to it—

(a) paragraphs 2 and 4 do not apply, or cease to apply, in relation to the complaint except to the extent provided for by paragraph 4(7), and

(b) paragraphs 5, 6, 6A, 15 and 25 apply in relation to the complaint as if it had been referred to the Commission by the appropriate authority under paragraph 4.

(3) The Commission must notify the following that it is treating a complaint as having been referred to it—

(a) the appropriate authority;

(b) the complainant;

(c) except in a case where it appears to the Commission that to do so might prejudice an investigation of the complaint (whether an existing investigation or a possible future one), the person complained against (if any).

(4) Where an appropriate authority receives a notification under sub-paragraph (3) in respect of a complaint and the complaint has not yet been recorded, the appropriate authority must record the complaint."

(4) In paragraph 11 (recording etc of conduct matters otherwise than where conduct matters arise in civil proceedings), omit sub-paragraph (5).

(5) In paragraph 13 (reference of conduct matters to the Commission), in sub-paragraph (7), in the words before paragraph (a), after "occasion" insert ", or that has been treated as having been so referred by virtue of paragraph 13A".

(6) After paragraph 13 insert—

"13A Power of Commission to treat conduct matter as having been referred

13A (1) The Commission may treat a conduct matter that comes to its attention otherwise than by having been referred to it under paragraph 13 as having been so referred.

(2) Where the Commission treats a conduct matter as having been referred to it—

(a) paragraphs 10, 11 and 13 do not apply, or cease to apply, in relation to the matter except to the extent provided for by paragraph 13(7), and

(b) paragraphs 14 and 15 apply in relation to the matter as if it had been referred to the Commission by the appropriate authority under paragraph 13.

(3) The Commission must notify the following that it is treating a conduct matter as having been referred to it—

(a) the appropriate authority;

(b) except in a case where it appears to the Commission that to do so might prejudice an investigation of the matter (whether an existing investigation or a possible future one), the person to whose conduct the matter relates.

(4) Where an appropriate authority receives a notification under sub-paragraph (3) in respect of a conduct matter and the matter has not yet been recorded, the appropriate authority must record the matter."

(7) In paragraph 14A (duty to record DSI matters), omit sub-paragraph (2).

(8) In paragraph 14C (reference of DSI matters to the Commission), in sub-paragraph (3), after "occasion" insert ", or that has been treated as having been so referred by virtue of paragraph 14CA,".

(9) After paragraph 14C insert—

"14CA Power of Commission to treat DSI matter as having been referred

14CA (1) The Commission may treat a DSI matter that comes to its attention otherwise than by having been referred to it under paragraph 14C as having been so referred.

(2) Where the Commission treats a DSI matter as having been referred to it—

(a) paragraphs 14A and 14C do not apply, or cease to apply, in relation to the matter except to the extent provided for by paragraph 14C(3), and

(b) paragraphs 14D and 15 apply in relation to the matter as if it had been referred to the Commission by the appropriate authority under paragraph 14C.

(3) The Commission must notify the appropriate authority that it is treating a DSI matter as having been referred to it.

(4) Where an appropriate authority receives a notification under sub-paragraph (3) in respect of a DSI matter and the matter has not yet been recorded, the appropriate authority must record the matter."

(10) In section 29 of the Police Reform Act 2002 (interpretation of Part 2 of that Act), in subsection (1), in paragraph (a) of the definition of "recordable conduct matter", for "or 11" substitute ", 11 or 13A".

18 IPCC power to require re-investigation

(1) In Part 2 of the Police Reform Act 2002 (complaints and misconduct), after section 13A (as inserted by section 13) insert—

"13B Power of the Commission to require re-investigation

(1) This section applies where—

(a) a report on an investigation of a complaint, recordable conduct matter or DSI matter carried out under the direction of the Commission has been submitted to it under paragraph 22(3) or 24A of Schedule 3, or

(b) a report on an investigation of a complaint, recordable conduct matter or DSI matter carried out by a person designated by the Commission has been submitted to it under paragraph 22(5) or 24A of Schedule 3.

(2) The Commission may at any time determine that the complaint, recordable conduct matter or DSI matter is to be re-investigated if it is satisfied that there are compelling reasons for doing so.

(3) Where the Commission makes a determination under subsection (2), it must determine that the re-investigation is to take the form of an investigation by the Commission unless subsection (4) applies, in which case the Commission must determine that the re-investigation is to take the form described in that subsection.

(4) This subsection applies where the Commission determines that it would be more appropriate for the re-investigation to take the form of an investigation by the appropriate authority under the direction of the Commission.

(5) Where—

(a) the Commission determines under subsection (3) or (7) that a re-investigation is to take the form of an investigation by the Commission, and

(b) at any time after that the Commission determines that subsection (4) applies in relation to the re-investigation,

the Commission may make a further determination under this section (to replace the earlier one) that the re-investigation is instead to take the form of an investigation by the appropriate authority under the direction of the Commission.

(6) Where the Commission determines under subsection (3) or (5) that a re-investigation is to take the form of an investigation by the appropriate authority under the direction of the Commission, the Commission must keep under review whether subsection (4) continues to apply in relation to the re-investigation.

(7) If, on such a review, the Commission determines that subsection (4) no longer applies in relation to a re-investigation, the Commission must make a further determination under this section (to replace the earlier one) that the re-investigation is instead to take the form of an investigation by the Commission.

(8) Sub-paragraphs (6) and (7) of paragraph 15 of Schedule 3 shall apply in relation to a further determination under subsection (5) or (7) as they apply in the case of a further determination under sub-paragraph (5A) or (5B) of that paragraph.

(9) The other provisions of Schedule 3 shall apply in relation to any re-investigation in pursuance of a determination under this section as they apply in relation to any investigation in pursuance of a determination under paragraph 15.

(10) The Commission shall notify the appropriate authority of any determination that it makes under this section and of its reasons for making the determination.

(11) The Commission shall also notify the following of any determination that it makes under this section and of its reasons for making the determination—

(a) every person entitled to be kept properly informed in relation to the complaint, recordable conduct matter or DSI matter (as the case may be) under section 21;

(b) where the determination is made in relation to a complaint, the complainant;

(c) the person to whose conduct the re-investigation will relate.

(12) The duty imposed by subsection (11) on the Commission shall have effect subject to such exceptions as may be provided for by regulations made by the Secretary of State.

(13) Subsections (6) to (8) of section 20 apply for the purposes of subsection (12) as they apply for the purposes of that section.

(14) In relation to a matter that was formerly a DSI matter but was recorded as a conduct matter in pursuance of paragraph 21A(5) of Schedule 3, the reference in subsection (10) to the appropriate authority is a reference to the appropriate authority in relation to the person whose conduct was in question.

(15) The reference to a report in subsection (1) includes a report on a re-investigation by virtue of this section or paragraph 25 of Schedule 3."

(2) Part 3 of Schedule 3 to the Police Reform Act 2002 (handling of complaints and conduct matters etc: investigations and subsequent proceedings) is amended as follows.

(3) In paragraph 23 (action by the Commission in response to an investigation report under paragraph 22), after sub-paragraph (1) insert—

"(1A) But if, following the submission of such a report, the Commission determines under section 13B that the complaint or recordable conduct matter is to be re-investigated the provisions of this paragraph other than sub-paragraph (2)(a) do not apply, or cease to apply, in relation to that report."

(4) In paragraph 24A (final reports on investigations: DSI matters), after sub-paragraph (5) (as inserted by Schedule 5) insert—

"(6) But sub-paragraphs (4) and (5) and paragraphs 24B and 24C do not apply, or cease to apply, in relation to a report submitted under sub-paragraph (2) if, following the submission of the report, the Commission determines under section 13B that the DSI matter is to be re-investigated."

(5) In paragraph 27 (duties with respect to disciplinary proceedings etc), after sub-paragraph (1) insert—

"(1A) But where this paragraph would otherwise apply by virtue of sub-paragraph (1)(c), it does not apply, or ceases to apply, in relation to the investigation if the Commission determines under section 13B that the DSI matter is to be re-investigated."

(6) In paragraph 28B (response to recommendation by the Commission under paragraph 28A), at the end insert—

"(12) This paragraph does not apply, or ceases to apply, in relation to a recommendation made by virtue of paragraph 28A(1) if the Commission determines under section 13B that the complaint, recordable conduct matter or DSI matter that the Commission received a report on is to be re-investigated."

19 Sensitive information received by IPCC: restriction on disclosure

(1) Part 2 of the Police Reform Act 2002 (complaints and misconduct) is amended as follows.

(2) After section 21 insert—

"21A Restriction on disclosure of sensitive information

(1) Where the Commission receives information within subsection (3), the Commission must not disclose (whether under section 11, 20 or 21 or otherwise) the information, or the fact that it has been received, unless the relevant authority consents to the disclosure.

(2) Where a person appointed under paragraph 18 of Schedule 3 to investigate a complaint or matter (a "paragraph 18 investigator") receives information within subsection (3), the paragraph 18 investigator must not disclose the information, or the fact that it has been received, to any person other than the Commission unless the relevant authority consents to the disclosure.

(3) The information is—

(a) intelligence service information;

(b) protected information relating to a relevant warrant;

(c) information obtained from a government department which, at the time it is provided to the Commission or the paragraph 18 investigator, is identified by the department as information the disclosure of which may, in the opinion of the relevant authority—

(i) cause damage to national security, international relations or the economic interests of the United Kingdom or any part of the United Kingdom, or

(ii) jeopardise the safety of any person.

(4) Where the Commission or a paragraph 18 investigator discloses to another person information within subsection (3), or the fact that the Commission or the paragraph 18 investigator has received it, the other person must not disclose that information or that fact unless the relevant authority consents to the disclosure.

(5) In this section—

"government department" means a department of Her Majesty's Government but does not include—

(a) the Security Service,

(b) the Secret Intelligence Service, or

(c) the Government Communications Headquarters ("GCHQ");

"intelligence service information" means information that was obtained (directly or indirectly) from or that relates to—

(a) the Security Service,

(b) the Secret Intelligence Service,

(c) GCHQ, or

(d) any part of Her Majesty's forces, or of the Ministry of Defence, which engages in intelligence activities;

"Minister of the Crown" includes the Treasury;

"paragraph 18 investigator" has the meaning given by subsection (2);

"protected information", in relation to a relevant warrant, means information relating to any of the matters mentioned in section 57(4) of the Investigatory Powers Act 2016 in relation to the warrant;

"relevant authority" means—

(a) in the case of intelligence service information obtained (directly or indirectly) from or relating to the Security Service, the Director-General of the Security Service;

(b) in the case of intelligence service information obtained (directly or indirectly) from or relating to the Secret Intelligence Service, the Chief of the Secret Intelligence Service;

(c) in the case of intelligence service information obtained (directly or indirectly) from or relating to GCHQ, the Director of GCHQ;

(d) in the case of intelligence service information obtained (directly or indirectly) from or relating to Her Majesty's forces or the Ministry of Defence, the Secretary of State;

(e) in the case of protected information relating to a relevant warrant, the person to whom the relevant warrant is or was addressed;

(f) in the case of information within subsection (3)(c)—

(i) the Secretary of State, or

(ii) the Minister of the Crown in charge of the government department from which the information was obtained (if that Minister is not a Secretary of State);

"relevant warrant" means—

(a) a warrant under Chapter 1 of Part 2 of the Investigatory Powers Act 2016, or

(b) a warrant under Chapter 1 of Part 6 of that Act.

21B Provision of sensitive information to the Commission and certain investigators

(1) A person who provides information that is intelligence service information or protected information relating to a relevant warrant to the Commission or a paragraph 18 investigator (whether under a provision of this Part or otherwise) must—

(a) make the Commission or the paragraph 18 investigator aware that the information is intelligence service information or (as the case may be) protected information relating to a relevant warrant, and

(b) provide the Commission or the paragraph 18 investigator with such additional information as will enable the Commission or the paragraph 18 investigator to identify the relevant authority in relation to the information.

(2) In this section, "intelligence service information", "protected information relating to a relevant warrant", "paragraph 18 investigator" and "relevant authority" have the same meaning as in section 21A."

(3) In Schedule 3 (handling of complaints and conduct matters etc), in Part 3 (investigations and subsequent proceedings)—

(a) omit paragraph 19ZD (sensitive information: restriction on further disclosure of information received under an information notice);

(b) in paragraph 22 (final reports on investigations: complaints, conduct matters and certain DSI matters)—

(i) after sub-paragraph (6) insert—

"(6A) Where a person would contravene section 21A by submitting, or (as the case may be) sending a copy of, a report in its entirety to the appropriate authority under sub-paragraph (2) or (3)(b), the person must instead submit, or send a copy of, the report after having removed or obscured the information which by virtue of section 21A the person must not disclose.";

(ii) in sub-paragraph (8), at the end insert "except so far as the person is prevented from doing so by section 21A";

(c) in paragraph 23 (action by the Commission in response to an investigation report under paragraph 22)—

(i) in sub-paragraph (1A) (as inserted by section 18), after "sub-paragraph (2)(a)" insert "(read with sub-paragraph (2ZA))";

(ii) after sub-paragraph (2) insert—

"(2ZA) Where the Commission would contravene section 21A by sending a copy of a report in its entirety to the appropriate authority under sub-paragraph (2)(a) or to the Director of Public Prosecutions under sub-paragraph (2)(c), the Commission must instead send a copy of the report after having removed or obscured the information which by virtue of section 21A the Commission must not disclose.";

(d) in paragraph 24A (final reports on investigations: other DSI matters), after sub-paragraph (3) insert—

"(3A) Where a person would contravene section 21A by sending a copy of a report in its entirety to the appropriate authority under sub-paragraph (2)(b), the person must instead send a copy of the report after having removed or obscured the information which by virtue of section 21A the person must not disclose.";

(e) in paragraph 24B (action by the Commission in response to an investigation report under paragraph 24A), after sub-paragraph (1) insert—

"(1A) Sub-paragraph (3A) of paragraph 24A applies for the purposes of sub-paragraph (1) of this paragraph as it applies for the purposes of sub-paragraph (2)(b) of that paragraph."

20 Investigations by IPCC: powers of seizure and retention

(1) In Schedule 3 to the Police Reform Act 2002 (handling of complaints and conduct matters etc), in Part 3 (investigations and subsequent proceedings), before paragraph 19A insert—

"19ZE Investigations by the Commission: power of seizure

19ZE (1) The powers conferred by this paragraph are exercisable by a person—

(a) who is designated under paragraph 19(2) in relation to an investigation (the "designated person"), and

(b) who is lawfully on any premises for the purposes of the investigation.

(2) The designated person may seize anything which is on the premises if the designated person has reasonable grounds for believing—

(a) that it is evidence relating to the conduct or other matter to which the investigation relates, and

(b) that it is necessary to seize it in order to prevent the evidence being concealed, lost, altered or destroyed.

(3) The designated person may require any information which is stored in any electronic form and is accessible from the premises to be produced in a form in which it can be taken away and in which it is visible and legible, or from which it can readily be produced in a visible and legible form, if the designated person has reasonable grounds for believing—

(a) that it is evidence relating to the conduct or other matter to which the investigation relates, and

(b) that it is necessary to do so in order to prevent the evidence being concealed, lost, tampered with or destroyed.

(4) The powers conferred by this paragraph do not authorise the seizure of an item which the designated person exercising the power has reasonable grounds for believing to be an item subject to legal privilege within the meaning of the 1984 Act (see section 10 of that Act).

(5) Where a designated person has the power to seize a thing or require information to be produced under this paragraph and under section 19 of the 1984 Act (by virtue of section 97(8) of the 1996 Act or paragraph 19(4)), the designated person is to be treated for all purposes as acting in exercise of the power conferred by section 19 of the 1984 Act.

(6) In this paragraph "premises" has the same meaning as in the 1984 Act (see section 23 of that Act).

19ZF Further provision about seizure under paragraph 19ZE

19ZF (1) This paragraph applies where a designated person seizes anything under paragraph 19ZE(2).

(2) The designated person must provide a notice in relation to the thing seized if requested to do so by a person showing himself—

(a) to be the occupier of the premises on which it was seized, or

(b) to have had custody or control of it immediately before the seizure.

(3) The notice must state what has been seized and the reason for its seizure.

(4) The notice must be provided within a reasonable time from the making of the request for it.

(5) In this paragraph "designated person" has the same meaning as in paragraph 19ZE.

19ZG Investigations by the Commission: power of retention

19ZG (1) This paragraph applies to anything which, for the purposes of an investigation in accordance with paragraph 19—

(a) has been seized under paragraph 19ZE(2) or taken away following a requirement imposed under paragraph 19ZE(3), or

(b) is otherwise lawfully in the possession of the Commission.

(2) Anything to which this paragraph applies may be retained by the Commission for as long as is necessary in all the circumstances, including (amongst other things) so that it may be used as evidence in criminal or disciplinary proceedings or in an inquest held under Part 1 of the Coroners and Justice Act 2009.

(3) For the purposes of sub-paragraph (2), the retention of anything to which this paragraph applies is not necessary if having a photograph or copy of the thing would suffice (and the Commission may arrange for the thing to be photographed or copied before it ceases to be retained).

19ZH Further provision about things retained under paragraph 19ZG

19ZH (1) This paragraph applies to anything which—

(a) has been seized (whether under paragraph 19ZE(2) or otherwise), and

(b) is being retained by the Commission under paragraph 19ZG.

(2) If a request for permission to be granted access to a thing to which this paragraph applies is made to the Commission by—

(a) a person who had custody or control of the thing immediately before it was seized, or

(b) someone acting on behalf of such a person,

the Commission must allow the person who made the request access to it under the supervision of a member of the Commission's staff.

(3) Sub-paragraph (4) applies if a request for a photograph or copy of a thing to which this paragraph applies is made to the Commission by—

(a) a person who had custody or control of the thing immediately before it was seized, or

(b) someone acting on behalf of such a person.

(4) The Commission must either—

(a) allow the person who made the request access to the thing under the supervision of a member of the Commission's staff for the purpose of photographing or copying it, or

(b) arrange for the thing to be photographed or copied.

(5) If the Commission acts under sub-paragraph (4)(b), the Commission must supply the photograph or copy to the person who made the request within a reasonable time from the making of the request.

(6) The Commission is not obliged to do anything in response to a request under sub-paragraph (2) or (3) if the Commission has reasonable grounds for believing that to do so would prejudice—

(a) any investigation being carried out in accordance with this Schedule, or

(b) any criminal or disciplinary proceedings or any inquest held under Part 1 of the Coroners and Justice Act 2009."

(2) In section 21 of the Police and Criminal Evidence Act 1984 (access and copying), at the end insert—

"(10) The references to a constable in subsections (1) and (2) do not include a constable who has seized a thing under paragraph 19ZE of Schedule 3 to the Police Reform Act 2002."

21 References to England and Wales in connection with IPCC functions

(1) In section 29 of the Police Reform Act 2002 (interpretation of Part 2), at the end insert—

"(8) References in sections 26, 26BA and 26C to England and Wales include the sea and other waters within the seaward limits of the territorial sea adjacent to England and Wales."

(2) In section 28 of the Commissioners for Revenue and Customs Act 2005 (complaints and misconduct: England and Wales), in subsection (6), at the end insert ", including the sea and other waters within the seaward limits of the territorial sea adjacent to England and Wales".

(3) In section 41 of the Police and Justice Act 2006 (immigration and asylum enforcement functions and customs functions: complaints and misconduct), in subsection (7), at the end insert ", including the sea and other waters within the seaward limits of the territorial sea adjacent to England and Wales".

22 Oversight functions of local policing bodies

(1) In section 1 of the Police Reform and Social Responsibility Act 2011 (police and crime commissioners), in subsection (8) (duty to hold chief constable to account), after paragraph (c) insert—

"(ca) the exercise of the chief constable's functions under Part 2 of the Police Reform Act 2002 in relation to the handling of complaints;".

(2) In section 3 of that Act (Mayor's Office for Policing and Crime), in subsection (8) (duty to hold Commissioner of Police of the Metropolis to account), after paragraph (c) insert—

"(ca) the exercise of the Commissioner's functions under Part 2 of the Police Reform Act 2002 in relation to the handling of complaints;".

(3) In section 6ZA of the Police Act 1996 (power to confer particular functions on the Common Council), in subsection (2), after paragraph (a) insert—

"(aa) to hold the Commissioner of Police for the City of London to account for the exercise of the Commissioner's functions under Part 2 of the Police Reform Act 2002 in relation to the handling of complaints;".

23 Delegation of functions by local policing bodies

(1) In section 23 of the Police Reform Act 2002 (Part 2 regulations), in subsection (2), after paragraph (p) insert—

"(pa) for local policing bodies to have power to delegate the exercise or performance of powers and duties conferred or imposed on them by or under this Part (including powers and duties that are acquired by virtue of giving a notice under section 13A);".

(2) In section 18 of the Police Reform and Social Responsibility Act 2011 (delegation of functions by police and crime commissioners), in subsection (3), after paragraph (a) insert—

"(aa) arrange, under subsection (1)(b) or (2), for the deputy police and crime commissioner or any other person to exercise a function that the police and crime commissioner has under or by virtue of Part 2 of the Police Reform Act 2002 (see instead section 23(2)(pa) of that Act and regulations made under that provision);".

(3) In section 19 of the Police Reform and Social Responsibility Act 2011 (delegation of functions by Mayor's Office for Policing and Crime), in subsection (3), after paragraph (a) insert—

"(aa) arrange, under subsection (1)(b) or (2), for the Deputy Mayor for Policing and Crime or any other person to exercise a function that the Mayor's Office for Policing and Crime has under or by virtue of Part 2 of the Police Reform Act 2002 (see instead section 23(2)(pa) of that Act and regulations made under that provision);".

(4) In section 107 of the Local Government Act 1972 (application of sections 101 to 106 of that Act to the Common Council)—

(a) in subsection (2), omit the words from the beginning to "and" in the first place it occurs;

(b) after subsection (2) insert—

"(2A) The Common Council may not, under section 101(1)(a), arrange for any person to exercise a function that the Common Council has under or by virtue of Part 2 of the Police Reform Act 2002 (see instead section 23(2)(pa) of that Act and regulations made under that provision)."

24 Transfer of staff to local policing bodies

(1) A local policing body may make one or more schemes for the transfer to itself from the chief officer of police of the police force maintained by the local policing body of rights and liabilities under, or in connection with, a relevant contract of employment

provided that the condition in subsection (2) is satisfied in relation to each such scheme.

(2) The condition referred to in subsection (1) is that it is desirable to make the scheme to enable the local policing body to discharge functions that are, or are to be, conferred on it under or by virtue of the Police Reform Act 2002 as a result of the amendments of that Act made by section 13 of, and paragraph 39 of Schedule 5 to, this Act.

(3) For the purposes of this section a contract of employment is a relevant contract of employment if it is a contract of employment of a member of the civilian staff of the police force (within the meaning of Part 1 of the Police Reform and Social Responsibility Act 2011) and the staff member is not designated under section 38 of the Police Reform Act 2002.

(4) The local policing body must obtain the consent of the chief officer of police to the making of the scheme.

(5) Where the chief officer of police does not consent to the making of the scheme, the local policing body may make the scheme notwithstanding subsection (4) if the Secretary of State consents to the making of the scheme.

(6) A scheme under subsection (1) must make provision that has the same or similar effect as the Transfer of Undertakings (Protection of Employment) Regulations 2006 (S.I. 2006/246) (so far as those regulations do not apply in relation to the transfer).

CHAPTER 2

POLICE SUPER-COMPLAINTS

25 Power to make super-complaints

After Part 2 of the Police Reform Act 2002 (complaints and misconduct) insert—

"PART 2A

SUPER-COMPLAINTS

29A Power to make super-complaints

(1) A designated body may make a complaint to Her Majesty's Chief Inspector of Constabulary that a feature, or combination of features, of policing in England and Wales by one or more than one police force is, or appears to be, significantly harming the interests of the public.

(2) See section 29B for the meaning of "designated body".

(3) In this section-

"England and Wales" includes the adjacent United Kingdom waters within the meaning of section 30 of the Police Act 1996,

"police force" means any of the following—

(a) the metropolitan police force,

(b) a police force maintained under section 2 of the Police Act 1996 (police forces in England and Wales outside London),
(c) the National Crime Agency,
(d) the City of London police force,
(e) the Ministry of Defence Police,
(f) the Civil Nuclear Constabulary,
(g) the British Transport Police."

26 Bodies who may make super-complaints

In Part 2A of the Police Reform Act 2002, after section 29A (for which see section 25 above), insert—

"29B Bodies who may make super-complaints

(1) In this Part "designated body" means a body designated in regulations made by the Secretary of State.

(2) The Secretary of State—
  (a) may make or revoke such a designation if the Secretary of State considers it appropriate to do so, and
  (b) must make or revoke such a designation if asked to do so by an authorised person.

(3) The Secretary of State must, in deciding whether to act under subsection (2)(a), apply criteria specified or described in regulations made by the Secretary of State.

(4) The authorised person must, in deciding whether to ask the Secretary of State to act under subsection (2)(b), apply criteria specified or described in regulations made by the Secretary of State.

(5) The Secretary of State must, before making regulations under subsection (3) or (4), consult such persons as the Secretary of State considers appropriate.

(6) In this section "authorised person" means any person specified or described in regulations made by the Secretary of State."

27 Regulations about super-complaints

(1) In Part 2A of the Police Reform Act 2002, after section 29B (for which see section 26 above), insert—

"29C Regulations about super-complaints

(1) The Secretary of State may by regulations make provision about complaints under section 29A.

(2) Such provision may, in particular, include provision about—
  (a) the procedure for dealing with a matter before a complaint is made under section 29A (including who is to deal with the matter),

(b) the procedure for dealing with a complaint under section 29A (including who is to deal with the matter),

(c) whether, or the extent to which, a matter is to be dealt with under this Part or Part 2.

(3) Regulations under this section may—

(a) confer (or enable the conferring of) functions on Her Majesty's Chief Inspector of Constabulary, the Independent Police Complaints Commission, the College of Policing or any other person,

(b) apply (with or without modifications), in relation to any matter to be dealt with by the Independent Police Complaints Commission under this Part, any provision made by or under Part 2."

(2) After section 10(3) of that Act (general functions of the Commission) insert—

"(3A) The Commission also has any functions conferred on it by regulations under section 29C of this Act (regulations about super-complaints)."

CHAPTER 3

WHISTLE-BLOWING: POWER OF IPCC TO INVESTIGATE

28 Investigations by the IPCC: whistle-blowing

(1) After Part 2A of the Police Reform Act 2002 (for which see sections 25 to 27 above) insert—

"PART 2B

INVESTIGATION OF CONCERNS RAISED BY WHISTLE-BLOWERS

29D Power to investigate concerns raised by whistle-blowers

(1) The Commission may investigate any concern raised by a whistle-blower of which it becomes aware (whether because the whistle-blower has contacted the Commission or for any other reason) but only if the whistle-blower informs the Commission, before the beginning of the investigation, that he or she consents to an investigation taking place.

(2) In deciding whether to investigate, the Commission must take into account the public interest.

(3) For the purposes of this Part, a person is a "whistle-blower" if—

(a) the person is, or was at any time, under the direction and control of a chief officer of police,

(b) the person raises a concern that is about a police force or a person serving with the police,

(c) the matter to which the concern relates is not—

(i) about the conditions of service of persons serving with the police, or

(ii) a matter that is, or could be, the subject of a complaint by the person under Part 2, and

(d) at the time the Commission first becomes aware of the concern, the matter to which it relates is not—

(i) under investigation under the direction of the Commission in accordance with paragraph 18 of Schedule 3,

(ii) under investigation by the Commission in accordance with paragraph 19 of that Schedule,

(iii) being dealt with as a complaint under section 29A under regulations under section 29C (regulations about super-complaints), or

(iv) under investigation under this Part.

(4) Subsection (1) is subject to section 29F (which deals with the position where the concern is a conduct matter for the purposes of Part 2) and to section 29G (which deals with the position where the concern is a DSI matter for the purposes of that Part).

(5) Schedule 3A (which makes provision about the procedure etc where the Commission decides to investigate under subsection (1)) has effect.

29E Commission's powers and duties where it decides not to investigate

(1) If the Commission decides not to carry out an investigation under section 29D(1), the Commission must inform the whistle-blower of the decision.

(2) In such a case, the Commission may, with the consent of the whistle-blower—

(a) disclose the nature of the concern to the appropriate authority, and

(b) make recommendations in the light of the concern.

(3) In this Part, except where otherwise provided, "appropriate authority" means—

(a) if the concern relates to a chief officer or an acting chief officer, the local policing body for the area of the police force of which he or she is a member;

(b) if the concern relates to any other person, the chief officer under whose direction and control that person is;

(c) if the concern does not relate to any particular persons, the chief officer of the police force to which the concern relates.

(4) The Secretary of State may by regulations make further provision about recommendations under subsection (2).

(5) The regulations may (amongst other things)—

(a) describe the kinds of recommendations that the Commission may make under subsection (2);

(b) specify the persons to whom the recommendations may be made;

(c) authorise the Commission to require a response to any recommendation made by the Commission under subsection (2).

29F Special provision for "conduct matters"

(1) Before deciding whether to carry out an investigation under section 29D(1), the Commission must consider whether the concern is about a conduct matter for the purposes of Part 2 (see section 12(2)).

(2) If the Commission determines that the concern is about a conduct matter for the purposes of Part 2—

(a) it may not carry out an investigation under section 29D(1), and

(b) it must notify the appropriate authority in relation to the person whose conduct is in question of its determination.

(3) Where the appropriate authority in relation to the person whose conduct is in question is notified under subsection (2), it must record the matter under paragraph 11 of Schedule 3 to this Act as a conduct matter.

(4) The Secretary of State may by regulations make provision modifying Schedule 3 in relation to a conduct matter that, in accordance with subsection (3), is recorded under paragraph 11 of that Schedule but only for the purpose of making provision for the protection of the anonymity of whistle-blowers.

29G Special provision for "DSI matters"

(1) Before deciding whether to carry out an investigation under section 29D(1), the Commission must consider whether the concern is about a death or serious injury matter ("a DSI matter") for the purposes of Part 2 (see section 12(2A)).

(2) If the Commission determines that the concern is about a DSI matter for the purposes of Part 2—

(a) it may not carry out an investigation under section 29D(1), and

(b) it must notify the appropriate authority in relation to the DSI matter.

(3) Where the appropriate authority in relation to the DSI matter is notified under subsection (2), it must record the matter under paragraph 14A of Schedule 3 to this Act as a DSI matter.

(4) The Secretary of State may by regulations make provision modifying Schedule 3 in relation to a DSI matter that, in accordance with subsection (3), is recorded under paragraph 14A of that Schedule but only for the purpose of making provision for the protection of the anonymity of whistle-blowers.

(5) In this section, references to the appropriate authority in relation to a DSI matter have the same meaning as in Part 2 (see section 29).

29H Commission's powers and duties where whistle-blower is deceased

(1) The power of the Commission to carry out an investigation under section 29D(1) applies where the whistle-blower dies before the Commission becomes aware of the concern (or before it decides to investigate).

(2) Any investigation begun by the Commission under section 29D(1) before the death of the whistle-blower may be continued after the death.

(3) Where a whistle-blower dies—

(a) any requirement under this Part to obtain the consent of the whistle-blower may be satisfied by obtaining the consent of that person's approved representative;

(b) any requirement under this Part to give any document or other information to the whistle-blower may be satisfied by giving the document or other information to the person's approved representative;

(c) any requirement under this Part not to disclose the identity of the whistle-blower does not apply or (where the Commission became aware of the concern before the death) ceases to apply.

(4) For the purpose of this section, "approved representative" means a person who has been approved by the Commission for the purposes of this Part.

(5) The Commission may only approve a person who is—

(a) the widow or widower (or surviving civil partner) of the deceased whistle-blower,

(b) a personal representative (within the meaning of section 55(1)(xi) of the Administration of Estates Act 1925) of the deceased whistle-blower, or

(c) any other person appearing to the Commission to have, by reason of a family or similar relationship with the deceased whistle-blower, a relevant interest in the outcome of the concern.

29I Duty to keep whistle-blowers informed

(1) Where the Commission carries out an investigation under section 29D(1), it must keep the whistle-blower properly informed about the progress of the investigation and its outcome.

(2) The Secretary of State may by regulations provide for exceptions to the duty under subsection (1).

(3) The power conferred by subsection (2) may be exercised only to the extent that the Secretary of State considers necessary for any of the permitted non-disclosure purposes.

(4) "The permitted non-disclosure purposes" are—

(a) preventing the premature or inappropriate disclosure of information that is relevant to, or may be used in, any actual or prospective criminal proceedings;

(b) preventing the disclosure of information in any circumstances in which it has been determined in accordance with the regulations that its non-disclosure—

(i) is in the interests of national security,

(ii) is for the purposes of the prevention or detection of crime or the apprehension or prosecution of offenders,

(iii) is for the purposes of the investigation of an allegation of misconduct against the whistle-blower or the taking of disciplinary proceedings or other appropriate action in relation to such an allegation,

(iv) is for the purposes of an investigation under Part 2 that relates to the whistle-blower,

(v) is required on proportionality grounds, or

(vi) is otherwise necessary in the public interest.

(5) The non-disclosure of information is required on proportionality grounds if its disclosure would cause, directly or indirectly, an adverse effect which would be disproportionate to the benefits arising from its disclosure.

29J Protection of anonymity of whistle-blowers

(1) The Secretary of State may by regulations make provision setting out the circumstances in which the Commission is required or authorised to disclose information falling within subsection (2) (or any particular description of such information) to persons specified, or of a description specified, in the regulations.

(2) The information falling within this subsection is—

(a) the identity of a whistle-blower or information that might (whether alone or with other information) tend to reveal that identity;

(b) the nature of a concern raised by a whistle-blower.

(3) The power conferred by subsection (1) may be exercised only to the extent that the Secretary of State considers necessary for any of the permitted disclosure purposes.

(4) "The permitted disclosure purposes" are—

(a) the protection of the interests of national security;

(b) the prevention or detection of crime or the apprehension of offenders;

(c) the institution or conduct of criminal proceedings;

(d) the investigation of allegations of misconduct against whistle-blowers and the taking of disciplinary proceedings or other appropriate action in relation to such allegations;

(e) investigations under Part 2 that relate to whistle-blowers;

(f) investigations under this Part;

(g) any other purpose that is for the protection of the public interest.

(5) Except as provided by regulations under subsection (1) or by any other provision of this Part, the Commission may not disclose information falling within subsection (2) unless the whistle-blower consents to the disclosure.

29K Other restrictions on disclosure of information

(1) The Secretary of State may by regulations make provision setting out the circumstances in which the Commission is required or authorised to disclose information falling within subsection (2) (or any particular description of such information) to persons specified, or of a description specified, in the regulations.

(2) The information falling within this subsection is—

(a) information relating to an investigation under section 29D;

(b) information relating to the outcome of any such investigation.

(3) The power conferred by subsection (1) may be exercised only to the extent that the Secretary of State considers necessary for any of the permitted disclosure purposes.

(4) In this section, "the permitted disclosure purposes" has the same meaning as in section 29J.

(5) Except as provided by regulations under subsection (1) or by any other provision of this Part, the Commission may not disclose information falling within subsection (2).

29L Application of provisions of Part 2

(1) The following provisions of Part 2 apply in relation to the functions of the Commission under this Part as they apply in relation to the functions of the Commission under Part 2—

- (a) section 15 (general duties of local policing bodies, chief officers and inspectors);
- (b) section 16 (payment for assistance with investigation);
- (c) section 17 (provision of information to the Commission);
- (d) section 18 (inspection of police premises on behalf of the Commission);
- (e) section 19 (use of investigatory powers by or on behalf of the Commission);
- (f) section 21A (restriction on disclosure of sensitive information);
- (g) section 21B (provision of sensitive information to the Commission);
- (h) section 22 (power of the Commission to issue guidance);
- (i) section 26 (forces maintained otherwise than by local policing bodies);
- (j) section 26BA (College of Policing);
- (k) section 26C (the National Crime Agency).

(2) Except as provided by subsection (1), the provision made by sections 15 to 29 of Part 2 does not apply in relation to the functions of the Commission under this Part.

29M Regulation-making powers: consultation

Before making regulations under this Part, the Secretary of State must consult—

- (a) the Commission,
- (b) such persons as appear to the Secretary of State to represent the views of police and crime commissioners,
- (c) the Mayor's Office for Policing and Crime;
- (d) the Common Council,
- (e) the National Police Chiefs' Council, and
- (f) such other persons as the Secretary of State thinks fit.

29N Interpretation

(1) In this Part—

"the Commission" means the Independent Police Complaints Commission;

"appropriate authority" has the meaning given by section 29E(3);

"chief officer" means the chief officer of police of any police force; and "acting chief officer" means (as appropriate)—

(a) a person exercising or performing functions of a chief constable in accordance with section 41 of the Police Reform and Social Responsibility Act 2011,

(b) a person exercising powers or duties of the Commissioner of Police of the Metropolis in accordance with section 44 or 45(4) of that Act, or

(c) a person exercising duties of the Commissioner of Police for the City of London in accordance with section 25 of the City of London Police Act 1839;

"conduct" has the same meaning as in Part 2 (see section 29(1));

"whistle-blower" has the meaning given by section 29D(3).

(2) References in this Part to a person serving with the police have the same meaning as in Part 2 (see section 12(7))."

(2) After Schedule 3 to the Police Reform Act 2002 insert the new Schedule 3A set out in Schedule 6 to this Act.

(3) In section 10 of that Act, after subsection (3A) (for which see section 27 above), insert—

"(3B) The Commission also has the functions which are conferred on it by Part 2B (whistle-blowing)."

(4) In section 105 of that Act, in subsection (5), after "Part 2" insert "or 2B".

(5) In section 63 of the Police Act 1996 (Police Advisory Board for England and Wales), in subsection (3)(b), after "Part 2" insert "or 2B".

CHAPTER 4

POLICE DISCIPLINE

29 Disciplinary proceedings: former members of police forces and former special constables

(1) The Police Act 1996 is amended as follows.

(2) In section 50 (regulations for police forces), after subsection (3) (regulations concerning disciplinary proceedings) insert—

"(3A) Regulations under this section may provide for the procedures that are established by or under regulations made by virtue of subsection (3) to apply (with or without modifications) in respect of the conduct, efficiency or effectiveness of any person where—

(a) an allegation relating to the conduct, efficiency or effectiveness of the person comes to the attention of a chief officer of police, a local policing body or the Independent Police Complaints Commission,

(b) at the time of the alleged misconduct, inefficiency or ineffectiveness the person was a member of a police force, and

(c) condition A, B or C is satisfied in relation to the person.

(3B) Condition A is that the person ceases to be a member of a police force after the allegation first comes to the attention of a person mentioned in subsection (3A)(a).

(3C) Condition B is that the person had ceased to be a member of a police force before the allegation first came to the attention of a person mentioned in subsection (3A)(a) but the period between the person having ceased to be a member of a police force and the allegation first coming to the attention of a person mentioned in subsection (3A)(a) does not exceed the period specified in regulations under this section.

(3D) Condition C is that—

(a) the person had ceased to be a member of a police force before the allegation first came to the attention of a person mentioned in subsection (3A)(a),

(b) the period between the person having ceased to be a member of a police force and the allegation first coming to the attention of a person mentioned in subsection (3A)(a) exceeds the period specified for the purposes of condition B, and

(c) the alleged misconduct, inefficiency or ineffectiveness is such that, if proved, the person could have been dealt with by dismissal if the person had still been a member of a police force.

(3E) Regulations made by virtue of subsection (3A) as they apply in a case where condition C is satisfied in relation to a person must provide that disciplinary proceedings may be taken against the person in respect of the alleged misconduct, inefficiency or ineffectiveness only if the Independent Police Complaints Commission determines that taking such proceedings would be reasonable and proportionate having regard to—

(a) the seriousness of the alleged misconduct, inefficiency or ineffectiveness,

(b) the impact of the allegation on public confidence in the police, and

(c) the public interest.

(3F) Regulations made by virtue of subsection (3A) may make provision about matters to be taken into account by the Independent Police Complaints Commission for the purposes of subsection (3E)(a) to (c).

(3G) Regulations made by virtue of subsection (3A) must provide that disciplinary proceedings which are not the first disciplinary proceedings to be taken against the person in respect of the alleged misconduct, inefficiency or ineffectiveness may be taken only if they result from a re-investigation of the allegation (whether carried out under regulations under this section or under the Police Reform Act 2002) that begins within the period specified in the regulations.

The period specified must begin with the date when the person ceased to be a member of a police force."

(3) In section 51 (regulations for special constables), after subsection (2A) (regulations concerning disciplinary proceedings) insert—

"(2B) Regulations under this section may provide for the procedures that are established by or under regulations made by virtue of subsection (2A) to apply (with or without modifications) in respect of the conduct, efficiency or effectiveness of any person where—

(a) an allegation relating to the conduct, efficiency or effectiveness of the person comes to the attention of a chief officer of police, a local policing body or the Independent Police Complaints Commission,

(b) at the time of the alleged misconduct, inefficiency or ineffectiveness the person was a special constable, and

(c) condition A, B or C is satisfied in relation to the person.

(2C) Condition A is that the person ceases to be a special constable after the allegation first comes to the attention of a person mentioned in subsection (2B)(a).

(2D) Condition B is that the person had ceased to be a special constable before the allegation first came to the attention of a person mentioned in subsection (2B)(a) but the period between the person having ceased to be a special constable and the allegation first coming to the attention of a person mentioned in subsection (2B)(a) does not exceed the period specified in regulations under this section.

(2E) Condition C is that—

(a) the person had ceased to be a special constable before the allegation first came to the attention of a person mentioned in subsection (2B)(a),

(b) the period between the person having ceased to be a special constable and the allegation first coming to the attention of a person mentioned in subsection (2B)(a) exceeds the period specified for the purposes of condition B, and

(c) the alleged misconduct, inefficiency or ineffectiveness is such that, if proved, the person could have been dealt with by dismissal if the person had still been a special constable.

(2F) Regulations made by virtue of subsection (2B) as they apply in a case where condition C is satisfied in relation to a person must provide that disciplinary proceedings may be taken against the person in respect of the alleged misconduct, inefficiency or ineffectiveness only if the Independent Police Complaints Commission determines that taking such proceedings would be reasonable and proportionate having regard to—

(a) the seriousness of the alleged misconduct, inefficiency or ineffectiveness,

(b) the impact of the allegation on public confidence in the police, and

(c) the public interest.

(2G) Regulations made by virtue of subsection (2B) may make provision about matters to be taken into account by the Independent Police Complaints Commission for the purposes of subsection (2F)(a) to (c).

(2H) Regulations made by virtue of subsection (2B) must provide that disciplinary proceedings which are not the first disciplinary proceedings to be taken against the person in respect of the alleged misconduct, inefficiency or ineffectiveness may be taken only if they result from a re-investigation of the allegation (whether carried out under regulations under this section or under the Police Reform Act 2002) that begins within the period specified in the regulations.

The period specified must begin with the date when the person ceased to be a special constable."

(4) In section 84 (representation etc at disciplinary and other proceedings)—

(a) in subsection (1)—

(i) after "50(3)" insert "or (3A)";

(ii) after "51(2A)" insert "or (2B)";

(b) in subsection (4)—

(i) in the definition of "the officer concerned", after "constable" insert "or, as the case may be, the former member of a police force or the former special constable,";

(ii) in the definition of "relevant authority", after "authority"" insert ", in relation to proceedings conducted under regulations made in pursuance of section 50(3) or section 51(2A),";

(iii) after the definition of "relevant authority" insert—

""relevant authority", in relation to proceedings conducted under regulations made in pursuance of section 50(3A) or section 51(2B), means—

(a) where the officer concerned is a former member of a police force (other than a former chief officer of police), or a former special constable, the chief officer of police of the police force of which the officer was last a member, or for which the officer was last appointed as a special constable;

(b) where the officer concerned is a former chief officer of police, the local policing body for the police force of which the officer was last a member;".

(5) In section 85 (appeals against dismissal etc), in subsection (1), after "constable" insert ", or a former member of a police force or a former special constable,".

(6) In Schedule 6 (appeals to Police Appeals Tribunals), in paragraph 10—

(a) in paragraph (b), before "means" insert ", except in relation to an appeal under section 85 that relates to proceedings conducted under regulations made in pursuance of section 50(3A) or section 51(2B),";

(b) after paragraph (b) insert—

"(ba) the relevant local policing body", in relation to an appeal under section 85 that relates to proceedings conducted under regulations made in pursuance of section 50(3A) or section 51(2B), means the local policing body which maintains—

(i) the police force of which the appellant was last a member, or

(ii) the police force for the area for which the appellant was last appointed as a special constable,

as the case may be."

(7) Regulations made in pursuance of section 50(3A) or 51(2B) of the Police Act 1996 (as inserted by subsections (2) and (3))—

(a) may not make provision in relation to a person who ceases to be a member of a police force or a special constable (as the case may be) before the coming into force of subsections (2) and (3);

(b) may make provision in relation to a person who ceases to be a member of a police force or a special constable (as the case may be) after the coming into force of this section even though the alleged misconduct, inefficiency or ineffectiveness occurred at a time before the coming into force of subsections (2) and (3), but only if the alleged misconduct, inefficiency or ineffectiveness is such that, if proved, there could be a finding in relation to the person in disciplinary proceedings that the person would have been dismissed if the person had still been a member of a police force or a special constable.

(8) Schedule 7 makes amendments of the Ministry of Defence Police Act 1987, the Railways and Transport Safety Act 2003 and the Energy Act 2004 which produce an equivalent effect to the amendments made by this section.

30 Police barred list and police advisory list

(1) After Part 4 of the Police Act 1996, insert the Part set out in Schedule 8 to this Act.

(2) In consequence of the new Part 4A of the Police Act 1996 (as inserted by Schedule 8), the Police Reform and Social Responsibility Act 2011 is amended as follows.

(3) In section 42 (appointment of Commissioner of Police of the Metropolis), after subsection (3A) insert—

"(3AA) But a person who would be eligible for appointment by virtue of subsection (3A) is not eligible for appointment at a time when the person is included in the police barred list maintained under section 88B of the Police Act 1996."

(4) In section 43 (Deputy Commissioner of Police of the Metropolis), after subsection (3) insert—

"(3A) The Secretary of State may not recommend to Her Majesty that She appoint a person as the Deputy Commissioner of Police of the Metropolis unless that person is eligible for appointment.

(3B) A person is not eligible for appointment at a time when the person is included in the police barred list maintained under section 88B of the Police Act 1996."

(5) In Part 1 of Schedule 8 (appointment of Chief Constables), in paragraph 1—

(a) the existing text becomes sub-paragraph (1);

(b) after that sub-paragraph insert—

"(2) The police and crime commissioner also has duties under section 88C of the Police Act 1996 (effect of inclusion in police barred list) in relation to the appointment of a chief constable."

(6) The Secretary of State may by regulations made by statutory instrument make provision that—

(a) corresponds or is similar to that made by or under Part 4A of the Police Act 1996 (as inserted by Schedule 8), and

(b) relates to a person who is, or has been, employed or appointed by a person with functions of a public nature exercisable in, or in relation to, England and Wales that relate to policing or law enforcement (other than a chief officer of police or a local policing body, within the meaning of the Police Act 1996).

(7) A statutory instrument containing regulations under subsection (6) is subject to annulment in pursuance of a resolution of either House of Parliament.

31 Appeals to Police Appeals Tribunals

(1) Schedule 6 to the Police Act 1996 (appeals to Police Appeals Tribunals) is amended as follows.

(2) In paragraph 1 (appeal by a senior officer), in sub-paragraph (1), in the words before paragraph (a), for "Secretary of State" substitute "relevant person".

(3) In paragraph 2 (appeal by a member of a police force other than a senior officer or by a special constable), in sub-paragraph (1)—

(a) in the words before paragraph (a), for "relevant local policing body" substitute "relevant person";

(b) omit paragraph (d);

(c) at the end insert—

"(e) one shall be a lay person."

(4) After paragraph 2 insert—

"2A (1) For the purposes of paragraphs 1 and 2, "the relevant person" means the person determined in accordance with rules made by the Secretary of State.

(2) Rules under sub-paragraph (1) may make—

(a) different provision for different cases and circumstances;

(b) provision for the relevant person to be able to delegate the power to appoint the members of a tribunal.

(3) A statutory instrument containing rules under sub-paragraph (1) is subject to annulment in pursuance of a resolution of either House of Parliament."

(5) In paragraph 10 (interpretation)—

(a) after paragraph (a) insert—

"(aa) lay person" means a person who is not, and has never been—

(i) a member of a police force or a special constable,

(ii) a member of the civilian staff of a police force, including the metropolitan police force, within the meaning of Part 1 of the Police Reform and Social

Responsibility Act 2011 (see section 102(4) and (6) of that Act),

(iii) a person employed by the Common Council of the City of London in its capacity as police authority who is under the direction and control of the Commissioner of Police for the City of London,

(iv) a police and crime commissioner,

(v) a member of staff of a police and crime commissioner, or of the Mayor's Office for Policing and Crime, within the meaning of Part 1 of the Police Reform and Social Responsibility Act 2011 (see section 102(3) and (5) of that Act),

(vi) a constable within the meaning of Part 1 of the Police and Fire Reform (Scotland) Act 2012 (2012 asp 8) (see section 99 of that Act),

(vii) a member of the Police Service of Northern Ireland or the Police Service of Northern Ireland Reserve,

(viii) a member of the British Transport Police Force or a special constable appointed under section 25 of the Railways and Transport Safety Act 2003,

(ix) an employee of the British Transport Police Authority appointed under section 27 of the Railways and Transport Safety Act 2003,

(x) a member of the Ministry of Defence Police,

(xi) a person (other than a member of the Ministry of Defence Police) who is under the direction and control of the chief constable for the Ministry of Defence Police,

(xii) a member of the Civil Nuclear Constabulary, or

(xiii) an employee of the Civil Nuclear Police Authority appointed under paragraph 6 of Schedule 10 to the Energy Act 2004,";

(b) omit sub-paragraph (c).

(6) In consequence of the other provision made by this section—

(a) in the Criminal Justice and Immigration Act 2008, in Part 1 of Schedule 22, omit paragraph 11(6)(b);

(b) in the Police Reform and Social Responsibility Act 2011, in Part 1 of Schedule 16, omit paragraph 47(2)(b).

32 Guidance concerning disciplinary proceedings and conduct etc

(1) Section 87 of the Police Act 1996 (guidance concerning disciplinary proceedings etc) is amended as follows.

(2) For subsections (1) to (1A) substitute—

"(1) The Secretary of State may issue guidance as to the discharge of their disciplinary functions to—

(a) local policing bodies,

(b) chief officers of police,

(c) other members of police forces,

(d) civilian police employees, and

(e) the Independent Police Complaints Commission."

(3) Before subsection (2) insert—

"(1B) The College of Policing may, with the approval of the Secretary of State, issue guidance to the persons mentioned in subsection (1)(a) to (c) as to the discharge of their disciplinary functions in relation to members of police forces and special constables and former members of police forces and former special constables."

(4) After subsection (4) insert—

"(4A) In this section "disciplinary functions" means—

(a) functions in relation to the conduct, efficiency and effectiveness of, and the maintenance of discipline of, the following persons (including functions in relation to disciplinary proceedings)—

(i) members of police forces;

(ii) special constables;

(iii) civilian police employees;

(b) functions in relation to disciplinary proceedings against persons who were, but have ceased to be, persons falling within paragraph (a)."

(5) For subsection (5) substitute—

"(5) In this section—

"civilian police employee" means—

(a) a member of the civilian staff of a police force, including the metropolitan police force (within the meaning of Part 1 of the Police Reform and Social Responsibility Act 2011), or

(b) a person employed by the Common Council of the City of London in its capacity as police authority who is under the direction and control of the Commissioner of Police for the City of London;

"disciplinary proceedings"—

(a) in relation to a member of a police force or a special constable, or a former member of a police force or a former special constable, means any proceedings under regulations under section 50 or 51 that are identified as disciplinary proceedings by those regulations;

(b) in relation to any other person, means any proceedings identified as disciplinary proceedings by regulations made by the Secretary of State for the purposes of this section."

(6) After subsection (5) insert—

"(6) A statutory instrument containing regulations under paragraph (b) of the definition of "disciplinary proceedings" in subsection (5) is subject to annulment in pursuance of a resolution of either House of Parliament."

(7) After section 87 of the Police Act 1996 insert—

"87A Guidance concerning conduct etc

(1) The Secretary of State may issue guidance as to matters of conduct, efficiency and effectiveness to—

(a) members of police forces,
(b) special constables, and
(c) civilian police employees.

(2) The College of Policing may, with the approval of the Secretary of State, issue guidance of the type described in subsection (1) to the persons mentioned in paragraphs (a) and (b) of that subsection.

(3) It shall be the duty of every person to whom any guidance under this section is issued to have regard to the guidance.

(4) A failure by a person to whom guidance under this section is issued to have regard to the guidance shall be admissible in evidence in any disciplinary proceedings brought against the person.

(5) In this section "civilian police employees" and "disciplinary proceedings" have the same meaning as in section 87."

CHAPTER 5

IPCC: RE-NAMING AND ORGANISATIONAL CHANGE

33 Independent Office for Police Conduct

(1) The body corporate known as the Independent Police Complaints Commission—

(a) is to continue to exist, and
(b) is to be known instead as the Independent Office for Police Conduct.

(2) Section 9 of the Police Reform Act 2002 (which established the Independent Police Complaints Commission) is amended in accordance with subsections (3) to (8).

(3) For the heading substitute "The Independent Office for Police Conduct".

(4) For subsection (1) substitute—

"(1) The body corporate previously known as the Independent Police Complaints Commission—

(a) is to continue to exist, and
(b) is to be known instead as the Independent Office for Police Conduct."

(5) For subsection (2) substitute—

"(2) The Office is to consist of—

(a) a Director General appointed by Her Majesty, and
(b) at least six other members.

(2A) The other members must consist of—

(a) persons appointed as non-executive members (see paragraph 1A of Schedule 2), and

(b) persons appointed as employee members (see paragraph 1B of that Schedule),

but the powers of appointment under those paragraphs must be exercised so as to secure that a majority of members of the Office (including the Director General) are non-executive members."

(6) In subsection (3)—

(a) for "chairman of the Commission" substitute "Director General";

(b) omit ", or as another member of the Commission,".

(7) In subsection (5)—

(a) for "The Commission shall not—" substitute "Neither the Office nor the Director General shall—";

(b) for "Commission's" substitute "Office's".

(8) In subsection (6) for "Commission" substitute "Office".

(9) Schedule 9 makes further provision in relation to the Independent Office for Police Conduct.

34 Exercise of functions

(1) Section 10 of the Police Reform Act 2002 (general functions of the Commission) is amended in accordance with subsections (2) to (5) (see also paragraph 17 of Schedule 9 for further minor and consequential amendments).

(2) For "Commission", in each place except as otherwise provided by subsection (5) (including in the heading and in provisions inserted by amendments made by this Act), substitute "Director General".

(3) In subsection (2)—

(a) in paragraph (a), at the end insert "or other concerns raised by virtue of Part 2B (whistle-blowing)";

(b) in paragraph (c), after "complaints" insert "or other concerns".

(4) After subsection (5) insert—

"(5A) In carrying out functions the Director General must have regard to any advice provided to the Director General by the Office (see section 10A(1)(c))."

(5) In subsection (7), for "Commission", in the first place it occurs, substitute "Office".

(6) After that section insert—

"10A General functions of the Office

(1) The functions of the Office are—

(a) to secure that the Office has in place appropriate arrangements for good governance and financial management,

(b) to determine and promote the strategic aims and values of the Office,

(c) to provide support and advice to the Director General in the carrying out of the Director General's functions, and

(d) to monitor and review the carrying out of such functions.

(2) The Office also has such other functions as are conferred on it by any other enactment (whenever passed or made).

(3) The Office is to perform its functions for the general purpose of improving the way in which the Director General's functions are carried out (including by encouraging the efficient and effective use of resources in the carrying out of those functions).

(4) In carrying out its functions the Office must in particular have regard to public confidence in the existence of suitable arrangements with respect to the matters mentioned in section 10(2) and with the operation of the arrangements that are in fact maintained with respect to those matters.

(5) The Office may do anything which appears to it to be calculated to facilitate, or is incidental or conducive to, the carrying out of its functions.

10B Efficiency etc in exercise of functions

The Director General and the Office must carry out their functions efficiently and effectively.

10C Strategy for exercise of functions

(1) The Director General and the Office must jointly—

(a) prepare a strategy for the carrying out of their functions, and

(b) review the strategy (and revise it as appropriate) at least once every 12 months.

(2) The strategy must set out how the Director General and the Office propose to carry out their functions in the relevant period.

(3) The strategy must also include a plan for the use during the relevant period of resources for the carrying out of functions of the Director General and the Office.

(4) The Director General and the Office must each give effect to the strategy in carrying out their functions.

(5) The Director General and the Office must jointly publish a strategy (or revised strategy) prepared under this section (stating the time from which it takes effect).

(6) In this section "relevant period", in relation to a strategy, means the period of time that is covered by the strategy.

10D Code of practice

(1) The Director General and the Office must jointly prepare a code of practice dealing with the relationship between the Director General and the Office.

(2) In doing so, they must (in particular) seek to reflect the principle that the Director General is to act independently when making decisions in connection with the carrying out of the Director General's functions.

(3) The code must include provision as to the following—

(a) how the strategy required by section 10C is to be prepared, reviewed and revised;

(b) the matters to be covered by the strategy and the periods to be covered by it from time to time;

(c) how the carrying out of functions by the Director General is to be monitored and reviewed by other members of the Office;

(d) the giving of advice to the Director General by other members of the Office in connection with the carrying out of functions by the Director General;

(e) the keeping of written records of instances where the Director General has not followed advice given by other members of the Office and the reasons for not doing so;

(f) how non-executive members of the Office are to give practical effect to the requirement imposed by subsection (2).

(4) The Code may include whatever other provision the Director General and the Office think appropriate.

(5) The Director General and the Office must jointly review the code regularly and revise it as appropriate.

(6) The Director General and the Office must each comply with the code.

(7) The Director General and the Office must jointly publish a code (or revised code) prepared under this section (stating the time from which it takes effect)."

35 Public records

(1) In Schedule 1 to the Public Records Act 1958 (definition of public records), in Part 2 of the Table at the end of paragraph 3, insert at the appropriate place—

"Independent Office for Police Conduct."

(2) The records that become public records for the purposes of that Act as a result of the amendment made by subsection (1) include all records of the Independent Office for Police Conduct of the kind mentioned in paragraph 3(1) of Schedule 1 to that Act (whether created before or after the coming into force of this section, and whether created under that name or under the name of the Independent Police Complaints Commission).

(3) If the amendment made by subsection (1) comes into force before subsection (1) of section 33 comes into force, the reference in that amendment to the Independent Office for Police Conduct is, until subsection (1) of that section comes into force, to be read as a reference to the Independent Police Complaints Commission.

CHAPTER 6

INSPECTION

36 Powers of inspectors to obtain information, access to police premises etc

(1) In Schedule 4A to the Police Act 1996 (further provision about Her Majesty's Inspectors of Constabulary), for paragraphs 6A and 6B substitute—

"6A Powers of inspectors to obtain information etc

6A (1) An inspector may serve on a person a notice requiring the person—

(a) to provide the inspector with any information or documents that the inspector reasonably requires for the purposes of an inspection under section 54;

(b) to produce or deliver up to the inspector any evidence or other things that the inspector reasonably requires for those purposes.

This is subject to sub-paragraphs (6) to (9).

(2) A notice under this paragraph must—

(a) specify or describe the information, documents, evidence or other things that are required by the inspector;

(b) specify the period within which the information, documents, evidence or other things must be provided, produced or delivered up;

(c) where the notice is served on a person who has a right of appeal under paragraph 6D, give details of that right of appeal.

(3) In a case where a notice is served on a person who has a right of appeal under paragraph 6D, a period specified under sub-paragraph (2)(b) must not end before the end of the period within which the appeal could be brought.

(4) A notice under this paragraph may specify the form and manner in which any information, documents, evidence or other things are to be provided, produced or delivered up.

(5) An inspector may cancel a notice under this paragraph by written notice to the person on whom it was served.

(6) A notice under this paragraph must not be used to obtain information, or any document or other thing, from—

(a) the Security Service,

(b) the Secret Intelligence Service,

(c) the Government Communications Headquarters,

(d) any part of Her Majesty's forces, or of the Ministry of Defence, which engages in intelligence activities,

(e) the Crown Prosecution Service,

(f) the Service Prosecuting Authority, or

(g) the Serious Fraud Office.

(7) A notice under this paragraph must also not be used to obtain information, or any document or other thing, from any person if—

(a) the information, or the document or other thing, was obtained by that person (directly or indirectly) from a body or other entity mentioned in sub-paragraph (6), or

(b) the information, or the document or other thing, relates to a body or other entity mentioned in that sub-paragraph.

(8) A notice under this paragraph must not require a person—

(a) to provide information that might incriminate the person;

(b) to provide an item subject to legal privilege within the meaning of the Police and Criminal Evidence Act 1984 (see section 10 of that Act);

(c) to make a disclosure that would be prohibited by any of Parts 1 to 7 or Chapter 1 of Part 9 of the Investigatory Powers Act 2016;

(d) to provide information that was provided to the person by, or by an agency of, the government of a country or territory outside the United Kingdom where that government does not consent to the disclosure of the information.

(9) A notice under this paragraph must not require a postal or telecommunications operator to provide communications data.

(10) In sub-paragraph (9), "communications data", "postal operator" and "telecommunications operator" have the same meanings as in the Investigatory Powers Act 2016 (see sections 261 and 262 of that Act).

(11) In this paragraph—

"document" means anything in which information of any description is recorded;

"inspector" means—

(a) an inspector of constabulary,

(b) a person appointed under section 56 as an assistant inspector of constabulary or staff officer to the inspectors of constabulary, or

(c) a person authorised by an inspector of constabulary to act on behalf of the inspector for the purposes of this paragraph.

6B Powers of inspectors to obtain access to police premises

6B (1) An inspector may serve on a person a notice requiring the person to allow the inspector access, which the inspector reasonably requires for the purposes of an inspection under section 54, to—

(a) premises that are occupied (wholly or partly) for the purposes of—

(i) a police force,

(ii) a local policing body,

(iii) a person providing services, in pursuance of contractual arrangements (but without being employed by a chief officer of police of the police force or its local policing body), to assist a police force in relation to the discharge of its chief officer's functions, or

(iv) any other person who is, by virtue of any enactment, carrying out any of the activities of a police force, and

(b) documents and other things on those premises.

(2) A notice under this paragraph must—

(a) specify or describe the premises to which the inspector requires access;

(b) specify the time when access is required (which may be immediately after the service of the notice).

(3) Where there are reasonable grounds for not allowing the inspector to have access to the premises at the time specified under sub-paragraph (2)(b), the requirement under this paragraph has effect as a requirement to secure that access is allowed to the inspector at the earliest practicable time specified by the inspector after there cease to be such grounds.

(4) An inspector may cancel a notice under this paragraph by written notice to the person on whom it was served.

(5) In this paragraph "document" and "inspector" have the same meanings as in paragraph 6A (and, for that purpose, the reference in paragraph (c) of the definition of "inspector" in paragraph 6A(11) to paragraph 6A is to be read as a reference to this paragraph).

6C Failure to comply with notice under paragraph 6A or 6B

6C (1) If a person who has received a notice under paragraph 6A or 6B—

(a) fails or refuses without reasonable excuse to do what is required by the notice, or

(b) (in the case of a notice under paragraph 6A) knowingly or recklessly provides information in response to the notice that is false in a material respect,

the chief inspector of constabulary may certify in writing to the High Court that the person has failed to comply with the notice.

(2) The High Court may then inquire into the matter and, after hearing any witness who may be produced against or on behalf of the person, and after hearing any statement offered in defence, deal with the person as if the person had committed a contempt of court.

6D Appeals against notices under paragraph 6A

6D (1) A person on whom a notice is served under paragraph 6A may appeal against the notice to the First-tier Tribunal on the ground that the notice is not in accordance with the law.

(2) The right of appeal conferred by sub-paragraph (1) does not apply where the notice is served on a person who is—

(a) a member of a police force;

(b) a special constable;

(c) a member of the civilian staff of a police force, including the metropolitan police force (within the meaning of Part 1 of the Police Reform and Social Responsibility Act 2011);

(d) a local policing body or a person employed by a local policing body;

(e) a person providing services, in pursuance of contractual arrangements (but without being employed by a chief officer of police of a police force or its local policing body), to assist a police force in relation to the discharge of its chief officer's functions;

(f) a person employed by a person providing services as mentioned in paragraph (e);

(g) any other person who is, by virtue of any enactment, carrying out any of the activities of a police force.

(3) If an appeal is brought, any requirement imposed by the notice is of no effect pending the determination or withdrawal of the appeal.

(4) If the Tribunal considers that the notice is not in accordance with the law—

(a) it must quash the notice, and

(b) it may give directions regarding the service of a further notice under paragraph 6A.

6E Sensitive information: restriction on further disclosure

6E (1) Where an inspector receives information within sub-paragraph (2), the inspector must not disclose the information, or the fact that it has been received, unless the relevant authority consents to the disclosure.

(2) The information is—

(a) intelligence service information;

(b) protected information relating to a relevant warrant;

(c) information obtained from a government department which, at the time it is provided to the inspector, is identified by the department as information the disclosure of which may, in the opinion of the relevant authority—

(i) cause damage to national security, international relations or the economic interests of the United Kingdom or any part of the United Kingdom, or

(ii) jeopardise the safety of any person.

(3) Where an inspector discloses to another person information within sub-paragraph (2), or the fact that the inspector has received it, the other person must not disclose that information or that fact unless the relevant authority consents to the disclosure.

(4) A prohibition on disclosure in sub-paragraph (1) or (3) does not apply to disclosure by one inspector to another.

(5) In this paragraph—

"government department" means a department of Her Majesty's Government but does not include—

(a) the Security Service,

(b) the Secret Intelligence Service, or

(c) the Government Communications Headquarters ("GCHQ");

"inspector" means—

(a) an inspector of constabulary,

(b) a person appointed under section 56 as an assistant inspector of constabulary or staff officer to the inspectors of constabulary, or

(c) a person authorised by an inspector of constabulary to act on behalf of the inspector in receiving information (whether under paragraph 6A or otherwise);

"intelligence service information" means information that was obtained (directly or indirectly) from or that relates to—

(a) the Security Service,

(b) the Secret Intelligence Service,

(c) GCHQ, or

(d) any part of Her Majesty's forces, or of the Ministry of Defence, which engages in intelligence activities;

"Minister of the Crown" includes the Treasury;

"protected information", in relation to a relevant warrant, means information relating to any of the matters mentioned in section 57(4) of the Investigatory Powers Act 2016 in relation to the warrant;

"relevant authority" means—

(a) in the case of intelligence service information obtained (directly or indirectly) from or relating to the Security Service, the Director-General of the Security Service;

(b) in the case of intelligence service information obtained (directly or indirectly) from or relating to the Secret Intelligence Service, the Chief of the Secret Intelligence Service;

(c) in the case of intelligence service information obtained (directly or indirectly) from or relating to GCHQ, the Director of GCHQ;

(d) in the case of intelligence service information obtained (directly or indirectly) from or relating to Her Majesty's forces or the Ministry of Defence, the Secretary of State;

(e) in the case of protected information relating to a relevant warrant, the person to whom the relevant warrant is or was addressed;

(f) in the case of information within sub-paragraph (2)(c)—

 (i) the Secretary of State, or

 (ii) the Minister of the Crown in charge of the government department from which the information was obtained (if that Minister is not a Secretary of State);

"relevant warrant" means—

(a) a warrant under Chapter 1 of Part 2 of the Investigatory Powers Act 2016, or

(b) a warrant under Chapter 1 of Part 6 of that Act.

6F Provision of sensitive information to inspectors

6F (1) A person who provides information that is intelligence service information or protected information relating to a relevant warrant to an inspector (whether under a provision of this Schedule or otherwise) must—

(a) make the inspector aware that the information is intelligence service information or (as the case may be) protected information relating to a relevant warrant, and

(b) provide the inspector with such additional information as will enable the inspector to identify the relevant authority in relation to the information.

(2) In this paragraph, "inspector", "intelligence service information", "protected information relating to a relevant warrant" and "relevant authority" have the same meaning as in paragraph 6E."

(2) Omit section 86 of the Police Reform and Social Responsibility Act 2011 (which is spent as a result of subsection (1) above).

37 Inspectors and inspections: miscellaneous

(1) In section 54 of the Police Act 1996 (appointment and functions of inspectors of constabulary), after subsection (6) insert—

"(7) For the purposes of this section, a police force includes—

(a) staff appointed by the chief officer of police of the police force;

(b) staff appointed by a local policing body if, or to the extent that, they are employed to assist the police force;

(c) persons providing services, in pursuance of contractual arrangements (but without being employed by the chief officer of police of the police force or its local policing body), to assist the police force in relation to the discharge of its chief officer's functions;

(d) any other persons if, or to the extent that, they are engaged by virtue of any enactment in carrying out the activities of the police force."

(2) In section 55 of that Act (publication of reports of inspections), after subsection (5) insert—

"(5A) The comments of the local policing body, together with any comments submitted by the chief officer of police and any response to those comments by the local policing body, must be published before the end of the period of 56 days beginning with the day on which the report is published.

(5B) If the published report includes a recommendation, the comments of the local policing body must include an explanation of—

(a) the action the local policing body has taken or proposes to take in response to the recommendation, or

(b) why the local policing body has not taken, or does not propose to take, any action in response."

(3) In that section, in subsection (6), for the words after "subsection (5)" substitute "to—

(a) the inspectors of constabulary, and

(b) the Secretary of State."

(4) In section 56 of that Act (assistant inspectors and staff officers), in subsections (1) and (2), for "Secretary of State" substitute "chief inspector of constabulary".

(5) In paragraph 2 of Schedule 4A to that Act (inspection programmes and inspection frameworks)—

(a) in sub-paragraph (1)(a), for "he proposes" substitute "the inspectors of constabulary propose";

(b) in sub-paragraph (1)(b), for "he proposes to carry out his" substitute "they propose to carry out their";

(c) after sub-paragraph (5) insert—

"(6) The chief inspector of constabulary or, at the request of the chief inspector, any other inspector may carry out inspections that have not been set out in an inspection programme (and have not been required under section 54(2B) or requested under section 54(2BA)).

(7) Before deciding to carry out, or to request another inspector to carry out, an inspection that has not been set out in an inspection programme, the chief inspector of constabulary must consult —

(a) the Secretary of State, and

(b) the local policing body for the police force to which the inspection relates."

(6) In Schedule 6 to the Crime and Courts Act 2013 (inspection and complaints), in paragraph 4, after sub-paragraph (1) insert—

"(1A) The comments must be published before the end of the period of 56 days beginning with the day on which the HMIC report is published by the Secretary of State.

(1B) If the HMIC report includes a recommendation, the comments must include an explanation of—

(a) the action the Director General has taken or proposes to take in response to the recommendation, or

(b) why the Director General has not taken, or does not propose to take, any action in response."

PART 3

POLICE WORKFORCE AND REPRESENTATIVE INSTITUTIONS

CHAPTER 1

POLICE WORKFORCE

Powers of police civilian staff and volunteers

38 Powers of police civilian staff and police volunteers

(1) Chapter 1 of Part 4 of the Police Reform Act 2002 (exercise of police powers etc by civilians) is amended as follows.

(2) In section 38 (police powers for civilian staff), for subsections (1) and (2) substitute—

"(1) The chief officer of police of any police force may designate a relevant employee as either or both of the following—

(a) a community support officer;

(b) a policing support officer.

(1A) The chief officer of police of any police force may designate a police volunteer as either or both of the following—

(a) a community support volunteer;

(b) a policing support volunteer."

(3) In that section, omit subsections (5A) to (6A).

(4) In that section, before subsection (7) insert—

"(6B) The powers and duties that may be conferred or imposed on a person designated under this section are—

(a) any power or duty of a constable, other than a power or duty specified in Part 1 of Schedule 3B (excluded powers and duties);

(b) where the person is designated as a community support officer or a community support volunteer, any power or duty that is described in Schedule 3C as a power or duty of a community support officer or community support volunteer.

(6C) The Secretary of State may by regulations amend Part 1 of Schedule 3B so as to add to the list of powers and duties specified in it.

(6D) Part 2 of Schedule 3B makes provision about the application of legislation in relation to powers or duties of a constable that may be exercised or performed by a person designated under this section.

(6E) Any power or duty of a constable that is conferred or imposed on a person designated under this section by a chief officer of police of a police force may (subject to provision included in the designation under subsection (6F)) be exercised or performed by the person—

(a) in the area of that police force, and

(b) in any cases or circumstances in which it could be exercised or performed by a constable who is a member of that force.

(6F) A designation under this section may provide that any power or duty of a constable that is conferred or imposed by the designation may be exercised or performed by the person designated—

(a) in such areas outside the area of the police force in question as are specified in the designation (as well as within the area of the police force);

(b) only in such parts of the area of that police force as are specified in the designation;

(c) only in cases or circumstances so specified."

(5) In that section, after subsection (7) insert—

"(7A) A police volunteer authorised or required to do anything by virtue of a designation under this section —

(a) shall not be authorised or required by virtue of that designation to engage in any conduct otherwise than while acting as a police volunteer;

(b) shall be so authorised or required subject to such restrictions and conditions (if any) as may be specified in the designation."

(6) In that section, after subsection (9) insert—

"(9A) The chief officer of police of a police force must ensure that no person designated by the chief officer under this section is authorised to use a firearm, within the meaning given by section 57(1) of the Firearms Act 1968, in carrying out functions for the purposes of the designation.

(9B) However, subsection (9A) does not apply to—

(a) the use of a weapon, designed or adapted for the discharge of either of the following substances, for the purpose of discharging either of those substances—

(i) the substance, commonly known as "CS spray", that is produced by the use of 2-chlorobenzalmalononitrile;

(ii) the substance, commonly known as PAVA spray, that is produced by the use of pelargonic acid vanillylamide;

(b) the use of a weapon for a purpose specified in regulations made by the Secretary of State;

(c) the use of a weapon of a description specified in regulations made by the Secretary of State, whether generally or for a purpose so specified."

(7) In that section, after subsection (9B) (as inserted by subsection (6) above) insert—

"(9C) A statutory instrument containing regulations under subsection (6C) or (9B)(b) or (c) may not be made unless a draft of the instrument has been laid before and approved by a resolution of each House of Parliament."

(8) In that section, at the end insert—

"(12) In this section, "police volunteer" means a person who is under the direction and control of the chief officer making a designation under subsection (1A) otherwise than because the person is a constable, a special constable or a relevant employee.

(13) For the purpose of subsection (12), a person is to be treated as a relevant employee only in relation to times when the person is acting in the course of the person's employment."

(9) In the heading to section 38, after "civilian staff" insert "and volunteers".

(10) Omit section 38A (standard powers and duties of community support officers).

(11) After Schedule 3 insert —

(a) the new Schedule 3B set out in Schedule 10 to this Act, and

(b) (after that new Schedule) the new Schedule 3C set out in Schedule 11 to this Act.

39 Application of Firearms Act 1968 to the police: special constables and volunteers

(1) The Firearms Act 1968 is amended as follows.

(2) In section 54 of that Act (Application of Parts 1 and 2 to Crown servants), in subsection (3)—

(a) after paragraph (b) insert—

"(ba) a community support volunteer or a policing support volunteer designated under section 38 of the Police Reform Act 2002 by the chief constable of a police force in England and Wales,";

(b) after paragraph (f) insert ", or

(g) a community support volunteer or a policing support volunteer designated under section 38 of the Police Reform Act 2002 (as it applies by virtue of section 28 of the Railways and Transport Safety Act 2003) by the Chief Constable of the British Transport Police Force."

(3) In section 57 of that Act (interpretation), in subsection (4), after the definition of "imitation firearm" insert—

"""member of a police force" means—

(a) as respects England and Wales, a constable who is a member of a police force or a special constable appointed under section 27 of the Police Act 1996;

(b) as respects Scotland, a constable within the meaning of section 99 of the Police and Fire Reform (Scotland) Act 2012 (2012 asp 8);

"member of the British Transport Police Force" includes a special constable appointed under section 25 of the Railways and Transport Safety Act 2003;".

40 Training etc of police volunteers

(1) After section 53E of the Police Act 1996 (guidance about civilian staff employed by local policing bodies and chief officers) insert—

"53F Guidance about designated police volunteers

(1) The College of Policing may issue guidance to chief officers of police about—

(a) the experience or qualifications that it would be appropriate for a person to have before being designated as a community support volunteer or a policing support volunteer under section 38 of the Police Reform Act 2002;

(b) the training to be undertaken by a person before being so designated or after being so designated.

(2) The College may from time to time revise the whole or any part of any guidance issued under this section.

(3) The College must publish any guidance issued under this section and any revision of it.

(4) Each chief officer of police must have regard to guidance issued under this section."

(2) In section 97 of the Criminal Justice and Police Act 2001 (regulations for police forces about police training etc), in subsection (6)(c)—

(a) omit the "or" at the end of sub-paragraph (ii);

(b) after sub-paragraph (iii) insert "or

(iv) a person designated as a community support volunteer or a policing support volunteer under section 38 of the Police Reform Act 2002."

41 Police volunteers: complaints and disciplinary matters

(1) In section 12 of the Police Reform Act 2002 (complaints, matters and persons to which Part 2 of the Act applies), in subsection (7) (what it means to be a person serving with the police)—

(a) omit the "or" at the end of paragraph (b);

(b) at the end of paragraph (c) insert "; or

(d) he is a person designated as a community support volunteer or a policing support volunteer under section 38."

(2) In section 87 of the Police Act 1996 (guidance concerning disciplinary proceedings etc), in subsection (4A)(a) (as inserted by section 32), after sub-paragraph (iii) insert—

"(iv) persons designated as community support volunteers or policing support volunteers under section 38 of the Police Reform Act 2002;".

(3) In section 87A of the Police Act 1996 (guidance concerning conduct etc) (as inserted by section 32), in subsection (1)—

(a) omit the "and" at the end of paragraph (b);

(b) at the end of paragraph (c) insert ", and

(d) persons designated as community support volunteers or policing support volunteers under section 38 of the Police Reform Act 2002."

(4) In Schedule 6 to the Police Act 1996 (appeals to Police Appeals Tribunals), in paragraph 10(aa) (as inserted by section 31), after paragraph (iii) insert—

"(iiia) a person designated as a community support volunteer or a policing support volunteer under section 38 of the Police Reform Act 2002,".

42 Police volunteers: police barred list and police advisory list

(1) Part 4A of the Police Act 1996 (police barred list and police advisory list) (as inserted by Schedule 8) is amended as follows.

(2) In section 88C (effect of inclusion in police barred list), at the end insert—

"(9) Before designating a person as a community support volunteer or a policing support volunteer under section 38 of the Police Reform Act 2002, a chief officer of police must check with the College of Policing whether the person is a barred person.

(10) A chief officer of police may not designate a barred person as a community support volunteer or a policing support volunteer under section 38 of the Police Reform Act 2002."

(3) In section 88I (duty to report resignations and retirements to College of Policing)—

(a) in the heading, after "retirements" insert "etc";

(b) in subsection (1), after paragraph (b) insert—

"(c) the person's designation as a community support volunteer or a policing support volunteer under section 38 of the Police Reform Act 2002 is withdrawn and the reason, or one of the reasons, for the withdrawal of the designation relates to conduct, efficiency or effectiveness;

(d) the person, having been designated as a community support volunteer or a policing support volunteer under section 38 of the Police Reform Act 2002, decides to stop volunteering as a police volunteer (within the meaning of that section) after a relevant allegation about the person comes to the attention of the relevant authority.";

(c) in subsection (4), after paragraph (d) insert—

"(e) in relation to a person falling within subsection (1)(c) or (d), the chief officer of police by whom the person was designated.";

(d) in subsection (6)(b), at the end insert "or (as the case may be) the person's designation as a community support volunteer or a policing support volunteer being withdrawn if the person had not decided to stop volunteering".

(4) In section 88K (effect of inclusion in police advisory list), at the end insert—

"(8) Before designating a person as a community support volunteer or a policing support volunteer under section 38 of the Police Reform Act 2002, a chief officer of police must check with the College of Policing whether the person is included in the police advisory list."

(5) In section 88L (removal from police advisory list), in subsection (7)—

(a) the words from "a person who," to the end of the subsection become paragraph (a);

(b) after that paragraph insert—

"(b) a person who was designated as a community support volunteer or a policing support volunteer under section 38 of the Police Reform Act 2002."

43 Police volunteers: inspection

(1) In section 54 of the Police Act 1996 (appointment and functions of inspectors of constabulary), in subsection (7) (as inserted by section 37), after paragraph (a) insert—

"(aa) persons designated as community support volunteers or policing support volunteers under section 38 of the Police Reform Act 2002;".

(2) In Schedule 4A to the Police Act 1996 (further provision about Her Majesty's Inspectors of Constabulary), in paragraph 6D (as inserted by section 36), after sub-paragraph (2)(c) insert—

"(ca) a person designated as a community support volunteer or a policing support volunteer under section 38 of the Police Reform Act 2002;".

44 Restrictions on designated persons acting as covert human intelligence sources

In section 29 of the Regulation of Investigatory Powers Act 2000 (authorisation of covert human intelligence sources), after subsection (6) insert—

"(6A) An authorisation under this section may not have the effect of authorising a covert human intelligence source who is a person designated under section 38 of the Police Reform Act 2002 to establish contact in person with another person."

45 Further amendments consequential on section 38 etc

Schedule 12—

(a) makes further amendments in consequence of the amendments made by section 38 (see Parts 1 and 2 of that Schedule), and

(b) makes minor correcting amendments of the Police Reform Act 2002 (see Part 3 of that Schedule).

Removal of powers of police to appoint traffic wardens

46 Removal of powers of police in England and Wales to appoint traffic wardens

(1) Sections 95 to 97 of the Road Traffic Regulation Act 1984 (traffic wardens), so far as extending to England and Wales, are repealed.

(2) Those sections, so far as extending to Scotland, are amended as follows.

(3) In section 95 (appointment of traffic wardens), omit subsection (1).

(4) In subsection (2) of that section, for "any such functions as are mentioned in subsection (1) above" substitute ", in aid of the police, functions normally undertaken by the police in connection with the control and regulation of, or the enforcement of the law relating to, traffic (including pedestrians) or stationary vehicles".

(5) In subsection (3) of that section, omit "under subsection (1) or".

(6) In subsection (4) of that section—

(a) omit "(whether in England and Wales or in Scotland)";

(b) for "subsection (1)" substitute "subsection (2)";

(c) in paragraph (b)—

(i) omit "or (in England and Wales) with the Secretary of State";

(ii) omit "or, as the case may be, by the Secretary of State".

(7) Omit subsection (4A) of that section.

(8) In section 96 (additional powers of traffic wardens), in subsection (2), omit paragraphs (a), (b) and (d).

(9) In section 97 (supplementary provisions as to traffic wardens), in subsection (3), omit, in both places where it occurs, "the Common Council or".

(10) Schedule 13 makes further amendments consequential on the repeal made by subsection (1).

Police rank structure

47 Power to make regulations about police ranks

After section 50 of the Police Act 1996 insert—

"50A Regulations for police forces: ranks

(1) The Secretary of State may by regulations specify the ranks that may be held by members of police forces, other than chief officers of police.

(2) The ranks must include the rank of constable.

(3) The Secretary of State may by regulations make provision that is consequential on, or incidental or supplemental to, regulations under subsection (1).

(4) The power conferred by subsection (3) includes power to—

(a) repeal, revoke or otherwise amend legislation that (in relation to members of police forces in England and Wales) makes provision with respect to ranks that are not specified in regulations under subsection (1);

(b) make other amendments of legislation that are consequential on regulations under subsection (1).

(5) In subsection (4), "legislation" means any provision of—

(a) an Act (including this Act),

(b) subordinate legislation within the meaning of the Interpretation Act 1978,

(c) an Act of the Scottish Parliament or an instrument made under such an Act,

(d) a Measure or Act of the National Assembly for Wales or an instrument made under a Measure or Act of that Assembly, or

(e) Northern Ireland legislation or an instrument made under Northern Ireland legislation.

(6) Regulations under this section may include transitional, transitory or saving provision.

(7) Regulations under this section may make different provision for different cases or circumstances.

(4) After subsection (1) insert—

"(1A) This subsection applies if—

(a) the constable is satisfied that releasing the person on bail is necessary and proportionate in all the circumstances (having regard, in particular, to any conditions of bail which would be imposed), and

(b) a police officer of the rank of inspector or above authorises the release on bail (having considered any representations made by the person)."

(5) In subsection (2) omit "on bail".

53 Section 52: consequential amendments

(1) The Police and Criminal Evidence Act 1984 is amended as follows.

(2) In section 18(5)(a) (circumstances in which a search after arrest may be conducted) omit "on bail".

(3) In section 30 (arrest elsewhere than at police station)—

(a) in subsection (1B) for "on bail" substitute "of a person arrested elsewhere than at police station",

(b) in subsection (7A) omit the words from "or releasing" to the end, and

(c) in subsections (10) and (11) for "on bail" substitute "under section 30A".

(4) Section 30B (section 30A: notices) is amended as follows.

(5) In the heading omit "Bail under".

(6) In subsection (1) for "grants bail to" substitute "releases".

(7) In subsection (2)—

(a) omit the "and" before paragraph (b), and

(b) after paragraph (b) insert "and

(c) whether the person is being released without bail or on bail".

(8) In subsection (3) for "The notice" substitute "A notice given to a person who is released on bail".

(9) In section 30C (section 30A: supplemental)—

(a) in the heading omit "Bail under", and

(b) in subsection (4) omit "on bail".

54 Release from detention at a police station

(1) Section 34 of the Police and Criminal Evidence Act 1984 (limitations on police detention) is amended as follows.

(2) In subsection (5) for the words from "without" to the end substitute "—

(a) without bail unless subsection (5A) applies, or

(b) on bail if subsection (5A) applies."

(3) After subsection (5) insert—

"(5A) This subsection applies if—

(a) it appears to the custody officer—

(i) that there is need for further investigation of any matter in connection with which the person was detained at any time during the period of the person's detention, or

(ii) that, in respect of any such matter, proceedings may be taken against the person or the person may be given a youth caution under section 66ZA of the Crime and Disorder Act 1998, and

(b) the pre-conditions for bail are satisfied."

(4) Section 37 of the Police and Criminal Evidence Act 1984 (duties of custody officer before charge) is amended as follows.

(5) In subsection (2) for the words from "either" to the end substitute "—

(a) without bail unless the pre-conditions for bail are satisfied, or

(b) on bail if those pre-conditions are satisfied,

(subject to subsection (3))".

(6) In subsection (3) for "so believing" substitute "believing that the person's detention without being charged is necessary to secure or preserve evidence relating to an offence for which the person is under arrest or to obtain such evidence by questioning the person".

(7) In subsection (7) for paragraphs (b) and (c) substitute—

"(b) shall be released without charge and without bail unless the pre-conditions for bail are satisfied,

(c) shall be released without charge and on bail if those pre-conditions are satisfied but not for the purpose mentioned in paragraph (a), or".

(8) In subsection (8A)(b) for "(b)" substitute "(c)".

55 Release following arrest for breach of bail etc

(1) Section 37CA of the Police and Criminal Evidence Act 1984 (release following arrest for breach of bail) is amended as follows.

(2) In the heading and subsection (1) for "section 37(7)(b)" substitute "section 37(7)(c)".

(3) In subsection (2)(b) for the words from ", either" to the end substitute "—

(i) without bail unless the pre-conditions for bail are satisfied, or

(ii) on bail if those pre-conditions are satisfied."

(4) In subsection (4) at the end insert "(and the reference in section 50A to any conditions of bail which would be imposed is to be read accordingly)".

(5) In section 37D(4A) of the Police and Criminal Evidence Act 1984 (power to keep a person in police detention) for "section 37(7)(b)" substitute "section 37(7)(c)".

56 Release from further detention at police station

(1) In section 41(7) of the Police and Criminal Evidence Act 1984 (limits on period of detention without charge) for the words from "either" to the end substitute "—

(a) without bail unless the pre-conditions for bail are satisfied, or

(b) on bail if those pre-conditions are satisfied."

(2) Section 42 of the Police and Criminal Evidence Act 1984 (authorisation of continued detention) is amended as follows.

(3) In subsection (10)—

(a) omit ", either on bail or without bail", and

(b) for the words from ", unless" to the end substitute "—

(a) without bail unless the pre-conditions for bail are satisfied, or

(b) on bail if those pre-conditions are satisfied,

(subject to subsection (10A))".

(4) After subsection (10) insert—

"(10A) Subsection (10) does not apply if—

(a) the person has been charged with an offence, or

(b) the person's continued detention is authorised or otherwise permitted in accordance with section 43."

57 Warrants of further detention: release

(1) Section 43 of the Police and Criminal Evidence Act 1984 (warrants of further detention) is amended as follows.

(2) In subsection (15) for the words from ", either" to the end substitute "—

(a) without bail unless the pre-conditions for bail are satisfied, or

(b) on bail if those pre-conditions are satisfied."

(3) In subsection (18) for the words from "be released" to the end substitute ", unless the person is charged, be released from police detention upon or before the expiry of the warrant—

(a) without bail unless the pre-conditions for bail are satisfied, or

(b) on bail if those pre-conditions are satisfied."

(4) In section 44(7) of the Police and Criminal Evidence Act 1984 (extension of warrants of further detention) for the words from ", either" to the end substitute "—

(a) without bail unless the pre-conditions for bail are satisfied, or

(b) on bail if those pre-conditions are satisfied."

58 Meaning of "pre-conditions for bail"

After section 50 of the Police and Criminal Evidence Act 1984 insert—

"50A Interpretation of references to pre-conditions for bail

For the purposes of this Part the following are the pre-conditions for bail in relation to the release of a person by a custody officer—

(a) that the custody officer is satisfied that releasing the person on bail is necessary and proportionate in all the circumstances (having regard, in particular, to any conditions of bail which would be imposed), and

(b) that an officer of the rank of inspector or above authorises the release on bail (having considered any representations made by the person or the person's legal representative)."

59 Release without bail: fingerprinting and samples

(1) The Police and Criminal Evidence Act 1984 is amended as follows.

(2) In section 61(5A) (fingerprinting of person arrested for a recordable offence) —
- (a) in paragraph (a) omit "in the case of a person who is on bail,", and
- (b) in paragraph (b) omit "in any case,".

(3) In section 63(3ZA) (taking of non-intimate sample from person arrested for a recordable offence)—
- (a) in paragraph (a) omit "in the case of a person who is on bail,", and
- (b) in paragraph (b) omit "in any case,".

60 Release under section 24A of the Criminal Justice Act 2003

(1) Section 24A of the Criminal Justice Act 2003 (arrest for failure to comply with conditions attached to conditional caution) is amended as follows.

(2) In subsection (2) for paragraphs (b) and (c) substitute—

"(b) released without charge and without bail (with or without any variation in the conditions attached to the caution) unless paragraph (c)(i) and (ii) applies, or

(c) released without charge and on bail if—

(i) the release is to enable a decision to be made as to whether the person should be charged with the offence, and

(ii) the pre-conditions for bail are satisfied."

(3) In subsections (3)(a) and (4) for "subsection (2)(b)" substitute "subsection (2)(c)".

(4) After subsection (8) insert—

"(8A) In subsection (2) the reference to the pre-conditions for bail is to be read in accordance with section 50A of the 1984 Act."

Conditions of bail

61 Bail before charge: conditions of bail etc

(1) The Police and Criminal Evidence Act 1984 is amended as follows.

(2) In section 46A(1A) (power of arrest for failure to answer police bail) for "section 37, 37C(2)(b) or 37CA(2)(b) above" substitute "this Part".

(3) Section 47 (bail after arrest) is amended as follows.

(4) In subsection (1A) for the words from "section 37" to "cases" substitute "this Part (except sections 37C(2)(b) and 37CA(2)(b))".

(5) In subsections (1B) and (1C) omit "37,".

Time limits on period of bail

62 Limit on period of bail under section 30A of PACE

(1) The Police and Criminal Evidence Act 1984 is amended as follows.

(2) Section 30B (section 30A: notices) is amended as follows.

(3) For subsection (4) substitute—

"(4) The notice must also specify—

(a) the police station which the person is required to attend, and

(b) the time on the bail end date when the person is required to attend the police station."

(4) Omit subsection (4A)(c) and the "and" before it.

(5) Omit subsection (5).

(6) In subsection (6) for the words from "(5)" to the end substitute "to attend at a different time or an additional time".

(7) After subsection (6) insert—

"(6A) A person may not be required under subsection (6) to attend a police station at a time which is after the bail end date in relation to the person."

(8) After subsection (7) insert—

"(8) In this section "bail end date", in relation to a person, means the last day of the period of 28 days beginning with the day after the day on which the person was arrested for the offence in relation to which bail is granted under section 30A."

(9) In section 30CA (bail under section 30A: variation of conditions by police) omit subsection (1)(b) and the "or" before it.

(10) In section 30D(3) (meaning of "specified" in section 30D(1)) omit "or (5)".

63 Limits on period of bail without charge under Part 4 of PACE

After section 47 of the Police and Criminal Evidence Act 1984 insert—

"47ZA Limits on period of bail without charge

(1) This section applies in relation to the power conferred on a custody officer, when releasing a person on bail under this Part, to appoint a time for the person to attend at a police station in accordance with section 47(3)(c).

(2) The power must be exercised so as to appoint a time on the day on which the applicable bail period in relation to the person ends, unless subsection (3) or (4) applies.

(3) This subsection applies where—

(a) at the time of the exercise of the power the person is on bail under this Part in relation to one or more offences other than the relevant offence, and

(b) the custody officer believes that it is appropriate to align the person's attendance in relation to the relevant offence with the person's attendance in relation to the one or more other offences.

(4) This subsection applies where the custody officer believes that a decision as to whether to charge the person with the relevant offence would be made before the end of the applicable bail period in relation to the person.

(5) Where subsection (3) or (4) applies, the power may be exercised so as to appoint a time on a day falling before the end of the applicable bail period in relation to the person.

(6) This section is subject to section 47ZL.

(7) In this section references to attendance are to attendance at a police station in accordance with section 47(3)(c).

(8) In this Part the "relevant offence", in relation to a person, means the offence in respect of which the power mentioned in subsection (1) is exercised in relation to the person.

47ZB Applicable bail period: initial limit

(1) In this Part the "applicable bail period", in relation to a person, means—

(a) in an SFO case, the period of 3 months beginning with the person's bail start date, or

(b) in an FCA case or any other case, the period of 28 days beginning with the person's bail start date.

(2) The applicable bail period in relation to a person may be extended under sections 47ZD to 47ZG or treated as extended under section 47ZJ(3).

(3) Subsection (1) and sections 47ZD to 47ZG are subject to sections 47ZL and 47ZM.

(4) For the purposes of this Part—

(a) a person's bail start date is the day after the day on which the person was arrested for the relevant offence,

(b) an "FCA case" is a case in which—

(i) the relevant offence in relation to the person is being investigated by the Financial Conduct Authority, and

(ii) a senior officer confirms that sub-paragraph (i) applies,

(c) an "SFO case" is a case in which—

(i) the relevant offence in relation to the person is being investigated by the Director of the Serious Fraud Office, and

(ii) a senior officer confirms that sub-paragraph (i) applies, and

(d) "senior officer" means a police officer of the rank of superintendent or above.

47ZC Applicable bail period: conditions A to D in sections 47ZD to 47ZG

(1) This section applies for the purposes of sections 47ZD to 47ZG.

(2) Condition A is that the decision-maker has reasonable grounds for suspecting the person in question to be guilty of the relevant offence.

(3) Condition B is that the decision-maker has reasonable grounds for believing—

(a) in a case where the person in question is or is to be released on bail under section 37(7)(c) or 37CA(2)(b), that further time is needed for making a decision as to whether to charge the person with the relevant offence, or

(b) otherwise, that further investigation is needed of any matter in connection with the relevant offence.

(4) Condition C is that the decision-maker has reasonable grounds for believing—

(a) in a case where the person in question is or is to be released on bail under section 37(7)(c) or 37CA(2)(b), that the decision as to whether to charge the person with the relevant offence is being made diligently and expeditiously, or

(b) otherwise, that the investigation is being conducted diligently and expeditiously.

(5) Condition D is that the decision-maker has reasonable grounds for believing that the release on bail of the person in question is necessary and proportionate in all the circumstances (having regard, in particular, to any conditions of bail which are, or are to be, imposed).

(6) In this section "decision-maker" means—

(a) in relation to a condition which falls to be considered by virtue of section 47ZD, the senior officer in question;

(b) in relation to a condition which falls to be considered by virtue of section 47ZE, the appropriate decision-maker in question;

(c) in relation to a condition which falls to be considered by virtue of section 47ZF or 47ZG, the court in question.

47ZD Applicable bail period: extension of initial limit in standard cases

(1) This section applies in relation to a person if—

(a) the applicable bail period in relation to the person is the period mentioned in section 47ZB(1)(b),

(b) that period has not ended, and

(c) a senior officer is satisfied that conditions A to D are met in relation to the person.

(2) The senior officer may authorise the applicable bail period in relation to the person to be extended so that it ends at the end of the period of 3 months beginning with the person's bail start date.

(3) Before determining whether to give an authorisation under subsection (2) in relation to a person, the senior officer must arrange for the person or the person's legal representative to be informed that a determination is to be made.

(4) In determining whether to give an authorisation under subsection (2) in relation to a person, the senior officer must consider any representations made by the person or the person's legal representative.

(5) The senior officer must arrange for the person or the person's legal representative to be informed whether an authorisation under subsection (2) has been given in relation to the person.

47ZE Applicable bail period: extension of limit in designated cases

(1) This section applies in relation to a person if—

(a) the person's case is an SFO case, or

(b) a senior officer has authorised an extension of the applicable bail period in relation to the person under section 47ZD.

(2) A qualifying prosecutor may designate the person's case as being an exceptionally complex case (a "designated case").

(3) If an appropriate decision-maker is satisfied that conditions A to D are met in relation to the person in a designated case, the decision-maker may authorise the applicable bail period in relation to the person to be extended so that it ends at the end of the period of 6 months beginning with the person's bail start date.

(4) An appropriate decision-maker is—

(a) a member of staff of the Financial Conduct Authority who is of the description designated for the purposes of this paragraph by the Chief Executive of the Authority (in an FCA case),

(b) a member of the Serious Fraud Office who is of the Senior Civil Service (in an SFO case), or

(c) a qualifying police officer (in any other case).

(5) Before determining whether to give an authorisation under subsection (3) in relation to a person—

(a) the appropriate decision-maker must arrange for the person or the person's legal representative to be informed that a determination is to be made, and

(b) if the appropriate decision-maker is a qualifying police officer, the officer must consult a qualifying prosecutor.

(6) In determining whether to give an authorisation under subsection (3) in relation to a person, the appropriate decision-maker must consider any representations made by the person or the person's legal representative.

(7) The appropriate decision-maker must arrange for the person or the person's legal representative to be informed whether an authorisation under subsection (3) has been given in relation to the person.

(8) Any designation under subsection (2) must be made, and any authorisation under subsection (3) must be given, before the applicable bail period in relation to the person has ended.

(9) In this section—

"qualifying police officer" means a police officer of the rank of commander or assistant chief constable or above, and

"qualifying prosecutor" means a prosecutor of the description designated for the purposes of this section by the Chief Executive of the

Financial Conduct Authority, the Director of the Serious Fraud Office or the Director of Public Prosecutions.

47ZF Applicable bail period: first extension of limit by court

(1) This section applies in relation to a person if—

(a) the person's case is an SFO case,

(b) a senior officer has authorised an extension of the applicable bail period in relation to the person under section 47ZD, or

(c) an appropriate decision-maker has authorised an extension of the applicable bail period in relation to the person under section 47ZE.

(2) Before the applicable bail period in relation to the person ends a qualifying applicant may apply to a magistrates' court for it to authorise an extension of the applicable bail period in relation to the person under this section.

(3) If the court is satisfied that—

(a) conditions B to D are met in relation to the person, and

(b) the case does not fall within subsection (7),

it may authorise the applicable bail period to be extended as specified in subsection (4).

(4) The applicable bail period is to end—

(a) in a case falling within subsection (1)(a) or (b), at the end of the period of 6 months beginning with the person's bail start date;

(b) in a case falling within subsection (1)(c), at the end of the period of 9 months beginning with the person's bail start date.

(5) If the court is satisfied that—

(a) conditions B to D are met in relation to the person, and

(b) the case falls within subsection (7),

it may authorise the applicable bail period to be extended as specified in subsection (6).

(6) The applicable bail period is to end—

(a) in a case falling within subsection (1)(a) or (b), at the end of the period of 9 months beginning with the person's bail start date;

(b) in a case falling within subsection (1)(c), at the end of the period of 12 months beginning with the person's bail start date.

(7) A case falls within this subsection if the nature of the decision or further investigations mentioned in condition B means that that decision is unlikely to be made or those investigations completed if the applicable bail period in relation to the person is not extended as specified in subsection (6).

(8) In this section "qualifying applicant" means—

(a) a constable,

(b) a member of staff of the Financial Conduct Authority who is of the description designated for the purposes of this subsection by the Chief Executive of the Authority,

(c) a member of the Serious Fraud Office, or

(d) a Crown Prosecutor.

47ZG Applicable bail period: subsequent extensions of limit by court

(1) Subsections (2) to (6) apply where a court has authorised an extension of the applicable bail period in relation to a person under section 47ZF.

(2) Before the applicable bail period in relation to the person ends a qualifying applicant may apply to a magistrates' court for it to authorise an extension of the applicable bail period in relation to the person under this section.

(3) If the court is satisfied that—

(a) conditions B to D are met in relation to the person, and

(b) the case does not fall within subsection (8),

it may authorise the applicable bail period to be extended as specified in subsection (4).

(4) The applicable bail period is to end at the end of the period of 3 months beginning with the end of the current applicable bail period in relation to the person.

(5) If the court is satisfied that—

(a) conditions B to D are met in relation to the person, and

(b) the case falls within subsection (8),

it may authorise the applicable bail period to be extended as specified in subsection (6).

(6) The applicable bail period is to end at the end of the period of 6 months beginning with the end of the current applicable bail period in relation to the person.

(7) Where a court has authorised an extension of the applicable bail period in relation to a person under subsection (3) or (5), a qualifying applicant may make further applications under subsection (2) (and subsections (3) to (6) apply accordingly).

(8) A case falls within this subsection if the nature of the decision or further investigations mentioned in condition B means that that decision is unlikely to be made or those investigations completed if the current applicable bail period in relation to the person is not extended as specified in subsection (6).

(9) For the purposes of this section—

(a) references to the current applicable bail period in relation to a person are to the applicable bail period applying to the person when the application under this section is made (subject to section 47ZJ(3)), and

(b) "qualifying applicant" has the same meaning as in section 47ZF.

47ZH Sections 47ZF and 47ZG: withholding sensitive information

(1) This section applies where a qualifying applicant makes an application to a magistrates' court under section 47ZF or 47ZG in relation to a person.

(2) The qualifying applicant may apply to the court for it to authorise the specified information to be withheld from the person and any legal representative of the person.

(3) The court may grant an application under subsection (2) only if satisfied that there are reasonable grounds for believing that the specified information is sensitive information.

(4) For the purposes of this section information is sensitive information if its disclosure would have one or more of the following results—

(a) evidence connected with an indictable offence would be interfered with or harmed;

(b) a person would be interfered with or physically injured;

(c) a person suspected of having committed an indictable offence but not yet arrested for the offence would be alerted;

(d) the recovery of property obtained as a result of an indictable offence would be hindered.

(5) In this section "specified information" means the information specified in the application under subsection (2).

47ZI Sections 47ZF to 47ZH: proceedings in magistrates' court

(1) An application made to a magistrates' court under section 47ZF or 47ZG in relation to a person is to be determined by a single justice of the peace on written evidence unless subsection (2) or (3) applies.

(2) This subsection applies if—

(a) the effect of the application would be to extend the applicable bail period in relation to the person so that it ends at or before the end of the period of 12 months beginning with the person's bail start date, and

(b) a single justice of the peace considers that the interests of justice require an oral hearing.

(3) This subsection applies if—

(a) the effect of the application would be to extend the applicable bail period in relation to the person so that it ends after the end of the period of 12 months beginning with the person's bail start date, and

(b) the person, or the person who made the application, requests an oral hearing.

(4) If subsection (2) or (3) applies, the application is to be determined by two or more justices of the peace sitting otherwise than in open court.

(5) Where an application under section 47ZF or 47ZG in relation to a person is to be determined as mentioned in subsection (4), the justices may direct that the person and any legal representative of the person be excluded from any part of the hearing.

(6) The justices may give a direction under subsection (5) only if satisfied that there are reasonable grounds for believing that sensitive information would be disclosed at the part of the hearing in question.

(7) An application under section 47ZH is to be determined by a single justice of the peace on written evidence unless the justice determines that the interests of justice require an oral hearing.

(8) If the justice makes a determination under subsection (7)—

(a) the application is to be determined by two or more justices of the peace sitting otherwise than in open court, and

(b) the justices hearing the application must direct that the person to whom the application relates and any legal representative of the person be excluded from the hearing.

(9) In this section "sensitive information" has the meaning given in section 47ZH(4).

47ZJ Sections 47ZF and 47ZG: late applications to magistrates' court

(1) This section applies where—

(a) an application under section 47ZF or 47ZG is made to a magistrates' court before the end of the applicable bail period in relation to a person, but

(b) it is not practicable for the court to determine the application before the end of that period.

(2) The court must determine the application as soon as is practicable.

(3) The applicable bail period in relation to the person is to be treated as extended until the application is determined.

(4) If it appears to the court that it would have been reasonable for the application to have been made in time for it to have been determined by the court before the end of the applicable bail period in relation to the person, it may refuse the application.

47ZK Rules

Criminal Procedure Rules may make provision in connection with applications under sections 47ZF, 47ZG and 47ZH and the proceedings for determining such applications.

47ZL Applicable bail period and bail return date: special case of release on bail under section 37(7)(a) or 37C(2)(b)

(1) This section applies where a person is released on bail under section 37(7)(a) or 37C(2)(b).

(2) The running of the applicable bail period in relation to the person—

(a) does not begin (in the case of a first release on bail), or

(b) is suspended (in any other case),

(subject to subsection (6)).

(3) Accordingly section 47ZA does not apply to the exercise of the power mentioned in section 47ZA(1) when releasing the person on bail.

(4) Subsections (5) and (6) apply if a DPP request is made in relation to the person.

(5) A custody officer must exercise the power mentioned in section 47(4A) to appoint a different time for the person to attend at the police station (and section 47(4B) to (4D) applies accordingly).

(6) The applicable bail period in relation to the person—

(a) begins to run on the day on which the DPP request is made (in the case of a first release on bail), or

(b) resumes running on that day (in any other case).

(7) Subsection (8) applies where—

(a) a DPP request has been made in relation to the person, and

(b) the applicable bail period in relation to the person would end before the end of the period of 7 days beginning with the day on which the DPP request was made.

(8) The running of the applicable bail period in relation to the person is suspended for the number of days necessary to secure that the applicable bail period ends at the end of the period of 7 days beginning with the day on which the DPP request was made.

(9) Subsections (10) and (11) apply if the DPP request made in relation to the person is met.

(10) The running of the applicable bail period in relation to the person is suspended.

(11) Accordingly section 47(4D) does not apply to any exercise of the power under section 47(4A).

(12) For the purposes of this section—

(a) a "DPP request", in relation to a person, means a request by the Director of Public Prosecutions for the further information specified in the request to be provided before the Director decides under section 37B(2) whether there is sufficient evidence to charge the person with the relevant offence,

(b) a DPP request is met when the further information specified in the request is provided, and

(c) references to the case of a first release on bail are to a case where the person has not been released on bail in relation to the relevant offence under any other provision of this Part or under section 30A.

47ZM Applicable bail period: special cases of release on bail under section 30A and periods in hospital

(1) Subsections (2) and (3) apply where a person was released on bail under section 30A.

(2) The period of 28 days mentioned in section 30B(8) in relation to the person is to be treated as being the period of 28 days mentioned in section 47ZB(1)(b) in relation to the person.

(3) Any reference to the relevant offence, in relation to the person, is to be read as a reference to the offence in respect of which the power in section 30A(1) was exercised.

(4) Subsection (5) applies if, at any time on the day on which the applicable bail period in relation to a person would end, the person is in hospital as an in-patient.

(5) The running of the applicable bail period in relation to the person is to be treated as having been suspended for any day on which the patient was in hospital as an in-patient."

64 Section 63: consequential amendments

(1) The Police and Criminal Evidence Act 1984 is amended as follows.

(2) Section 37D (release on bail under section 37) is amended as follows.

(3) Omit subsections (1) to (3).

(4) In subsections (4) to (5) for "subsection (1) above" substitute "section 47(4A)".

(5) Section 47 (bail after arrest) is amended as follows.

(6) In subsection (3)(c) at the end insert "(subject to section 47ZA)".

(7) After subsection (4) insert—

"(4A) Where a person has been granted bail under this Part subject to a duty to attend at a police station, a custody officer may subsequently appoint a different time, or an additional time, at which the person is to attend at the police station to answer bail.

(4B) The custody officer must give the person notice in writing of the exercise of the power under subsection (4A).

(4C) The exercise of the power under subsection (4A) does not affect the conditions of bail (if any).

(4D) A custody officer may not appoint a time for a person's attendance under subsection (4A) which is after the end of the applicable bail period in relation to the person.

(4E) Subsection (4D) is subject to section 47ZL."

(8) In the Criminal Justice Act 2003—

(a) in section 24A(5)(b) (purposes for which person may be kept in police detention) for "section 37D(1)" substitute "section 47(4A)", and

(b) in section 24B(5) (application of provisions of the Police and Criminal Evidence Act 1984)—

(i) omit paragraph (a), and

(ii) in paragraph (c) at the end insert "except subsections (4D) and (4E)".

Re-arrest of person released under provisions of PACE

65 Release under provisions of PACE: re-arrest

(1) The Police and Criminal Evidence Act 1984 is amended as follows.

(2) In section 30C(4) (re-arrest without warrant of person released under section 30A) for the words from "new" to the end substitute ", since the person's release, new evidence has come to light or an examination or analysis of existing evidence has been made which could not reasonably have been made before the person's release".

(3) In section 41(9) (re-arrest without warrant of person released under section 41(7)) for the words from "new" to "since" substitute ", since the person's release, new evidence has come to light or an examination or analysis of existing evidence has been made which could not reasonably have been made before".

(4) In section 42(11) (re-arrest without warrant of person released under section 42(10)) for the words from "new" to "since" substitute ", since the person's release, new evidence has come to light or an examination or analysis of existing evidence has been made which could not reasonably have been made before".

(5) In section 43(19) (re-arrest without warrant of person released under section 43(18)) for the words from "new" to "since" substitute ", since the person's release, new evidence has come to light or an examination or analysis of existing evidence has been made which could not reasonably have been made before".

(6) In section 47(2) (re-arrest without warrant of person released on bail subject to a duty to attend at a police station) for the words from "new" to the end substitute ", since the person's release, new evidence has come to light or an examination or analysis of existing evidence has been made which could not reasonably have been made before the person's release".

Notification of decision not to prosecute

66 Duty to notify person released under section 34, 37 or 37CA of PACE that not to be prosecuted

(1) The Police and Criminal Evidence Act 1984 is amended as follows.

(2) In section 34 (limitations on police detention) after subsection (5A) (inserted by section 54 of this Act) insert—

"(5B) Subsection (5C) applies where—

(a) a person is released under subsection (5), and

(b) the custody officer determines that—

(i) there is not sufficient evidence to charge the person with an offence, or

(ii) there is sufficient evidence to charge the person with an offence but the person should not be charged with an offence or given a caution in respect of an offence.

(5C) The custody officer must give the person notice in writing that the person is not to be prosecuted.

(5D) Subsection (5C) does not prevent the prosecution of the person for an offence if new evidence comes to light after the notice was given.

(5E) In this Part "caution" includes—

(a) a conditional caution within the meaning of Part 3 of the Criminal Justice Act 2003;

(b) a youth conditional caution within the meaning of Chapter 1 of Part 4 of the Crime and Disorder Act 1998;

(c) a youth caution under section 66ZA of that Act."

(3) Section 37 (duties of custody officer before charge) is amended as follows.

(4) After subsection (6) insert—

"(6A) Subsection (6B) applies where—

(a) a person is released under subsection (2), and

(b) the custody officer determines that—

(i) there is not sufficient evidence to charge the person with an offence, or

(ii) there is sufficient evidence to charge the person with an offence but the person should not be charged with an offence or given a caution in respect of an offence.

(6B) The custody officer must give the person notice in writing that the person is not to be prosecuted.

(6C) Subsection (6B) does not prevent the prosecution of the person for an offence if new evidence comes to light after the notice was given."

(5) After subsection (8) insert—

"(8ZA) Where—

(a) a person is released under subsection (7)(b) or (c), and

(b) the custody officer makes a determination as mentioned in subsection (6A)(b),

subsections (6B) and (6C) apply."

(6) Section 37B (consultation with Director of Public Prosecutions) is amended as follows.

(7) After subsection (5) insert—

"(5A) Subsection (5) does not prevent the prosecution of the person for an offence if new evidence comes to light after the notice was given."

(8) Omit subsection (9).

(9) In section 37CA (release following arrest for breach of bail) after subsection (4) insert—

"(5) Subsection (6) applies where—

(a) a person is released under subsection (2), and

(b) a custody officer determines that—

(i) there is not sufficient evidence to charge the person with an offence, or

(ii) there is sufficient evidence to charge the person with an offence but the person should not be charged with an offence or given a caution in respect of an offence.

(6) The custody officer must give the person notice in writing that the person is not to be prosecuted.

(7) Subsection (6) does not prevent the prosecution of the person for an offence if new evidence comes to light after the notice was given."

(10) In section 24B(2) of the Criminal Justice Act 2003 (application of provisions of Police and Criminal Evidence Act 1984)—

(a) in paragraph (d) for "(5)" substitute "(5E)", and

(b) in paragraph (f) for "(6)" substitute "(6C)".

67 Duty to notify person released under any of sections 41 to 44 of PACE that not to be prosecuted

(1) The Police and Criminal Evidence Act 1984 is amended as follows.

(2) In section 41 (limits on period of detention without charge) after subsection (9) insert—

"(10) Subsection (11) applies where—

(a) a person is released under subsection (7), and

(b) a custody officer determines that—

(i) there is not sufficient evidence to charge the person with an offence, or

(ii) there is sufficient evidence to charge the person with an offence but the person should not be charged with an offence or given a caution in respect of an offence.

(11) The custody officer must give the person notice in writing that the person is not to be prosecuted.

(12) Subsection (11) does not prevent the prosecution of the person for an offence if new evidence comes to light after the notice was given."

(3) In section 42 (authorisation of continued detention) after subsection (11) insert—

"(12) Subsection (13) applies where—

(a) a person is released under subsection (10), and

(b) a custody officer determines that—

(i) there is not sufficient evidence to charge the person with an offence, or

(ii) there is sufficient evidence to charge the person with an offence but the person should not be charged with an offence or given a caution in respect of an offence.

(13) The custody officer must give the person notice in writing that the person is not to be prosecuted.

(14) Subsection (13) does not prevent the prosecution of the person for an offence if new evidence comes to light after the notice was given."

(4) In section 43 (warrants of further detention) after subsection (19) insert—

"(20) Subsection (21) applies where—

(a) a person is released under subsection (15) or (18), and

(b) a custody officer determines that—

(i) there is not sufficient evidence to charge the person with an offence, or

(ii) there is sufficient evidence to charge the person with an offence but the person should not be charged with an offence or given a caution in respect of an offence.

(21) The custody officer must give the person notice in writing that the person is not to be prosecuted.

(22) Subsection (21) does not prevent the prosecution of the person for an offence if new evidence comes to light after the notice was given."

(5) In section 44 (extension of warrants of further detention) after subsection (8) insert—

"(9) Subsection (10) applies where—

(a) a person is released under subsection (7), and

(b) a custody officer determines that—

(i) there is not sufficient evidence to charge the person with an offence, or

(ii) there is sufficient evidence to charge the person with an offence but the person should not be charged with an offence or given a caution in respect of an offence.

(10) The custody officer must give the person notice in writing that the person is not to be prosecuted.

(11) Subsection (10) does not prevent the prosecution of the person for an offence if new evidence comes to light after the notice was given."

Breach of pre-charge bail conditions relating to travel

68 Offence of breach of pre-charge bail conditions relating to travel

(1) This section applies where—

(a) a person is arrested under section 24 of the Police and Criminal Evidence Act 1984, or under Article 26 of the Police and Criminal Evidence (Northern Ireland) Order 1989 (S.I. 1989/1341 (N.I.12), in respect of an offence mentioned in section 41(1) or (2) of the Counter-Terrorism Act 2008,

(b) the person is released without charge and on bail under Part 4 of the 1984 Act or (as the case may be) Part 5 of the 1989 Order, and

(c) the release on bail is subject to a travel restriction condition.

(2) Each of the following is a travel restriction condition—

(a) a condition that the person must not leave the United Kingdom,

(b) a condition that the person must not enter any port, or one or more particular ports, in the United Kingdom,

(c) a condition that the person must not go to a place in Northern Ireland that is within one mile of the border between Northern Ireland and the Republic of Ireland,

(d) a condition that the person must surrender all of his or her travel documents or all of his or her travel documents that are of a particular kind,

(e) a condition that the person must not have any travel documents, or travel documents of a particular kind, in his or her possession (whether the documents relate to that person or to another person),

(f) a condition that the person must not obtain, or seek to obtain, any travel documents (whether relating to that person or to another person) or travel documents of a particular kind.

(3) The person commits an offence if—

(a) the person's release on bail is subject to the travel restriction condition mentioned in subsection (2)(a) and he or she fails to comply with the condition, or

(b) the person's release on bail is subject to a travel restriction condition mentioned in subsection (2)(b) to (f) and he or she fails, without reasonable excuse, to comply with the condition.

(4) A person guilty of an offence under subsection (3) is liable—

(a) on summary conviction—

(i) in England and Wales, to imprisonment for a term not exceeding 12 months (or, in relation to offences committed before section 154(1) of the Criminal Justice Act 2003 comes into force, 6 months) or to a fine, or to both;

(ii) in Northern Ireland, to imprisonment for a term not exceeding 6 months, or to a fine not exceeding the statutory maximum, or to both;

(b) on conviction on indictment, to imprisonment for a term not exceeding 12 months or to a fine, or to both.

(5) Where an offence under this section is committed by a person released without charge and on bail under Part 4 of the Police and Criminal Evidence Act 1984, the offence is to be treated as having been committed in England and Wales (whether or not the conduct constituting the offence took place there).

(6) Where an offence under this section is committed by a person released without charge and on bail under Part 5 of the Police and Criminal Evidence (Northern Ireland) Order 1989 (S.I. 1989/1341 (N.I.12)), the offence is to be treated as having been committed in Northern Ireland (whether or not the conduct constituting the offence took place there).

(7) Section 69 defines words used in subsection (2).

69 Offence of breach of pre-charge bail conditions relating to travel: interpretation

(1) This section defines words used in section 68(2).

(2) "Travel document" means anything that is or appears to be—

(a) a passport, or

(b) a ticket or other document that permits a person to make a journey by any means from a place within the United Kingdom to a place outside the United Kingdom.

(3) "Passport" means—

(a) a United Kingdom passport (within the meaning of the Immigration Act 1971),

(b) a passport issued by or on behalf of the authorities of a country or territory outside the United Kingdom, or by or on behalf of an international organisation, or

(c) a document that can be used (in some or all circumstances) instead of a passport.

(4) "Port" means—

(a) an airport,
(b) a sea port,
(c) a hoverport,
(d) a heliport,
(e) a railway station where passenger trains depart for places outside the United Kingdom, or
(f) any other place at which a person is able, or attempting, to get on or off any craft, vessel or vehicle in connection with leaving the United Kingdom.

CHAPTER 2

RETENTION OF BIOMETRIC MATERIAL

70 Retention of fingerprints and DNA profiles: PACE

(1) Part 5 of the Police and Criminal Evidence Act 1984 (questioning and treatment of persons by police) is amended as follows.

(2) In section 63F (retention of section 63D material: persons arrested for or charged with a qualifying offence), after subsection (2) insert—

"(2A) In subsection (2), references to a recordable offence include an offence under the law of a country or territory outside England and Wales where the act constituting the offence would constitute a recordable offence if done in England and Wales (and, in the application of subsection (2) where a person has previously been convicted, this applies whether or not the act constituted such an offence when the person was convicted)."

(3) In that section, after subsection (11) insert—

"(12) For the purposes of the definition of "excluded offence" in subsection (11)—

(a) references to a recordable offence or a qualifying offence include an offence under the law of a country or territory outside England and Wales where the act constituting the offence would constitute a recordable offence or (as the case may be) a qualifying offence if done in England and Wales (whether or not it constituted such an offence when the person was convicted), and
(b) in the application of paragraph (b) of that definition in relation to an offence under the law of a country or territory outside England and Wales, the reference to a relevant custodial sentence of 5 years or more is to be read as a reference to a sentence of imprisonment or other form of detention of 5 years or more."

(4) In section 63H (retention of section 63D material: persons arrested for or charged with a minor offence), after subsection (2) insert—

"(2A) In subsection (2), the reference to a recordable offence includes an offence under the law of a country or territory outside England and Wales where the act constituting the offence would constitute a recordable offence if done in England and Wales (whether or not it constituted such an offence when the person was convicted)."

(5) In that section, in subsection (3), after "section 63F(11)" insert "(read with section 63F(12))".

(6) After section 63I insert—

"63IA Retention of material: persons convicted of an offence outside England and Wales after taking of section 63D material

(1) This section applies where—

(a) section 63D material is taken (or, in the case of a DNA profile, derived from a sample taken) in connection with the investigation of an offence,

(b) at any time before the material is required to be destroyed by virtue of this Part of this Act, the person is convicted of an offence under the law of a country or territory outside England and Wales, and

(c) the act constituting the offence mentioned in paragraph (b) would constitute a recordable offence if done in England and Wales.

(2) The material may be retained indefinitely.

(3) This section does not apply where section 63KA applies."

(7) In the heading of section 63J, at the end insert ": other cases".

(8) In section 63K (retention of section 63D material: exception for persons under 18 convicted of minor offence), after subsection (1) insert—

"(1A) In subsection (1)(a)(ii), the reference to a recordable offence includes an offence under the law of a country or territory outside England and Wales where the act constituting the offence would constitute a recordable offence if done in England and Wales (whether or not it constituted such an offence when the person was convicted)."

(9) In that section, after subsection (5) insert—

"(5A) In subsection (5), the reference to a recordable offence includes an offence under the law of a country or territory outside England and Wales where the act constituting the offence would constitute a recordable offence if done in England and Wales."

(10) After section 63K insert—

"63KA Retention of section 63D material under section 63IA: exception for persons under 18 convicted of first minor offence outside England and Wales

(1) This section applies where—

(a) section 63D material is taken (or, in the case of a DNA profile, derived from a sample taken) in connection with the investigation of an offence,

(b) at any time before the material is required to be destroyed by virtue of this Part of this Act, the person is convicted of an offence under the law of a country or territory outside England and Wales,

(c) the act constituting the offence mentioned in paragraph (b) would constitute a recordable offence if done in England and Wales but would not constitute a qualifying offence,

(d) the person is aged under 18 at the time of the offence mentioned in paragraph (b), and

(e) the person has not previously been convicted of a recordable offence.

(2) In subsection (1)(e), the reference to a recordable offence includes an offence under the law of a country or territory outside England and Wales where the act constituting the offence would constitute a recordable offence if done in England and Wales (whether or not it constituted such an offence when the person was convicted).

(3) Where the person is sentenced to imprisonment or another form of detention for less than 5 years in respect of the offence mentioned in subsection (1)(b), the section 63D material may be retained until the end of the period consisting of the term of the sentence plus 5 years.

(4) Where the person is sentenced to imprisonment or another form of detention for 5 years or more in respect of the offence mentioned in subsection (1)(b), the material may be retained indefinitely.

(5) Where the person is given a sentence other than a sentence of imprisonment or other form of detention in respect of the offence mentioned in subsection (1)(b), the material may be retained until the end of the period of 5 years beginning with the date on which the person was arrested for the offence (or, if the person was not arrested for the offence, the date on which the person was charged with it).

(6) But if, before the end of the period within which material may be retained by virtue of this section, the person is again convicted of a recordable offence, the material may be retained indefinitely.

(7) In subsection (6), the reference to a recordable offence includes an offence under the law of a country or territory outside England and Wales where the act constituting the offence would constitute a recordable offence if done in England and Wales."

(11) In section 63N (retention of section 63D material given voluntarily), after subsection (4) insert—

"(5) The reference to a recordable offence in subsection (3)(a) includes an offence under the law of a country or territory outside England and Wales where the act constituting the offence would constitute a recordable offence if done in England and Wales.

(6) The reference to a recordable offence in subsections (3)(b) and (4), and the reference to a qualifying offence in subsection (4), includes an offence under the law of a country or territory outside England and Wales where the act constituting the offence would constitute a recordable offence or (as the case may be) a qualifying offence if done in England and Wales (whether or not it constituted such an offence when the person was convicted)."

71 Retention of fingerprints and DNA profiles: Terrorism Act 2000

(1) Schedule 8 to the Terrorism Act 2000 (detention) is amended as follows.

(2) In paragraph 20B (retention of paragraph 20A material: persons detained under section 41), after sub-paragraph (2) insert—

"(2A) In sub-paragraph (2) —

(a) the reference to a recordable offence includes an offence under the law of a country or territory outside the United Kingdom where the act constituting the offence would constitute—

(i) a recordable offence under the law of England and Wales if done there, or

(ii) a recordable offence under the law of Northern Ireland if done there,

(and, in the application of sub-paragraph (2) where a person has previously been convicted, this applies whether or not the act constituted such an offence when the person was convicted);

(b) the reference to an offence in Scotland which is punishable by imprisonment includes an offence under the law of a country or territory outside the United Kingdom where the act constituting the offence would constitute an offence under the law of Scotland which is punishable by imprisonment if done there (and, in the application of sub-paragraph (2) where a person has previously been convicted, this applies whether or not the act constituted such an offence when the person was convicted)."

(3) In paragraph 20C (retention of paragraph 20A material: persons detained under Schedule 7), after sub-paragraph (2) insert—

"(2A) In sub-paragraph (2) —

(a) the reference to a recordable offence includes an offence under the law of a country or territory outside the United Kingdom where the act constituting the offence would constitute—

(i) a recordable offence under the law of England and Wales if done there, or

(ii) a recordable offence under the law of Northern Ireland if done there,

(and, in the application of sub-paragraph (2) where a person has previously been convicted, this applies whether or not the act constituted such an offence when the person was convicted);

(b) the reference to an offence in Scotland which is punishable by imprisonment includes an offence under the law of a country or territory outside the United Kingdom where the act constituting the offence would constitute an offence under the law of Scotland which is punishable by imprisonment if done there (and, in the application of sub-paragraph (2) where a person has previously been convicted, this applies whether or not the act constituted such an offence when the person was convicted)."

(4) In paragraph 20D (interpretation), after sub-paragraph (5) insert—

"(5A) For the purposes of sub-paragraph (4)—

(a) a person is to be treated as having previously been convicted in England and Wales of a recordable offence if—
(i) the person has previously been convicted of an offence under the law of a country or territory outside the United Kingdom, and
(ii) the act constituting the offence would constitute a recordable offence under the law of England and Wales if done there (whether or not it constituted such an offence when the person was convicted);
(b) a person is to be treated as having previously been convicted in Northern Ireland of a recordable offence if—
(i) the person has previously been convicted of an offence under the law of a country or territory outside the United Kingdom, and
(ii) the act constituting the offence would constitute a recordable offence under the law of Northern Ireland if done there (whether or not it constituted such an offence when the person was convicted);
(c) a person is to be treated as having previously been convicted in Scotland of an offence which is punishable by imprisonment if—
(i) the person has previously been convicted of an offence under the law of a country or territory outside the United Kingdom, and
(ii) the act constituting the offence would constitute an offence punishable by imprisonment under the law of Scotland if done there (whether or not it constituted such an offence when the person was convicted);
(d) the reference in sub-paragraph (4)(b) to a qualifying offence includes a reference to an offence under the law of a country or territory outside the United Kingdom where the act constituting the offence would constitute a qualifying offence under the law of England and Wales if done there or (as the case may be) under the law of Northern Ireland if done there (whether or not it constituted such an offence when the person was convicted).

(5B) For the purposes of paragraphs 20B and 20C and this paragraph—
(a) offence, in relation to any country or territory outside the United Kingdom, includes an act punishable under the law of that country or territory, however it is described;
(b) a person has in particular been convicted of an offence under the law of a country or territory outside the United Kingdom if—
(i) a court exercising jurisdiction under the law of that country or territory has made in respect of such an offence a finding equivalent to a finding that the person is not guilty by reason of insanity, or
(ii) such a court has made in respect of such an offence a finding equivalent to a finding that the person is under a disability and did the act charged against the person in respect of the offence."

CHAPTER 3

POWERS UNDER PACE: MISCELLANEOUS

72 PACE: entry and search of premises for the purpose of arrest

In section 17 of the Police and Criminal Evidence Act 1984 (entry for the purpose of arrest) after subsection (1)(caa) insert—

"(cab) of arresting a person under any of the following provisions—

(i) section 30D(1) or (2A);

(ii) section 46A(1) or (1A);

(iii) section 5B(7) of the Bail Act 1976 (arrest where a person fails to surrender to custody in accordance with a court order);

(iv) section 7(3) of the Bail Act 1976 (arrest where a person is not likely to surrender to custody etc);

(v) section 97(1) of the Legal Aid, Sentencing and Punishment of Offenders Act 2012 (arrest where a child is suspected of breaking conditions of remand);".

73 PACE: treatment of those aged 17

(1) The Police and Criminal Evidence Act 1984 is amended as follows.

(2) In section 30A (bail elsewhere than at police station), in subsection (3B)(d), for "under the age of 17" substitute "under the age of 18".

(3) In section 63B (testing for presence of class A drugs)—

(a) in subsection (5A), for "has not attained the age of 17" substitute "has not attained the age of 18";

(b) in subsection (10), in the definition of "appropriate adult", for "has not attained the age of 17" substitute "has not attained the age of 18".

(4) In section 65 (which makes provision to supplement the provisions of Part 5 on the questioning and treatment of persons by the police), in subsection (1), in the definition of "appropriate consent", in paragraph (a), for "has attained the age of 17 years" substitute "has attained the age of 18 years".

74 PACE: detention: use of live links

(1) The Police and Criminal Evidence Act 1984 is amended as follows.

(2) After section 45 insert—

"Use of live links

45ZA Functions of extending detention: use of live links

(1) The functions of a police officer under section 42(1) or (2) may be performed, in relation to an arrested person who is held at a police station, by an officer who is not present at the police station but has access to the use of a live link if—

(a) a custody officer considers that the use of the live link is appropriate,

(b) the arrested person has had advice from a solicitor on the use of the live link, and

(c) the appropriate consent to the use of the live link has been given.

(2) In subsection (1)(c), "the appropriate consent" means—

(a) in relation to a person who has attained the age of 18, the consent of that person;

(b) in relation to a person who has not attained that age but has attained the age of 14, the consent of that person and of his or her parent or guardian;

(c) in relation to a person who has not attained the age of 14, the consent of his or her parent or guardian.

(3) The consent of a person who has not attained the age of 18 (but has attained the age of 14), or who is a vulnerable adult, may only be given in the presence of an appropriate adult.

(4) Section 42 applies with the modifications set out in subsections (5) to (7) below in any case where the functions of a police officer under that section are, by virtue of subsection (1), performed by an officer who is not at the police station where the arrested person is held.

(5) Subsections (5)(b) and (9)(iii) and (iv) of that section are each to be read as if, instead of requiring the officer to make a record, they required the officer to cause another police officer to make a record.

(6) Subsection (6) of that section is to be read as if it required the officer to give the persons mentioned in that subsection an opportunity to make representations—

(a) if facilities exist for the immediate transmission of written representations to the officer, either in writing by means of those facilities or orally by means of the live link, or

(b) in any other case, orally by means of the live link.

(7) Subsection (9) of that section is to be read as if the reference in paragraph (b) to the right conferred by section 58 were omitted.

(8) In this section—

"live link" means an arrangement by which an officer who is not present at the police station where an arrested person is held is able to see and hear, and to be seen and heard by, the arrested person and the arrested person's solicitor (and for this purpose any impairment of eyesight or hearing is to be disregarded);

"vulnerable adult" means a person aged 18 or over who may have difficulty understanding the purpose of an authorisation under section 42(1) or (2) or anything that occurs in connection with a decision whether to give such an authorisation (whether because of a mental disorder or for any other reason);

"appropriate adult", in relation to a person who has not attained the age of 18, means—

(a) the persons's parent or guardian or, if the person is in the care of a local authority or voluntary organisation, a person representing that authority or organisation,

(b) a social worker of a local authority, or

(c) if no person falling within paragraph (a) or (b) is available, any responsible person aged 18 or over who is not a police officer or a person employed for, or engaged on, police purposes;

"appropriate adult", in relation to a vulnerable adult, means—

(a) a relative, guardian or other person responsible for the vulnerable adult's care,

(b) a person who is experienced in dealing with vulnerable adults but who is not a police officer or a person employed for, or engaged on, police purposes, or

(c) if no person falling within paragraph (a) or (b) is available, any responsible person aged 18 or over who is not a police officer or a person employed for, or engaged on, police purposes.

(9) In subsection (8), in both definitions of "appropriate adult", "police purposes" has the meaning given by section 101(2) of the Police Act 1996.

45ZB Warrants for further detention: use of live links

(1) A magistrates' court may give a live link direction for the purpose of the hearing of an application under section 43 for a warrant authorising further detention of a person, or the hearing of an application under section 44 for an extension of such a warrant, if—

(a) a custody officer considers that the use of a live link for that purpose is appropriate,

(b) the person to whom the application relates has had legal advice on the use of the live link,

(c) the appropriate consent to the use of the live link has been given, and

(d) it is not contrary to the interests of justice to give the direction.

(2) In subsection (1)(c), "the appropriate consent" means—

(a) in relation to a person who has attained the age of 18, the consent of that person;

(b) in relation to a person who has not attained that age but has attained the age of 14, the consent of that person and of his or her parent or guardian;

(c) in relation to a person who has not attained the age of 14, the consent of his or her parent or guardian.

(3) Where a live link direction is given, the requirement under section 43(2)(b) for the person to whom the application relates to be brought before the court for the hearing does not apply.

(4) In this section—

"live link direction" means a direction that a live link be used for the purposes of the hearing;

"live link" means an arrangement by which a person (when not in the place where the hearing is being held) is able to see and hear, and to be seen and heard by, the court during a hearing (and for this purpose any impairment of eyesight or hearing is to be disregarded);

"vulnerable adult" means a person aged 18 or over who may have difficulty understanding the purpose of the hearing or what occurs at it (whether because of a mental disorder or for any other reason);

"appropriate adult", in relation to a person aged under 18, means—

(a) the person's parent or guardian or, if the person is in the care of a local authority or voluntary organisation, a person representing that authority or organisation,

(b) a social worker of a local authority, or

(c) if no person falling within paragraph (a) or (b) is available, any responsible person aged 18 or over who is not a police officer or a person employed for, or engaged on, police purposes;

"appropriate adult", in relation to a vulnerable adult, means—

(a) a relative, guardian or other person responsible for the appropriate adult's care,

(b) a person who is experienced in dealing with vulnerable adults but who is not a police officer or a person employed for, or engaged on, police purposes, or

(c) if no person falling within paragraph (a) or (b) is available, any responsible person aged 18 or over who is not a police officer or a person employed for, or engaged on, police purposes.

(5) In subsection (4), in both definitions of "appropriate adult", "police purposes" has the meaning given by section 101(2) of the Police Act 1996."

(3) In section 45 (detention before charge-supplementary), in subsection (1), for "sections 43 and 44" substitute "sections 43, 44 and 45ZB".

(4) In section 45A—

(a) for the heading substitute "Use of live links for other decisions about detention";

(b) in subsection (1)(b), for the words from "video-conferencing facilities" to the end substitute "a live link";

(c) in subsection (3), for "the facilities mentioned in subsection (1) above" substitute "a live link";

(d) in subsection (7), in each of paragraphs (a)(i) and (b), for "the video-conferencing facilities" substitute "the live link";

(e) for subsection (10) substitute—

"(10) In this section, "live link", in relation to any functions, means an arrangement by which the functions may be performed by an officer who is not present at the police station where an arrested person is held but who is able (for the purpose of the functions) to see and hear, and to be seen and heard by, the arrested person and any legal representative of that person (and for this purpose any impairment of eyesight or hearing is to be disregarded)."

(5) In consequence of the amendments made by subsection (4), in section 40A—

(a) in subsection (2)(a), for "video-conferencing facilities" substitute "a live link";

(b) in subsection (5), for "video-conferencing facilities" substitute "live link".

75 PACE: interviews: use of live links

(1) Section 39 of the Police and Criminal Evidence Act 1984 (responsibilities in relation to persons detained) is amended as follows.

(2) In subsection (2)(a), for "a police officer investigating an offence for which that person is in police detention" substitute "another police officer at the police station where the person is in police detention, for the purpose of an interview that is part of the investigation of an offence for which the person is in police detention or otherwise in connection with the investigation of such an offence".

(3) After subsection (3) insert—

"(3A) Subsections (3B) and (3C) apply if the custody officer, in accordance with any code of practice issued under this Act, transfers or permits the transfer of a person in police detention to an officer mentioned in subsection (2)(a) for the purpose of an interview that is to be conducted to any extent by means of a live link by another police officer who is investigating the offence but is not at the police station where the person in police detention is held at the time of the interview.

(3B) The officer who is not at the police station has the same duty as the officer mentioned in subsection (2)(a) to ensure that the person is treated in accordance with the provisions of this Act and of any such codes of practice as are mentioned in subsection (1).

(3C) If the person detained is subsequently returned to the custody of the custody officer, the officer who is not at the police station also has the same duty under subsection (3) as the officer mentioned in subsection (2)(a).

(3D) For the purpose of subsection (3C), subsection (3) applies as if the reference to "in his custody" were a reference to "being interviewed".

(3E) In subsection (3A), "live link" means an arrangement by which the officer who is not at the police station is able to see and hear, and to be seen and heard by, the person in police detention, any legal representative of that person and the officer who has custody of that person at the police station (and for this purpose any impairment of eyesight or hearing is to be disregarded)."

76 PACE: audio recording of interviews

(1) The Police and Criminal Evidence Act 1984 is amended as follows.

(2) In section 60 (which currently makes provision about the tape-recording of interviews) —

(a) in subsection (1), in each of paragraphs (a) and (b), for "tape-recording" substitute "audio recording";

(b) in the heading of the section, for "Tape-recording" substitute "Audio recording".

(3) In section 113 (application of Act to armed forces), in subsection (4)(a), for "tape-recording" substitute "audio recording".

77 PACE: duty to notify person interviewed that not to be prosecuted

After section 60A of the Police and Criminal Evidence Act 1984 insert—

"60B Notification of decision not to prosecute person interviewed

(1) This section applies where—

(a) a person suspected of the commission of a criminal offence is interviewed by a police officer but is not arrested for the offence, and

(b) the police officer in charge of investigating the offence determines that—

(i) there is not sufficient evidence to charge the person with an offence, or

(ii) there is sufficient evidence to charge the person with an offence but the person should not be charged with an offence or given a caution in respect of an offence.

(2) A police officer must give the person notice in writing that the person is not to be prosecuted.

(3) Subsection (2) does not prevent the prosecution of the person for an offence if new evidence comes to light after the notice was given.

(4) In this section "caution" includes—

(a) a conditional caution within the meaning of Part 3 of the Criminal Justice Act 2003;

(b) a youth conditional caution within the meaning of Chapter 1 of Part 4 of the Crime and Disorder Act 1998;

(c) a youth caution under section 66ZA of that Act."

78 PACE: consultation on codes of practice

In section 67 of the Police and Criminal Evidence Act 1984 (codes of practice: supplementary), after subsection (4) insert—

"(4A) The duty to consult under subsection (4) does not apply to a revision of a code where the Secretary of State considers that—

(a) the revision is necessary in consequence of legislation, and

(b) the Secretary of State has no discretion as to the nature of the revision.

(4B) Where, in consequence of subsection (4A), a revision of a code is issued without prior consultation with the persons mentioned in subsection (4), the Secretary of State must (at the same time as issuing the revision) publish a statement that, in his or her opinion, paragraphs (a) and (b) of subsection (4A) apply to the revision.

(4C) In subsection (4A), "legislation" means any provision of—

(a) an Act,

(b) subordinate legislation within the meaning of the Interpretation Act 1978."

79 Definition of "appropriate adult" in criminal justice legislation

(1) In section 63B of the Police and Criminal Evidence Act 1984 (testing for presence of Class A drugs), in subsection (10), in paragraph (c), in the definition of "appropriate adult", for "a person employed by the police" substitute "a person employed for, or engaged on, police purposes; and "police purposes" has the meaning given by section 101(2) of the Police Act 1996".

(2) In section 66ZA of the Crime and Disorder Act 1998 (youth cautions), in subsection (7) (which defines "appropriate adult"), in paragraph (d), for "a person employed by the police" substitute "a person employed for, or engaged on, police purposes; and "police purposes" has the meaning given by section 101(2) of the Police Act 1996".

(3) In section 161 of the Criminal Justice Act 2003 (pre-sentence drug testing), in subsection (8) (which defines "appropriate adult"), in paragraph (c), for "a person employed by the police" substitute "a person employed for, or engaged on, police purposes; and "police purposes" has the meaning given by section 101(2) of the Police Act 1996".

CHAPTER 4

POWERS UNDER THE MENTAL HEALTH ACT 1983

80 Extension of powers under sections 135 and 136 of the Mental Health Act 1983

(1) The Mental Health Act 1983 is amended as follows.

(2) In section 135 (warrant to search for and remove patients), after subsection (1) insert—

> "(1A) If the premises specified in the warrant are a place of safety, the constable executing the warrant may, instead of removing the person to another place of safety, keep the person at those premises for the purpose mentioned in subsection (1)."

(3) In subsection (3) of that section—

(a) for "under this section" substitute "under subsection (1)";

(b) before "may" insert ", or kept at the premises specified in the warrant under subsection (1A),".

(4) In section 136 (mentally disordered persons found in public places), for subsection (1) substitute—

> "(1) If a person appears to a constable to be suffering from mental disorder and to be in immediate need of care or control, the constable may, if he thinks it necessary to do so in the interests of that person or for the protection of other persons—
>
> (a) remove the person to a place of safety within the meaning of section 135, or
>
> (b) if the person is already at a place of safety within the meaning of that section, keep the person at that place or remove the person to another place of safety.

(1A) The power of a constable under subsection (1) may be exercised where the mentally disordered person is at any place, other than—

(a) any house, flat or room where that person, or any other person, is living, or

(b) any yard, garden, garage or outhouse that is used in connection with the house, flat or room, other than one that is also used in connection with one or more other houses, flats or rooms.

(1B) For the purpose of exercising the power under subsection (1), a constable may enter any place where the power may be exercised, if need be by force."

(5) After subsection (1B) of that section (inserted by subsection (4) above) insert—

"(1C) Before deciding to remove a person to, or to keep a person at, a place of safety under subsection (1), the constable must, if it is practicable to do so, consult—

(a) a registered medical practitioner,

(b) a registered nurse,

(c) an approved mental health professional, or

(d) a person of a description specified in regulations made by the Secretary of State."

(6) In subsection (2) of that section, for "removed to" substitute "removed to, or kept at,".

(7) For the heading of that section substitute "Removal etc of mentally disordered persons without a warrant".

81 Restrictions on places that may be used as places of safety

(1) The Mental Health Act 1983 is amended as follows.

(2) In section 135 (warrant to search for and remove patients), in subsection (6), omit the words "the occupier of which is willing temporarily to receive the patient".

(3) After subsection (6) of that section insert—

"(7) For the purpose of subsection (6)—

(a) a house, flat or room where a person is living may not be regarded as a suitable place unless—

(i) if the person believed to be suffering from a mental disorder is the sole occupier of the place, that person agrees to the use of the place as a place of safety;

(ii) if the person believed to be suffering from a mental disorder is an occupier of the place but not the sole occupier, both that person and one of the other occupiers agree to the use of the place as a place of safety;

(iii) if the person believed to be suffering from a mental disorder is not an occupier of the place, both that person and the occupier (or, if more than one, one of the occupiers) agree to the use of the place as a place of safety;

(b) a place other than one mentioned in paragraph (a) may not be regarded as a suitable place unless a person who appears to the constable exercising powers under this section to be responsible for the management of the place agrees to its use as a place of safety."

(4) After subsection (7) of that section (inserted by subsection (3) above) insert—

"(8) This section is subject to section 136A which makes provision about the removal and taking of persons to a police station under this section."

(5) In section 136, after subsection (4) insert—

"(5) This section is subject to section 136A which makes provision about the removal and taking of persons to a police station, and the keeping of persons at a police station, under this section."

(6) After section 136 insert—

"136A Use of police stations as places of safety

(1) A child may not, in the exercise of a power to which this section applies, be removed to, kept at or taken to a place of safety that is a police station.

(2) The Secretary of State may by regulations—

(a) provide that an adult may be removed to, kept at or taken to a place of safety that is a police station, in the exercise of a power to which this section applies, only in circumstances specified in the regulations;

(b) make provision about how adults removed to, kept at or taken to a police station, in the exercise of a power to which this section applies, are to be treated while at the police station, including provision for review of their detention.

(3) Regulations under this section—

(a) may make different provision for different cases;

(b) may make provision that applies subject to specified exceptions;

(c) may include incidental, supplementary or consequential provision or transitional, transitory or saving provision.

(4) The powers to which this section applies are—

(a) the power to remove a person to a place of safety under a warrant issued under section 135(1);

(b) the power to take a person to a place of safety under section 135(3A);

(c) the power to remove a person to, or to keep a person at, a place of safety under section 136(1);

(d) the power to take a person to a place of safety under section 136(3).

(5) In this section—

(a) "child" means a person aged under 18;

(b) "adult" means a person aged 18 or over."

82 Periods of detention in places of safety etc

(1) The Mental Health Act 1983 is amended as follows.

(2) In section 135 (warrant to search for and remove patients)—

(a) in subsection (3), for "72 hours" substitute "the permitted period of detention";

(b) after subsection (3) insert—

"(3ZA) In subsection (3), "the permitted period of detention" means—

(a) the period of 24 hours beginning with—

(i) in a case where the person is removed to a place of safety, the time when the person arrives at that place;

(ii) in a case where the person is kept at the premises specified in the warrant, the time when the constable first entered the premises to execute the warrant; or

(b) where an authorisation is given in relation to the person under section 136B, that period of 24 hours and such further period as is specified in the authorisation.";

(c) in subsection (3A), for "the period of 72 hours" substitute "the permitted period of detention";

(d) in subsection (3B), for "the period of 72 hours" substitute "the permitted period of detention".

(3) In section 136 (mentally disordered persons found in public places)—

(a) in subsection (2), for "72 hours" substitute "the permitted period of detention";

(b) after subsection (2) insert—

"(2A) In subsection (2), "the permitted period of detention" means—

(a) the period of 24 hours beginning with—

(i) in a case where the person is removed to a place of safety, the time when the person arrives at that place;

(ii) in a case where the person is kept at a place of safety, the time when the constable decides to keep the person at that place; or

(b) where an authorisation is given in relation to the person under section 136B, that period of 24 hours and such further period as is specified in the authorisation.";

(c) in subsection (3), for "the period of 72 hours" substitute "the permitted period of detention";

(d) in subsection (4), for "the period of 72 hours" substitute "the permitted period of detention".

(4) After section 136A (inserted by section 81) insert—

"136B Extension of detention

(1) The registered medical practitioner who is responsible for the examination of a person detained under section 135 or 136 may, at any time before the expiry of the period of 24 hours mentioned in section 135(3ZA) or (as the case may be) 136(2A), authorise the detention of the person for a further period not exceeding 12 hours (beginning immediately at the end of the period of 24 hours).

(2) An authorisation under subsection (1) may be given only if the registered medical practitioner considers that the extension is necessary because the condition of the person detained is such that it would not be practicable for the assessment of the person for the purpose of section 135 or (as the case may be) section 136 to be carried out before the end of the period of 24 hours (or, if the assessment began within that period, for it to be completed before the end).

(3) If the person is detained at a police station, and the assessment would be carried out or completed at the station, the registered medical practitioner may give an authorisation under subsection (1) only if an officer of the rank of superintendent or above approves it."

(5) In section 138 (retaking of patients escaping from custody), in subsection (3), for the words from "after the expiration of the period" to the end of the subsection substitute "—

(a) in a case where the person escapes while being removed to a place of safety in the execution of a warrant under section 135(1) or under section 136(1), after the end of the period of 24 hours beginning with the escape;

(b) in a case where the person escapes after the beginning of the period that is the permitted period of detention in relation to the person under section 135(3ZA) or 136(2A), after the end of that period (taking into account any authorisation under section 136B(1) that was given before the person escaped)."

83 Protective searches: individuals removed etc under section 135 or 136 of the Mental Health Act 1983

After section 136B of the Mental Health Act 1983 (inserted by section 82) insert—

"136C Protective searches

(1) Where a warrant is issued under section 135(1) or (2), a constable may search the person to whom the warrant relates if the constable has reasonable grounds for believing that the person—

(a) may present a danger to himself or herself or to others, and

(b) is concealing on his or her person an item that could be used to cause physical injury to himself or herself or to others.

(2) The power to search conferred by subsection (1) may be exercised—

(a) in a case where a warrant is issued under section 135(1), at any time during the period beginning with the time when a constable enters the premises specified in the warrant and ending when the person ceases to be detained under section 135;

(b) in a case where a warrant is issued under section 135(2), at any time while the person is being removed under the authority of the warrant.

(3) Where a person is detained under section 136(2) or (4), a constable may search the person, at any time while the person is so detained, if the constable has reasonable grounds for believing that the person—

(a) may present a danger to himself or herself or to others, and

(b) is concealing on his or her person an item that could be used to cause physical injury to himself or herself or to others.

(4) The power to search conferred by subsection (1) or (3) is only a power to search to the extent that is reasonably required for the purpose of discovering the item that the constable believes the person to be concealing.

(5) The power to search conferred by subsection (1) or (3)—

(a) does not authorise a constable to require a person to remove any of his or her clothing other than an outer coat, jacket or gloves, but

(b) does authorise a search of a person's mouth.

(6) A constable searching a person in the exercise of the power to search conferred by subsection (1) or (3) may seize and retain anything found, if he or she has reasonable grounds for believing that the person searched might use it to cause physical injury to himself or herself or to others.

(7) The power to search a person conferred by subsection (1) or (3) does not affect any other power to search the person."

CHAPTER 5

MARITIME ENFORCEMENT: ENGLISH AND WELSH OFFENCES

Application of maritime enforcement powers: general

84 Application of maritime enforcement powers: general

(1) A law enforcement officer may, for the purpose of preventing, detecting, investigating or prosecuting an offence under the law of England and Wales, exercise any of the maritime enforcement powers in relation to—

(a) a United Kingdom ship in England and Wales waters, foreign waters or international waters,

(b) a ship without nationality in England and Wales waters or international waters,

(c) a foreign ship in England and Wales waters or international waters, or

(d) a ship, registered under the law of a relevant territory, in England and Wales waters or international waters.

(2) In this Chapter, "the maritime enforcement powers" are the powers set out in—

(a) section 88 (power to stop, board, divert and detain);

(b) section 89 (power to search and obtain information);

(c) section 90 (power of arrest and seizure).

(3) The following persons are "law enforcement officers" for the purpose of this Chapter—

(a) a constable who is a member of a police force in England and Wales,

(b) a special constable appointed under section 27 of the Police Act 1996,

(c) a constable who is a member of the British Transport Police Force,

(d) a port constable, within the meaning of section 7 of the Marine Navigation Act 2013, or a person appointed to act as a constable under provision made by virtue of section 16 of the Harbours Act 1964,

(e) a designated customs official within the meaning of Part 1 of the Borders, Citizenship and Immigration Act 2009 (see section 14(6) of that Act),

(f) a designated NCA officer who is authorised by the Director General of the National Crime Agency (whether generally or specifically) to exercise the powers of a law enforcement officer under this Chapter, or

(g) a person of a description specified in regulations made by the Secretary of State.

(4) Regulations under subsection (3)(g) are to be made by statutory instrument.

(5) A statutory instrument containing regulations under subsection (3)(g) is subject to annulment in pursuance of a resolution of either House of Parliament.

(6) This section is subject to section 85 (which makes provision about when the authority of the Secretary of State is required before the maritime enforcement powers are exercised in reliance on this section).

85 Restriction on exercise of maritime enforcement powers

(1) The authority of the Secretary of State is required before a law enforcement officer exercises any of the maritime enforcement powers, in reliance on section 84(1), in relation to a United Kingdom ship in foreign waters.

(2) The Secretary of State may give authority under subsection (1) only if the State, or the relevant territory, in whose waters the powers would be exercised consents to the exercise of the powers.

(3) The authority of the Secretary of State is required before a law enforcement officer exercises any of the maritime enforcement powers, in reliance on section 84(1), in relation to a foreign ship, or a ship registered under the law of a relevant territory, within the territorial sea adjacent to England and Wales or in international waters.

(4) The Secretary of State may give authority under subsection (3) in relation to a foreign ship only if—

- (a) the home state has requested the assistance of the United Kingdom for the purpose of preventing, detecting, investigating or prosecuting an offence under the law of England and Wales,
- (b) the home state has authorised the United Kingdom to act for that purpose, or
- (c) the United Nations Convention on the Law of the Sea 1982 (Cmnd 8941) otherwise permits the exercise of the powers in relation to the ship.

Ships in Scotland waters: hot pursuit

86 Hot pursuit of ships in Scotland waters

(1) A law enforcement officer may, for the purpose of preventing, detecting, investigating or prosecuting an offence under the law of England and Wales, exercise any of the maritime enforcement powers in relation to a ship in Scotland waters if—

- (a) the ship is pursued there,
- (b) immediately before the pursuit of the ship, the ship was in England and Wales waters or international waters,
- (c) before the pursuit of the ship, a signal was given for it to stop,
- (d) the signal was given in such a way as to be audible or visible from the ship, and
- (e) the pursuit of the ship is not interrupted.

(2) For the purposes of subsection (1)(e), pursuit is not interrupted by reason only of the fact that—

- (a) the method of carrying out the pursuit, or
- (b) the identity of the ship or aircraft carrying out the pursuit,

changes during the course of the pursuit.

(3) This section is subject to section 87 (which requires the authority of the Secretary of State before the maritime enforcement powers are exercised in relation to a foreign ship, or a ship registered under the law of a relevant territory, within the territorial sea adjacent to Scotland).

87 Restriction on exercise of maritime enforcement powers in hot pursuit

(1) The authority of the Secretary of State is required before a law enforcement officer exercises any of the maritime enforcement powers, in reliance on section 86, in relation to a foreign ship, or a ship registered under the law of a relevant territory, within the territorial sea adjacent to Scotland.

(2) The Secretary of State may give authority under subsection (1) in relation to a foreign ship only if—

(a) the home state has requested the assistance of the United Kingdom for the purpose of preventing, detecting, investigating or prosecuting an offence under the law of England and Wales,

(b) the home state has authorised the United Kingdom to act for that purpose, or

(c) the United Nations Convention on the Law of the Sea 1982 (Cmnd 8941) otherwise permits the exercise of the powers in relation to the ship.

The maritime enforcement powers

88 Power to stop, board, divert and detain

(1) This section applies if a law enforcement officer has reasonable grounds to suspect that—

(a) an offence under the law of England and Wales is being, or has been, committed on a ship in relation to which the powers conferred by this section are exercisable by virtue of section 84 or 86, or

(b) a ship in relation to which those powers are so exercisable is otherwise being used in connection with the commission of an offence under that law.

(2) The law enforcement officer may—

(a) stop the ship;

(b) board the ship;

(c) require the ship to be taken to a port in England and Wales or elsewhere and detained there.

(3) Except as provided by subsection (5), the authority of the Secretary of State is required before a law enforcement officer may exercise the power conferred by subsection (2)(c) to require the ship to be taken to a port outside the United Kingdom.

(4) The Secretary of State may give authority for the purposes of subsection (3) only if the State, or the relevant territory, in which the port is located is willing to receive the ship.

(5) If the law enforcement officer is acting under authority given for the purposes of section 85(3) or 87(1), the law enforcement officer may require the ship to be taken to—

(a) a port in the home state or relevant territory in question, or

(b) if the home state or relevant territory requests, a port in any other State or relevant territory willing to receive the ship.

(6) The law enforcement officer may require the master of the ship, or any member of its crew, to take such action as is necessary for the purposes of subsection (2)(c).

(7) A law enforcement officer must give notice in writing to the master of any ship detained under this section.

(8) The notice must state that the ship is to be detained until the notice is withdrawn by the giving of a further notice in writing signed by a law enforcement officer.

89 Power to search and obtain information

(1) This section applies if a law enforcement officer has reasonable grounds to suspect that there is evidence relating to an offence under the law of England and Wales (other than items subject to legal privilege) on a ship in relation to which the powers conferred by this section are exercisable by virtue of section 84 or 86.

(2) The law enforcement officer may search—
(a) the ship;
(b) anyone found on the ship;
(c) anything found on the ship (including cargo).

(3) The law enforcement officer may require a person found on the ship to give information about himself or herself or about anything found on the ship.

(4) The power to search conferred by subsection (2) is a power to search only to the extent that it is reasonably required for the purpose of discovering evidence of the kind mentioned in subsection (1).

(5) The power to search a person conferred by subsection (2) does not authorise a law enforcement officer to require the person to remove any clothing in public other than an outer coat, jacket or gloves.

(6) In exercising a power conferred by subsection (2) or (3), a law enforcement officer may (amongst other things)—
(a) open any containers;
(b) require the production of documents, books or records relating to the ship or anything on it, other than anything that the law enforcement officer has reasonable grounds to believe to be an item subject to legal privilege;
(c) make photographs or copies of anything the production of which the law enforcement officer has power to require.

(7) The power in subsection (6)(b) to require the production of documents, books or records includes, in relation to documents, books or records kept in electronic form, power to require the provision of the documents, books or records in a form in which they are legible and can be taken away.

(8) The power of a law enforcement officer under subsection (2)(b) or (c) or (3) may be exercised on the ship or elsewhere.

90 Power of arrest and seizure

(1) This section applies if a law enforcement officer has reasonable grounds to suspect that an offence under the law of England and Wales has been, or is being, committed on a ship in relation to which the powers conferred by this section are exercisable by virtue of section 84 or 86.

(2) The law enforcement officer may arrest without warrant anyone whom the officer has reasonable grounds for suspecting to be guilty of the offence.

(3) The law enforcement officer may seize and retain anything found on the ship which appears to the officer to be evidence of the offence, other than anything that the officer has reasonable grounds to believe to be an item subject to legal privilege.

(4) The power of a law enforcement officer under subsection (2) or (3) may be exercised on the ship or elsewhere.

Supplementary provision

91 Maritime enforcement powers: supplementary: protective searches

(1) This section applies where a power conferred by section 88 is exercised in relation to a ship.

(2) A law enforcement officer may search any person found on the ship for anything which the officer has reasonable grounds to believe the person might use to—

(a) cause physical injury,

(b) cause damage to property, or

(c) endanger the safety of any ship.

(3) The power under subsection (2) may be exercised on board the ship or elsewhere.

(4) A law enforcement officer searching a person under subsection (2) may seize and retain anything found if the law enforcement officer has reasonable grounds to believe that the person might use it for a purpose mentioned in paragraphs (a) to (c) of that subsection.

(5) Anything seized under subsection (4) may be retained only for so long as there are reasonable grounds to believe that it might be used as mentioned in that subsection.

(6) The power to search a person conferred by subsection (2) does not authorise a law enforcement officer to require the person to remove any clothing in public, other than an outer coat, jacket or gloves.

92 Maritime enforcement powers: other supplementary provision

(1) A law enforcement officer may—

(a) be accompanied by other persons, and

(b) take equipment or materials,

to assist the officer in the exercise of powers under this Chapter.

(2) A law enforcement officer may use reasonable force, if necessary, in the performance of functions under this Chapter.

(3) A person accompanying a law enforcement officer under subsection (1) may perform any of the officer's functions under this Chapter, but only under the officer's supervision.

(4) A law enforcement officer must produce evidence of the officer's authority if asked to do so.

(5) A law enforcement officer is not liable in any criminal or civil proceedings for anything done in the purported performance of functions under this Chapter if the court is satisfied that—

(a) the act was done in good faith, and

(b) there were reasonable grounds for doing it.

(6) The powers conferred by this Chapter do not affect any other powers that a law enforcement officer may have.

93 Maritime enforcement powers: offences

(1) A person commits an offence if the person—

(a) intentionally obstructs a law enforcement officer in the performance of functions under this Chapter, or

(b) fails without reasonable excuse to comply with a requirement imposed by a law enforcement officer in the performance of those functions.

(2) A person who provides information in response to a requirement imposed by a law enforcement officer in the performance of functions under this Chapter commits an offence if—

(a) the information is false in a material particular, and the person either knows it is or is reckless as to whether it is, or

(b) the person intentionally fails to disclose any material particular.

(3) A law enforcement officer may arrest without warrant anyone whom the officer has reasonable grounds for suspecting to be guilty of an offence under this section.

(4) A person guilty of an offence under this section is liable on summary conviction to a fine.

94 Maritime enforcement powers: code of practice

(1) The Secretary of State must prepare and issue a code of practice in respect of the practice to be followed by law enforcement officers when arresting a person under the power conferred by section 90.

(2) The code must, in particular, provide guidance as to the information to be given to the person at the time of arrest (whether about procedural rights or other matters).

(3) A failure of a law enforcement officer to comply with any provision of the code does not of itself render the law enforcement officer liable to any criminal or civil proceedings.

(4) The code—

(a) is admissible in evidence in criminal and civil proceedings, and

(b) may be taken into account by a court or tribunal in any case in which it appears to the court or tribunal to be relevant.

(5) The Secretary of State may at any time revise the whole or any part of the code.

(6) The code, or any revision of the code, does not come into operation until the Secretary of State so provides by regulations.

(7) Regulations under this section are to be made by statutory instrument.

(8) A statutory instrument containing regulations under this section that bring the code into operation may not be made unless a draft of the instrument has been laid before, and approved by a resolution of, each House of Parliament.

(9) A statutory instrument containing regulations under this section that bring a revision of the code into operation must be laid before Parliament (if the regulations are made without a draft having been laid and approved as mentioned in subsection (8)).

(10) Where a statutory instrument, or draft of a statutory instrument, is laid under this section, the code or revision of the code to which it relates must also be laid.

95 Interpretation

(1) In this Chapter—

"designated NCA officer" means a National Crime Agency officer who is either or both of the following—

(a) an officer designated under section 10 of the Crime and Courts Act 2013 as having the powers and privileges of a constable;

(b) an officer designated under that section as having the powers of a general customs official;

"England and Wales waters" means the sea and other waters within the seaward limits of the territorial sea adjacent to England and Wales;

"foreign ship" means a ship which—

(a) is registered in a State other than the United Kingdom, or

(b) is not so registered but is entitled to fly the flag of a State other than the United Kingdom;

"foreign waters" means the sea and other waters within the seaward limits of the territorial sea adjacent to any relevant territory or State other than the United Kingdom;

"home state", in relation to a foreign ship, means—

(a) the State in which the ship is registered, or

(b) the State whose flag the ship is otherwise entitled to fly;

"international waters" means waters beyond the territorial sea of the United Kingdom or of any other State or relevant territory;

"items subject to legal privilege" has the same meaning as in the Police and Criminal Evidence Act 1984 (see section 10 of that Act);

"law enforcement officer" has the meaning given by section 84(3);

"maritime enforcement powers" has the meaning given by section 84(2);

"relevant territory" means—

(a) the Isle of Man;

(b) any of the Channel Islands;

(c) a British overseas territory;

"Scotland waters" means the sea and other waters within the seaward limits of the territorial sea adjacent to Scotland;

"ship" includes every description of vessel (including a hovercraft) used in navigation;

"ship without nationality" means a ship which—

(a) is not registered in, or otherwise entitled to fly the flag of, any State or relevant territory, or

(b) sails under the flags of two or more States or relevant territories, or under the flags of a State and relevant territory, using them according to convenience;

"United Kingdom ship" means a ship which—

(a) is registered under Part 2 of the Merchant Shipping Act 1995,

(b) is a Government ship within the meaning of that Act,

(c) is not registered in any State or relevant territory but is wholly owned by persons each of whom has a United Kingdom connection, or

(d) is registered under an Order in Council under section 1 of the Hovercraft Act 1968.

(2) For the purposes of paragraph (c) of the definition of "United Kingdom ship" in subsection (1), a person has a "United Kingdom connection" if the person is—

(a) a British citizen, a British overseas territories citizen or a British Overseas citizen,

(b) an individual who is habitually resident in the United Kingdom, or

(c) a body corporate which is established under the law of a part of the United Kingdom and has its principal place of business in the United Kingdom.

(3) References in this Chapter to the United Nations Convention on the Law of the Sea include references to any modifications of that Convention agreed after the passing of this Act that have entered into force in relation to the United Kingdom.

CHAPTER 6

Maritime enforcement: Scottish offences

Application of maritime enforcement powers: general

96 Application of maritime enforcement powers: general

(1) A law enforcement officer may, for the purpose of preventing, detecting or investigating an offence under the law of Scotland, exercise any of the maritime enforcement powers in relation to—

(a) a United Kingdom ship in Scotland waters, foreign waters or international waters,

(b) a ship without nationality in Scotland waters or international waters,

(c) a foreign ship in Scotland waters or international waters, or

(d) a ship, registered under the law of a relevant territory, in Scotland waters or international waters.

(2) In this Chapter, "the maritime enforcement powers" are the powers set out in—

(a) section 100 (power to stop, board, divert and detain);

(b) section 101 (power to search and obtain information);

(c) section 102 (power of arrest and seizure).

(3) The following persons are "law enforcement officers" for the purpose of this Chapter—

(a) a constable within the meaning of section 99 of the Police and Fire Reform (Scotland) Act 2012 (2012 asp 8),

(b) a constable who is a member of the British Transport Police Force,

(c) a designated customs official within the meaning of Part 1 of the Borders, Citizenship and Immigration Act 2009 (see section 14(6) of that Act),

(d) a designated NCA officer who is authorised by the Director General of the National Crime Agency (whether generally or specifically) to exercise the powers of a law enforcement officer under this Chapter, or

(e) a person of a description specified in regulations made by the Secretary of State.

(4) Regulations under subsection (3)(e) are to be made by statutory instrument.

(5) A statutory instrument containing regulations under subsection (3)(e) is subject to annulment in pursuance of a resolution of either House of Parliament.

(6) Regulations under subsection (3)(e) may not make devolved provision except with the consent of the Scottish Ministers.

(7) For the purpose of subsection (6), regulations under subsection (3)(e) make devolved provision if and to the extent that the effect of the regulations is to confer functions under this Chapter on a person of a description specified in the regulations and it would be within the legislative competence of the Scottish Parliament to confer those functions on persons of that description in an Act of the Scottish Parliament.

(8) This section is subject to section 97 (which makes provision about when the authority of the Secretary of State is required before the maritime enforcement powers are exercised in reliance on this section).

97 Restriction on exercise of maritime enforcement powers

(1) The authority of the Secretary of State is required before a law enforcement officer exercises any of the maritime enforcement powers, in reliance on section 96(1), in relation to a United Kingdom ship in foreign waters.

(2) The Secretary of State may give authority under subsection (1) only if the State, or the relevant territory, in whose waters the powers would be exercised consents to the exercise of the powers.

(3) The authority of the Secretary of State is required before a law enforcement officer exercises any of the maritime enforcement powers, in reliance on section 96(1), in relation to a foreign ship, or a ship registered under the law of a relevant territory, within the territorial sea adjacent to Scotland or in international waters.

(4) The Secretary of State may give authority under subsection (3) in relation to a foreign ship only if—

(a) the home state has requested the assistance of the United Kingdom for the purpose of preventing, detecting or investigating an offence under the law of Scotland,

(b) the home state has authorised the United Kingdom to act for that purpose, or

(c) the United Nations Convention on the Law of the Sea 1982 (Cmnd 8941) otherwise permits the exercise of the powers in relation to the ship.

Ships in England and Wales waters: hot pursuit

98 Hot pursuit of ships in England and Wales waters

(1) A law enforcement officer may, for the purpose of preventing, detecting or investigating an offence under the law of Scotland, exercise any of the maritime enforcement powers in relation to a ship in England and Wales waters if—

(a) the ship is pursued there,

(b) immediately before the pursuit of the ship, the ship was in Scotland waters or international waters,

(c) before the pursuit of the ship, a signal was given for it to stop,

(d) the signal was given in such a way as to be audible or visible from the ship, and

(e) the pursuit of the ship is not interrupted.

(2) For the purposes of subsection (1)(e), pursuit is not interrupted by reason only of the fact that—

(a) the method of carrying out the pursuit, or

(b) the identity of the ship or aircraft carrying out the pursuit,

changes during the course of the pursuit.

(3) This section is subject to section 99 (which requires the authority of the Secretary of State before the maritime enforcement powers are exercised in relation to a foreign ship, or a ship registered under the law of a relevant territory, within the territorial sea adjacent to England and Wales).

99 Restriction on exercise of maritime enforcement powers in hot pursuit

(1) The authority of the Secretary of State is required before a law enforcement officer exercises any of the maritime enforcement powers, in reliance on section 98 in relation to a foreign ship, or a ship registered under the law of a relevant territory, within the territorial sea adjacent to England and Wales.

(2) The Secretary of State may give authority under subsection (1) in relation to a foreign ship only if—

(a) the home state has requested the assistance of the United Kingdom for the purpose of preventing, detecting or investigating an offence under the law of Scotland,

(b) the home state has authorised the United Kingdom to act for that purpose, or

(c) the United Nations Convention on the Law of the Sea 1982 (Cmnd 8941) otherwise permits the exercise of the powers in relation to the ship.

The maritime enforcement powers

100 Power to stop, board, divert and detain

(1) This section applies if a law enforcement officer has reasonable grounds to suspect that—

- (a) an offence under the law of Scotland is being, or has been, committed on a ship in relation to which the powers conferred by this section are exercisable by virtue of section 96 or 98, or
- (b) a ship in relation to which those powers are so exercisable is otherwise being used in connection with the commission of an offence under that law.

(2) The law enforcement officer may—

- (a) stop the ship;
- (b) board the ship;
- (c) require the ship to be taken to a port in Scotland or elsewhere and detained there.

(3) Except as provided by subsection (5), the authority of the Secretary of State is required before a law enforcement officer may exercise the power conferred by subsection (2)(c) to require the ship to be taken to a port outside the United Kingdom.

(4) The Secretary of State may give authority for the purposes of subsection (3) only if the State, or the relevant territory, in which the port is located is willing to receive the ship.

(5) If the law enforcement officer is acting under authority given for the purposes of section 97(3) or 99(1), the law enforcement officer may require the ship to be taken to—

- (a) a port in the home state or relevant territory in question, or
- (b) if the home state or relevant territory requests, a port in any other State or relevant territory willing to receive the ship.

(6) The law enforcement officer may require the master of the ship, or any member of its crew, to take such action as is necessary for the purposes of subsection (2)(c).

(7) A law enforcement officer must give notice in writing to the master of any ship detained under this section.

(8) The notice must state that the ship is to be detained until the notice is withdrawn by the giving of a further notice in writing signed by a law enforcement officer.

101 Power to search and obtain information

(1) This section applies if a law enforcement officer has reasonable grounds to suspect that there is evidence relating to an offence under the law of Scotland (other than items subject to legal privilege) on a ship in relation to which the powers conferred by this section are exercisable by virtue of section 96 or 98.

(2) The law enforcement officer may search—

- (a) the ship;
- (b) anyone found on the ship;
- (c) anything found on the ship (including cargo).

(3) The law enforcement officer may require a person found on the ship to give information about himself or herself.

(4) The power to search conferred by subsection (2) is a power to search only to the extent that it is reasonably required for the purpose of discovering evidence of the kind mentioned in subsection (1).

(5) The power to search a person conferred by subsection (2) does not authorise a law enforcement officer to require the person to remove any clothing in public other than an outer coat, jacket or gloves.

(6) In exercising a power conferred by subsection (2) or (3), a law enforcement officer may (amongst other things)—

(a) open any containers;

(b) require the production of documents, books or records relating to the ship or anything on it, other than anything that the law enforcement officer has reasonable grounds to believe to be an item subject to legal privilege;

(c) make photographs or copies of anything the production of which the law enforcement officer has power to require.

(7) The power in subsection (6)(b) to require the production of documents, books or records includes, in relation to documents, books or records kept in electronic form, power to require the provision of the documents, books or records in a form in which they are legible and can be taken away.

(8) The power of a law enforcement officer under subsection (2)(b) or (c) or (3) may be exercised on the ship or elsewhere.

102 Power of arrest and seizure

(1) This section applies if a law enforcement officer has reasonable grounds to suspect that an offence under the law of Scotland has been, or is being, committed on a ship in relation to which the powers conferred by this section are exercisable by virtue of section 96 or 98.

(2) The law enforcement officer may arrest without warrant anyone whom the officer has reasonable grounds for suspecting to be guilty of the offence.

(3) The law enforcement officer may seize and retain anything found on the ship which appears to the officer to be evidence of the offence, other than anything that the officer has reasonable grounds to believe to be an item subject to legal privilege.

(4) The power of a law enforcement officer under subsection (2) or (3) may be exercised on the ship or elsewhere.

Supplementary provision

103 Maritime enforcement powers: supplementary: protective searches

(1) This section applies where a power conferred by section 100 is exercised in relation to a ship.

(2) A law enforcement officer may search any person found on the ship for anything which the officer has reasonable grounds to believe the person might use to—

(a) cause physical injury,

(b) cause damage to property, or

(c) endanger the safety of any ship.

(3) The power under subsection (2) may be exercised on board the ship or elsewhere.

(4) A law enforcement officer searching a person under subsection (2) may seize and retain anything found if the law enforcement officer has reasonable grounds to believe that the person might use it for a purpose mentioned in paragraphs (a) to (c) of that subsection.

(5) Anything seized under subsection (4) may be retained only for so long as there are reasonable grounds to believe that it might be used as mentioned in that subsection.

(6) The power to search a person conferred by subsection (2) does not authorise a law enforcement officer to require the person to remove any clothing in public, other than an outer coat, jacket or gloves.

104 Maritime enforcement powers: other supplementary provision

(1) A law enforcement officer may—

(a) be accompanied by other persons, and

(b) take equipment or materials,

to assist the officer in the exercise of powers under this Chapter.

(2) A law enforcement officer may use reasonable force, if necessary, in the performance of functions under this Chapter.

(3) A person accompanying a law enforcement officer under subsection (1) may perform any of the officer's functions under this Chapter, but only under the officer's supervision.

(4) A law enforcement officer must produce evidence of the officer's authority if asked to do so.

(5) The powers conferred by this Chapter do not affect any other powers that a law enforcement officer may have.

105 Maritime enforcement powers: offences

(1) A person commits an offence if the person—

(a) intentionally obstructs a law enforcement officer in the performance of functions under this Chapter, or

(b) fails without reasonable excuse to comply with a requirement imposed by a law enforcement officer in the performance of those functions.

(2) A person who provides information in response to a requirement imposed by a law enforcement officer in the performance of functions under this Chapter commits an offence if—

(a) the information is false in a material particular, and the person either knows it is or is reckless as to whether it is, or

(b) the person intentionally fails to disclose any material particular.

(3) A law enforcement officer may arrest without warrant anyone whom the officer has reasonable grounds for suspecting to be guilty of an offence under this section.

(4) A person guilty of an offence under this section is liable on summary conviction to a fine not exceeding level 5 on the standard scale.

106 Interpretation

(1) In this Chapter—

"designated NCA officer" means a National Crime Agency officer who is either or both of the following—

(a) an officer designated under section 10 of the Crime and Courts Act 2013 as having the powers and privileges of a constable who is entitled to exercise the powers and privileges of a Scottish constable (see paragraph 11(3) to (5) of Schedule 5 to that Act);

(b) an officer designated under that section as having the powers of a general customs official;

"England and Wales waters" means the sea and other waters within the seaward limits of the territorial sea adjacent to England and Wales;

"foreign ship" means a ship which—

(a) is registered in a State other than the United Kingdom, or

(b) is not so registered but is entitled to fly the flag of a State other than the United Kingdom;

"foreign waters" means the sea and other waters within the seaward limits of the territorial sea adjacent to any relevant territory or State other than the United Kingdom;

"home state", in relation to a foreign ship, means—

(a) the State in which the ship is registered, or

(b) the State whose flag the ship is otherwise entitled to fly;

"international waters" means waters beyond the territorial sea of the United Kingdom or of any other State or relevant territory;

"items subject to legal privilege" has the same meaning as in Chapter 3 of Part 8 of the Proceeds of Crime Act 2002 (see section 412 of that Act);

"law enforcement officer" has the meaning given by section 96(3);

"maritime enforcement powers" has the meaning given by section 96(2);

"relevant territory" means—

(a) the Isle of Man;

(b) any of the Channel Islands;

(c) a British overseas territory;

"Scotland waters" means the sea and other waters within the seaward limits of the territorial sea adjacent to Scotland;

"ship" includes every description of vessel (including a hovercraft) used in navigation;

"ship without nationality" means a ship which—

(a) is not registered in, or otherwise entitled to fly the flag of, any State or relevant territory, or

(b) sails under the flags of two or more States or relevant territories, or under the flags of a State and relevant territory, using them according to convenience;

"United Kingdom ship" means a ship which—

(a) is registered under Part 2 of the Merchant Shipping Act 1995,

(b) is a Government ship within the meaning of that Act,

(c) is not registered in any State or relevant territory but is wholly owned by persons each of whom has a United Kingdom connection, or

(d) is registered under an Order in Council under section 1 of the Hovercraft Act 1968.

(2) For the purposes of paragraph (c) of the definition of "United Kingdom ship" in subsection (1), a person has a "United Kingdom connection" if the person is—

(a) a British citizen, a British overseas territories citizen or a British Overseas citizen,

(b) an individual who is habitually resident in the United Kingdom, or

(c) a body corporate which is established under the law of a part of the United Kingdom and has its principal place of business in the United Kingdom.

(3) References in this Chapter to the United Nations Convention on the Law of the Sea include references to any modifications of that Convention agreed after the passing of this Act that have entered into force in relation to the United Kingdom.

CHAPTER 7

MARITIME ENFORCEMENT: NORTHERN IRISH OFFENCES

Application of maritime enforcement powers: general

107 Application of maritime enforcement powers: general

(1) A law enforcement officer may, for the purpose of preventing, detecting or investigating an offence under the law of Northern Ireland, exercise any of the maritime enforcement powers in relation to—

(a) a United Kingdom ship in Northern Ireland waters,

(b) a ship without nationality in Northern Ireland waters,

(c) a foreign ship in Northern Ireland waters, or

(d) a ship, registered under the law of a relevant territory, in Northern Ireland waters.

(2) In this Chapter, "the maritime enforcement powers" are the powers set out in—

(a) section 109 (power to stop, board, divert and detain);

(b) section 110 (power to search and obtain information);

(c) section 111 (power of arrest and seizure).

(3) The following persons are "law enforcement officers" for the purpose of this Chapter—

(a) a constable who is a member of the Police Service of Northern Ireland or the Police Service of Northern Ireland Reserve,

(b) a person appointed as a special constable in Northern Ireland by virtue of provision incorporating section 79 of the Harbours, Docks, and Piers Clauses Act 1847,

(c) a designated customs official within the meaning of Part 1 of the Borders, Citizenship and Immigration Act 2009 (see section 14(6) of that Act),

(d) a designated NCA officer who is authorised by the Director General of the National Crime Agency (whether generally or specifically) to exercise the powers of a law enforcement officer under this Chapter, or

(e) a person of a description specified in regulations made by the Secretary of State.

(4) Regulations under subsection (3)(e) are to be made by statutory instrument.

(5) A statutory instrument containing regulations under subsection (3)(e) is subject to annulment in pursuance of a resolution of either House of Parliament.

(6) Regulations under subsection (3)(e) may not make devolved provision except with the consent of the Department of Justice in Northern Ireland.

(7) For the purposes of subsection (6), regulations under subsection (3)(e) make devolved provision if and to the extent that—

(a) the effect of the regulations is to confer functions under this Chapter on a person of a description specified in the regulations,

(b) it would be within the legislative competence of the Northern Ireland Assembly to confer those functions on persons of that description in an Act of the Northern Ireland Assembly, and

(c) the consent of the Secretary of State would not be required under section 8 of the Northern Ireland Act 1998 in relation to a Bill conferring such functions.

(8) This section is subject to section 108 (which makes provision about when the authority of the Secretary of State is required before the maritime enforcement powers are exercised in reliance on this section).

108 Restriction on exercise of maritime enforcement powers

(1) The authority of the Secretary of State is required before a law enforcement officer exercises any of the maritime enforcement powers, in reliance on section 107(1), in relation to a foreign ship, or a ship registered under the law of a relevant territory, within the territorial sea adjacent to Northern Ireland.

(2) The Secretary of State may give authority under subsection (1) in relation to a foreign ship only if—

(a) the home state has requested the assistance of the United Kingdom for the purpose of preventing, detecting or investigating an offence under the law of Northern Ireland,

(b) the home state has authorised the United Kingdom to act for that purpose, or

(c) the United Nations Convention on the Law of the Sea 1982 (Cmnd 8941) otherwise permits the exercise of the powers in relation to the ship.

The maritime enforcement powers

109 Power to stop, board, divert and detain

(1) This section applies if a law enforcement officer has reasonable grounds to suspect that—

(a) an offence under the law of Northern Ireland is being, or has been, committed on a ship in relation to which the powers conferred by this section are exercisable by virtue of section 107, or

(b) a ship in relation to which those powers are so exercisable is otherwise being used in connection with the commission of an offence under that law.

(2) The law enforcement officer may—

(a) stop the ship;

(b) board the ship;

(c) require the ship to be taken to a port in Northern Ireland.

(3) The law enforcement officer may require the master of the ship, or any member of its crew, to take such action as is necessary for the purposes of subsection (2)(c).

(4) A law enforcement officer must give notice in writing to the master of any ship detained under this section.

(5) The notice must state that the ship is to be detained until the notice is withdrawn by the giving of a further notice in writing signed by a law enforcement officer.

110 Power to search and obtain information

(1) This section applies if a law enforcement officer has reasonable grounds to suspect that there is evidence relating to an offence under the law of Northern Ireland (other than items subject to legal privilege) on a ship in relation to which the powers conferred by this section are exercisable by virtue of section 107.

(2) The law enforcement officer may search—

(a) the ship;

(b) anyone found on the ship;

(c) anything found on the ship (including cargo).

(3) The law enforcement officer may require a person found on the ship to give information about himself or herself.

(4) The power to search conferred by subsection (2) is a power to search only to the extent that it is reasonably required for the purpose of discovering evidence of the kind mentioned in subsection (1).

(5) The power to search a person conferred by subsection (2) does not authorise a law enforcement officer to require the person to remove any clothing in public other than an outer coat, jacket or gloves.

(6) In exercising a power conferred by subsection (2) or (3), a law enforcement officer may (amongst other things)—

(a) open any containers;

(b) require the production of documents, books or records relating to the ship or anything on it, other than anything that the law enforcement officer has reasonable grounds to believe to be an item subject to legal privilege;

(c) make photographs or copies of anything the production of which the law enforcement officer has power to require.

(7) The power in subsection (6)(b) to require the production of documents, books or records includes, in relation to documents, books or records kept in electronic form, power to require the provision of the documents, books or records in a form in which they are legible and can be taken away.

(8) The power of a law enforcement officer under subsection (2)(b) or (c) or (3) may be exercised on the ship or elsewhere.

111 Power of arrest and seizure

(1) This section applies if a law enforcement officer has reasonable grounds to suspect that an offence under the law of Northern Ireland has been, or is being, committed on a ship in relation to which the powers conferred by this section are exercisable by virtue of section 107.

(2) The law enforcement officer may arrest without warrant anyone whom the officer has reasonable grounds for suspecting to be guilty of the offence.

(3) The law enforcement officer may seize and retain anything found on the ship which appears to the officer to be evidence of the offence, other than anything that the officer has reasonable grounds to believe to be an item subject to legal privilege.

(4) The power of a law enforcement officer under subsection (2) or (3) may be exercised on the ship or elsewhere.

Supplementary provision

112 Maritime enforcement powers: supplementary: protective searches

(1) This section applies where a power conferred by section 109 is exercised in relation to a ship.

(2) A law enforcement officer may search any person found on the ship for anything which the officer has reasonable grounds to believe the person might use to—

(a) cause physical injury,

(b) cause damage to property, or

(c) endanger the safety of any ship.

(3) The power under subsection (2) may be exercised on board the ship or elsewhere.

(4) A law enforcement officer searching a person under subsection (2) may seize and retain anything found if the law enforcement officer has reasonable grounds to believe that the person might use it for a purpose mentioned in paragraphs (a) to (c) of that subsection.

(5) Anything seized under subsection (4) may be retained only for so long as there are reasonable grounds to believe that it might be used as mentioned in that subsection.

(6) The power to search a person conferred by subsection (2) does not authorise a law enforcement officer to require the person to remove any clothing in public, other than an outer coat, jacket or gloves.

113 Maritime enforcement powers: other supplementary provision

(1) A law enforcement officer may—
  (a) be accompanied by other persons, and
  (b) take equipment or materials,

to assist the officer in the exercise of powers under this Chapter.

(2) A law enforcement officer may use reasonable force, if necessary, in the performance of functions under this Chapter.

(3) A person accompanying a law enforcement officer under subsection (1) may perform any of the officer's functions under this Chapter, but only under the officer's supervision.

(4) A law enforcement officer must produce evidence of the officer's authority if asked to do so.

(5) The powers conferred by this Chapter do not affect any other powers that a law enforcement officer may have.

114 Maritime enforcement powers: offences

(1) A person commits an offence if the person—
  (a) intentionally obstructs a law enforcement officer in the performance of functions under this Chapter, or
  (b) fails without reasonable excuse to comply with a requirement imposed by a law enforcement officer in the performance of those functions.

(2) A person who provides information in response to a requirement imposed by a law enforcement officer in the performance of functions under this Chapter commits an offence if—
  (a) the information is false in a material particular, and the person either knows it is or is reckless as to whether it is, or
  (b) the person intentionally fails to disclose any material particular.

(3) A law enforcement officer may arrest without warrant anyone whom the officer has reasonable grounds for suspecting to be guilty of an offence under this section.

(4) A person guilty of an offence under this section is liable on summary conviction to a fine not exceeding level 5 on the standard scale.

115 Interpretation

(1) In this Chapter—

"designated NCA officer" means a National Crime Agency officer who is either or both of the following—
  (a) an officer designated under section 10 of the Crime and Courts Act 2013 as having the powers and privileges of a constable who is entitled to

exercise the powers and privileges of a Northern Ireland constable (see paragraph 11(6) of Schedule 5 to that Act);

(b) an officer designated under that section as having the powers of a general customs official;

"foreign ship" means a ship which—

(a) is registered in a State other than the United Kingdom, or

(b) is not so registered but is entitled to fly the flag of a State other than the United Kingdom;

"home state", in relation to a foreign ship, means—

(a) the State in which the ship is registered, or

(b) the State whose flag the ship is otherwise entitled to fly;

"items subject to legal privilege" has the same meaning as in the Police and Criminal Evidence (Northern Ireland) Order 1989 (S.I. 1989/1341 (N.I. 12)) (see article 12 of that Order);

"law enforcement officer" has the meaning given by section 107(3);

"maritime enforcement powers" has the meaning given by section 107(2);

"Northern Ireland waters" means the sea and other waters within the seaward limits of the territorial sea adjacent to Northern Ireland;

"relevant territory" means—

(a) the Isle of Man;

(b) any of the Channel Islands;

(c) a British overseas territory;

"ship" includes every description of vessel (including a hovercraft) used in navigation;

"ship without nationality" means a ship which—

(a) is not registered in, or otherwise entitled to fly the flag of, any State or relevant territory, or

(b) sails under the flags of two or more States or relevant territories, or under the flags of a State and relevant territory, using them according to convenience;

"United Kingdom ship" means a ship which—

(a) is registered under Part 2 of the Merchant Shipping Act 1995,

(b) is a Government ship within the meaning of that Act,

(c) is not registered in any State or relevant territory but is wholly owned by persons each of whom has a United Kingdom connection, or

(d) is registered under an Order in Council under section 1 of the Hovercraft Act 1968.

(2) For the purposes of paragraph (c) of the definition of "United Kingdom ship" in subsection (1), a person has a "United Kingdom connection" if the person is—

(a) a British citizen, a British overseas territories citizen or a British Overseas citizen,

(b) an individual who is habitually resident in the United Kingdom, or

(c) a body corporate which is established under the law of a part of the United Kingdom and has its principal place of business in the United Kingdom.

(3) References in this Chapter to the United Nations Convention on the Law of the Sea include references to any modifications of that Convention agreed after the passing of this Act that have entered into force in relation to the United Kingdom.

CHAPTER 8

CROSS-BORDER ENFORCEMENT

116 Extension of cross-border powers of arrest: urgent cases

(1) In Part 10 of the Criminal Justice and Public Order Act 1994 (cross-border enforcement), after section 137 insert—

"137A Additional cross-border powers of arrest etc: urgent cases

(1) A constable of a police force in England and Wales may arrest a person in England and Wales without a warrant if—

(a) the constable has reasonable grounds for suspecting that the person has committed a specified offence in Scotland or in Northern Ireland, and

(b) the constable also has reasonable grounds for believing that it is necessary to arrest the person—

(i) to allow the prompt and effective investigation of the offence, or

(ii) to prevent any prosecution for the offence from being hindered by the disappearance of the person.

(2) A constable of a police force in Scotland may arrest a person in Scotland without a warrant if—

(a) the constable has reasonable grounds for suspecting that the person has committed a specified offence in England and Wales or in Northern Ireland, and

(b) the constable is satisfied that it would not be in the interests of justice to delay the arrest either to enable a warrant for the person's arrest to be obtained and then executed under section 136 or to enable a power of arrest under section 137 to be exercised.

(3) Without prejudice to the generality of subsection (2)(b), it would not be in the interests of justice to delay an arrest for a purpose mentioned in that subsection if the constable reasonably believes that, unless the person is arrested without delay, the person will obstruct the course of justice in any way, including by seeking to avoid arrest or interfering with witnesses or evidence.

(4) A constable of a police force in Northern Ireland may arrest a person in Northern Ireland without a warrant if—

(a) the constable has reasonable grounds for suspecting that the person has committed a specified offence in England and Wales or in Scotland, and

(b) the constable also has reasonable grounds for believing that it is necessary to arrest the person—

(i) to allow the prompt and effective investigation of the offence, or

(ii) to prevent any prosecution for the offence from being hindered by the disappearance of the person.

(5) The power conferred by subsection (1) or (2) may be exercised by a constable appointed under section 24 of the Railways and Transport Safety Act 2003 in England and Wales or (as the case may be) in Scotland.

(6) The following provisions apply in relation to an arrest under this section by a constable of a person suspected of having committed a specified offence in England and Wales or in Northern Ireland—

(a) where the arrest is in England and Wales under subsection (1) or in Northern Ireland under subsection (4), the constable has the powers of entry and search conferred by section 137E;

(b) where the arrest is in Scotland under subsection (2), the constable has the same powers of entry and search for the purpose of the arrest as a constable of a police force in Scotland would have if there were reasonable grounds for suspecting that the offence had been committed in Scotland;

(c) the constable has the powers conferred by section 139 in relation to the arrested person;

(d) the constable may use reasonable force, if necessary, in arresting the person or in exercising the powers conferred by sections 137E and 139.

(7) Where a constable is arresting under this section a person suspected of having committed a specified offence in Scotland, the constable has the same powers as a constable of a police force in Scotland would have if arresting the person for the offence in Scotland.

(8) In this section—

"constable of a police force", in relation to Northern Ireland, means a member of the Police Service of Northern Ireland or the Police Service of Northern Ireland Reserve;

"specified offence" has the meaning given by section 137B.

137B Meaning of "specified offence" for the purposes of section 137A

(1) In section 137A, "specified offence" has the meaning given by this section.

(2) An offence committed in England and Wales is a specified offence if it is—

(a) an offence (including an offence under the common law) that is punishable by virtue of any statutory provision with imprisonment or another form of detention for a term of 10 years or with a greater punishment,

(b) an offence specified in Part 1 of Schedule 7A,

(c) an offence of attempting or conspiring to commit, or of inciting the commission of, an offence mentioned in paragraph (a) or (b), or

(d) an offence under Part 2 of the Serious Crime Act 2007 (encouraging or assisting crime) in relation to an offence mentioned in paragraph (a) or (b).

(3) An offence committed in Scotland is a specified offence if it is—

(a) an offence (including an offence under the common law) that is punishable by virtue of any statutory provision with imprisonment or another form of detention for a term of 10 years or with a greater punishment,

(b) an offence specified in Part 2 of Schedule 7A, or

(c) an offence of attempting or conspiring to commit, or of inciting the commission of, an offence mentioned in paragraph (a) or (b).

(4) An offence committed in Northern Ireland is a specified offence if it is—

(a) an offence (including an offence under the common law) that is punishable by virtue of any statutory provision with imprisonment or another form of detention for a term of 10 years or with a greater punishment,

(b) an offence specified in Part 3 of Schedule 7A,

(c) an offence of attempting or conspiring to commit, or of inciting the commission of, an offence mentioned in paragraph (a) or (b), or

(d) an offence under Part 2 of the Serious Crime Act 2007 (encouraging or assisting crime) in relation to an offence mentioned in paragraph (a) or (b).

(5) The Secretary of State may by regulations made by statutory instrument amend Part 1, 2 or 3 of Schedule 7A so as to add an offence to, or remove an offence from, the offences for the time being specified in the Part.

(6) Regulations under subsection (5) may add an offence to a Part of Schedule 7A only if—

(a) the offence is indictable, and

(b) the Secretary of State considers that it is necessary in the interests of justice to add the offence to the Part.

(7) For the purpose of subsection (6)(a), an offence is indictable if—

(a) in the case of an offence under the law of England and Wales, it is an indictable offence in England and Wales;

(b) in the case of an offence under the law of Scotland, it may be tried on indictment in Scotland;

(c) in the case of an offence under the law of Northern Ireland, it is an indictable offence in Northern Ireland.

(8) The Secretary of State may not make regulations under subsection (5) unless the Scottish Ministers and the Department of Justice in Northern Ireland consent to the making of the regulations.

(9) A statutory instrument containing regulations under subsection (5) may not be made unless a draft of the instrument has been laid before, and approved by a resolution of, each House of Parliament.

(10) In this section—

(a) a description of an offence in subsection (2)(a) or (b) or (4)(a) or (b) includes such an offence committed by aiding, abetting, counselling or procuring;

(b) a description of an offence in subsection (3)(a) or (b) includes such an offence committed by involvement art and part or by aiding, abetting, counselling or procuring;

(c) "statutory provision" means any provision of—

(i) an Act or subordinate legislation within the meaning of the Interpretation Act 1978;

(ii) an Act of the Scottish Parliament or an instrument made under such an Act;

(iii) a Measure or Act of the National Assembly for Wales or an instrument made under such a Measure or Act;

(iv) Northern Ireland legislation or an instrument made under Northern Ireland legislation.

137C Detention for the purpose of re-arrest

(1) A person arrested under section 137A in respect of a specified offence may be detained but only for the purpose of—

(a) enabling a warrant for the person's arrest in respect of the offence to be obtained and then executed under section 136, or

(b) enabling the person to be re-arrested under section 137.

(2) The person may be detained for that purpose—

(a) for an initial period of 3 hours beginning with the time of the arrest;

(b) for a second period of no more than 21 hours beginning with the end of the initial period, but only if detention for that period is authorised by both an officer of at least the rank of inspector in the arresting force and an officer of at least the rank of inspector in the investigating force;

(c) for a third period of no more than 12 hours beginning with the end of the second period, but only if detention for that period is authorised by both an officer of a rank above that of inspector in the arresting force and an officer of a rank above that of inspector in the investigating force.

(3) An officer of the arresting force may give an authorisation for the purpose of subsection (2)(b) or (c) only if satisfied that it is in the interests of justice to do so.

(4) An officer of the investigating force may give an authorisation for the purpose of subsection (2)(b) only if satisfied that—

(a) there are reasonable grounds to suspect that the person has committed the specified offence,

(b) a constable intends that the person be arrested as soon as is reasonably practicable (whether by the obtaining and execution of a warrant under section 136 or under section 137) and is acting expeditiously for that purpose, and

(c) it is in the interests of justice to give the authorisation.

(5) An officer of the investigating force may give an authorisation for the purpose of subsection (2)(c) only if satisfied that—

(a) there continue to be reasonable grounds to suspect that the person has committed the specified offence,

(b) a constable intends that the person be arrested as soon as is reasonably practicable (whether by the obtaining and execution of a warrant under section 136 or under section 137) and is acting expeditiously for that purpose, and

(c) it is in the interests of justice to give the authorisation.

(6) If, at any time while the person is detained, an appropriate officer in the investigating force is satisfied that it is no longer in the interests of justice for the person to be detained—

(a) the officer must notify the arresting force, and

(b) the person must be released immediately.

(7) In subsection (6), "appropriate officer" means—

(a) in relation to the person's detention for the initial period, any constable;

(b) in relation to the person's detention for the second period, an officer of at least the rank of inspector;

(c) in relation to the person's detention for the third period, an officer of a rank above that of inspector.

(8) In this section—

"arresting force" means the police force of which the constable who arrested the person under section 137A is a member;

"investigating force" means the police force that is investigating the specified offence which the person arrested under section 137A is suspected of having committed;

"specified offence" has the same meaning as in section 137A (see sections 137A(8) and 137B).

(9) In subsection (8), in the definition of "investigating force", the reference to a police force includes a reference to—

(a) the National Crime Agency;

(b) any of the following (to the extent that their functions relate to the investigation of offences)—

(i) officers of Revenue and Customs;

(ii) immigration officers;

(iii) designated customs officials within the meaning of Part 1 of the Borders, Citizenship and Immigration Act 2009 (see section 14(6) of that Act).

(10) In the application of this section in a case where the investigating force is a police force mentioned in subsection (9)(a) or (b)—

(a) the reference to a constable in subsections (4)(b) and (5)(b), and the reference to a constable in the investigating force in subsection (7)(a), is to be read as a reference to a National Crime Agency officer designated under section 9 or 10 of the Crime and Courts Act 2013 ("a designated NCA officer"), an officer of Revenue and Customs, an immigration officer or a designated customs official (as the case may be);

(b) any reference to an officer of at least, or above, the rank of inspector in the investigating force is to be read as a reference to a designated NCA officer, an officer of Revenue and Customs, an immigration officer or a designated customs official (as the case may be) of at least, or above, the equivalent grade.

137D Rights of persons arrested under section 137A

(1) A person arrested under section 137A must be informed of the following matters as soon as is practicable after the arrest—

- (a) the purpose for which the person may be detained under section 137C;
- (b) the provision made by that section about the periods for which the person may be detained.

(2) The following provisions apply in relation to persons arrested under section 137A in respect of a specified offence committed in England and Wales (subject to the modifications made by Part 1 of Schedule 7B)—

- (a) section 28 of the Police and Criminal Evidence Act 1984 (information to be given on arrest);
- (b) section 56 of that Act (right to have someone informed when arrested);
- (c) section 58 of that Act (access to legal advice);
- (d) section 31 of the Children and Young Persons Act 1933 (separation of children and young persons from adults in police stations, courts etc);
- (e) section 34 of that Act (additional protection for children and young persons).

(3) The following provisions apply in relation to persons arrested under section 137A in respect of a specified offence committed in Scotland (subject to the modifications made by Part 2 of Schedule 7B)—

- (a) section 3 of the Criminal Justice (Scotland) Act 2016 (asp 1) (information to be given on arrest);
- (b) Chapter 5 of Part 1 of that Act (rights of suspects in police custody);
- (c) section 51 of that Act (duty to consider child's well-being);
- (d) section 52 of that Act (duties in relation to children in custody).

(4) The following provisions apply in relation to persons arrested under section 137A in respect of a specified offence committed in Northern Ireland (subject to the modifications made by Part 3 of Schedule 7B)—

- (a) Article 30 of the Police and Criminal Evidence (Northern Ireland) Order 1989 (S.I. 1989/1341 (N.I.12)) (information to be given on arrest);
- (b) Article 57 of that Order (right to have someone informed when arrested);
- (c) Article 59 of that Order (access to legal advice);
- (d) Article 9 of the Criminal Justice (Children) (Northern Ireland) Order 1998 (S.I. 1998/1504 (N.I.9)) (separation of child in police detention from adults charged with offences);
- (e) Article 10 of that Order (additional protection for children and young persons).

(5) The Secretary of State may by regulations made by statutory instrument—

- (a) amend this section so as to add to the provisions that for the time being apply as mentioned in subsection (2), (3) or (4);
- (b) amend this section so as to remove any of those provisions that were added by virtue of paragraph (a);

(c) amend Schedule 7B so as to alter the modifications for the time being made by that Schedule, including by adding a modification or removing one;

(d) amend Schedule 7B so as to provide that any of the provisions that for the time being apply as mentioned in subsection (2), (3) or (4) do not apply in cases or circumstances set out in the Schedule.

(6) Regulations under subsection (5) may include consequential provision, including provision amending any statutory provision; and, for that purpose, statutory provision has the same meaning as in section 137B (see subsection (10)(c) of that section).

(7) The Secretary of State may not make regulations under subsection (5) unless the Scottish Ministers and the Department of Justice in Northern Ireland consent to the making of the regulations.

(8) A statutory instrument containing regulations under subsection (5) may not be made unless a draft of the instrument has been laid before, and approved by a resolution of, each House of Parliament.

(9) In the application of Schedule 7B in a case where the investigating force is a police force mentioned in section 137C(9)(a) or (b), any reference to an officer of at least, or above, a particular rank in the investigating force is to be read as a reference to a designated NCA officer, an officer of Revenue and Customs, an immigration officer or a designated customs official (as the case may be) of at least, or above, the equivalent grade."

(2) After Schedule 7 to that Act insert, as Schedule 7A to that Act, the Schedule set out in Schedule 15 to this Act.

(3) After Schedule 7A to that Act (as inserted by subsection (2) above) insert, as Schedule 7B to that Act, the Schedule set out in Schedule 16 to this Act.

117 Cross-border enforcement: powers of entry to effect arrest

In Part 10 of the Criminal Justice and Public Order Act 1994 (cross-border enforcement), after section 137D (as inserted by section 116) insert—

"137E Entry and search for the purposes of arrest

(1) A constable may enter and search any premises—

(a) for the purpose of executing in England and Wales under section 136(2)(b) a warrant issued in Northern Ireland;

(b) for the purpose of executing in Northern Ireland under section 136(3)(a) a warrant issued in England and Wales;

(c) for the purpose of arresting a person in Northern Ireland under section 137(1) in respect of a relevant England and Wales offence;

(d) for the purpose of arresting a person in England and Wales under section 137(3) in respect of a relevant Northern Ireland offence;

(e) for the purpose of arresting a person in England and Wales under section 137A(1) in respect of a specified offence committed in Northern Ireland;

(f) for the purpose of arresting a person in Northern Ireland under section 137A(4) in respect of a specified offence committed in England and Wales.

(2) In subsection (1)—

(a) "relevant England and Wales offence" means—

(i) an offence that is an indictable offence in England and Wales;

(ii) an offence mentioned in section 17(1)(c) or (caa) of the Police and Criminal Evidence Act 1984;

(b) "relevant Northern Ireland offence" means—

(i) an offence that is an indictable offence in Northern Ireland;

(ii) an offence mentioned in Article 19(1)(ba) to (c) of the Police and Criminal Evidence (Northern Ireland) Order 1989 (S.I. 1989/1341 (N.I.12)).

(3) The powers of entry and search conferred by subsection (1)—

(a) are exercisable only if the constable has reasonable grounds for believing that the person whom he is seeking is on the premises, and

(b) are limited, in relation to premises consisting of two or more separate dwellings, to powers to enter and search—

(i) any part of the premises which the occupier of any dwelling comprised in the premises uses in common with the occupier of any other such dwelling, and

(ii) any such dwelling in which the constable has reasonable grounds for believing that the person whom he is seeking may be.

(4) The power of search conferred by subsection (1) is only a power to search to the extent that is reasonably required for the purpose for which the power of entry is exercised.

(5) In this section, "premises" includes any place and, in particular, includes—

(a) any vehicle, vessel, aircraft or hovercraft,

(b) any offshore installation,

(c) any renewable energy installation, and

(d) any tent or movable structure.

"Offshore installation" has the meaning given to it by section 44 of the Petroleum Act 1998.

"Renewable energy installation" has the same meaning as in Chapter 2 of Part 2 of the Energy Act 2004 (see section 104 of that Act)."

118 Cross-border enforcement: officers of Revenue and Customs

In section 87 of the Finance Act 2007 (cross-border exercise of powers: officers of Revenue and Customs), in subsection (4) for "only in the exercise of a function relating to tax (including duties and tax credits)" substitute "in the exercise of any function of the Commissioners for Her Majesty's Revenue and Customs or of officers of Revenue and Customs, within the meaning of the Commissioners for Revenue and Customs Act 2005 (see section 51(2) to (2B) of that Act)".

119 Cross-border enforcement: minor and consequential amendments

Schedule 17—

(a) makes minor amendments of Part 10 of the Criminal Justice and Public Order Act 1994 (cross-border enforcement), and

(b) makes amendments consequential on the other amendments of that Part made by this Chapter.

CHAPTER 9

MISCELLANEOUS

120 Powers to require removal of disguises: oral authorisation

In section 60AA of the Criminal Justice and Public Order Act 1994 (powers to require removal of disguises), for subsection (6) substitute—

"(6) Subject to subsection (6A), an authorisation under subsection (3)—

(a) shall be in writing and signed by the officer giving it; and

(b) shall specify—

(i) the grounds on which it is given;

(ii) the locality in which the powers conferred by this section are exercisable; and

(iii) the period during which those powers are exercisable.

(6A) An authorisation under subsection (3) need not be given in writing where it is not practicable to do so but any oral authorisation—

(a) must state the matters which would otherwise have to be specified under subsection (6); and

(b) must be recorded in writing as soon as it is practicable to do so.

(6B) A direction under subsection (4) shall be given in writing or, where that is not practicable, recorded in writing as soon as it is practicable to do so."

PART 5

POLICE AND CRIME COMMISSIONERS AND POLICE AREAS

Deputy PCCs etc: terms and eligibility

121 Term of office of deputy police and crime commissioners

(1) Schedule 1 to the Police Reform and Social Responsibility Act 2011 (police and crime commissioners) is amended in accordance with subsections (2) and (3).

(2) In paragraph 8 (the deputy police and crime commissioner), for sub-paragraph (3) substitute—

"(3) The terms and conditions of a person appointed as the deputy police and crime commissioner must ensure that the term of office ends no later than the sixth day after the day of the poll at the next ordinary election of police and crime commissioners (that is, the day on which the term of office of the appointing police and crime commissioner would, if there were no vacancy in the office before then, end in accordance with section 50(7)(b)).

(3A) The terms and conditions must also provide for the deputy police and crime commissioner's appointment to end when, following an election held under section 51 to fill a vacancy in the office of the appointing police and crime commissioner, the person elected makes and delivers a declaration of acceptance of office under section 70(1).

(3B) Subject to sub-paragraphs (3) and (3A), the terms and conditions may make such provision about termination as the appointing police and crime commissioner thinks appropriate."

(3) In that paragraph, omit sub-paragraph (5).

(4) The amendments made by this section apply in relation to the terms and conditions of a person appointed as a deputy police and crime commissioner before this section comes into force (as well as to the terms and conditions of a person appointed after it comes into force).

(5) But the amendments do not apply in relation to the terms and conditions of a person appointed as a deputy police and crime commissioner before this section comes into force if, at the time when it comes into force, an election held under section 51 of the 2011 Act to fill a vacancy in the office of police and crime commissioner for the police area in question is in progress.

(6) For the purpose of subsection (5), an election held under section 51 of the 2011 Act is in progress during the period—

(a) beginning with the time when the vacancy in the office of police and crime commissioner occurred, and

(b) ending immediately after the person elected to fill the vacancy has made and delivered a declaration of acceptance under section 70(1) of that Act.

122 Eligibility of deputy police and crime commissioners for election

(1) In section 65 of the Police Reform and Social Responsibility Act 2011 (disqualification from election or holding office as police and crime commissioner: police grounds), after subsection (1) insert—

"(1A) Subsection (1)(e)(i) does not prevent a deputy police and crime commissioner—

(a) from being elected as police and crime commissioner at an ordinary election of police and crime commissioners;

(b) from being elected at an election held under section 51 to fill a vacancy in the office of police and crime commissioner if, on the day on which the person is nominated as a candidate at the election and at all times between that day and the declaration of the result of the election, the deputy is acting as police and crime commissioner under section 62."

(2) Section 65(1A)(b) of the 2011 Act (as inserted by subsection (1) above) does not apply in relation to an election held under section 51 of that Act to fill a vacancy in the office

of police and crime commissioner if the election is in progress at the time this section comes into force.

(3) For the purpose of subsection (2), an election held under section 51 of the 2011 Act is in progress during the period—

(a) beginning with the time when the vacancy in the office of police and crime commissioner occurred, and

(b) ending immediately after the person elected to fill the vacancy has made and delivered a declaration of acceptance under section 70(1) of that Act.

123 Deputy Mayor for Policing and Crime as member of local authority

(1) Section 1 of the Local Government and Housing Act 1989 (disqualification and political restriction of certain local authority officers and staff) is amended as follows.

(2) In subsection (9) (references to a person holding a politically restricted post under a local authority include every member of the staff of an elected local policing body) omit ", except for a deputy police and crime commissioner".

(3) After that subsection insert—

"(10) The reference in subsection (9) to every member of the staff of an elected local policing body does not include a deputy police and crime commissioner.

(11) For the purposes of subsection (1) only, the reference in subsection (9) to every member of the staff of an elected local policing body does not include the Deputy Mayor for Policing and Crime appointed under section 19(1)(a) of the Police Reform and Social Responsibility Act 2011."

Names of police areas

124 Amendments to the names of police areas

(1) After section 31 of the Police Act 1996 insert—

"Amendment of names of police areas

31A Power to amend names of police areas

(1) The Secretary of State may by regulations amend any name of a police area specified in the first column of Schedule 1 (police areas).

(2) A statutory instrument containing regulations under subsection (1) may not be made unless a draft of the instrument has been laid before and approved by a resolution of each House of Parliament."

(2) In consequence of the amendment made by subsection (1), in section 1(2)(a) of that Act (police areas), in the words in brackets, for "any amendment made to that Schedule by an order" substitute "any amendment made to the first column of that Schedule by regulations under section 31A or any amendment made to the second column, or to the first and second columns, by an order".

PART 6

FIREARMS AND PYROTECHNIC ARTICLES

Firearms

125 Firearms Act 1968: meaning of "firearm" etc

(1) The Firearms Act 1968 is amended as follows.

(2) In section 57 (interpretation), in subsection (1), for the words from the beginning to the end of paragraph (c) substitute—

"(1) In this Act, the expression "firearm" means—

(a) a lethal barrelled weapon (see subsection (1B));

(b) a prohibited weapon;

(c) a relevant component part in relation to a lethal barrelled weapon or a prohibited weapon (see subsection (1D));

(d) an accessory to a lethal barrelled weapon or a prohibited weapon where the accessory is designed or adapted to diminish the noise or flash caused by firing the weapon;".

(3) In that section, before subsection (2) insert—

"(1B) In subsection (1)(a), "lethal barrelled weapon" means a barrelled weapon of any description from which a shot, bullet or other missile, with kinetic energy of more than one joule at the muzzle of the weapon, can be discharged.

(1C) Subsection (1) is subject to section 57A (exception for airsoft guns)."

(4) In that section, after subsection (1C) (as inserted by subsection (3) above) insert—

"(1D) For the purposes of subsection (1)(c), each of the following items is a relevant component part in relation to a lethal barrelled weapon or a prohibited weapon—

(a) a barrel, chamber or cylinder,

(b) a frame, body or receiver,

(c) a breech block, bolt or other mechanism for containing the pressure of discharge at the rear of a chamber,

but only where the item is capable of being used as a part of a lethal barrelled weapon or a prohibited weapon."

(5) After section 57 insert—

"57A Exception for airsoft guns

(1) An "airsoft gun" is not to be regarded as a firearm for the purposes of this Act.

(2) An "airsoft gun" is a barrelled weapon of any description which—

(a) is designed to discharge only a small plastic missile (whether or not it is also capable of discharging any other kind of missile), and

(b) is not capable of discharging a missile (of any kind) with kinetic energy at the muzzle of the weapon that exceeds the permitted level.

(3) "Small plastic missile" means a missile that—
(a) is made wholly or partly from plastics,
(b) is spherical, and
(c) does not exceed 8 millimetres in diameter.

(4) The permitted kinetic energy level is—
(a) in the case of a weapon which is capable of discharging two or more missiles successively without repeated pressure on the trigger, 1.3 joules;
(b) in any other case, 2.5 joules."

(6) After section 57A (as inserted by subsection (5) above) insert—

"57B Power to amend section 57(1D)

(1) The Secretary of State may by regulations made by statutory instrument amend section 57(1D) so as to make different provision for the purposes of section 57(1)(c) about the meaning of a relevant component part in relation to a lethal barrelled weapon or a prohibited weapon.

(2) Regulations under this section may include—
(a) incidental, supplementary or consequential provision;
(b) transitional, transitory or saving provision.

(3) A statutory instrument containing regulations under this section may not be made unless a draft of the instrument has been laid before and approved by a resolution of each House of Parliament."

126 Firearms Act 1968: meaning of "antique firearm"

(1) Section 58 of the Firearms Act 1968 (particular savings) is amended in accordance with subsections (2) and (3).

(2) After subsection (2) (which makes provision about antique firearms) insert—

"(2A) For the purposes of subsection (2), a firearm is an "antique firearm" if—
(a) either the conditions in subsection (2B) are met or the condition in subsection (2C) is met, and
(b) if an additional condition is specified in regulations under subsection (2D), that condition is also met.

(2B) The conditions in this subsection are that—
(a) the firearm's chamber or, if the firearm has more than one chamber, each of its chambers is either—
(i) a chamber that the firearm had when it was manufactured, or
(ii) a replacement for such a chamber that is identical to it in all material respects;
(b) the firearm's chamber or (as the case may be) each of the firearm's chambers is designed for use with a cartridge of a description specified in regulations made by statutory instrument by the Secretary of State (whether or not it is also capable of being used with other cartridges).

(2C) The condition in this subsection is that the firearm's propulsion system is of a description specified in regulations made by statutory instrument by the Secretary of State.

(2D) The Secretary of State may by regulations made by statutory instrument specify either of the following conditions for the purposes of subsection (2A)(b)—

(a) a condition that a number of years specified in the regulations has elapsed since the date on which the firearm was manufactured;

(b) a condition that the firearm was manufactured before a date specified in the regulations.

(2E) In its application to Scotland, subsection (2C) does not apply in relation to a firearm that is an air weapon.

(2F) Regulations under subsection (2B), (2C) or (2D) may make different provision for different purposes.

(2G) Subject to subsection (2H), a statutory instrument containing regulations under subsection (2B), (2C) or (2D) may not be made unless a draft of the instrument has been laid before and approved by a resolution of each House of Parliament.

(2H) A statutory instrument containing regulations under subsection (2B) or (2C) which contain only provision amending regulations previously made under that subsection so as to remove a description of cartridge or a description of propulsion system from the descriptions specified in those regulations is subject to annulment in pursuance of a resolution of either House of Parliament."

(3) In subsection (2)—

(a) in paragraph (a), for "section 21" substitute "sections 19, 20 and 21";

(b) in paragraph (b), for "section 21" substitute "section 19, 20 or 21".

(4) Subsections (5) to (7) apply where—

(a) immediately before the coming into force of regulations under section 58(2B), (2C) or (2D) of the Firearms Act 1968 (as inserted by subsection (2) above), a person has in his or her possession a firearm that is an antique firearm for the purposes of section 58(2) of that Act, and

(b) in consequence of the coming into force of the regulations, the firearm ceases to be an antique firearm for those purposes.

(5) Section 5 of the Firearms Act 1968 does not apply in relation to the possession of the firearm by the person unless—

(a) the person carries on a business as a firearms dealer, and

(b) the firearm is in his or her possession for the purpose of the business.

(6) An application by the person for a certificate under section 1 or 2 of that Act in respect of possession of the firearm may not be refused on the ground that the person does not have a good reason for having the firearm in his or her possession.

(7) An application by the person for the renewal of a certificate issued under section 1 or 2 of that Act in respect of possession of the firearm may not be refused on the ground that the person does not have a good reason for having the firearm in his or her possession.

(8) The provision made by subsections (4) to (7) does not prevent additional transitional provision being made (under the power conferred by section 183(9)) in connection with the coming into force of this section (including provision for enabling certificates and authorisations under the Firearms Act 1968 to be issued or granted before this section comes fully into force).

127 Possession of articles for conversion of imitation firearms

After section 4 of the Firearms Act 1968 (conversion of weapons) insert—

"4A Possession of articles for use in connection with conversion

(1) A person, other than a registered firearms dealer, commits an offence if—

(a) the person has in his or her possession or under his or her control an article that is capable of being used (whether by itself or with other articles) to convert an imitation firearm into a firearm, and

(b) the person intends to use the article (whether by itself or with other articles) to convert an imitation firearm into a firearm.

(2) A person guilty of an offence under this section is liable—

(a) on summary conviction—

(i) in England and Wales, to imprisonment for a term not exceeding 12 months (or, in relation to offences committed before section 154(1) of the Criminal Justice Act 2003 comes into force, 6 months) or to a fine, or to both;

(ii) in Scotland, to imprisonment for a term not exceeding 12 months, or to a fine not exceeding the statutory maximum, or to both;

(b) on conviction on indictment, to imprisonment for a term not exceeding 5 years or to a fine, or to both."

128 Controls on defectively deactivated weapons

After section 8 of the Firearms (Amendment) Act 1988 insert—

"8A Controls on defectively deactivated weapons

(1) It is an offence for a person who owns or claims to own a defectively deactivated weapon—

(a) to make the weapon available for sale or as a gift to another person, or

(b) to sell it or give it (as a gift) to another person.

(2) Subsection (1)(a) does not apply if—

(a) the weapon is made available for sale or as a gift only to a person who is outside the EU (or to persons all of whom are outside the EU), and

(b) it is made so available on the basis that, if a sale or gift were to take place, the weapon would be transferred to a place outside the EU.

(3) Subsection (1)(b) does not apply if—

(a) the weapon is sold or given to a person who is outside the EU (or to persons all of whom are outside the EU), and

(b) in consequence of the sale or gift, it is (or is to be) transferred to a place outside the EU.

(4) For the purpose of this section, something is a "defectively deactivated weapon" if—

(a) it was at any time a firearm,

(b) it has been rendered incapable of discharging any shot, bullet or other missile (and, accordingly, has either ceased to be a firearm or is a firearm only by virtue of the Firearms Act 1982), but

(c) it has not been rendered so incapable in a way that meets the technical specifications for the deactivation of the weapon that apply at the time when the weapon is made available for sale or as a gift or (as the case may be) when it is sold or given as a gift.

(5) The Secretary of State must publish a document setting out the technical specifications that apply for the purposes of subsection (4)(c) ("the technical specifications document").

(6) The technical specifications document may set out different technical specifications for different kinds of weapon.

(7) The Secretary of State—

(a) may from time to time revise the technical specifications document, and

(b) where it is revised—

(i) must publish the document as revised, and

(ii) specify in it the date on which any changes to the technical specifications that apply for the purposes of subsection (4)(c) take effect.

(8) In the case of a weapon rendered incapable as mentioned in subsection (4)(b) before 8 April 2016, subsection (1)(a) or (b) does not apply if the weapon is made available for sale or as a gift, or (as the case may be) sold or given, by or on behalf of a museum in respect of which a museum firearms licence is in force to another museum in respect of which such a licence is in force.

(9) References in this section to "sale" include exchange or barter (and references to sell are to be construed accordingly).

(10) In this section, "museum firearms licence" means a licence granted under the Schedule to the Firearms (Amendment) Act 1988.

(11) A person guilty of an offence under this section is liable—

(a) on summary conviction—

(i) in England and Wales, to imprisonment for a term not exceeding 12 months (or, in relation to offences committed before section 154(1) of the Criminal Justice Act 2003 comes into force, 6 months) or to a fine, or to both;

(ii) in Scotland, to imprisonment for a term not exceeding 12 months, or to a fine not exceeding the statutory maximum, or to both;

(b) on conviction on indictment, to imprisonment for a term not exceeding 5 years or to a fine, or to both."

129 Controls on ammunition which expands on impact

(1) The Firearms Act 1968 is amended in accordance with subsections (2) and (3).

(2) In section 5 (weapons subject to general prohibition), in subsection (1A), for paragraph (f) substitute—

"(f) any ammunition which is designed to be used with a pistol and incorporates a missile designed or adapted to expand on impact;".

(3) In section 5A (exemptions from requirement of authority under section 5), in subsection (8)(a), after "which", in the first place it occurs, insert "is designed to be used with a pistol and".

(4) In consequence of the amendment made by subsection (2), omit section 9 of the Firearms (Amendment) Act 1997.

130 Authorised lending and possession of firearms for hunting etc

(1) After section 11 of the Firearms Act 1968 insert—

"11A Authorised lending and possession of firearms for hunting etc

(1) A person ("the borrower") may, without holding a certificate under this Act, borrow a rifle or shot gun from another person on private premises ("the lender") and have the rifle or shot gun in his or her possession on those premises if—

(a) the four conditions set out in subsections (2) to (5) are met, and

(b) in the case of a rifle, the borrower is aged 17 or over.

(2) The first condition is that the borrowing and possession of the rifle or shot gun are for either or both of the following purposes—

(a) hunting animals or shooting game or vermin;

(b) shooting at artificial targets.

(3) The second condition is that the lender—

(a) is aged 18 or over,

(b) holds a certificate under this Act in respect of the rifle or shot gun, and

(c) is either—

(i) a person who has a right to allow others to enter the premises for the purposes of hunting animals or shooting game or vermin, or

(ii) a person who is authorised in writing by a person mentioned in sub-paragraph (i) to lend the rifle or shot gun on the premises (whether generally or to persons specified in the authorisation who include the borrower).

(4) The third condition is that the borrower's possession and use of the rifle or shot gun complies with any conditions as to those matters specified in the lender's certificate under this Act.

(5) The fourth condition is that, during the period for which the rifle or shot gun is borrowed, the borrower is in the presence of the lender or—

(a) where a rifle is borrowed, a person who, although not the lender, is aged 18 or over, holds a certificate under this Act in respect of that rifle and is a person described in subsection (3)(c)(i) or (ii);

(b) where a shot gun is borrowed, a person who, although not the lender, is aged 18 or over, holds a certificate under this Act in respect of that shot gun or another shot gun and is a person described in subsection (3)(c)(i) or (ii).

(6) Where a rifle is borrowed on any premises in reliance on subsection (1), the borrower may, without holding a firearm certificate, purchase or acquire ammunition on the premises, and have the ammunition in his or her possession on those premises for the period for which the firearm is borrowed, if—

(a) the ammunition is for use with the firearm,

(b) the lender's firearm certificate authorises the lender to have in his or her possession during that period ammunition of a quantity not less than that purchased or acquired by, and in the possession of, the borrower, and

(c) the borrower's possession and use of the ammunition complies with any conditions as to those matters specified in the certificate."

(2) In consequence of the amendment made by subsection (1), omit the following—

(a) section 11(5) of the Firearms Act 1968;

(b) section 16 of the Firearms (Amendment) Act 1988.

131 Limited extension of firearm certificates etc

(1) After section 28A of the Firearms Act 1968 (certificates: supplementary) insert—

"28B Certificates: limited extension

(1) This section applies where—

(a) an application is made for the renewal of a certificate on or before the day which falls 8 weeks before the day at the end of which the certificate is due to expire, but

(b) the chief officer of police does not determine whether or not to grant the application before the certificate is due to expire.

(2) The certificate continues in force by virtue of this subsection until whichever of the following events occurs first—

(a) the chief officer determines whether or not to grant the application;

(b) the extension period ends.

(3) In subsection (2), "the extension period" means the period of 8 weeks beginning with the day after the day at the end of which the certificate was due to expire.

(4) If the event mentioned in subsection (2)(a) occurs first, and the chief officer grants the application, any period for which the certificate continued in force under subsection (2) is to be treated for the purposes of section 28A(1) as part of the period for which the renewed certificate is in force.

(5) This section does not apply in relation to the renewal of a certificate granted or last renewed in Northern Ireland."

(2) In consequence of the amendment made by subsection (1), in section 28A of that Act (certificates: supplementary), after subsection (1) insert—

"(1A) Subsection (1) is subject to the provision made by section 28B for circumstances in which a certificate may continue in force after the period of five years from the date when it was granted or last renewed."

132 Applications under the Firearms Acts: fees

(1) After section 32 of the Firearms Act 1968 (fee for certificate and exemption from paying it in certain cases) insert—

"32ZA Fees in connection with authority under section 5

(1) The Secretary of State may by regulations authorise the appropriate national authority to require payment of a fee before an authority under section 5 is granted, varied or renewed.

(2) Regulations under subsection (1) must specify the amount of any fee that may be charged.

(3) The regulations may make different provision for different cases (including specifying different fees for different cases).

(4) The regulations may include—

(a) incidental, supplementary or consequential provision;

(b) transitional, transitory or saving provision.

(5) Regulations under this section are to be made by statutory instrument.

(6) A statutory instrument containing regulations under this section is subject to annulment in pursuance of a resolution of either House of Parliament.

(7) In this section, "the appropriate national authority" means—

(a) in or as regards England and Wales, the Secretary of State;

(b) in or as regards Scotland, the Scottish Ministers."

(2) Before section 16 of the Firearms (Amendment) Act 1988 insert—

"15B Fees in connection with approvals under section 15

(1) The Secretary of State may by regulations authorise the appropriate national authority to require payment of a fee before an approval under section 15 is granted, varied or renewed.

(2) Regulations under subsection (1) must specify the amount of any fee that may be charged.

(3) The regulations may make different provision for different cases (including specifying different fees for different cases).

(4) The regulations may include—

(a) incidental, supplementary or consequential provision;

(b) transitional, transitory or saving provision.

(5) Regulations under this section are to be made by statutory instrument.

(6) A statutory instrument containing regulations under this section is subject to annulment in pursuance of a resolution of either House of Parliament.

(7) In this section, "the appropriate national authority" means—

(a) in or as regards England and Wales, the Secretary of State;

(b) in or as regards Scotland, the Scottish Ministers."

(3) In the Schedule to the Firearms (Amendment) Act 1988 (firearms and ammunition in museums), omit paragraph 3.

(4) In that Schedule, before paragraph 4 insert—

"3A (1) The Secretary of State may by regulations authorise the appropriate national authority to require payment of a fee before a licence is granted, varied or renewed.

(2) Regulations under sub-paragraph (1) must specify the amount of any fee that may be charged.

(3) The regulations may make different provision for different cases (including specifying different fees for different cases).

(4) The regulations may include—

(a) incidental, supplementary or consequential provision;

(b) transitional, transitory or saving provision.

(5) Regulations under this paragraph are to be made by statutory instrument.

(6) A statutory instrument containing regulations under this paragraph is subject to annulment in pursuance of a resolution of either House of Parliament.

(7) In this section, "the appropriate national authority" means—

(a) in or as regards England and Wales, the Secretary of State;

(b) in or as regards Scotland, the Scottish Ministers."

(5) In consequence of the amendment made by subsection (2), omit section 15(6) of the Firearms (Amendment) Act 1988.

133 Guidance to police officers in respect of firearms

(1) The Firearms Act 1968 is amended as follows.

(2) After section 55 insert—

"55A Guidance as to exercise of police functions

(1) The Secretary of State may issue guidance to chief officers of police as to the exercise of their functions under, or in connection with, this Act.

(2) The Secretary of State may revise any guidance issued under this section.

(3) The Secretary of State must arrange for any guidance issued under this section, and any revision of it, to be published.

(4) A chief officer of police must have regard to any guidance issued under this section.

(5) Before issuing guidance under this section, the Secretary of State must consult—

(a) the National Police Chiefs' Council, and

(b) the chief constable of the Police Service of Scotland."

(3) In section 44 (appeals against police decisions), after subsection (3) insert—

"(3A) The court or sheriff hearing an appeal must have regard to any guidance issued under section 55A that is relevant to the appeal."

Pyrotechnic articles

134 Possession of pyrotechnic articles at musical events

(1) It is an offence for a person to have a pyrotechnic article in his or her possession at any time when the person is—

(a) at a place where a qualifying musical event is being held, or

(b) at any other place that is being used by a person responsible for the organisation of a qualifying musical event for the purpose of—

(i) regulating entry to, or departure from, the event, or

(ii) providing sleeping or other facilities for those attending the event.

(2) Subsection (1) does not apply—

(a) to a person who is responsible for the organisation of the event, or

(b) to a person who has the article in his or her possession with the consent of a person responsible for the organisation of the event.

(3) A person guilty of an offence under this section is liable on summary conviction to imprisonment for a term not exceeding 51 weeks (or, in relation to offences committed before section 281(5) of the Criminal Justice Act 2003 comes into force, 3 months), or to a fine not exceeding level 3 on the standard scale, or to both.

(4) In this section, "pyrotechnic article" means an article that contains explosive substances, or an explosive mixture of substances, designed to produce heat, light, sound, gas or smoke, or a combination of such effects, through self-sustained exothermic chemical reactions, other than—

(a) a match, or

(b) an article specified, or of a description specified, in regulations made by statutory instrument by the Secretary of State.

(5) In this section, "qualifying musical event" means an event at which one or more live musical performances take place and which is specified, or of a description specified, in regulations made by statutory instrument by the Secretary of State.

(6) A statutory instrument containing regulations under this section is subject to annulment in pursuance of a resolution of either House of Parliament.

PART 7

ALCOHOL AND LATE NIGHT REFRESHMENT

Licensing

135 Meaning of "alcohol": inclusion of alcohol in any state

In the Licensing Act 2003, in section 191(1) (meaning of "alcohol") after "liquor" insert "(in any state)".

136 Interim steps pending review: representations

(1) In the Licensing Act 2003, section 53B (interim steps pending review) is amended as follows.

(2) In subsection (6) at the beginning insert "Subject to subsection (9A),".

(3) After subsection (9) insert—

"(9A) Where the relevant licensing authority has determined under subsection (8) whether to withdraw or modify the interim steps taken, the holder of the premises licence may only make further representations under subsection (6) if there has been a material change in circumstances since the authority made its determination."

137 Summary reviews of premises licences: review of interim steps

(1) The Licensing Act 2003 is amended as follows.

(2) Section 53C (review of premises licence following review notice) is amended as follows.

(3) In subsection (2)—

(a) at the end of paragraph (a) insert "and",

(b) in paragraph (b) omit "and", and

(c) omit paragraph (c).

(4) After subsection (11) insert—

"(12) Section 53D makes provision about the application and review of any interim steps that have been taken under section 53B in relation to a premises licence before a decision under this section comes into effect in relation to the licence."

(5) After section 53C insert—

"53D Interim steps pending section 53C decision coming into effect

(1) At the hearing to consider an application for a review under section 53A, the relevant licensing authority must review any interim steps that have been taken by the relevant licensing authority under section 53B that have effect on the date of the hearing.

(2) In conducting the review under this section, the relevant licensing authority must—

(a) consider whether the interim steps are appropriate for the promotion of the licensing objectives;

(b) consider any relevant representations; and

(c) determine whether to withdraw or modify the interim steps taken.

(3) The power of the relevant licensing authority on a review under this section includes a power to take any of the following interim steps—

(a) the modification of the conditions of the premises licence;

(b) the exclusion of the sale of alcohol by retail from the scope of the licence;

(c) the removal of the designated premises supervisor from the licence;

(d) the suspension of the licence;

and for this purpose the conditions of the licence are modified if any of them is altered or omitted or any new condition is added.

(4) Any interim steps taken under subsection (3) apply until—

(a) the end of the period given for appealing against a decision made under section 53C,

(b) if the decision under section 53C is appealed against, the time the appeal is disposed of, or

(c) the end of a period determined by the relevant licensing authority (which may not be longer than the period of time for which such interim steps could apply under paragraph (a) or (b)).

(5) Any interim steps taken under section 53B in relation to a premises licence cease to have effect when the decision made under section 53C comes into effect.

(6) In subsection (2) "relevant representations" means representations which—

(a) are relevant to one or more of the licensing objectives, and

(b) meet the requirements of subsection (7).

(7) The requirements are—

(a) that the representations are made by the holder of the premises licence, a responsible authority or any other person within the period prescribed under subsection 53A(3)(e),

(b) that they have not been withdrawn, and

(c) if they are made by a person who is not a responsible authority, that they are not, in the opinion of the relevant licensing authority, frivolous or vexatious.

(8) Where the relevant licensing authority determines that any representations are frivolous or vexatious, it must notify the person who made them of the reasons for that determination.

(9) A decision under this section may be appealed (see paragraph 8B of Part 1 of Schedule 5 (appeals: premises licences))."

(6) Part 1 of Schedule 5 (appeals: premises licences) is amended as follows.

(7) After paragraph 8A (summary review of premises licence) insert—

"8B Review of interim steps

8B (1) This paragraph applies where a review of interim steps is decided under section 53D (review of interim steps at a summary review of a premises licence).

(2) An appeal may be made against that decision by—

(a) the chief officer of police for the police area (or each police area) in which the premises are situated, or

(b) the holder of the premises licence.

(3) An appeal under this paragraph must be heard by the magistrates' court within the period of 28 days beginning with the day on which the appellant commenced the appeal (see paragraph 9(2))."

(8) This section does not apply to an application made under section 53A of the Licensing Act 2003 (summary reviews on application of senior police officer) where a decision in relation to that application has been made under section 53C (review of premises licence following review notice) before the coming into force of this section.

138 Personal licences: licensing authority powers in relation to convictions

(1) The Licensing Act 2003 is amended as follows.

(2) In section 10(4)(a) (functions that may not be delegated to an officer) after sub-paragraph (xii) insert—

"(xiii) section 132A(8) and (12) (revocation or suspension of licence by local authority where it becomes aware of convictions or immigration penalties),".

(3) After section 132 (licence holder's duty to notify licensing authority of convictions) insert—

"132A Convictions etc of licence-holder: powers of licensing authority

(1) This section applies where a licensing authority has granted a personal licence and it becomes aware (whether by virtue of section 123(1), 131 or 132 or otherwise) that the holder of the licence ("the licence holder") has been, at any time before or after the grant of the licence—

(a) convicted of any relevant offence or foreign offence, or

(b) required to pay an immigration penalty.

(2) But this section does not apply at any time when in the case of a licence holder who has been convicted of any relevant offence or foreign offence—

(a) the licence holder has appealed against a conviction for, or any sentence imposed in relation to, a relevant offence or foreign offence and that appeal has not been disposed of, or

(b) the time limit for appealing against such a conviction or sentence has not expired.

(3) The relevant licensing authority may—

(a) suspend the licence for a period not exceeding six months, or
(b) revoke the licence.

(4) If the relevant licensing authority is considering whether to suspend or revoke the licence, the authority must give notice to the licence holder.

(5) A notice under subsection (4) must invite the licence holder to make representations regarding—
(a) the relevant offence, foreign offence or immigration penalty that has caused the relevant licensing authority to issue the notice,
(b) any decision of a court under section 129 or 130 in relation to the licence, and
(c) any other relevant information (including information regarding the licence holder's personal circumstances).

(6) The licence holder may make representations under subsection (5) to the relevant licensing authority within the period of 28 days beginning with the day the notice was issued.

(7) Before deciding whether to suspend or revoke the licence the relevant licensing authority must take into account—
(a) any representations made by the licence holder under this section,
(b) any decision of a court under section 129 or 130 of which the licensing authority is aware, and
(c) any other information which the authority considers relevant.

(8) Having taken into account the matters described in subsection (7) the relevant licensing authority may make a decision whether to suspend or revoke a licence, unless subsection (9) applies.

(9) This subsection applies where the relevant licensing authority has taken into account the matters described in subsection (7) and proposes not to revoke the licence.

(10) Where subsection (9) applies the authority must—
(a) give notice to the chief officer of police for its area that it proposes not to revoke the licence, and
(b) invite the officer to make representations regarding the issue of whether the licence should be suspended or revoked having regard to the crime prevention objective.

(11) The chief officer of police may make representations under subsection (10)(b) to the relevant licensing authority within the period of 14 days beginning with the day the notice was received.

(12) Where the relevant licensing authority has given notice to the chief officer of police under subsection (10)(a), the authority must take into account—
(a) any representations from the officer, and
(b) the matters described in subsection (7),

and then make a decision whether to suspend or revoke the licence.

(13) The relevant licensing authority must give notice of any decision made under subsection (8) or (12) to the licence holder and the chief officer of police, including reasons for the decision.

(14) A decision under this section does not have effect—

(a) until the end of the period given for appealing against the decision, or

(b) if the decision is appealed against, until the appeal is disposed of.

(15) A decision under subsection (8) or (12) may be appealed (see paragraph 17(5A) of Part 3 of Schedule 5 (appeals: personal licences))."

(4) In paragraph 17 of Part 3 of Schedule 5 (appeals: personal licences) after sub-paragraph (5A) insert—

"(5B) Where a licensing authority revokes or suspends a personal licence under section 132A(8) or (12) the holder of the licence may appeal against that decision."

139 Licensing Act 2003: addition of further relevant offences

(1) Schedule 4 to the Licensing Act 2003 (personal licence: relevant offences) is amended as follows.

(2) In paragraph 18 (sexual offences), after paragraph (a) insert—

"(aa) listed in Schedule 3 to the Sexual Offences Act 2003 (sexual offences for the purposes of notification and orders);".

(3) After paragraph 19 (violent offences) insert—

"19A An offence listed in Part 1 of Schedule 15 to the Criminal Justice Act 2003 (specified violent offences)."

(4) After paragraph 22 (fraud offences) insert—

"22ZA An offence under any of the following provisions of the Violent Crime Reduction Act 2006—

(a) section 28 (using someone to mind a weapon);

(b) section 36 (manufacture, import and sale of realistic imitation firearms)."

(5) After paragraph 23A (offences under the Psychoactive Substances Act 2016) insert—

"23B An offence listed in section 41 of the Counter-Terrorism Act 2008 (terrorism offences)."

140 Licensing Act 2003: guidance

In the Licensing Act 2003, in section 182 (guidance) omit subsections (2) and (4) to (6).

141 Cumulative impact assessments

(1) The Licensing Act 2003 is amended as follows.

(2) In section 5 (statement of licensing policy), after subsection (6C) insert—

"(6D) In determining or revising its policy, a licensing authority must have regard to any cumulative impact assessments published by it under section 5A.

(6E) A licensing statement must—

(a) summarise any cumulative impact assessments published by the licensing authority under section 5A, and

(b) explain how the licensing authority has discharged its duty under subsection (6D)."

(3) After section 5 insert—

"5A Cumulative impact assessments

(1) A licensing authority may publish a document ("a cumulative impact assessment") stating that the licensing authority considers that the number of relevant authorisations in respect of premises in one or more parts of its area described in the assessment is such that it is likely that it would be inconsistent with the authority's duty under section 4(1) to grant any further relevant authorisations in respect of premises in that part or those parts.

(2) A cumulative impact assessment must set out the evidence for the authority's opinion as set out in the assessment in accordance with subsection (1).

(3) For the purposes of this section, "relevant authorisations" means—

(a) premises licences;

(b) club premises certificates.

(4) A cumulative impact assessment may relate to all relevant authorisations or only to relevant authorisations of a kind described in the assessment.

(5) Before publishing a cumulative impact assessment, the licensing authority must consult the persons mentioned in section 5(3).

(6) For the purposes of the consultation, the licensing authority must provide the persons mentioned in section 5(3) with the following information—

(a) the reasons why it is considering publishing a cumulative impact assessment;

(b) a general indication of the part or parts of its area which it is considering describing in the assessment;

(c) whether it considers that the assessment will relate to all relevant authorisations or only to relevant authorisations of a particular kind.

(7) Where a licensing authority publishes a cumulative impact assessment, it must, before the end of each relevant period, consider whether it remains of the opinion stated in the assessment.

(8) Before deciding whether it remains of that opinion, the licensing authority must consult the persons mentioned in section 5(3).

(9) If the licensing authority is no longer of that opinion—

(a) it must publish a statement to that effect, and

(b) the duties in section 5(6D) and (6E) and subsection (7) of this section cease to apply in relation to the assessment.

(10) If the licensing authority remains of that opinion, it must revise the cumulative impact assessment so that it—

(a) includes a statement to that effect, and

(b) sets out the evidence as to why the authority remains of that opinion.

(11) A licensing authority must publish any revision of a cumulative impact assessment.

(12) In subsection (7), "relevant period" means the period of three years beginning with the publication of the cumulative impact assessment or a revision of the cumulative impact assessment."

Late night levy

142 Late night levy requirements

(1) Section 125 of the Police Reform and Social Responsibility Act 2011 (late night levy requirement) is amended as follows.

(2) For subsections (1) and (2) substitute—

"(1) In this Chapter, "a late night levy requirement" means a requirement to pay a late night levy in accordance with this Chapter.

(2) A licensing authority may decide that a late night levy requirement is to apply in its area or in a part of its area in respect of—

(a) relevant late night alcohol authorisations relating to premises in the area or the part, or

(b) relevant late night alcohol authorisations and relevant late night refreshment authorisations relating to premises in the area or the part.

(2A) Accordingly, references in this Chapter to a late night authorisation to which a late night levy requirement relates are references to any relevant late night alcohol authorisation or relevant late night refreshment authorisation in respect of which the late night levy requirement applies.

(2B) A licensing authority may decide under subsection (2) that different late night levy requirements are to apply in different parts of its area."

(3) In subsection (3)(a), after "supply of alcohol" insert "or late night refreshment".

(4) Omit subsection (4).

(5) Schedule 18 makes further amendments of Chapter 2 of Part 2 of the Police Reform and Social Responsibility Act 2011 (late night levy).

PART 8

FINANCIAL SANCTIONS

Interpretation

143 Interpretation

(1) This section sets out definitions that apply for the purposes of this Part.

(2) "EU financial sanctions Regulation" means an EU Regulation adopted under Article 215 of the Treaty on the Functioning of the European Union to the extent that the Regulation—

(a) imposes prohibitions or obligations for one or more of the following purposes—

(i) freezing funds or economic resources;

(ii) preventing funds or economic resources being made available;

(iii) prohibiting or restricting access to financial markets or financial services;

(b) makes provision to supplement prohibitions or obligations of the kind mentioned in paragraph (a).

(3) "UN financial sanctions Resolution" means a resolution adopted by the Security Council of the United Nations to the extent that the resolution provides under article 41 of the Charter of the United Nations for States to take measures that—

(a) impose prohibitions or obligations for one or more of the following purposes—

(i) freezing funds or economic resources;

(ii) preventing funds or economic resources being made available;

(iii) prohibiting or restricting access to financial markets or financial services;

(b) make provision to supplement prohibitions or obligations of the kind mentioned in paragraph (a).

(4) "Financial sanctions legislation" means—

(a) an EU financial sanctions Regulation;

(b) an instrument made under section 2(2) of the European Communities Act 1972 for the purpose of implementing, or otherwise in relation to, EU obligations created or arising by or under an EU financial sanctions Regulation;

(c) a provision of an Act or of subordinate legislation (within the meaning of the Interpretation Act 1978) where the purpose of the provision is to implement a UN financial sanctions Resolution;

(d) a freezing order under section 4 of the Anti-terrorism, Crime and Security Act 2001;

(e) a direction under Schedule 7 to the Counter-Terrorism Act 2008 to the extent that it contains a requirement of a kind mentioned in paragraph 13 of that Schedule (limiting or ceasing business), paragraph 17 of that Schedule and Part 5 of that Schedule so far as it relates to the enforcement of a requirement of a kind mentioned in paragraph 13 of that Schedule.

(5) The reference in subsection (2) to Article 215 of the Treaty on the Functioning of the European Union includes a reference to any of Articles 60, 301 and 308 of the Treaty establishing the European Community (as it had effect before 1 December 2009).

Enhanced maximum penalties

144 Powers to create offences under section 2(2) ECA 1972: maximum term of imprisonment

(1) Paragraph 1(1)(d) of Schedule 2 to the European Communities Act 1972 applies with the following modifications in relation to the exercise of the powers conferred by section 2(2) of that Act ("the section 2(2) powers") to make provision for the purposes of implementing, or otherwise in relation to, EU obligations created or arising by or under an EU financial sanctions Regulation.

(2) The prohibition arising under paragraph 1(1)(d) on the creation of offences punishable by imprisonment for more than a period specified in that paragraph does not apply to the exercise of the section 2(2) powers for those purposes.

(3) Instead, the section 2(2) powers may not be exercised for those purposes to create an offence punishable by imprisonment for a period exceeding—

(a) in the case of conviction on indictment, 7 years;

(b) in the case of summary conviction—

(i) in relation to England and Wales, 12 months or, in relation to offences committed before section 154(1) of the Criminal Justice Act 2003 comes into force, 6 months;

(ii) in relation to Scotland, 12 months;

(iii) in relation to Northern Ireland, 6 months.

(4) Subsection (5) applies where, at any time before this section comes into force, the section 2(2) powers have been exercised for those purposes to create an offence punishable by imprisonment.

(5) The section 2(2) powers may (at any time after this section comes into force) be exercised for those purposes to vary the provision made for the maximum period of imprisonment by making any provision that could (by virtue of subsections (2) and (3)) be made if the offence were created after this section comes into force.

(6) A variation made in reliance on subsection (5) does not affect the penalty for an offence if any act or other event proof of which is required for conviction of the offence takes place before this section comes into force.

145 Other offences: maximum term of imprisonment

(1) Schedule 3 to the Anti-terrorism, Crime and Security Act 2001 (freezing orders) is amended in accordance with subsections (2) and (3).

(2) In paragraph 7 (offences), for sub-paragraph (6)(a) and (b) substitute—

"(a) on summary conviction—

(i) in England and Wales, to imprisonment for a term not exceeding 12 months (or, in relation to offences committed before section 154(1) of the Criminal Justice Act 2003 comes into force, 6 months) or to a fine, or to both;

(ii) in Scotland, to imprisonment for a term not exceeding 12 months, or to a fine not exceeding the statutory maximum, or to both;

(iii) in Northern Ireland, to imprisonment for a term not exceeding 6 months, or to a fine not exceeding the statutory maximum, or to both;

(b) on conviction on indictment, to imprisonment for a term not exceeding 7 years or to a fine, or to both."

(3) In that paragraph, in sub-paragraph (7), for the words from "on summary conviction" to the end of the sub-paragraph substitute "—

(a) on summary conviction—

(i) in England and Wales, to imprisonment for a term not exceeding 12 months (or, in relation to offences committed before section 154(1) of the Criminal Justice Act 2003 comes into force, 6 months) or to a fine, or to both;

(ii) in Scotland, to imprisonment for a term not exceeding 12 months, or to a fine not exceeding the statutory maximum, or to both;

(iii) in Northern Ireland, to imprisonment for a term not exceeding 6 months, or to a fine not exceeding the statutory maximum, or to both;

(b) on conviction on indictment, to imprisonment for a term not exceeding 2 years or to a fine, or to both."

(4) Schedule 7 to the Counter-Terrorism Act 2008 (terrorist financing and money laundering) is amended in accordance with subsections (5) to (9).

(5) In paragraph 30 (offence of failure to comply with requirement imposed by direction), after sub-paragraph (4) insert—

"(4A) In a case where a person is guilty of an offence under this paragraph by failing to comply with a requirement of a kind mentioned in paragraph 13, the person is liable—

(a) on summary conviction—

(i) in England and Wales, to imprisonment for a term not exceeding 12 months (or, in relation to offences committed before section 154(1) of the Criminal Justice Act 2003 comes into force, 6 months) or to a fine, or to both;

(ii) in Scotland, to imprisonment for a term not exceeding 12 months, or to a fine not exceeding the statutory maximum, or to both;

(iii) in Northern Ireland, to imprisonment for a term not exceeding 6 months, or to a fine not exceeding the statutory maximum, or to both;

(b) on conviction on indictment, to imprisonment for a term not exceeding 7 years or to a fine, or to both."

(6) In sub-paragraph (5) of that paragraph, at the beginning insert "In any other case,".

(7) In paragraph 30A (offence of relevant person circumventing requirements), after sub-paragraph (1) insert—

"(1A) In a case where a person is guilty of an offence under this paragraph in relation to a requirement of a kind mentioned in paragraph 13, the person is liable—

(a) on summary conviction—

(i) in England and Wales, to imprisonment for a term not exceeding 12 months (or, in relation to offences committed before section 154(1) of the Criminal Justice Act 2003 comes into force, 6 months) or to a fine, or to both;

(ii) in Scotland, to imprisonment for a term not exceeding 12 months, or to a fine not exceeding the statutory maximum, or to both;

(iii) in Northern Ireland, to imprisonment for a term not exceeding 6 months, or to a fine not exceeding the statutory maximum, or to both;

(b) on conviction on indictment, to imprisonment for a term not exceeding 7 years or to a fine, or to both."

(8) In sub-paragraph (2) of that paragraph, at the beginning insert "In any other case,".

(9) In paragraph 31 (offences in connection with licences), in sub-paragraph (2), for the words from "on conviction on indictment" to the end of the sub-paragraph substitute "—

(a) on summary conviction—

(i) in England and Wales, to imprisonment for a term not exceeding 12 months (or, in relation to offences committed before section 154(1) of the Criminal Justice Act 2003 comes into force, 6 months) or to a fine, or to both;

(ii) in Scotland, to imprisonment for a term not exceeding 12 months, or to a fine not exceeding the statutory maximum, or to both;

(iii) in Northern Ireland, to imprisonment for a term not exceeding 6 months, or to a fine not exceeding the statutory maximum, or to both;

(b) on conviction on indictment, to imprisonment for a term not exceeding 2 years or to a fine, or to both."

(10) The amendments made by this section do not affect the penalty for an offence if any act or other event proof of which is required for conviction of the offence takes place before this section comes into force.

Civil sanctions

146 Power to impose monetary penalties

(1) The Treasury may impose a monetary penalty on a person if it is satisfied, on the balance of probabilities, that—

(a) the person has breached a prohibition, or failed to comply with an obligation, that is imposed by or under financial sanctions legislation, and

(b) the person knew, or had reasonable cause to suspect, that the person was in breach of the prohibition or (as the case may be) had failed to comply with the obligation.

(2) The amount of the penalty is to be such amount as the Treasury may determine but it may not exceed the permitted maximum.

(3) In a case where the breach or failure relates to particular funds or economic resources and it is possible to estimate the value of the funds or economic resources, the permitted maximum is the greater of—
   (a) £1,000,000, and
   (b) 50% of the estimated value of the funds or resources.

(4) In any other case, the permitted maximum is £1,000,000.

(5) In subsection (3), "funds" and "economic resources" have the same meanings as they have in the financial sanctions legislation that contains the prohibition or obligation in respect of which the monetary penalty is imposed.

(6) The Treasury must keep the amount for the time being specified in subsection (3)(a) or (4) under review.

(7) The Treasury may by regulations made by statutory instrument amend subsection (3)(a) or (4) so as to substitute another amount for the amount for the time being specified in it.

(8) Regulations under subsection (7) may include transitional provision.

(9) Before making regulations under subsection (7), the Treasury must consult such persons as it considers appropriate.

(10) A statutory instrument containing regulations under subsection (7) may not be made unless a draft of the instrument has been laid before and approved by a resolution of each House of Parliament.

(11) Any monetary penalty payable under this section is recoverable by the Treasury as a civil debt.

(12) Any monetary penalty received by the Treasury by virtue of this section must be paid into the Consolidated Fund.

(13) This section does not authorise the imposition of a monetary penalty on the Crown.

147 Monetary penalties: procedural rights

(1) Before imposing a monetary penalty on a person under section 146, the Treasury must inform the person of its intention to do so.

(2) The Treasury must also—
   (a) explain the grounds for imposing the penalty,
   (b) specify the amount of the penalty,
   (c) explain that the person is entitled to make representations, and
   (d) specify the period within which any such representations must be made.

(3) If (having considered any representations), the Treasury decides to impose the penalty, the Treasury must—
   (a) inform the person of its decision,
   (b) explain that the person is entitled to seek a review by a Minister of the Crown, and
   (c) specify the period within which the person must inform the Treasury that the person wishes to seek such a review.

(4) If the person seeks a review, the Minister may—

(a) uphold the decision to impose the penalty and its amount,

(b) uphold the decision to impose the penalty but substitute a different amount, or

(c) cancel the decision to impose the penalty.

(5) A review under subsection (4) must be carried out by the Minister personally.

(6) If on a review under subsection (4) the Minister decides to uphold the Treasury's decision to impose the penalty and its amount, or to uphold the Treasury's decision to impose the penalty but to substitute a different amount, the person may appeal (on any ground) to the Upper Tribunal.

(7) On an appeal under subsection (6), the Upper Tribunal may quash the Minister's decision and if it does so may—

(a) quash the Treasury's decision to impose the penalty;

(b) uphold that decision but substitute a different amount for the amount determined by the Treasury (or, in a case where the Minister substituted a different amount, by the Minister).

(8) In this section, "Minister of the Crown" means the holder of an office in Her Majesty's Government in the United Kingdom.

148 Monetary penalties: bodies corporate and unincorporated associations

(1) If a monetary penalty is payable under section 146 by a body, the Treasury may also impose a monetary penalty on an officer of the body if it is satisfied, on the balance of probabilities, that the breach or failure in respect of which the monetary penalty is payable by the body—

(a) took place with the consent or connivance of the officer, or

(b) was attributable to any neglect on the part of the officer.

(2) In subsection (1)—

"body" means a body corporate, a partnership or an unincorporated body other than a partnership;

"officer of a body" means—

(a) in relation to a body corporate, a director, manager, secretary or other similar officer of the body or a person purporting to act in any such capacity;

(b) in relation to a partnership, a partner or a person purporting to act as a partner;

(c) in relation to an unincorporated body other than a partnership, a person who is concerned in the management or control of the body or purports to act in the capacity of a person so concerned.

(3) Sections 146(2) to (5), (11) and (12) and 147 apply in relation to a monetary penalty that may be imposed under subsection (1) as they apply in relation to a monetary penalty that may be imposed under section 146(1).

149 Monetary penalties: supplementary

(1) The Treasury must issue guidance as to—

(a) the circumstances in which it may consider it appropriate to impose a monetary penalty under section 146 or 148, and
(b) how it will determine the amount of the penalty.

(2) The Treasury must, at such intervals as it considers appropriate, publish reports about the imposition of monetary penalties under section 146 or 148.

Other provisions about enforcement

150 Deferred prosecution agreements

In Part 2 of Schedule 17 to the Crime and Courts Act 2013 (which lists the offences in relation to which a deferred prosecution agreement may be entered into), after paragraph 26 insert—

"26A (1) An offence under an instrument made under section 2(2) of the European Communities Act 1972 for the purpose of implementing, or otherwise in relation to, EU obligations created or arising by or under an EU financial sanctions Regulation.

(2) An offence under an Act or under subordinate legislation where the offence was created for the purpose of implementing a UN financial sanctions Resolution.

(3) An offence under paragraph 7 of Schedule 3 to the Anti-terrorism, Crime and Security Act 2001 (freezing orders).

(4) An offence under paragraph 30 or 30A of Schedule 7 to the Counter-Terrorism Act 2008 where the offence relates to a requirement of the kind mentioned in paragraph 13 of that Schedule.

(5) An offence under paragraph 31 of Schedule 7 to the Counter-Terrorism Act 2008.

(6) In this paragraph—

"EU financial sanctions Regulation" and "UN financial sanctions Resolution" have the same meanings as in Part 8 of the Policing and Crime Act 2017 (see section 143 of that Act);

"subordinate legislation" has the same meaning as in the Interpretation Act 1978."

151 Serious crime prevention orders

(1) Schedule 1 to the Serious Crime Act 2007 (which lists the offences in respect of which serious crime prevention orders may be made) is amended as follows.

(2) In Part 1 (England and Wales), after paragraph 13A insert—

"13B Financial sanctions legislation

13B (1) An offence under an instrument made under section 2(2) of the European Communities Act 1972 for the purpose of implementing, or otherwise in relation to, EU obligations created or arising by or under an EU financial sanctions Regulation.

(2) An offence under an Act or under subordinate legislation where the offence was created for the purpose of implementing a UN financial sanctions Resolution.

(3) An offence under paragraph 7 of Schedule 3 to the Anti-terrorism, Crime and Security Act 2001 (freezing orders).

(4) An offence under paragraph 30 or 30A of Schedule 7 to the Counter-Terrorism Act 2008 where the offence relates to a requirement of the kind mentioned in paragraph 13 of that Schedule.

(5) An offence under paragraph 31 of Schedule 7 to the Counter-Terrorism Act 2008.

(6) In this paragraph—

"EU financial sanctions Regulation" and "UN financial sanctions Resolution" have the same meanings as in Part 8 of the Policing and Crime Act 2017 (see section 143 of that Act);

"subordinate legislation" has the same meaning as in the Interpretation Act 1978."

(3) In Part 1A (Scotland), after paragraph 16M —

"16MA Financial sanctions legislation

16MA (1) An offence under an instrument made under section 2(2) of the European Communities Act 1972 for the purpose of implementing, or otherwise in relation to, EU obligations created or arising by or under an EU financial sanctions Regulation.

(2) An offence under an Act or under subordinate legislation where the offence was created for the purpose of implementing a UN financial sanctions Resolution.

(3) An offence under paragraph 7 of Schedule 3 to the Anti-terrorism, Crime and Security Act 2001 (freezing orders).

(4) An offence under paragraph 30 or 30A of Schedule 7 to the Counter-Terrorism Act 2008 where the offence relates to a requirement of the kind mentioned in paragraph 13 of that Schedule.

(5) An offence under paragraph 31 of Schedule 7 to the Counter-Terrorism Act 2008.

(6) In this paragraph—

"EU financial sanctions Regulation" and "UN financial sanctions Resolution" have the same meanings as in Part 8 of the Policing and Crime Act 2017 (see section 143 of that Act);

"subordinate legislation" has the same meaning as in the Interpretation Act 1978."

(4) In Part 2 (Northern Ireland), after paragraph 29 insert—

"29A Financial sanctions legislation

29A (1) An offence under an instrument made under section 2(2) of the European Communities Act 1972 for the purpose of implementing, or otherwise in relation to, EU obligations created or arising by or under an EU financial sanctions Regulation.

(2) An offence under an Act or under subordinate legislation where the offence was created for the purpose of implementing a UN financial sanctions Resolution.

(3) An offence under paragraph 7 of Schedule 3 to the Anti-terrorism, Crime and Security Act 2001 (freezing orders).

(4) An offence under paragraph 30 or 30A of Schedule 7 to the Counter-Terrorism Act 2008 where the offence relates to a requirement of the kind mentioned in paragraph 13 of that Schedule.

(5) An offence under paragraph 31 of Schedule 7 to the Counter-Terrorism Act 2008.

(6) In this paragraph—

"EU financial sanctions Regulation" and "UN financial sanctions Resolution" have the same meanings as in Part 8 of the Policing and Crime Act 2017 (see section 143 of that Act);

"subordinate legislation" has the same meaning as in the Interpretation Act 1978."

Avoidance of delay: temporary regulations

152 Implementation of UN financial sanctions Resolutions: temporary regulations

(1) Where a UN financial sanctions Resolution is adopted, the Treasury may by regulations made by statutory instrument make such provision as it considers appropriate for the implementation of the Resolution.

(2) Regulations under this section must provide for the regulations to cease to have effect at whichever of the following times first occurs—

(a) the time when an EU financial sanctions Regulation made for the purpose of implementing the UN financial sanctions Resolution enters into force;

(b) the end of a day specified in the regulations, which may not be a day that falls more than 30 days after the day on which the UN financial sanctions Resolution is adopted.

(3) At any time before the end of the day specified in the regulations under subsection (2)(b), the Treasury may amend the regulations (by making further regulations) so as to substitute for the day specified in the regulations in accordance with subsection (2)(b) a different day, which may not be a day that falls more than 60 days after the day on which the UN financial sanctions Resolution is adopted.

(4) The power conferred by subsection (3) may be exercised on only one occasion.

(5) Subsection (3) does not affect the power (by virtue of section 14 of the Interpretation Act 1978) to amend regulations under subsection (1) for a purpose other than that mentioned in subsection (3).

(6) A statutory instrument containing regulations under this section is subject to annulment in pursuance of a resolution of either House of Parliament.

(7) Section 153 makes further provision about regulations under this section.

153 Content of regulations under section 152

(1) Regulations under section 152 may impose prohibitions for such of the following purposes as are relevant to the UN financial sanctions Resolution that is being implemented by the regulations—

(a) freezing funds or economic resources owned, held or controlled by designated persons;

(b) preventing funds or economic resources being made available to, or for the benefit, of designated persons.

(2) In subsection (1), "designated person" means a person who is specified in any of the following instruments as a person in relation to whom the measures required by the UN financial sanctions Resolution are to be taken—

(a) the UN financial sanctions Resolution or any other UN financial sanctions Resolution;

(b) an instrument made by an organ of the United Nations for the purpose of specifying the persons in relation to whom the measures required by the Resolution are to be taken.

For the purpose of this subsection, "person" includes (in addition to an individual and a body of persons corporate or unincorporate) any organisation and any association or combination of persons.

(3) Regulations under section 152 must describe the designated persons to whom the prohibitions in the regulations relate but may do so by referring to any of the instruments mentioned in subsection (2) or in any other way; and, where the persons are described by referring to any of those instruments, the regulations may provide for the reference in the regulations to the instrument to have effect as a reference to the instrument as varied or supplemented from time to time.

(4) The regulations may create exceptions to any prohibitions included in the regulations by virtue of subsection (1), including provision for any of those prohibitions not to apply to anything done under the authority of a licence issued by the Treasury under the regulations.

(5) The regulations may make provision—

(a) for requiring a person who is subject to a prohibition, or any other person of a description specified in the regulations, to provide information to the Treasury;

(b) authorising or restricting the disclosure of information so provided.

(6) The regulations may make provision for the enforcement of any prohibitions or requirements set out in the regulations, including provision for preventing any prohibitions from being circumvented.

(7) The provision that may be made under subsection (6) includes—
(a) the creation of offences;
(b) provision corresponding or similar to sections 146 to 149 (civil sanctions).

(8) The regulations may not create an offence punishable by imprisonment for a period exceeding—
(a) in the case of conviction on indictment, 7 years;
(b) in the case of summary conviction—
(i) in relation to England and Wales, 12 months or, in relation to offences committed before section 154(1) of the Criminal Justice Act 2003 comes into force, 6 months;
(ii) in relation to Scotland, 12 months;
(iii) in relation to Northern Ireland, 6 months.

(9) The regulations may provide that a person is not to be subject to any form of liability in consequence of anything done by that person under the regulations.

(10) The regulations may bind the Crown but they may not—
(a) provide for the Crown to be criminally liable, or
(b) provide for the Crown to be liable to pay a monetary penalty.

(11) The regulations may include—
(a) incidental, supplementary or consequential provision;
(b) transitional or transitory provision.

(12) The regulations may—
(a) make different provision for different purposes;
(b) confer a discretion on any person.

Avoidance of delay: temporary listing

154 Linking of UN financial sanctions Resolutions with EU financial sanctions Regulations

(1) For the purposes of section 155, the Treasury may by regulations made by statutory instrument provide that a United Nations financial sanctions Resolution specified in the regulations is linked to an EU financial sanctions Regulation specified in the regulations.

(2) The regulations may provide for any reference in the regulations to a United Nations financial sanctions Resolution or to an EU financial sanctions Regulation to have effect as a reference to the United Nations financial sanctions Resolution or (as the case may be) to the EU financial sanctions Regulation as varied or supplemented from time to time.

(3) A statutory instrument containing regulations under subsection (1) is subject to annulment in pursuance of a resolution of either House of Parliament.

155 Implementation of UN financial sanctions Resolutions: temporary listing

(1) This section applies where—

(a) regulations under section 154 provide that a UN financial sanctions Resolution is linked to an EU financial sanctions Regulation,

(b) a person is designated for the purposes of the UN financial sanctions Resolution, and

(c) at the time the person is designated for those purposes, the person is not included in the list of persons, set out in the EU financial sanctions Regulation, to whom the prohibitions contained in the Regulation relate ("the EU list").

(2) The person is to be treated for a temporary period as if the person were included in the EU list (as well as being designated for the purposes of the UN financial sanctions Resolution).

(3) The temporary period referred to in subsection (2) begins at the time the person is designated for the purposes of the UN financial sanctions Regulation.

(4) The temporary period ends—

(a) at the end of the day on which the person is (otherwise than under subsection (2)) included in the EU list;

(b) if the person is not included in the EU list before the end of the period of 30 days beginning with the day after the day on which the person is designated for the purposes of the UN financial sanctions Resolution, at the end of that period of 30 days.

(5) For the purposes of this section, a person is designated for the purposes of a UN financial sanctions Resolution if the person is specified in any of the following instruments as a person in relation to whom the measures required by the UN financial sanctions Resolution are to be taken—

(a) the UN financial sanctions Resolution or any other UN financial sanctions Resolution;

(b) an instrument made by an organ of the United Nations for the purpose of specifying the persons in relation to whom the measures required by the Resolution are to be taken.

For the purpose of this subsection, "person" includes (in addition to an individual and a body corporate or unincorporate) any organisation and any association or combination of persons.

(6) This section applies where a person is designated for the purposes of the UN financial sanctions Resolution before this section comes into force (as well as where the person is designated after this section comes into force) but, in such a case, the temporary period begins on the day on which this section comes into force.

Power to extend to Bailiwick of Guernsey etc

156 Extension to the Bailiwick of Guernsey, Isle of Man and BOTs

(1) Her Majesty may by Order in Council provide for regulations under section 152(1) (whether made before or after the making of the Order in Council) to extend with or without modifications to—

(a) the Bailiwick of Guernsey;

(b) the Isle of Man;

(c) any of the British overseas territories.

(2) Her Majesty may by Order in Council provide for section 143, regulations under section 154 (whether made before or after the making of the Order in Council) and section 155 to extend with or without modifications to—

(a) the Bailiwick of Guernsey;

(b) the Isle of Man;

(c) any of the British overseas territories.

(3) The power conferred by subsection (1) or (2), so far as relating to regulations, includes power to provide for the regulations as amended from time to time to extend as mentioned in that subsection.

(4) The modifications that may be specified in an Order in Council under subsection (1) include a modification of any provision included in the regulations about the time at which the regulations are to cease to have effect.

(5) A modification included in an Order in Council by virtue of subsection (4)—

(a) may have the effect that the regulations (as extended by the Order in Council) continue to have effect after the time when the regulations have ceased to have effect under the law of England and Wales, Scotland and Northern Ireland, but

(b) must secure that the regulations (as so extended) cease to have effect on a day that falls no later than 120 days after the day on which the relevant UN financial sanctions Resolution is adopted.

(6) In subsection (5), "the relevant UN financial sanctions Resolution" means the UN financial sanctions Resolution that is being implemented by the regulations.

PART 9

MISCELLANEOUS AND GENERAL

CHAPTER 1

MISCELLANEOUS

Police collaboration

157 Power to enter into police collaboration agreements

(1) The Police Act 1996 is amended in accordance with subsections (2) to (4).

(2) In section 22A (collaboration agreements)—

(a) in subsection (1)(b), for "and two or more policing bodies" substitute "and—

(i) one or more policing bodies together with one or more other persons, or

(ii) if no other person is a party to the agreement, two or more policing bodies.";

(b) in subsection (6), for "(1)" substitute "(1)(a)".

(3) In section 23F (collaboration agreements: guidance), after subsection (2) insert—

"(3) The Secretary of State may give other persons who exercise functions of a public nature guidance about collaboration agreements or related matters, and those persons must have regard to the guidance in exercising such functions."

(4) In section 23G (collaboration agreements: directions), after subsection (2) insert—

"(2A) The Secretary of State may give one or more other persons who exercise functions of a public nature directions about collaboration agreements or related matters."

(5) Schedule 19 contains amendments in relation to cases where the Director General of the National Crime Agency is a party to a collaboration agreement under section 22A of the Police Act 1996 (as amended by this section).

NCA powers

158 Powers of NCA officers in relation to customs matters

(1) The Crime and Courts Act 2013 is amended as follows.

(2) In section 9 (Director General: customs powers of Commissioners & operational powers)—

(a) in subsection (2), after paragraph (b) insert—

"(ba) the powers of a general customs official;";

(b) in subsection (8), in the definition of "operational power", after paragraph (b) insert—

"(ba) a power of a general customs official;".

(3) In section 10 (operational powers of other NCA officers), in subsection (1) after paragraph (b) insert—

"(ba) the powers of a general customs official;".

(4) In Schedule 5 (police, customs and immigration powers), after Part 5 (designation: powers of officers of Revenue and Customs) insert—

"**PART 5A**

DESIGNATIONS: POWERS OF GENERAL CUSTOMS OFFICIALS

18A (1) If an NCA officer is designated as a person having the powers of a general customs official, the NCA officer has, in relation to any customs matter, the same powers as a general customs official would have.

(2) But that is subject to any limitation included in the designation.

18B If a power of a general customs official is exercisable both—

(a) in relation to a customs matter, and

(b) in relation to any other matter,

the power is exercisable by a designated officer only in relation to the customs matter.

18C (1) This paragraph applies to an enactment if it provides for the issuing of warrants which authorise a general customs official to exercise any power in relation to a customs matter.

(2) For the purpose of enabling a designated officer to exercise that power in relation to a customs matter, the enactment has effect as if the designated officer were a general customs official."

(5) In paragraph 26 of that Schedule (modification of references), after paragraph (c) insert—

"(ca) a power of a general customs official is exercisable by any NCA officer, a reference to a general customs official in any enactment which relates to that power is to be taken to be, or to include, a reference to any NCA officer by whom that power is exercisable;".

(6) In paragraph 27 of that Schedule (power to make further provision), in sub-paragraph (2), after paragraph (d)(ii) insert—

"(iia) one or more grades of, or pay scales applicable to, general customs officials;".

(7) In paragraph 28 of that Schedule (functions of third parties relating to constables etc: extension to NCA), in sub-paragraph (2), after paragraph (c) insert—

"(ca) a general customs official,".

Requirements to confirm nationality

159 Requirement to state nationality

In the UK Borders Act 2007, after section 43 (supply of police information) insert—

"43A Requirement to state nationality

(1) An individual who is arrested for an offence must state his or her nationality if required to do so by an immigration officer or a constable in accordance with this section.

(2) A requirement may be imposed on an individual under subsection (1) only if the immigration officer or constable suspects that the individual may not be a British citizen.

(3) When imposing a requirement under subsection (1) the immigration officer or constable must inform the individual that an offence may be committed if the individual fails to comply with a requirement imposed under this section.

(4) The immigration officer or constable must make a written record of the imposition of a requirement under subsection (1) as soon as practicable.

(5) The written record is to be made in the presence of the individual where this is practicable.

43B Offence of not giving nationality

(1) A person commits an offence if, without reasonable excuse, the person fails to comply with a requirement imposed in accordance with section 43A, whether by providing false or incomplete information or by providing no information.

(2) Information provided by a person in response to a requirement imposed in accordance with section 43A is not admissible in evidence in criminal proceedings against that person other than proceedings for an offence under this section.

(3) A person who is guilty of an offence under subsection (1) is liable—

(a) on summary conviction in England and Wales, to either or both of the following—

(i) imprisonment for a term not exceeding 51 weeks (or 6 months if the offence was committed before the commencement of section 281(5) of the Criminal Justice Act 2003);

(ii) a fine;

(b) on summary conviction in Northern Ireland, to either or both of the following—

(i) imprisonment for a term not exceeding 6 months;

(ii) a fine not exceeding level 5 on the standard scale."

160 Requirement to produce nationality document

In the UK Borders Act 2007, after section 46 (seizure of nationality documents) insert—

"46A Requirement to produce nationality document

(1) This section applies where—

(a) an individual has been arrested on suspicion of the commission of an offence, and

(b) the individual is to be released after arrest (whether or not on bail)—

(i) before a decision is taken on whether the individual should be charged with an offence, or

(ii) after being charged with an offence.

(2) Before the individual is released an immigration officer or a constable may give the individual a notice requiring the production of a nationality document not later than 72 hours after the individual is released.

(3) A notice may be given under subsection (2) only if the immigration officer or constable giving it suspects that the individual may not be a British citizen.

(4) A notice under subsection (2) must be given in writing.

(5) The notice must include statements that—

(a) the individual to whom it is given must produce the nationality document not later than 72 hours after the individual is released, and

(b) an offence may be committed if an individual fails to comply with a notice given under this section.

(6) The notice must also set out—

(a) the person to whom the document must be produced, and

(b) the means by which the document must be produced.

(7) In this section, and in sections 46B and 46C—

"nationality document" means a passport relating to the individual or, if there is no passport relating to the individual, one or more documents that enable the individual's nationality or citizenship to be established;

"passport" means—

(a) a United Kingdom passport (within the meaning of the Immigration Act 1971),

(b) a passport issued by or on behalf of the authorities of a country or territory outside the United Kingdom, or by or on behalf of an international organisation, or

(c) a document that can be used (in some or all circumstances) instead of a passport.

46B Retention of nationality document etc

(1) An immigration officer or constable may retain a nationality document produced in response to a notice under section 46A(2) while the immigration officer or constable suspects that—

(a) the individual to whom the document relates may be liable to removal from the United Kingdom in accordance with a provision of the Immigration Acts, and

(b) retention of the document may facilitate the individual's removal.

(2) Section 28I of the Immigration Act 1971 (seized material: access and copying) has effect in relation to a nationality document produced by an individual in response to a notice under section 46A(2) and retained by an immigration officer as if the nationality document had been seized when the individual had custody or control of it.

(3) Section 21 of the Police and Criminal Evidence Act 1984 or Article 23 of the Police and Criminal Evidence (Northern Ireland) Order 1989 (S.I. 1989/1341 (N.I. 12)) (seized material: access and copying) has effect in relation to a nationality document produced by an individual in response to a notice under section 46A(2) and retained by a constable in England and Wales or Northern Ireland as if the nationality document had been seized when the individual had custody or control of it.

46C Offence of failing to produce nationality document

(1) A person commits an offence if, without reasonable excuse, the person fails to comply with a notice given in accordance with section 46A.

(2) The fact that a person deliberately destroyed or disposed of a nationality document is not a reasonable excuse for the purposes of subsection (1) unless the destruction or disposal was—

(a) for a reasonable cause, or

(b) beyond the control of the person charged with the offence.

(3) In subsection (2)(a) "reasonable cause" does not include the purpose of—

(a) delaying the handling or resolution of a claim or application or the taking of a decision,

(b) increasing the chances of success of a claim or application, or

(c) complying with instructions given by a person who offers advice about, or facilitates, immigration into the United Kingdom, unless in the circumstances of the case it is unreasonable to expect non-compliance with the instructions or advice.

(4) A person who is guilty of an offence under subsection (1) is liable—

(a) on summary conviction in England and Wales, to either or both of the following—

(i) imprisonment for a term not exceeding 51 weeks (or 6 months if the offence was committed before the commencement of section 281(5) of the Criminal Justice Act 2003);

(ii) a fine;

(b) on summary conviction in Scotland, to either or both of the following—

(i) imprisonment for a term not exceeding 12 months;

(ii) a fine not exceeding level 5 on the standard scale;

(c) on summary conviction in Northern Ireland, to either or both of the following—

(i) imprisonment for a term not exceeding 6 months;

(ii) a fine not exceeding level 5 on the standard scale."

161 Pilot schemes

(1) The Secretary of State may by regulations made by statutory instrument provide for any provision of sections 159 and 160 to come into force for a period of time to be specified in or under the regulations for the purpose of assessing the effectiveness of the provision.

(2) Regulations under subsection (1) may make different provision for different purposes or different areas.

(3) More than one set of regulations may be made under subsection (1).

(4) Provision included in regulations under subsection (1) does not affect the provision that may be included in relation to sections 159 and 160 in regulations under section 183 (commencement).

162 Requirement to give information in criminal proceedings

In the Courts Act 2003, after section 86 (alteration of place fixed for Crown Court trial) insert—

"86A Requirement to give information in criminal proceedings

(1) A person who is a defendant in proceedings in a criminal court must provide his or her name, date of birth and nationality if required to do so at any stage of proceedings by the court.

(2) Criminal Procedure Rules must specify the stages of proceedings at which requirements are to be imposed by virtue of subsection (1) (and may specify other stages of proceedings when such requirements may be imposed).

(3) A person commits an offence if, without reasonable excuse, the person fails to comply with a requirement imposed by virtue of subsection (1), whether by providing false or incomplete information or by providing no information.

(4) Information provided by a person in response to a requirement imposed by virtue of subsection (1) is not admissible in evidence in criminal proceedings against that person other than proceedings for an offence under this section.

(5) A person guilty of an offence under subsection (3) is liable on summary conviction to either or both of the following—

(a) imprisonment for a term not exceeding 51 weeks (or 6 months if the offence was committed before the commencement of section 281(5) of the Criminal Justice Act 2003), or

(b) a fine.

(6) The criminal court before which a person is required to provide his or her name, date of birth and nationality may deal with any suspected offence under subsection (3) at the same time as dealing with the offence for which the person was already before the court.

(7) In this section a "criminal court" is, when dealing with any criminal cause or matter—

(a) the Crown Court;

(b) a magistrates' court."

Seizure etc of travel documents

163 Powers to seize etc invalid travel documents

(1) Schedule 8 to the Anti-social Behaviour, Crime and Policing Act 2014 (Powers to seize invalid passports etc) is amended as follows.

(2) For the italic heading before paragraph 3 substitute "Powers of search and seizure etc: places other than ports".

(3) In paragraph 3, for sub-paragraph (1) substitute—

"(1) An examining officer who is a constable or a person appointed as an immigration officer under paragraph 1 of Schedule 2 to the Immigration Act 1971 may exercise any of the powers under this paragraph, at a place that is not a port, if the examining officer reasonably believes that a person is in possession of a cancelled UK passport or an invalid non-UK travel document."

(4) In that paragraph, in sub-paragraph (2)—

(a) for "This paragraph applies to a passport" substitute "A passport is "a cancelled UK passport";

(b) at the end of paragraph (a) insert "and";

(c) omit the "and" at the end of paragraph (b);

(d) omit paragraph (c).

(5) After sub-paragraph (2) insert—

"(2A) An invalid travel document is "an invalid non-UK travel document" if it is, or appears to be, a passport or other document which has been issued by or for the government of a state other than the United Kingdom."

(6) In that paragraph—

(a) in sub-paragraph (3)—

(i) in paragraph (a), for "the constable" substitute "the examining officer";

(ii) in paragraph (b), for "the constable" substitute "the examining officer";

(iii) in paragraph (d), for "the constable believes" substitute "the examining officer reasonably believes";

(b) in sub-paragraph (4)—

(i) in paragraph (c), for "the constable believes" substitute "the examining officer reasonably believes";

(ii) in paragraph (d), for "the constable" substitute "the examining officer";

(c) in sub-paragraph (5)—

(i) in the opening words, for "A constable" substitute "An examining officer";

(ii) in sub-paragraph (b), for "the constable's behalf" substitute "the examining officer's behalf".

(7) After paragraph 3 insert—

"3A Powers of entry, search and seizure etc: constables

3A (1) A constable may exercise any of the powers under this paragraph in relation to any premises, other than premises forming part of a port, if the constable reasonably believes that a cancelled UK passport or an invalid non-UK travel document is on the premises (whether or not in the possession of a person who is also on the premises).

(2) The powers are—

(a) to enter the premises;

(b) to search the premises for travel documents and to take possession of any that the constable finds;

(c) to inspect any travel document taken and to retain it while its validity is checked;

(d) (subject to paragraph 4) to retain any travel document taken that the constable reasonably believes to be invalid.

(3) A constable—

(a) may if necessary use reasonable force for the purpose of exercising a power under this paragraph;

(b) may authorise a person to carry out on the constable's behalf a search under this paragraph.

(4) This paragraph does not affect any power of a constable under paragraph 3(3), (4)(a) to (c) or (5) in relation to a person on any premises entered under sub-paragraph (2)(a)."

(8) In paragraph 4 (retention or return of documents seized)—

(a) in sub-paragraph (1), for "2(2)(c) or 3(3)(c)" substitute "2(2)(c), 3(3)(c) or 3A(2)(c)";

(b) after sub-paragraph (2) insert—

"(2A) If it is established that a travel document taken from any premises under paragraph 3A—

(a) is valid, or

(b) is invalid only because it has expired,

it must be returned to the person to whom it was issued straight away.";

(c) after sub-paragraph (3) insert—

"(3A) A travel document taken from premises under paragraph 3A must be returned to the person to whom it was issued before the end of the period of 7 days beginning with the day on which it was taken, unless during that period it is established that the document is invalid for some reason other than expiry.";

(d) in sub-paragraph (4), for "(2)(b) or (3)" substitute "(2)(b), (2A), (3) or (3A)";

(e) in that sub-paragraph, after "from whom he or she took the document" insert "or (as the case may be) to whom it was issued";

(f) in sub-paragraph (5), for "(2) or (3)" substitute "(2), (2A), (3) or (3A)".

(9) In paragraph 5 (offences), in sub-paragraph (2), for "a search under paragraph 2 or 3" substitute "the exercise of a power of search under paragraph 2, 3 or 3A, or the exercise of a power of entry under paragraph 3A,".

(10) In paragraph 6 (power of arrest), for "2" substitute "2 or 3".

Pardons for certain abolished offences etc

164 Posthumous pardons for convictions etc of certain abolished offences: England and Wales

(1) A person who has been convicted of, or cautioned for, an offence specified in subsection (3) and who has died before this section comes into force is pardoned for the offence if two conditions are met.

(2) Those conditions are that—

(a) the other person involved in the conduct constituting the offence consented to it and was aged 16 or over, and

(b) any such conduct at the time this section comes into force would not be an offence under section 71 of the Sexual Offences Act 2003 (sexual activity in a public lavatory).

(3) The offences to which subsection (1) applies are—

(a) an offence under section 12 of the Sexual Offences Act 1956 (buggery) or under section 13 of that Act (gross indecency between men);

(b) an offence under any of the following provisions (which made provision similar to section 12 of the Sexual Offences Act 1956)—

(i) 25 Hen. 8 c. 6 (1533) (an Act for the punishment of the vice of buggery);

(ii) 2 & 3 Edw. 6 c. 29 (1548) (an Act against sodomy);

(iii) 5 Eliz. 1 c. 17 (1562) (an Act for the punishment of the vice of buggery);

(iv) section 15 of 9 Geo. 4 c. 31 (1828) (an Act for consolidating and amending the law relating to offences against the person);

(v) section 61 of the Offences against the Person Act 1861;

(c) an offence under section 11 of the Criminal Law Amendment Act 1885 (which made provision similar to section 13 of the Sexual Offences Act 1956).

(4) The list of offences in subsection (3) is to be read as if it also included the corresponding service offences and, for that purpose, the corresponding service offences are—

(a) an offence under an enactment set out in subsection (5) which is such an offence by virtue of any of the enactments mentioned in subsection (3);

(b) an offence under section 32 of 13 Chas. 2 c. 9 (1661) (An Act for the regulation and better government of the navy);

(c) an offence under section 29 of 22 Geo. 2 c. 33 (1749) (An Act for amending and consolidating the laws relating to the navy);

(d) an offence of sodomy mentioned in, and punishable under, section 38 of the Naval Discipline Act 1860, section 38 of the Naval Discipline Act 1861, section 41 of the Naval Discipline Act 1864 or section 45 of the Naval Discipline Act 1866.

(5) The enactments referred to in subsection (4)(a) are—

(a) section 45 of the Naval Discipline Act 1866;

(b) section 41 of the Army Act 1881;

(c) section 41 of the Air Force Act 1917;

(d) section 70 of the Army Act 1955;

(e) section 70 of the Air Force Act 1955;

(f) section 42 of the Naval Discipline Act 1957.

(6) The reference in subsection (2)(b) to an offence under section 71 of the Sexual Offences Act 2003 is to be read as including a reference to an offence under section 42 of the Armed Forces Act 2006 which is such an offence by virtue of section 71 of that Act of 2003.

(7) Subject to subsection (8), the following provisions of section 101 of the Protection of Freedoms Act 2012 apply for the purposes of this section and section 167(1) (so far as relating to this section) as they apply for the purposes of Chapter 4 of Part 5 of that Act—

(a) in subsection (1), the definitions of "caution", "conviction", and "sentence" (and the related definition of "service disciplinary proceedings");
(b) subsections (2) and (5) to (7).

(8) The definition of "service disciplinary proceedings" in section 101(1) of the 2012 Act applies in accordance with subsection (7) with the modification that it also includes any proceedings (whether in England and Wales or elsewhere) under—
(a) 13 Chas. 2 c. 9 (1661) (An Act for the regulation and better government of the navy),
(b) 22 Geo. 2 c. 33 (1749) (An Act for amending and consolidating the laws relating to the navy), or
(c) the Naval Discipline Act 1860, the Naval Discipline Act 1861 or the Naval Discipline Act 1864.

(9) Except in relation to service disciplinary proceedings, this section applies only in relation to persons convicted or cautioned in England and Wales.

165 Other pardons for convictions etc of certain abolished offences: England and Wales

(1) This section applies to a person who has been convicted of, or cautioned for, an offence mentioned in section 92(1) of the Protection of Freedoms Act 2012 and who is living at the time this section comes into force.

(2) If, at the time this section comes into force, the person's conviction or caution has become a disregarded conviction or caution under Chapter 4 of Part 5 of the Protection of Freedoms Act 2012, the person is pardoned for the offence.

(3) If, at any time after this section comes into force, the person's conviction or caution becomes a disregarded conviction or caution under Chapter 4 of Part 5 of the Protection of Freedoms Act 2012, the person is also pardoned for the offence at that time.

(4) Expressions used in this section or section 167(1) (so far as relating to this section) and in Chapter 4 of Part 5 of the Protection of Freedoms Act 2012 have the same meaning in this section or (as the case may be) section 167(1) as in that Chapter (see section 101 of that Act).

166 Power to provide for disregards and pardons for additional abolished offences: England and Wales

(1) The Secretary of State may by regulations made by statutory instrument amend section 92 of the Protection of Freedoms Act 2012 (power of Secretary of State to disregard convictions or cautions) so as to add further offences to the list of offences specified in subsection (1) of that section.

(2) An offence may be added to that list only if—
(a) it was an offence under the law of England and Wales,
(b) it has been repealed or, in the case of an offence at common law, abolished, and
(c) either—
(i) the offence expressly regulated homosexual activity, or
(ii) although the offence did not expressly regulate homosexual activity, it appears to the Secretary of State that those responsible for

investigating occurrences of the offence targeted occurrences involving, or connected with, homosexual activity.

(3) Regulations under subsection (1) adding an offence may also amend section 92 so as to provide that, in relation to the offence, condition A is that it appears to the Secretary of State that matters specified in the amendment apply (in substitution for the matters specified in subsection (3)(a) and (b) of that section).

(4) Regulations under subsection (1) may make consequential amendments of Chapter 4 of Part 5 of the 2012 Act.

(5) Regulations under subsection (1) adding an offence must also provide for any person who has been convicted of, or cautioned for, the offence to be pardoned where—

(a) the person has died before the regulations come into force or the person dies during the period of 6 months beginning with the day on which they come into force, and

(b) the conditions specified in the regulations are met.

(6) Those conditions must correspond to the matters that are specified in condition A in section 92 of the 2012 Act as it applies in relation to the offence (that is, the matters which must appear to the Secretary of State to apply in order for condition A to be met).

(7) Subsection (5)(a) does not apply in relation to a person who dies during the period of 6 months if, before the person's death, the person's conviction of, or caution for, the offence becomes a disregarded conviction or caution under Chapter 4 of Part 5 of the 2012 Act (and, accordingly, the person is pardoned for the offence before death under section 165(3) of this Act).

(8) The regulations must make provision which has a comparable effect in relation to the pardons provided for by the regulations and the offences to which those pardons relate as section 164(4) to (9) of this Act has in relation to the pardons provided for by section 164(1) to (3) and the offences to which they relate.

(9) A statutory instrument containing regulations under this section may not be made unless a draft of the instrument has been laid before, and approved by a resolution of, each House of Parliament.

(10) In this section, "caution", "conviction", "disregarded caution" and "disregarded conviction" have the same meaning as in Chapter 4 of Part 5 of the 2012 Act (see section 101 of that Act).

167 Sections 164 to 166: supplementary

(1) A pardon under section 164 or 165, or under regulations under section 166, does not—

(a) affect any conviction, caution or sentence, or

(b) give rise to any right, entitlement or liability.

(2) Nothing in this section or in sections 164 to 166 or regulations under section 166 affects the prerogative of mercy.

168 Disregarding certain convictions etc for abolished offences: Northern Ireland

(1) After Chapter 4 of Part 5 of the Protection of Freedoms Act 2012 (disregarding certain convictions for buggery etc) insert—

"CHAPTER 5

DISREGARDING CERTAIN CONVICTIONS FOR BUGGERY ETC: NORTHERN IRELAND

General

101A Power of Department of Justice to disregard certain convictions or cautions

(1) A person who has in Northern Ireland been convicted of, or cautioned for, an offence under—

(a) Article 19 of the Criminal Justice (Northern Ireland) Order 2003 (S.I. 2003/1247 (N.I. 13)) (buggery),

(b) Article 7 of the Homosexual Offences (Northern Ireland) Order 1982 (S.I. 1982/1536 (N.I. 19)) (procuring others to commit homosexual acts),

(c) section 61 of the Offences against the Person Act 1861 (buggery), or

(d) section 11 of the Criminal Law Amendment Act 1885 (indecent acts between men),

may apply to the Department of Justice in Northern Ireland for the conviction or caution to become a disregarded conviction or caution.

(2) A conviction or caution becomes a disregarded conviction or caution when conditions A and B are met.

(3) In relation to an offence under Article 7 of the Homosexual Offences (Northern Ireland) Order 1982, Condition A is that the Department of Justice in Northern Ireland decides that it appears that—

(a) the conduct procured was conduct involving persons who consented to it and were aged 17 or over (whether or not that conduct occurred), and

(b) the conduct procured would not now be an offence under Article 75 of the Sexual Offences (Northern Ireland) Order 2008 (S.I. 2008/1769 (N.I. 2)) (sexual activity in a public lavatory).

(4) In relation to any other offence mentioned in subsection (1), Condition A is that the Department of Justice in Northern Ireland decides that it appears that—

(a) the other person involved in the conduct constituting the offence consented to it and was aged 17 or over, and

(b) any such conduct now would not be an offence under Article 75 of the Sexual Offences (Northern Ireland) Order 2008 (S.I. 2008/1769 (N.I. 2)).

(5) Condition B is that—

(a) the Department of Justice in Northern Ireland has given notice of the decision to the applicant under section 101C(4)(b), and

(b) the period of 14 days beginning with the day on which the notice was given has ended.

(6) Sections 101D to 101G explain the effect of a conviction or caution becoming a disregarded conviction or caution.

101B Applications to the Department of Justice

(1) An application under section 101A must be in writing.

(2) It must state—

(a) the name, address and date of birth of the applicant,

(b) the name and address of the applicant at the time of the conviction or caution,

(c) so far as known to the applicant, the time when and the place where the conviction was made or the caution given and, for a conviction, the case number, and

(d) such other information as the Department of Justice in Northern Ireland may require.

(3) It may include representations by the applicant or written evidence about the matters mentioned in condition A in section 101A.

101C Procedure for decisions by the Department of Justice

(1) In considering whether to make a decision of the kind mentioned in condition A in section 101A, the Department of Justice in Northern Ireland must, in particular, consider—

(a) any representations or evidence included in the application, and

(b) any available record of the investigation of the offence and of any proceedings relating to it that the Department of Justice in Northern Ireland considers to be relevant.

(2) The Department of Justice in Northern Ireland may not hold an oral hearing for the purpose of deciding whether to make a decision of the kind mentioned in condition A in section 101A.

(3) Subsection (4) applies if the Department of Justice in Northern Ireland—

(a) decides that it appears as mentioned in condition A in section 101A, or

(b) makes a different decision in relation to the matters mentioned in that condition.

(4) The Department of Justice in Northern Ireland must—

(a) record the decision in writing, and

(b) give notice of it to the applicant.

Effect of disregard

101D Effect of disregard on police and other records

(1) The Department of Justice in Northern Ireland must by notice direct the relevant data controller to delete details, contained in relevant official records, of a disregarded conviction or caution.

(2) A notice under subsection (1) may be given at any time after condition A in section 101A is met but no deletion may have effect before condition B in that section is met.

(3) Subject to that, the relevant data controller must delete the details as soon as reasonably practicable.

(4) Having done so, the relevant data controller must give notice to the person who has the disregarded conviction or caution that the details of it have been deleted.

(5) In this section—

"delete", in relation to such relevant official records as may be prescribed, means record with the details of the conviction or caution concerned—

(a) the fact that it is a disregarded conviction or caution, and

(b) the effect of it being such a conviction or caution,

"the general names database" means the names database held by the Secretary of State for the use of constables,

"the Northern Ireland names database" means the names database maintained by the Department of Justice in Northern Ireland for the purpose of recording convictions and cautions,

"official records" means records containing information about persons convicted of, or cautioned for, offences and kept by any court, police force, government department or local or other public authority in Northern Ireland for the purposes of its functions,

"prescribed" means prescribed by order of the Department of Justice in Northern Ireland,

"relevant data controller" means—

(a) in relation to the general names database or the Northern Ireland names database, the Chief Constable of the Police Service of Northern Ireland,

(b) in relation to other relevant official records, such persons as may be prescribed,

"relevant official records" means—

(a) the general names database,

(b) the Northern Ireland names database, and

(c) such other official records as may be prescribed.

(6) An order under this section may make different provision for different purposes.

(7) Any power to make an order under this section is exercisable by statutory rule for the purposes of the Statutory Rules (Northern Ireland) Order 1979 (S.I. 1979/1573 (N.I. 12)).

(8) A statutory rule containing an order under this section is subject to negative resolution (within the meaning of section 41(6) of the Interpretation Act (Northern Ireland) 1954 (c. 33 (N.I))).

101E Effect of disregard for disclosure and other purposes

(1) A person who has a disregarded conviction or caution is to be treated for all purposes in law as if the person has not—

(a) committed the offence,

(b) been charged with, or prosecuted for, the offence,

(c) been convicted of the offence,

(d) been sentenced for the offence, or

(e) been cautioned for the offence.

(2) In particular—

(a) no evidence is to be admissible in any proceedings before a judicial authority exercising its jurisdiction or functions in Northern Ireland to prove that the person has done, or undergone, anything within subsection (1)(a) to (e), and

(b) the person is not, in any such proceedings, to be asked (and, if asked, is not to be required to answer) any question relating to the person's past which cannot be answered without acknowledging or referring to the conviction or caution or any circumstances ancillary to it.

(3) Where a question is put to a person, other than in such proceedings, seeking information with respect to the previous convictions, cautions, offences, conduct or circumstances of any person—

(a) the question is to be treated as not relating to any disregarded conviction or caution, or any circumstances ancillary to it (and the answer to the question may be framed accordingly), and

(b) the person questioned is not to be subjected to any liability or otherwise prejudiced in law by reason of any failure to acknowledge or disclose that conviction or caution or any circumstances ancillary to it in answering the question.

(4) Any obligation imposed on any person by any enactment or rule of law or by the provisions of any agreement or arrangement to disclose any matters to any other person is not to extend to requiring the disclosure of a disregarded conviction or caution or any circumstances ancillary to it.

(5) A disregarded conviction or caution, or any circumstances ancillary to it, is not a proper ground for—

(a) dismissing or excluding a person from any office, profession, occupation or employment, or

(b) prejudicing the person in any way in any office, profession, occupation or employment.

(6) This section is subject to section 101F but otherwise applies despite any enactment or rule of law to the contrary.

(7) See also section 101G (meaning of "proceedings before a judicial authority" and "circumstances ancillary to a conviction or caution").

101F Saving for Royal pardons etc

Nothing in section 101E affects any right of Her Majesty, by virtue of Her Royal prerogative or otherwise, to grant a free pardon, to quash any conviction or sentence, or to commute any sentence.

101G Section 101E: supplementary

(1) In section 101E, "proceedings before a judicial authority" includes (in addition to proceedings before any of the ordinary courts of law) proceedings before any tribunal, body or person having power—

- (a) by virtue of any enactment, law, custom or practice,
- (b) under the rules governing any association, institution, profession, occupation or employment, or
- (c) under any provision of an agreement providing for arbitration with respect to questions arising under that agreement,

to determine any question affecting the rights, privileges, obligations or liabilities of any person, or to receive evidence affecting the determination of any such question.

(2) For the purposes of section 101E, circumstances ancillary to a conviction are any circumstances of—

- (a) the offence which was the subject of the conviction;
- (b) the conduct constituting the offence;
- (c) any process or proceedings preliminary to the conviction;
- (d) any sentence imposed in respect of the conviction;
- (e) any proceedings (whether by appeal or otherwise) for reviewing the conviction or any such sentence;
- (f) anything done in pursuance of, or undergone in compliance with, any such sentence.

(3) For the purposes of section 101E, circumstances ancillary to a caution are any circumstances of—

- (a) the offence which was the subject of the caution;
- (b) the conduct constituting the offence;
- (c) any process preliminary to the caution (including consideration by any person of how to deal with the offence and the procedure for giving the caution);
- (d) any proceedings for the offence which take place before the caution is given;
- (e) anything which happens after the caution is given for the purposes of bringing any such proceedings to an end;
- (f) any judicial review proceedings relating to the caution.

Appeals and other supplementary provision

101H Appeal against refusal to disregard convictions or caution

(1) The applicant may appeal to the High Court in Northern Ireland if—

(a) the Department of Justice in Northern Ireland makes a decision of the kind mentioned in section 101C(3)(b), and

(b) the High Court gives permission for an appeal against the decision.

(2) On such an appeal, the High Court must make its decision only on the basis of the evidence that was available to the Department of Justice in Northern Ireland.

(3) If the High Court decides that it appears as mentioned in condition A in section 101A, it must make an order to that effect.

(4) Otherwise, it must dismiss the appeal.

(5) A conviction or caution to which an order under subsection (3) relates becomes a disregarded conviction or caution when the period of 14 days beginning with the day on which the order was made has ended.

(6) There is no appeal from a decision of the High Court under this section.

101I Advisers

(1) The Department of Justice in Northern Ireland may appoint persons to advise whether, in any case referred to them by the Department of Justice in Northern Ireland, the Department of Justice in Northern Ireland should decide as mentioned in condition A in section 101A.

(2) The Department of Justice in Northern Ireland may disclose to a person so appointed such information (including anything within section 101C(1)(a) or (b)) as the Department of Justice considers relevant to the provision of such advice.

(3) The Department of Justice in Northern Ireland may pay expenses and allowances to a person so appointed.

101J Interpretation: Chapter 5

(1) In this Chapter—

"caution" means a caution or a warning given to a person in Northern Ireland in respect of an offence which, at the time the caution or warning is given, that person has admitted,

"conviction" includes—

(a) a conviction in respect of which an order has been made discharging the person concerned absolutely or conditionally, and

(b) a finding in any criminal proceedings (including a finding linked with a finding of insanity) that a person has committed an offence or done the act or made the omission charged,

"disregarded caution" is a caution which has become a disregarded caution by virtue of this Chapter,

"disregarded conviction" is a conviction which has become a disregarded conviction by virtue of this Chapter,

"document" includes information recorded in any form and, in relation to information recorded otherwise than in legible form, references to its provision or production include providing or producing a copy of the information in legible form,

"information" includes documents,

"notice" means notice in writing,

"official records" has the meaning given by section 101D(5).

(2) Paragraph (a) of the definition of "conviction" applies despite Article 6 of the Criminal Justice (Northern Ireland) Order 1996 (S.I. 1996/3160 (N.I. 24)) (which deems a conviction of a person discharged not to be a conviction).

(3) In this Chapter, a reference to an offence includes—

(a) a reference to an attempt, conspiracy or incitement to commit that offence, and

(b) a reference to aiding, abetting, counselling or procuring the commission of that offence.

(4) In the case of an attempt, conspiracy or incitement, the references in this Chapter to the conduct constituting the offence are references to the conduct to which the attempt, conspiracy or incitement related (whether or not that conduct occurred).

(5) For the purposes of subsections (3) and (4) an attempt to commit an offence includes conduct which—

(a) consisted of frequenting with intent to commit the offence any river, canal, street, highway, place of public resort or other location mentioned in section 4 of the Vagrancy Act 1824 (as it then had effect) in connection with frequenting by suspected persons or reputed thiefs, and

(b) was itself an offence under that section."

(2) In Article 2 of the Rehabilitation of Offenders (Northern Ireland) Order 1978 (S.I. 1978/1908 (N.I. 27)) (interpretation), after paragraph (3) insert—

"(3A) This Order does not apply to any disregarded conviction or caution within the meaning of Chapter 5 of Part 5 of the Protection of Freedoms Act 2012.

(3B) Accordingly, references in this Order to a conviction or caution do not include references to any such disregarded conviction or caution."

(3) In the heading of Chapter 4 of Part 5 of the Protection of Freedoms Act 2012, at the end insert ": England and Wales".

(4) In section 92 of that Act, after subsection (5) insert—

"(6) Except in relation to service disciplinary proceedings, this section applies only in relation to persons convicted or cautioned in England and Wales."

169 Posthumous pardons for convictions etc of certain abolished offences: Northern Ireland

(1) A person who has in Northern Ireland been convicted of, or cautioned for, an offence specified in subsection (2) and who has died before this section comes into force is pardoned for the offence if the conditions that apply under this section in relation to the offence are met.

(2) The offences to which subsection (1) applies are—

(a) an offence under Article 19 of the Criminal Justice (Northern Ireland) Order 2003 (S.I. 2003/1247 (N.I. 13)) (buggery);

(b) an offence under Article 7 of the Homosexual Offences (Northern Ireland) Order 1982 (S.I. 1982/1536 (N.I. 19)) (procuring others to commit homosexual acts);

(c) an offence under any of the following earlier provisions—

(i) 10 Chas. 1 sess. 2 c. 20 (1634) (an Act for the punishment of the vice of buggery);

(ii) section 18 of 10 Geo. 4 c. 34 (1829) (an Act for consolidating and amending the statutes in Ireland relating to offences against the person) (buggery);

(iii) section 61 of the Offences against the Person Act 1861 (buggery);

(iv) section 11 of the Criminal Law Amendment Act 1885 (gross indecency between men).

(3) In relation to an offence under Article 7 of the Homosexual Offences (Northern Ireland) Order 1982, the conditions that apply are that—

(a) the conduct procured was conduct involving persons who consented to it and were aged 17 or over (whether or not that conduct occurred), and

(b) the conduct procured would not now be an offence under Article 75 of the Sexual Offences (Northern Ireland) Order 2008 (S.I. 2008/1769 (N.I. 2)) (sexual activity in a public lavatory).

(4) In relation to any other offence mentioned in subsection (2), the conditions that apply are that—

(a) the other person involved in the conduct constituting the offence consented to it and was aged 17 or over, and

(b) any such conduct at the time this section comes into force would not be an offence under Article 75 of the Sexual Offences (Northern Ireland) Order 2008 (S.I. 2008/1769 (N.I. 2)) (sexual activity in a public lavatory).

(5) The following provisions of section 101J of the Protection of Freedoms Act 2012 apply for the purposes of this section and section 172(1) (so far as relating to this section) as they apply for the purposes of Chapter 5 of Part 5 of that Act—

(a) in subsection (1), the definitions of "caution" and "conviction";

(b) subsections (2) to (5).

170 Other pardons for convictions etc of certain abolished offences: Northern Ireland

(1) This section applies to a person who has in Northern Ireland been convicted of, or cautioned for, an offence mentioned in section 101A(1) of the Protection of Freedoms Act 2012 and who is living at the time this section comes into force.

(2) If, at any time after this section comes into force, the person's conviction or caution becomes a disregarded conviction or caution under Chapter 5 of Part 5 of the Protection of Freedoms Act 2012, the person is also pardoned for the offence at that time.

(3) Expressions used in this section or section 172(1) (so far as relating to this section) and in Chapter 5 of Part 5 of the Protection of Freedoms Act 2012 have the same meaning in this section or (as the case may be) section 172(1) as in that Chapter (see section 101J of that Act).

171 Power to provide for disregards and pardons for additional abolished offences: Northern Ireland

(1) The Department of Justice in Northern Ireland may by regulations amend section 101A of the Protection of Freedoms Act 2012 (power of Department of Justice to disregard convictions or cautions) so as to add further offences to the list of offences specified in subsection (1) of that section.

(2) An offence may be added to that list only if—

(a) it was an offence under the law of Northern Ireland (or, in the case of an offence that applied before Northern Ireland became a separate legal jurisdiction, an offence under the law of Ireland),

(b) it has been repealed or, in the case of an offence at common law, abolished, and

(c) either—

(i) the offence expressly regulated homosexual activity, or

(ii) although the offence did not expressly regulate homosexual activity, it appears to the Department of Justice that those responsible for investigating occurrences of the offence targeted occurrences involving, or connected with, homosexual activity.

(3) Regulations under subsection (1) adding an offence may also amend section 101A so as to provide that, in relation to the offence, condition A is that it appears to the Department of Justice that matters specified in the amendment apply (in substitution for the matters specified in subsection (4)(a) and (b) of that section).

(4) Regulations under subsection (1) may make consequential amendments of Chapter 5 of Part 5 of the 2012 Act.

(5) Regulations under subsection (1) adding an offence must also provide for any person who has been convicted of, or cautioned for, the offence to be pardoned where—

(a) the person has died before the regulations come into force or the person dies during the period of 6 months beginning with the day on which they come into force, and

(b) the conditions specified in the regulations are met.

(6) Those conditions must correspond to the matters that are specified in condition A in section 101A of the 2012 Act as it applies in relation to the offence (that is, the matters which must appear to the Department of Justice to apply in order for condition A to be met).

(7) Subsection (5)(a) does not apply in relation to a person who dies during the period of 6 months if, before the person's death, the person's conviction of, or caution for, the offence becomes a disregarded conviction or caution under Chapter 5 of Part 5 of the 2012 Act (and, accordingly, the person is pardoned for the offence before death under section 170(2) of this Act).

(8) The regulations must make provision which has a comparable effect in relation to the pardons provided for by the regulations and the offences to which those pardons

relate as section 169(5) of this Act has in relation to the pardons provided for by section 169(1) to (4) and the offences to which they relate.

(9) The power to make regulations under subsection (1) is exercisable by statutory rule for the purposes of the Statutory Rules (Northern Ireland) Order 1979 (S.I. 1979/1573) (N.I. 12)).

(10) Regulations under this section may not be made unless a draft of the regulations has been laid before, and approved by a resolution of, the Northern Ireland Assembly.

(11) In this section, "caution", "conviction", "disregarded caution" and "disregarded conviction" have the same meaning as in Chapter 5 of Part 5 of the 2012 Act (see section 101J of that Act).

172 Sections 169 to 171: supplementary

(1) A pardon under section 169 or 170, or under regulations under section 171, does not—

(a) affect any conviction, caution or sentence, or

(b) give rise to any right, entitlement or liability.

(2) Nothing in this section or in sections 169 to 171 or regulations under section 171 affects the prerogative of mercy.

Forced marriage: anonymity for victims

173 Anonymity of victims of forced marriage: England and Wales

(1) In Part 10 of the Anti-social Behaviour, Crime and Policing Act 2014 (forced marriage), after section 122 insert—

"122A Anonymity of victims of forced marriage: England and Wales

Schedule 6A (anonymity of victims of forced marriage) has effect."

(2) Insert, as Schedule 6A to that Act, the following Schedule—

"SCHEDULE 6A — Section 122A

ANONYMITY OF VICTIMS OF FORCED MARRIAGE

1 Prohibition on the identification of victims in publications

1 (1) This paragraph applies where an allegation has been made that an offence of forced marriage has been committed against a person.

(2) No matter likely to lead members of the public to identify the person, as the person against whom the offence is alleged to have been committed, may be included in any publication during the person's lifetime.

(3) In any criminal proceedings before a court, the court may direct that the restriction imposed by sub-paragraph (2) is not to apply (whether at all or to the extent specified in the direction) if the court is satisfied that either of the following conditions is met.

(4) The first condition is that the conduct of a person's defence at a trial of an offence of forced marriage would be substantially prejudiced if the direction were not given.

(5) The second condition is that—

(a) the effect of sub-paragraph (2) is to impose a substantial and unreasonable restriction on the reporting of the proceedings, and

(b) it is in the public interest to remove or relax the restriction.

(6) A direction under sub-paragraph (3) does not affect the operation of sub-paragraph (2) at any time before the direction is given.

(7) In this paragraph, "the court" means a magistrates' court or the Crown Court.

2 Penalty for breaching prohibition imposed by paragraph 1(2)

2 (1) If anything is included in a publication in contravention of the prohibition imposed by paragraph 1(2), each of the persons responsible for the publication is guilty of an offence.

(2) A person guilty of an offence under this paragraph is liable, on summary conviction, to a fine.

(3) The persons responsible for a publication are as follows—

Type of publication	*Persons responsible*
Newspaper or other periodical	Any person who is a proprietor, editor or publisher of the newspaper or periodical.
Relevant programme	Any person who— (a) is a body corporate engaged in providing the programme service in which the programme is included, or (b) has functions in relation to the programme corresponding to those of an editor of a newspaper.
Any other kind of publication	Any person who publishes the publication.

(4) If an offence under this paragraph is proved to have been committed with the consent or connivance of, or to be attributable to any neglect on the part of—

(a) a senior officer of a body corporate, or

(b) a person purporting to act in such a capacity,

the senior officer or person (as well as the body corporate) is guilty of the offence and liable to be proceeded against and punished accordingly.

(5) "Senior officer", in relation to a body corporate, means a director, manager, secretary or other similar officer of the body corporate; and for this purpose "director", in relation to a body corporate whose affairs are managed by its members, means a member of the body corporate.

(6) Proceedings for an offence under this paragraph may not be instituted except by, or with the consent of, the Attorney General.

3 Offence under paragraph 2: defences

3 (1) This paragraph applies where a person ("the defendant") is charged with an offence under paragraph 2 as a result of the inclusion of any matter in a publication.

(2) It is a defence for the defendant to prove that, at the time of the alleged offence, the defendant was not aware, and did not suspect or have reason to suspect, that—

(a) the publication included the matter in question, or

(b) the allegation in question had been made.

(3) It is a defence for the defendant to prove that the publication in which the matter appeared was one in respect of which the victim had given written consent to the appearance of matter of that description.

(4) The defence in sub-paragraph (3) is not available if—

(a) the victim was under the age of 16 at the time when his or her consent was given, or

(b) a person interfered unreasonably with the peace and comfort of the victim with a view to obtaining his or her consent.

(5) In this paragraph, "the victim" means the person against whom the offence of forced marriage in question is alleged to have been committed.

4 Special rules for providers of information society services

4 (1) Paragraph 2 applies to a domestic service provider who, in the course of providing information society services, publishes prohibited matter in an EEA state other than the United Kingdom (as well as to a person, of any description, who publishes prohibited matter in England and Wales).

(2) Proceedings for an offence under paragraph 2, as it applies to a domestic service provider by virtue of sub-paragraph (1), may be taken at any place in England and Wales.

(3) Nothing in this paragraph affects the operation of any of paragraphs 6 to 8.

5 (1) Proceedings for an offence under paragraph 2 may not be taken against a non-UK service provider in respect of anything done in the course of the provision of information society services unless the derogation condition is met.

(2) The derogation condition is that taking proceedings—

(a) is necessary for the purposes of the public interest objective,

(b) relates to an information society service that prejudices that objective or presents a serious and grave risk of prejudice to that objective, and

(c) is proportionate to that objective.

(3) "The public interest objective" means the pursuit of public policy.

6 (1) A service provider does not commit an offence under paragraph 2 by providing access to a communication network or by transmitting, in a communication network, information provided by a recipient of the service, if the service provider does not—

(a) initiate the transmission,

(b) select the recipient of the transmission, or

(c) select or modify the information contained in the transmission.

(2) For the purposes of sub-paragraph (1)—

(a) providing access to a communication network, and

(b) transmitting information in a communication network,

include the automatic, intermediate and transient storage of the information transmitted so far as the storage is solely for the purpose of carrying out the transmission in the network.

(3) Sub-paragraph (2) does not apply if the information is stored for longer than is reasonably necessary for the transmission.

7 (1) A service provider does not commit an offence under paragraph 2 by storing information provided by a recipient of the service for transmission in a communication network if the first and second conditions are met.

(2) The first condition is that the storage of the information—

(a) is automatic, intermediate and temporary, and

(b) is solely for the purpose of making more efficient the onward transmission of the information to other recipients of the service at their request.

(3) The second condition is that the service provider—

(a) does not modify the information,

(b) complies with any conditions attached to having access to the information, and

(c) if sub-paragraph (4) applies, promptly removes the information or disables access to it.

(4) This sub-paragraph applies if the service provider obtains actual knowledge that—

(a) the information at the initial source of the transmission has been removed from the network,

(b) access to it has been disabled, or

(c) a court or administrative authority has ordered the removal from the network of, or the disablement of access to, the information.

8 (1) A service provider does not commit an offence under paragraph 2 by storing information provided by a recipient of the service if—

(a) the service provider had no actual knowledge when the information was provided that it was, or contained, a prohibited publication, or

(b) on obtaining actual knowledge that the information was, or contained, a prohibited publication, the service provider promptly removed the information or disabled access to it.

(2) Sub-paragraph (1) does not apply if the recipient of the service is acting under the authority or control of the service provider.

9 Interpretation

9 (1) In this Schedule—

"domestic service provider" means a service provider established in England and Wales, Scotland or Northern Ireland;

"the E-Commerce Directive" means Directive 2000/31/EC of the European Parliament and of the Council of 8 June 2000 on certain legal aspects of information society services, in particular electronic commerce, in the Internal Market (Directive on electronic commerce);

"information society services"—

(a) has the meaning given in Article 2(a) of the E-Commerce Directive (which refers to Article 1(2) of Directive 98/34/EC of the European Parliament and of the Council of 22 June 1998 laying down a procedure for the provision of information in the field of technical standards and regulations), and

(b) is summarised in recital 17 of the E-Commerce Directive as covering "any service normally provided for remuneration, at a distance, by means of electronic equipment for the processing (including digital compression) and storage of data, and at the individual request of a recipient of a service";

"non-UK service provider" means a service provider established in an EEA state other than the United Kingdom;

"offence of forced marriage" means an offence under section 121;

"programme service" has the same meaning as in the Broadcasting Act 1990 (see section 201(1) of that Act);

"prohibited material" means any material the publication of which contravenes paragraph 1(2);

"publication" includes any speech, writing, relevant programme or other communication (in whatever form) which is addressed to, or is accessible by, the public at large or any section of the public;

"recipient", in relation to a service, means a person who, for professional ends or otherwise, uses an information society service, in particular for the purposes of seeking information or making it accessible;

"relevant programme" means a programme included in a programme service;

"service provider" means a person providing an information society service.

(2) For the purposes of the definition of "publication" in sub-paragraph (1)—

(a) an indictment or other document prepared for use in particular legal proceedings is not to be taken as coming within the definition;

(b) every relevant programme is to be taken as addressed to the public at large or to a section of the public.

(3) For the purposes of the definitions of "domestic service provider" and "non-UK service provider" in sub-paragraph (1)—

(a) a service provider is established in a particular part of the United Kingdom, or in a particular EEA state, if the service provider—

(i) effectively pursues an economic activity using a fixed establishment in that part of the United Kingdom, or that EEA state, for an indefinite period, and

(ii) is a national of an EEA state or a company or firm mentioned in Article 54 of the Treaty on the Functioning of the European Union;

(b) the presence or use in a particular place of equipment or other technical means of providing an information society service does not, of itself, constitute the establishment of a service provider;

(c) where it cannot be determined from which of a number of establishments a given information society service is provided, that service is to be regarded as provided from the establishment at the centre of the service provider's activities relating to that service."

174 Anonymity of victims of forced marriage: Northern Ireland

(1) After Part 4 of the Human Trafficking and Exploitation (Criminal Justice and Support for Victims) Act (Northern Ireland) 2015 (c.2 (N.I.)) insert—

"PART 4A

PROTECTION OF VICTIMS OF FORCED MARRIAGE

24A Anonymity of victims of forced marriage

Schedule 3A (anonymity of victims of forced marriage) has effect."

(2) Insert, as Schedule 3A to that Act, the following Schedule—

"SCHEDULE 3A — Section 24A

ANONYMITY OF VICTIMS OF FORCED MARRIAGE

1 Prohibition on the identification of victims in publications

1 (1) This paragraph applies where an allegation has been made that an offence of forced marriage has been committed against a person.

(2) No matter likely to lead members of the public to identify the person, as the person against whom the offence is alleged to have been committed, may be included in any publication during the person's lifetime.

(3) In any criminal proceedings before a court, the court may direct that the restriction imposed by sub-paragraph (2) is not to apply (whether at all or to the extent specified in the direction) if the court is satisfied that either of the following conditions is met.

(4) The first condition is that the conduct of a person's defence at a trial of an offence of forced marriage would be substantially prejudiced if the direction were not given.

(5) The second condition is that—

(a) the effect of sub-paragraph (2) is to impose a substantial and unreasonable restriction on the reporting of the proceedings, and

(b) it is in the public interest to remove or relax the restriction.

(6) A direction under sub-paragraph (3) does not affect the operation of sub-paragraph (2) at any time before the direction is given.

(7) In this paragraph, "the court" means a magistrates' court, a county court or the Crown Court.

2 Penalty for breaching prohibition imposed by paragraph 1(2)

2 (1) If anything is included in a publication in contravention of the prohibition imposed by paragraph 1(2), each of the persons responsible for the publication is guilty of an offence.

(2) A person guilty of an offence under this paragraph is liable, on summary conviction, to a fine not exceeding level 5 on the standard scale.

(3) The persons responsible for a publication are as follows—

Type of publication	*Persons responsible*
Newspaper or other periodical	Any person who is a proprietor, editor or publisher of the newspaper or periodical.
Relevant programme	Any person who— (a) is a body corporate engaged in providing the programme service in which the programme is included, or (b) has functions in relation to the programme corresponding to those of an editor of a newspaper.
Any other kind of publication	Any person who publishes the publication.

(4) Proceedings for an offence under this paragraph may not be instituted except by, or with the consent of, the Director of Public Prosecutions for Northern Ireland.

3 Offence under paragraph 2: defences

3 (1) This paragraph applies where a person ("the defendant") is charged with an offence under paragraph 2 as a result of the inclusion of any matter in a publication.

(2) It is a defence for the defendant to prove that, at the time of the alleged offence, the defendant was not aware, and did not suspect or have reason to suspect, that—

(a) the publication included the matter in question, or

(b) the allegation in question had been made.

(3) It is a defence for the defendant to prove that the publication in which the matter appeared was one in respect of which the victim had given written consent to the appearance of matter of that description.

(4) The defence in sub-paragraph (3) is not available if—

(a) the victim was under the age of 16 at the time when his or her consent was given, or

(b) a person interfered unreasonably with the peace and comfort of the victim with a view to obtaining his or her consent.

(5) In this paragraph, "the victim" means the person against whom the offence of forced marriage in question is alleged to have been committed.

4 Special rules for providers of information society services

4 (1) Paragraph 2 applies to a domestic service provider who, in the course of providing information society services, publishes prohibited matter in an EEA state other than the United Kingdom (as well as to a person, of any description, who publishes prohibited matter in Northern Ireland).

(2) Proceedings for an offence under paragraph 2, as it applies to a domestic service provider by virtue of sub-paragraph (1), may be taken at any place in Northern Ireland.

(3) Nothing in this paragraph affects the operation of any of paragraphs 6 to 8.

5 (1) Proceedings for an offence under paragraph 2 may not be taken against a non-UK service provider in respect of anything done in the course of the provision of information society services unless the derogation condition is met.

(2) The derogation condition is that taking proceedings—

(a) is necessary for the purposes of the public interest objective,

(b) relates to an information society service that prejudices that objective or presents a serious and grave risk of prejudice to that objective, and

(c) is proportionate to that objective.

(3) "The public interest objective" means the pursuit of public policy.

6 (1) A service provider does not commit an offence under paragraph 2 by providing access to a communication network or by transmitting, in

a communication network, information provided by a recipient of the service, if the service provider does not—

(a) initiate the transmission,

(b) select the recipient of the transmission, or

(c) select or modify the information contained in the transmission.

(2) For the purposes of sub-paragraph (1)—

(a) providing access to a communication network, and

(b) transmitting information in a communication network,

include the automatic, intermediate and transient storage of the information transmitted so far as the storage is solely for the purpose of carrying out the transmission in the network.

(3) Sub-paragraph (2) does not apply if the information is stored for longer than is reasonably necessary for the transmission.

7 (1) A service provider does not commit an offence under paragraph 2 by storing information provided by a recipient of the service for transmission in a communication network if the first and second conditions are met.

(2) The first condition is that the storage of the information—

(a) is automatic, intermediate and temporary, and

(b) is solely for the purpose of making more efficient the onward transmission of the information to other recipients of the service at their request.

(3) The second condition is that the service provider—

(a) does not modify the information,

(b) complies with any conditions attached to having access to the information, and

(c) if sub-paragraph (4) applies, promptly removes the information or disables access to it.

(4) This sub-paragraph applies if the service provider obtains actual knowledge that—

(a) the information at the initial source of the transmission has been removed from the network,

(b) access to it has been disabled, or

(c) a court or administrative authority has ordered the removal from the network of, or the disablement of access to, the information.

8 (1) A service provider does not commit an offence under paragraph 2 by storing information provided by a recipient of the service if—

(a) the service provider had no actual knowledge when the information was provided that it was, or contained, a prohibited publication, or

(b) on obtaining actual knowledge that the information was, or contained, a prohibited publication, the service provider promptly removed the information or disabled access to it.

(2) Sub-paragraph (1) does not apply if the recipient of the service is acting under the authority or control of the service provider.

9 Interpretation

9 (1) In this Schedule—

"domestic service provider" means a service provider established in England and Wales, Scotland or Northern Ireland;

"the E-Commerce Directive" means Directive 2000/31/EC of the European Parliament and of the Council of 8 June 2000 on certain legal aspects of information society services, in particular electronic commerce, in the Internal Market (Directive on electronic commerce);

"information society services"—

(a) has the meaning given in Article 2(a) of the E-Commerce Directive (which refers to Article 1(2) of Directive 98/34/EC of the European Parliament and of the Council of 22 June 1998 laying down a procedure for the provision of information in the field of technical standards and regulations), and

(b) is summarised in recital 17 of the E-Commerce Directive as covering "any service normally provided for remuneration, at a distance, by means of electronic equipment for the processing (including digital compression) and storage of data, and at the individual request of a recipient of a service";

"non-UK service provider" means a service provider established in an EEA state other than the United Kingdom;

"offence of forced marriage" means an offence under section 16;

"programme service" has the same meaning as in the Broadcasting Act 1990 (see section 201(1) of that Act);

"prohibited material" means any material the publication of which contravenes paragraph 1(2);

"publication" includes any speech, writing, relevant programme or other communication (in whatever form) which is addressed to, or is accessible by, the public at large or any section of the public;

"recipient", in relation to a service, means a person who, for professional ends or otherwise, uses an information society service, in particular for the purposes of seeking information or making it accessible;

"relevant programme" means a programme included in a programme service;

"service provider" means a person providing an information society service.

(2) For the purposes of the definition of "publication" in sub-paragraph (1)—

(a) an indictment or other document prepared for use in particular legal proceedings is not to be taken as coming within the definition;

(b) every relevant programme is to be taken as addressed to the public at large or to a section of the public.

(3) For the purposes of the definitions of "domestic service provider" and "non-UK service provider" in sub-paragraph (1)—

(a) a service provider is established in a particular part of the United Kingdom, or in a particular EEA state, if the service provider—

(i) effectively pursues an economic activity using a fixed establishment in that part of the United Kingdom, or that EEA state, for an indefinite period, and

(ii) is a national of an EEA state or a company or firm mentioned in Article 54 of the Treaty on the Functioning of the European Union;

(b) the presence or use in a particular place of equipment or other technical means of providing an information society service does not, of itself, constitute the establishment of a service provider;

(c) where it cannot be determined from which of a number of establishments a given information society service is provided, that service is to be regarded as provided from the establishment at the centre of the service provider's activities relating to that service."

Stalking

175 Sentences for offences of putting people in fear of violence etc

(1) In the Protection from Harassment Act 1997 —

(a) in section 4 (putting people in fear of violence), in subsection (4)(a), for "five years" substitute "ten years";

(b) in section 4A (stalking involving fear of violence or serious alarm or distress), in subsection (5)(a), for "five years" substitute "ten years".

(2) In the Crime and Disorder Act 1998, in section 32 (racially or religiously aggravated harassment etc), in subsection (4)(b) (which specifies the penalty on conviction on indictment for an offence under that section which consists of a racially or religiously aggravated offence under section 4 or 4A of the Protection from Harassment Act 1997), for "seven years" substitute "14 years".

(3) The amendments made by this section apply only in relation to an offence committed on or after the day on which this section comes into force.

(4) Where the course of conduct constituting an offence is found to have occurred over a period of 2 or more days, or at some time during a period of 2 or more days, the offence must be taken for the purposes of subsection (3) to have been committed on the last of those days.

Protection of children and vulnerable adults

176 Child sexual exploitation: streaming indecent images

In section 51(2) of the Sexual Offences Act 2003 (sexual exploitation of children: interpretation), in paragraph (b), at the end insert "or streamed or otherwise transmitted".

177 Licensing functions under taxi and PHV legislation: protection of children and vulnerable adults

(1) The Secretary of State may issue guidance to public authorities as to how their licensing functions under taxi and private hire vehicle legislation may be exercised so as to protect children, and vulnerable individuals who are 18 or over, from harm.

(2) The Secretary of State may revise any guidance issued under this section.

(3) The Secretary of State must arrange for any guidance issued under this section, and any revision of it, to be published.

(4) Any public authority which has licensing functions under taxi and private hire vehicle legislation must have regard to any guidance issued under this section.

(5) Before issuing guidance under this section, the Secretary of State must consult—

- (a) the National Police Chiefs' Council,
- (b) persons who appear to the Secretary of State to represent the interests of public authorities who are required to have regard to the guidance,
- (c) persons who appear to the Secretary of State to represent the interests of those whose livelihood is affected by the exercise of the licensing functions to which the guidance relates, and
- (d) such other persons as the Secretary of State considers appropriate.

(6) In this section, "taxi and private hire vehicle legislation" means—

- (a) the London Hackney Carriages Act 1843;
- (b) sections 37 to 68 of the Town Police Clauses Act 1847;
- (c) the Metropolitan Public Carriage Act 1869;
- (d) Part 2 of the Local Government (Miscellaneous Provisions) Act 1976;
- (e) the Private Hire Vehicles (London) Act 1998;
- (f) the Plymouth City Council Act 1975 (c.xx).

Coroners' investigations into deaths

178 Coroners' investigations into deaths: meaning of "state detention"

(1) Section 48 of the Coroners and Justice Act 2009 (interpretation of Part 1: general) is amended as follows.

(2) In subsection (1), in the definition of "state detention", after "subsection (2)" insert "(read with subsection (2A))".

(3) In subsection (2), at the beginning insert "Subject to subsection (2A),".

(4) After subsection (2) insert—

"(2A) But a person is not in state detention at any time when he or she is deprived of liberty under section 4A(3) or (5) or 4B of the Mental Capacity Act 2005."

Powers of Scottish litter authorities

179 Powers of litter authorities in Scotland

(1) In Part 4 of the Environmental Protection Act 1990 (litter etc), after section 91 insert—

"92 Summary proceedings by litter authorities

(1) Where a principal litter authority in Scotland other than a joint board is satisfied as respects—

(a) any relevant Crown land,

(b) any relevant land of a designated statutory undertaker,

(c) any relevant land of a designated educational institution, or

(d) any relevant land within a litter control area of a local authority,

that it is defaced by litter or refuse or that defacement of it by litter or refuse is likely to recur, the authority shall serve a notice (a "litter abatement notice") imposing either the requirement or the prohibition or both the requirement and the prohibition specified in subsection (2).

(2) The requirement and prohibition referred to in subsection (1) are as follows, namely—

(a) a requirement that the litter or refuse be cleared within a time specified in the notice;

(b) a prohibition on permitting the land to become defaced by litter or refuse.

(3) The litter abatement notice shall be served—

(a) as respects relevant Crown land, on the appropriate Crown authority;

(b) as respects relevant land of a designated statutory undertaker, on the undertaker;

(c) as respects relevant land of a designated educational institution, on the governing body of the institution or on the education authority responsible for the management of the institution;

(d) in any other case, on the occupier of the land or, if it is unoccupied, on the owner of the land.

(4) The person served with the notice may appeal against the notice to the sheriff by way of application within the period of 21 days beginning with the date on which the notice was served.

(5) If, on any appeal under subsection (4), the appellant proves that, as respects the land in question, he has complied with his duty under section 89(1), the court shall allow the appeal.

(6) If a person on whom a litter abatement notice is served, without reasonable excuse, fails to comply with or contravenes the requirement or prohibition imposed by the notice, he shall be guilty of an offence and liable on summary conviction to a fine not exceeding level 4 on the standard scale together with a further fine of an amount equal to one-twentieth of that level for each day on which the offence continues after the conviction.

(7) In any proceedings for an offence under subsection (6), it shall be a defence for the person charged to prove that he has complied, as respects the land in question, with his duty under section 89(1).

(8) A direction under section 89(6A) or a code of practice under section 89(7) shall be admissible in evidence in any proceedings under this section and, if any provision of such a direction or code appears to the court to be relevant to any question in the proceedings, it shall be taken into account in determining that question.

(9) If a person on whom a litter abatement notice is served fails to comply with the requirement imposed by the notice in respect of any land, the authority may, subject to subsection (10)—

(a) enter on the land and clear the litter or refuse, and

(b) recover from that person the expenditure attributable to their having done so, except such of the expenditure as that person shows was unnecessary in the circumstances.

(10) Subsection (9) does not apply in relation to relevant Crown land or relevant land of statutory undertakers.

93 Street litter control notices

(1) A principal litter authority in Scotland other than a joint board may, with a view to the prevention of accumulations of litter or refuse in and around any street or open land adjacent to any street, issue notices ("street litter control notices") imposing requirements on occupiers of premises in relation to such litter or refuse, in accordance with this section and section 94.

(2) If the authority is satisfied, in respect of any premises which are of a description prescribed under section 94(1)(a) and have a frontage on a street in their area, that—

(a) there is recurrent defacement by litter or refuse of any land, being part of the street or open land adjacent to the street, which is in the vicinity of the premises,

(b) the condition of any part of the premises which is open land in the vicinity of the frontage is, and if no notice is served is likely to continue to be, detrimental to the amenities of the locality by reason of the presence of litter or refuse, or

(c) there is produced, as a result of the activities carried on on the premises, quantities of litter or refuse of such nature and in such amounts as are likely to cause the defacement of any part of the street, or of open land adjacent to the street, which is in the vicinity of the premises,

the authority may serve a street litter control notice on the occupier or, if the premises are unoccupied, on the owner of the premises.

(3) A notice shall, subject to section 94(2), (3) and (4)—

(a) identify the premises and state the grounds under subsection (2) on which it is issued;

(b) specify an area of open land which adjoins or is in the vicinity of the frontage of the premises on the street;

(c) specify, in relation to that area or any part of it, such reasonable requirements as the authority considers appropriate in the circumstances;

and, for the purposes of paragraph (b), an area which includes land on both sides of the frontage of the premises shall be treated as an area adjoining that frontage.

(4) In this section and section 94—

"notice" means a street litter control notice;

"open land" means land in the open air;

"the premises", in relation to a notice, means the premises in respect of which the notice is issued;

"specified area" means the area specified in a notice under subsection (3)(b); and

"street" means a relevant highway, a relevant road or any other highway or road over which there is a right of way on foot.

94 Street litter: supplementary provisions

(1) The Scottish Ministers may by order prescribe—

(a) the descriptions of commercial or retail premises in respect of which a street litter control notice may be issued;

(b) the descriptions of land which may be included in a specified area; and

(c) the maximum area of land which may be included in a specified area;

and different descriptions or maximum dimensions may be prescribed under paragraph (b) or (c) for different cases or circumstances.

An order under this subsection is subject to the negative procedure.

(2) The power to describe premises or land under subsection (1)(a) or (b) includes power to describe the premises or land by reference to occupation or ownership or to the activities carried on there.

(3) The land comprised in a specified area

(a) shall include only land of one or more of the descriptions prescribed under subsection (1)(b);

(b) shall not include any land which is not—

(i) part of the premises,

(ii) part of a street,

(iii) relevant land of a principal litter authority, or

(iv) land under the direct control of any other local authority; and

(c) shall not exceed any applicable maximum area prescribed under subsection (1)(c);

but a specified area shall not include any part of the premises which is or is part of a litter control area.

(4) The requirements which may be imposed by a notice shall relate to the clearing of litter or refuse from the specified area and may in particular require—

(a) the provision or emptying of receptacles for litter or refuse;

(b) the doing within a period specified in the notice of any such thing as may be so specified (including the standards to which any such thing must be done); or

(c) the doing (while the notice remains in force) at such times or intervals, or within such period, of any such thing as may be so specified;

but a notice may not require the clearing of litter or refuse from any carriageway, except at a time when the carriageway is closed to all vehicular traffic.

(5) In relation to so much of the specified area as is not part of the premises the authority shall take account, in determining what requirements to impose, of their own duties under this Part or otherwise, and of any similar duties of any other local authority, in relation to that land.

(6) An authority proposing to serve a notice shall—

(a) inform the person on whom the notice is to be served;

(b) give him the opportunity to make representations about the notice within the period of 21 days beginning with the day on which he is so informed; and

(c) take any representations so made into account in making their decision.

(7) A person on whom a notice is served may appeal against the notice to the sheriff by way of application; and the court may quash the notice or may quash, vary or add to any requirement imposed by the notice.

(8) If it appears to the authority that a person has failed or is failing to comply with any requirement imposed by a notice, the authority may apply to the sheriff by way of application for an order requiring the person to comply with the requirement within such time as may be specified in the order.

(9) A person who, without reasonable excuse, fails to comply with an order under subsection (8) is guilty of an offence and liable on summary conviction to a fine not exceeding level 4 on the standard scale."

(2) Any order under section 94(1) of the Environmental Protection Act 1990 which had effect immediately before the coming into force of paragraph 21 of Schedule 11 to the Anti-social Behaviour, Crime and Policing Act 2014—

(a) is (so far as extending to Scotland) revived on the coming into force of this section, and

(b) has effect on its revival as if made under section 94(1) of that Act as re-enacted with modifications by this section.

CHAPTER 2

GENERAL

180 Consequential amendments, repeals and revocations

(1) The Secretary of State may by regulations made by statutory instrument make such provision as the Secretary of State considers appropriate in consequence of this Act other than Part 8.

(2) The Treasury may by regulations made by statutory instrument make such provision as the Treasury considers appropriate in consequence of Part 8.

(3) Regulations under subsection (1) or (2)—

(a) may include transitional, transitory or saving provision;

(b) may repeal, revoke or otherwise amend any provision of primary or subordinate legislation (including legislation passed or made in the same Session as this Act).

(4) A statutory instrument containing (whether alone or with other provision) regulations under this section that repeal, revoke or otherwise amend any provision of primary legislation is not to be made unless a draft of the instrument has been laid before, and approved by a resolution of, each House of Parliament.

(5) A statutory instrument containing regulations under this section that do not repeal, revoke or otherwise amend any provision of primary legislation is subject to annulment in pursuance of a resolution of either House of Parliament.

(6) In this section—

"primary legislation" means—

(a) an Act;

(b) an Act of the Scottish Parliament;

(c) a Measure or Act of the National Assembly for Wales;

(d) Northern Ireland legislation;

"subordinate legislation" means—

(a) subordinate legislation within the meaning of the Interpretation Act 1978;

(b) an instrument made under an Act of the Scottish Parliament;

(c) an instrument made under a Measure or Act of the National Assembly for Wales;

(d) an instrument made under Northern Ireland legislation.

181 Financial provision

The following are to be paid out of money provided by Parliament—

(a) any expenditure incurred under or by virtue of this Act by the Secretary of State;

(b) any increase attributable to this Act in the sums payable under any other Act out of money so provided.

182 Extent

(1) Except as provided by subsections (2) to (6), this Act extends only to England and Wales.

(2) The following provisions extend to England and Wales, Scotland and Northern Ireland—

(a) section 6, so far as relating to paragraphs 81, 95 and 96 of Schedule 1, and those paragraphs;

(b) section 8(11);

(c) section 9(3), so far as relating to paragraphs 108 and 121 of Schedule 2, and those paragraphs;
(d) section 16, so far as relating to paragraphs 22 and 47(h)(i) of Schedule 5, and those paragraphs;
(e) section 21(2) and (3);
(f) section 29(8), so far as relating to paragraphs 1 to 5 of Schedule 7, and those paragraphs;
(g) section 33(9), so far as relating to paragraphs 56(10), 59, 60, 61, 63, 64, 66, 68, 69 and 74 of Schedule 9, and those paragraphs;
(h) section 35;
(i) section 37(6);
(j) section 45, so far as relating to paragraphs 6, 13 and 14 of Schedule 12, and those paragraphs;
(k) section 46(10), so far as relating to paragraph 2 of Schedule 13, and that paragraph;
(l) section 47, so far as relating to the inserted sections 50A(3) to (7) and 50B of the Police Act 1996;
(m) section 50;
(n) section 71;
(o) section 76(3);
(p) sections 116 to 119 and Schedules 15, 16 and 17;
(q) sections 143 to 149 and 151 to 156;
(r) section 157(5) and Schedule 19;
(s) section 158;
(t) sections 160 and 161;
(u) section 163;
(v) this Chapter.

(3) The following provisions extend to England and Wales and Scotland (but not to Northern Ireland)—
(a) section 6, so far as relating to paragraphs 11, 14, 20 to 22, 33, 35, 52, 55, 59 to 66, 72 to 75, 80 and 85 of Schedule 1, and those paragraphs;
(b) section 7(8);
(c) section 8(5) and (8);
(d) section 9(3), so far as relating to paragraphs 30, 31, 33, 34, 48, 50, 74, 77, 80, 84 to 91, 99, 106 and 116 of Schedule 2, and those paragraphs;
(e) section 29(8), so far as relating to paragraphs 6 to 14 of Schedule 7, and those paragraphs;
(f) section 33(9), so far as relating to paragraphs 62 and 72 of Schedule 9, and those paragraphs;
(g) section 39;
(h) section 45, so far as relating to paragraphs 8, 12 and 17 of Schedule 12, and those paragraphs;
(i) section 46(10), so far as relating to paragraphs 4 and 6 of Schedule 13, and those paragraphs;
(j) section 49;

(k) section 51, so far as relating to paragraphs (a), (b) and (d) of paragraph 7 of Schedule 14, and those paragraphs;
(l) sections 84(2) to (5), 86 to 92 and 95;
(m) sections 96(2) to (7), 98 to 104 and 106;
(n) section 123;
(o) sections 125 to 133.

(4) The following provisions extend to England and Wales and Northern Ireland (but not to Scotland)—
(a) section 51, so far as relating to paragraphs 2(2), 3(2) and (3)(d) and 5(b) and (c) of Schedule 14, and those paragraphs;
(b) sections 68 and 69;
(c) section 159.

(5) The following provisions extend to Scotland only—
(a) section 46(2) to (9);
(b) sections 96(1) and (8), 97 and 105;
(c) section 179.

(6) The following provisions extend to Northern Ireland only—
(a) Chapter 7 of Part 4;
(b) sections 168(1) and (2) and 169 to 172;
(c) section 174.

(7) The power under section 60(4) of the UK Borders Act 2007 may be exercised so as to extend to any of the Channel Islands or the Isle of Man any amendment made by or under this Act of any part of that Act (with or without modification).

183 Commencement

(1) Except as provided by subsections (2) to (6), this Act comes into force on such day as the Secretary of State may by regulations made by statutory instrument appoint.

(2) Chapter 7 of Part 4 comes into force on such day as the Department of Justice in Northern Ireland appoints by order.

(3) Part 8 comes into force on such day as the Treasury may by regulations made by statutory instrument appoint.

(4) Sections 168 to 170 and 172 come into force on such day as the Department of Justice in Northern Ireland appoints by order.

(5) The following provisions come into force on the day on which this Act is passed—
(a) section 124;
(b) sections 164, 165 and 167;
(c) section 179;
(d) this Chapter;
(e) any other provision of this Act so far as is necessary for enabling the exercise on or after the day on which this Act is passed of any power to make provision by subordinate legislation (within the meaning of the Interpretation Act 1978) or to issue codes of practice or guidance.

(6) The following provisions come into force at the end of the period of 2 months beginning with the day on which this Act is passed—

(a) section 76;

(b) section 157 and Schedule 19;

(c) section 158;

(d) sections 173 and 174;

(e) section 176.

(7) Regulations under subsection (1) or (3), or an order under subsection (2) or (4), may appoint different days for different purposes.

(8) Before making regulations appointing a day for the coming into force of any provision of sections 96 to 106 the Secretary of State must consult the Scottish Ministers.

(9) The Secretary of State may by regulations made by statutory instrument make such transitional, transitory or saving provision as the Secretary of State considers appropriate in connection with the coming into force of any provision of this Act other than Chapter 7 of Part 4 , Part 8 or sections 168 to 172.

(10) The Department of Justice in Northern Ireland may by order make such transitional, transitory or saving provision as it considers appropriate in connection with the coming into force of any provision of Chapter 7 of Part 4 .

(11) The Treasury may by regulations made by statutory instrument make such transitional, transitory or saving provision as the Treasury considers appropriate in connection with the coming into force of any provision of Part 8 .

(12) The Department of Justice in Northern Ireland may by order make such transitional, transitory or saving provision as the Department of Justice in Northern Ireland considers appropriate in connection with the coming into force of sections 168, 169, 170 and 172.

(13) The power to make regulations under subsection (9) or (11), or an order under subsection (10) or (12), includes power to make different provision for different purposes.

(14) The powers conferred on the Department of Justice in Northern Ireland by subsections (2), (4), (10) and (12) are exercisable by statutory rule for the purposes of the Statutory Rules (Northern Ireland) Order 1979 (S.I. 1979/1573 (N.I. 12)).

184 Short title

This Act may be cited as the Policing and Crime Act 2017.

SCHEDULES

SCHEDULE 1

Section 6

PROVISION FOR POLICE AND CRIME COMMISSIONER TO BE FIRE AND RESCUE AUTHORITY

PART 1

AMENDMENTS TO THE FIRE AND RESCUE SERVICES ACT 2004

1 The Fire and Rescue Services Act 2004 is amended as follows.

2 Before section 1 insert—

"Fire and rescue authorities".

3 In section 1(4) (fire and rescue authorities) for the words from "sections" to the end substitute "—

(a) sections 2 and 4 (schemes constituting combined fire and rescue authorities for particular areas), and

(b) sections 4A and 4B (orders providing for police and crime commissioners to be fire and rescue authorities)."

4 Before section 2 insert—

"Combined fire and rescue authorities".

5 After section 4 insert—

"Fire and rescue authority involving police and crime commissioner

4A Power to provide for police and crime commissioner to be fire and rescue authority

4A 4A Power to provide for police and crime commissioner to be fire and rescue authority

(1) The Secretary of State may by order provide—

(a) for the creation of a corporation sole as the fire and rescue authority for the area specified in the order, and

(b) for the person who is for the time being the police and crime commissioner for the relevant police area to be for the time being that fire and rescue authority.

(2) In subsection (1) "the relevant police area" means the police area which—

(a) is the same as the area of the fire and rescue authority created by the order, or

(b) if the order creates two or more fire and rescue authorities, is the same as the areas of those authorities taken together.

(3) The whole of an area of a fire and rescue authority created by an order under this section must be—

(a) within England, and

(b) outside the metropolitan police district and the City of London police area.

(4) An order under this section may be made only if the relevant police and crime commissioner has submitted a proposal for the order to the Secretary of State.

(5) An order under this section may be made only if it appears to the Secretary of State that—

(a) it is in the interests of economy, efficiency and effectiveness for the order to be made, or

(b) it is in the interests of public safety for the order to be made.

(6) The Secretary of State may not make an order under this section in a case within subsection (5)(a) if the Secretary of State thinks that the order would have an adverse effect on public safety.

(7) In this section "relevant police and crime commissioner" has the same meaning as in Schedule A1; and that Schedule makes further provision about the procedure for an order under this section.

4B Changes to existing fire and rescue authorities

4B 4B Changes to existing fire and rescue authorities

(1) An order under section 4A may make alterations to the areas of fire and rescue authorities in England outside Greater London.

(2) The alterations that may be made by virtue of subsection (1) include alterations that result in a reduction or an increase in the number of such areas.

(3) An order under section 4A(1) may make provision for the abolition of—

(a) a metropolitan county fire and rescue authority,

(b) a combined fire and rescue authority constituted by a scheme under section 2,

(c) a combined fire and rescue authority constituted by a scheme to which section 4 applies, or

(d) a fire and rescue authority created by an order under section 4A(1).

4C Transfer of property, rights and liabilities

4C 4C Transfer of property, rights and liabilities

(1) This section applies if the Secretary of State makes an order under section 4A.

(2) The Secretary of State may make one or more schemes for the transfer of property, rights and liabilities from an existing fire and rescue authority

("the transferor") to the fire and rescue authority created by the order ("the transferee").

(3) The things that may be transferred under a transfer scheme include—

(a) property, rights and liabilities that could not otherwise be transferred;

(b) property acquired, and rights and liabilities arising, after the making of the scheme;

(c) criminal liabilities.

(4) A transfer scheme may make supplementary, incidental, transitional and consequential provision and may in particular—

(a) create rights, or impose liabilities, in relation to property or rights transferred;

(b) make provision about the continuing effect of things done by the transferor in respect of anything transferred;

(c) make provision about the continuation of things (including legal proceedings) in the process of being done by, on behalf of or in relation to the transferor in respect of anything transferred;

(d) make provision for references to the transferor in an instrument or other document in respect of anything transferred to be treated as references to the transferee;

(e) make provision for the shared ownership or use of property.

(5) A transfer scheme may provide—

(a) for the scheme to be modified by agreement after it comes into effect, and

(b) for any such modifications to have effect from the date when the original scheme comes into effect.

(6) In this section—

(a) references to the transfer of property include the grant of a lease;

(b) references to rights and liabilities include rights and liabilities under a contract of employment.

4D Further provision about authority created by section 4A order

4D 4D Further provision about authority created by section 4A order

(1) A person who is a fire and rescue authority created by an order under section 4A is to be paid allowances, in respect of expenses incurred by the person in the exercise of the authority's functions, which are of the kinds and amounts determined by the Secretary of State as payable in accordance with this subsection.

(2) A determination under subsection (1) may make different provision for different cases.

(3) Payments under subsection (1) are to be made by the fire and rescue authority.

(4) A fire and rescue authority created by an order under section 4A must appoint a person to be responsible for the proper administration of the authority's financial affairs (a "chief finance officer").

(5) A fire and rescue authority created by an order under section 4A must appoint a person to act as chief finance officer of the authority if and so long as—

(a) that post is vacant, or

(b) the holder of that post is, in the authority's opinion, unable to carry out the duties of that post.

(6) Section 113 of the Local Government Finance Act 1988 (qualifications of responsible officer) applies to a person appointed under subsection (4) or (5) as it applies to the persons having responsibility for the administration of financial affairs mentioned in that section.

(7) A fire and rescue authority created by an order under section 4A may—

(a) appoint such other staff as the authority thinks appropriate to enable the authority to exercise the functions of the authority;

(b) pay remuneration, allowances and gratuities to members of the authority's staff.

(8) In subsection (7) "allowances", in relation to a member of the authority's staff, means allowances in respect of expenses incurred by the member of staff in the course of employment as such a member of staff.

(9) A fire and rescue authority created by an order under section 4A may pay—

(a) pensions to, or in respect of, persons who are or have been members of the authority's staff, and

(b) amounts for or towards the provision of pensions to, or in respect of, persons who are or have been members of the authority's staff.

(10) An order under section 4A may make provision—

(a) about the delegation by the fire and rescue authority created by the order of the authority's functions to the person who is for the time being the relevant deputy police and crime commissioner;

(b) about the further delegation of such functions by that person to a member of staff of the authority or of the relevant police and crime commissioner;

(c) about the delegation by the authority of such functions to a member of staff of the authority or of the relevant police and crime commissioner.

(11) In subsection (10)—

"the relevant deputy police and crime commissioner" means the deputy police and crime commissioner for the police area—

(a) which corresponds to the area of the fire and rescue authority, or

(b) within which the area of the fire and rescue authority falls;

"the relevant police and crime commissioner" means the police and crime commissioner for that police area.

(12) References in subsection (10) to a member of staff of a police and crime commissioner are to any of the following persons appointed under Schedule 1 to the Police Reform and Social Responsibility Act 2011—

(a) the commissioner's chief executive;

(b) the commissioner's chief finance officer;

(c) other staff.

(13) Provision made under subsection (10) may—

(a) enable the delegation of any of the functions of the fire and rescue authority;

(b) enable the delegation of any of the functions of the authority other than those specified or described in the order;

(c) enable the delegation of the functions of the authority specified or described in the order.

(14) An order under section 4A may make provision about—

(a) the personal liability of a person who is the fire and rescue authority created by the order for acts or omissions done by the person in the exercise of the authority's functions;

(b) the personal liability of a person who is a member of staff of the fire and rescue authority created by the order for acts or omissions done by the person in the carrying out of duties as a member of staff.

(15) A fire and rescue authority created by an order under section 4A may acquire land compulsorily.

(16) The Acquisition of Land Act 1981 applies in relation to the compulsory purchase of land pursuant to subsection (15).

4E Requirement for authority created by section 4A order to have fire fund

4E 4E Requirement for authority created by section 4A order to have fire fund

(1) Each fire and rescue authority created by an order under section 4A must keep a fund to be known as the fire fund.

(2) All of the receipts of a fire and rescue authority created by an order under section 4A must be paid into the relevant fire fund.

(3) All of the expenditure of a fire and rescue authority created by an order under section 4A must be paid out of the relevant fire fund.

(4) A fire and rescue authority created by an order under section 4A must keep accounts of payments made into or out of the relevant fire fund.

(5) Subsections (2) and (3) are subject to the provisions of—

(a) the scheme established under section 26 of the Fire Services Act 1947 (Firemen's Pension Scheme) (as continued in force by order under section 36),

(b) a scheme under section 34 (pensions etc), or

(c) scheme regulations within the meaning of the Public Service Pensions Act 2013.

(6) In this section "relevant fire fund", in relation to a fire and rescue authority created by an order under section 4A, means the fire fund which that authority keeps.

4F Exercise of functions pursuant to section 4A order

4F 4F Exercise of functions pursuant to section 4A order

(1) A fire and rescue authority created by an order under section 4A must exercise its functions efficiently and effectively.

(2) A person who is the fire and rescue authority by virtue of an order under section 4A may not act in that office unless the person has made and delivered a declaration of acceptance of office under section 70 of the Police Reform and Social Responsibility Act 2011 in accordance with that section.

(3) Subsections (4) and (5) apply if—

(a) an order under section 4A has effect for the area of a fire and rescue authority, and

(b) an acting commissioner is appointed under section 62 of the Police Reform and Social Responsibility Act 2011 for the police area—

(i) which corresponds to the area of the fire and rescue authority, or

(ii) within which the area of the fire and rescue authority falls.

(4) The acting commissioner is to act as the fire and rescue authority for the period of the acting commissioner's appointment.

(5) Accordingly—

(a) all of the functions of the fire and rescue authority are exercisable by the acting commissioner during that period, and

(b) any property or rights vested in the fire and rescue authority may be dealt with by the acting commissioner in that period as if vested in the acting commissioner.

(6) Subsection (7) applies if a person elected as police and crime commissioner for a police area—

(a) is disqualified from being, or being elected as, a police and crime commissioner, or

(b) is disqualified from being, or being elected as, the police and crime commissioner for that area.

(7) Any acts of the person when acting in the office of fire and rescue authority are, despite that disqualification, as valid and effectual as if the person had not been disqualified.

4G Section 4A order: transitional provision

4G 4G Section 4A order: transitional provision

(1) The transitional provision which may be made by an order under section 4A by virtue of section 60(2)(b) includes, in particular, provision of the kind described in the following provisions of this section.

(2) An order under section 4A may make provision for a specified person to be the shadow fire and rescue authority for the area to which the order relates for a specified period.

(3) A shadow fire and rescue authority is a person who has the specified functions of a fire and rescue authority in relation to that area, but is not otherwise the fire and rescue authority for that area.

(4) An order under section 4A which includes provision by virtue of subsection (2) may make provision about the operation of any enactment in relation to—

(a) the shadow fire and rescue authority, or

(b) any other person to whom the enactment would otherwise apply.

(5) This includes provision for the enactment to apply with modifications in relation to a person within subsection (4)(a) or (b).

(6) An order under section 4A may make provision about the operation of the Local Government Finance Act 1992 in relation to the fire and rescue authority created by the order during a specified period beginning with the time when the authority becomes the fire and rescue authority for the area to which the order relates.

(7) This includes provision for that Act to apply for that period with modifications in relation to—

(a) the authority, or

(b) any other person to whom that Act would otherwise apply.

(8) Provision under subsection (4) or (6) may, in particular, make different provision for different parts of an authority's area.

(9) In this section—

(a) "specified" means specified in an order under section 4A;

(b) "enactment" includes an enactment contained in subordinate legislation within the meaning of the Interpretation Act 1978;

(c) references to the Local Government Finance Act 1992 include any provision made under that Act.

4H Delegation to chief constable for police area

4H 4H Delegation to chief constable for police area

(1) The Secretary of State may by order make provision about—

(a) the delegation of functions of a fire and rescue authority created, or to be created, by an order under section 4A to the chief constable of the police force for the police area—

(i) which corresponds to the area of the fire and rescue authority, or

(ii) within which the area of the fire and rescue authority falls;

(b) the delegation by such a chief constable of the chief constable's fire and rescue functions.

(2) Provision made under subsection (1) may—

(a) enable the delegation of any of the functions mentioned in that subsection;
(b) enable the delegation of any of the functions mentioned in that subsection other than those specified or described in the order;
(c) enable the delegation of such of the functions mentioned in that subsection as are specified or described in the order.

(3) Provision made under subsection (1)(b) may enable delegation to—
(a) members of the chief constable's police force;
(b) the civilian staff of that police force, as defined by section 102(4) of the Police Reform and Social Responsibility Act 2011;
(c) members of staff transferred to the chief constable under a scheme under section 4I(1);
(d) members of staff appointed by the chief constable under section 4I(4).

(4) An order under this section may be made only if the relevant police and crime commissioner has submitted a proposal for the order to the Secretary of State.

(5) An order under this section may be made only if it appears to the Secretary of State that—
(a) it is in the interests of economy, efficiency and effectiveness for the order to be made, or
(b) it is in the interests of public safety for the order to be made.

(6) The Secretary of State may not make an order under this section in a case within subsection (5)(a) if the Secretary of State thinks that the order would have an adverse effect on public safety.

(7) In this section "relevant police and crime commissioner" has the same meaning as in Schedule A1; and that Schedule makes provision about the procedure for an order under this section which is not combined, or not proposed to be combined, with an order under section 4A (see in particular paragraph 7 of that Schedule).

(8) In this section "fire and rescue functions", in relation to a chief constable, means—
(a) functions which are delegated to the chief constable under provision made under subsection (1)(a), and
(b) functions relating to fire and rescue services which are conferred on the chief constable by or by virtue of any enactment.

(9) This section is subject to section 37 (prohibition on employment of police in fire-fighting).

4I Further provision about chief constable covered by section 4H order

4I 4I Further provision about chief constable covered by section 4H order

(1) If an order is made under section 4H, the Secretary of State may make one or more schemes for the transfer of property, rights and liabilities—

(a) from a fire and rescue authority to the chief constable to whom the order applies, or

(b) from that chief constable to the fire and rescue authority to which the order applies.

(2) The fire and rescue authority mentioned in subsection (1)(a) may be one created by an order under section 4A or another kind of fire and rescue authority.

(3) Subsections (3) to (6) of section 4C apply to a transfer scheme under subsection (2) as they apply to a transfer scheme under that section.

(4) A chief constable to whom an order under section 4H applies may appoint staff for the purpose of the exercise of the chief constable's fire and rescue functions.

(5) A chief constable to whom an order under section 4H applies may—

(a) pay remuneration, allowances and gratuities to members of the chief constable's fire and rescue staff;

(b) pay pensions to, or in respect of, persons who are or have been such members of staff;

(c) pay amounts for or towards the provision of pensions to, or in respect of, persons who are or have been such members of staff.

(6) In subsection (5) "allowances", in relation to a member of staff, means allowances in respect of expenses incurred by the member of staff in the course of employment as such a member of staff.

(7) Subject to subsections (8) to (10), a person who is employed pursuant to a transfer by virtue of subsection (1) or an appointment under subsection (4) may not at the same time be employed pursuant to an appointment by a chief constable of the police force for a police area under Schedule 2 to the Police Reform and Social Responsibility Act 2011.

(8) Where an order under section 4H is in force in relation to the chief constable of the police force for a police area, the person who is for the time being the police force's chief finance officer is to be responsible for the proper administration of financial affairs relating to the exercise of the chief constable's fire and rescue functions.

(9) Subsection (7) does not prevent a person who is employed as a finance officer for fire functions from being at the same time employed as a finance officer for police functions.

(10) In subsection (9)—

"finance officer for fire functions" means a member of a chief constable's fire and rescue staff who—

(a) is not a chief finance officer of the kind mentioned in subsection (8), and

(b) is employed to carry out duties relating to the proper administration of financial affairs relating to the exercise of the chief constable's fire and rescue functions;

"finance officer for police functions" means a member of a chief constable's civilian staff within the meaning of the Police Reform and Social Responsibility Act 2011 who—

(a) is not a chief finance officer of the kind mentioned in subsection (8), and

(b) is employed to carry out duties relating to the proper administration of a police force's financial affairs.

(11) Where an order under section 4H is in force, the fire and rescue authority to which the order applies must pay—

(a) any damages or costs awarded against the chief constable to whom the order applies in any proceedings brought against the chief constable in respect of the acts or omissions of a member of the chief constable's fire and rescue staff;

(b) any costs incurred by the chief constable in any such proceedings so far as not recovered by the chief constable in the proceedings;

(c) any sum required in connection with the settlement of any claim made against the chief constable in respect of the acts or omissions of a member of the chief constable's fire and rescue staff, if the settlement is approved by the authority.

(12) Where an order under section 4H is in force, the fire and rescue authority to which the order applies may, in such cases and to such extent as appears to the authority to be appropriate, pay—

(a) any damages or costs awarded against a member of the fire and rescue staff of the chief constable to whom the order applies in proceedings for any unlawful conduct of that member of staff;

(b) costs incurred and not recovered by such a member of staff in such proceedings;

(c) sums required in connection with the settlement of a claim that has or might have given rise to such proceedings.

(13) In this section—

"fire and rescue functions" has the same meaning as in section 4H;

"fire and rescue staff", in relation to a chief constable to whom an order under section 4H applies, means—

(a) staff transferred to the chief constable under a scheme under subsection (1), and

(b) staff appointed by the chief constable under subsection (4).

4J Exercise of functions pursuant to section 4H order

4J 4J Exercise of functions pursuant to section 4H order

(1) This section applies if—

(a) an order under section 4H makes provision in relation to the area of a fire and rescue authority, and

(b) under the order, functions of the fire and rescue authority are delegated to the chief constable of the police force for the police area—

(i) which corresponds to the area of the fire and rescue authority, or

(ii) within which the area of the fire and rescue authority falls.

(2) The chief constable must secure that good value for money is obtained in exercising—

(a) functions which are delegated under the order, and

(b) functions relating to fire and rescue services which are conferred on the chief constable by or by virtue of any enactment.

(3) The chief constable must secure that persons exercising functions delegated by the chief constable under the order obtain good value for money in exercising those functions.

(4) The fire and rescue authority must—

(a) secure the exercise of the duties which are delegated to the chief constable under the order,

(b) secure the exercise of the duties relating to fire and rescue services which are imposed on the chief constable by or by virtue of any enactment,

(c) secure that functions which are delegated to the chief constable under the order are exercised efficiently and effectively, and

(d) secure that functions relating to fire and rescue services which are conferred or imposed on the chief constable by or by virtue of any enactment are exercised efficiently and effectively.

(5) The fire and rescue authority must hold the chief constable to account for the exercise of such functions.

4K Complaints and conduct matters etc

4K 4K Complaints and conduct matters etc

(1) If an order is made under section 4H(1)(b) that enables delegation to members of a police force or the civilian staff of a police force, the Secretary of State may by order amend Part 2 of the Police Reform Act 2002 (persons serving with the police: complaints and conduct matters etc) in consequence of that provision.

(2) If an order is made under section 4H(1)(b) that enables delegation to members of staff transferred to a chief constable under a scheme under section 4I(1) or appointed by a chief constable under section 4I(4), the Secretary of State may by order make provision of the type described in subsection (3) in relation to those members of staff.

(3) The provision referred to in subsection (2) is—

(a) provision corresponding or similar to any provision made by or under Part 2 of the Police Reform Act 2002;

(b) provision applying (with or without modifications) any provision made by or under Part 2 of that Act.

(4) The Secretary of State may by order, in consequence of any provision made under subsection (2), amend Part 2 of the Police Reform Act 2002.

(5) Before making an order under this section the Secretary of State must consult—

(a) the Police Advisory Board for England and Wales,

(b) the Independent Police Complaints Commission,

(c) such persons as appear to the Secretary of State to represent the views of police and crime commissioners,

(d) such persons as appear to the Secretary of State to represent the views of fire and rescue authorities, and

(e) such other persons as the Secretary of State considers appropriate.

4L Application of fire and rescue provisions

4L 4L Application of fire and rescue provisions

(1) The Secretary of State may by order—

(a) apply (with or without modifications) any provision of a fire and rescue enactment in relation to a person within subsection (2);

(b) make, in relation to a person within subsection (2), provision corresponding or similar to any provision of a fire and rescue enactment.

(2) Those persons are—

(a) a chief constable of a police force for a police area to whom an order under section 4H applies,

(b) a member of staff transferred to such a chief constable under a scheme under section 4I(1),

(c) a member of staff appointed by such a chief constable under section 4I(4),

(d) a member of such a chief constable's police force to whom functions have been delegated by virtue of section 4H(1)(b), and

(e) a member of the civilian staff of such a police force (as defined by section 102(4) of the Police Reform and Social Responsibility Act 2011) to whom functions have been delegated by virtue of section 4H(1)(b).

(3) The power conferred by subsection (1)(a) or (b) includes power to apply (with or without modifications) any provision made under a fire and rescue enactment or make provision corresponding or similar to any such provision.

(4) The Secretary of State may by order amend, revoke or repeal a provision of or made under an enactment in consequence of provision made by virtue of subsection (1).

(5) In this section "fire and rescue enactment" means an enactment relating to a fire and rescue authority (including, in particular, an enactment relating to an employee of such an authority or property of such an authority).

This includes an enactment contained in this Act.

(6) References in this section to an enactment or to provision made under an enactment are to an enactment whenever passed or (as the case may be) to provision whenever the instrument containing it is made.

4M Application of local policing provisions

4M 4M Application of local policing provisions

(1) Schedule A2 makes provision about the application, in relation to a fire and rescue authority created by an order under section 4A, of legislation relating to police and crime commissioners.

(2) The Secretary of State may by order—
   (a) apply (with or without modifications) any provision of a local policing enactment in relation to a fire and rescue authority created by an order under section 4A;
   (b) make, in relation to a fire and rescue authority created by an order under section 4A, provision corresponding or similar to any provision of a local policing enactment.

(3) The power conferred by subsection (2)(a) or (b) includes power to apply (with or without modifications) any provision made by or under a local policing enactment or make provision corresponding or similar to any such provision.

(4) The Secretary of State may by order amend, revoke or repeal a provision of or made under an enactment in consequence of provision made by virtue of subsection (2).

(5) In this section "local policing enactment" means an enactment relating to a police and crime commissioner.

(6) References in this section to an enactment or to provision made under an enactment are to an enactment whenever passed or (as the case may be) to provision whenever the instrument containing it is made."

6 Before section 5A insert—

"Powers of certain fire and rescue authorities".

7 In section 5A (powers of certain fire and rescue authorities) in subsection (3) (authorities to which powers apply)—
   (a) omit the "or" at the end of paragraph (c), and
   (b) at the end of paragraph (d) insert ", or
      (e) created by an order under section 4A."

8 After section 5L insert—

"Interpretation of Part 1

5M Interpretation of Part 1

5M 5M Interpretation of Part 1

In this Part—

"City of London police area" means the City of London as defined for the purposes of the Acts relating to the City of London police force;

"metropolitan police district" means that district as defined in section 76 of the London Government Act 1963;

"police area" means a police area listed in Schedule 1 to the Police Act 1996 (police areas outside London)."

9 In section 21 (Fire and Rescue National Framework) after subsection (2) insert—

"(2A) The Framework may contain different provision for different descriptions of fire and rescue authority."

10 After section 25 (but before the italic heading before section 26) insert—

"Police and crime plan

25A Police and crime plan

25A 25A Police and crime plan

A fire and rescue authority created by an order under section 4A must, in carrying out its functions, have regard to the police and crime plan issued by the police and crime commissioner for the police area—

(a) which corresponds to the area of the fire and rescue authority, or

(b) within which the area of the fire and rescue authority falls."

11 In section 34 (pensions etc) after subsection (10) insert—

"(11) References in subsection (1) to persons who are or have been employed by a fire and rescue authority include persons who are or have been employed by the chief constable of the police force for a police area having been—

(a) transferred to the chief constable under a scheme made under section 4I(1), or

(b) appointed by the chief constable under section 4I(4).

(12) References in the other provisions of this section to a fire and rescue authority include a chief constable of the police force for a police area who employs persons of the kind mentioned in subsection (11)."

12 For section 37 (prohibition on employment of police) substitute—

"37 Prohibition on employment of police in fire-fighting

"37 "37 Prohibition on employment of police in fire-fighting

(1) No member of a police force may be employed by a fire and rescue authority or a relevant chief constable for the purpose of—

(a) extinguishing fires, or

(b) protecting life and property in the event of fires.

(2) Subsection (1) does not prevent the exercise of functions under section 7 (fire-fighting) by—

(a) a relevant chief constable, or

(b) a deputy chief constable to whom such functions have been delegated by a relevant chief constable.

(3) In this section "relevant chief constable" means the chief constable of a police force for a police area to whom functions of a fire and rescue authority have been delegated under an order under section 4H."

13 Before Schedule 1 insert—

"SCHEDULE A1

Sections 4A(7) and 4H(7)

PROCEDURE FOR ORDERS UNDER SECTION 4A

1 Proposal for order under section 4A

1 (1) A proposal for an order under section 4A (a "section 4A proposal") must contain an assessment of why—

(a) it is in the interests of economy, efficiency and effectiveness for the order to be made, or

(b) it is in the interests of public safety for the order to be made.

(2) If the proposal suggests that an order under section 4A should be combined with an order under section 4H (delegation to chief constable for police area), the proposal must set out the reasons for that suggestion.

2 Duty of relevant fire and rescue authority to cooperate in preparation of proposal

2 (1) A relevant fire and rescue authority must cooperate with a relevant police and crime commissioner in the preparation of a section 4A proposal.

(2) A relevant fire and rescue authority must, in particular, provide a relevant police and crime commissioner with such information held by the authority as the commissioner reasonably requires for the purposes of the preparation of the proposal.

(3) Sub-paragraph (2) does not require the authority to provide information if to do so would breach—

(a) any obligation of confidence owed by the authority, or

(b) any other restriction on the disclosure of information (however imposed).

(4) Sub-paragraphs (1) and (2) do not apply if the proposal is for an order to create a fire and rescue authority for an area which, before the order is made, contains only the areas of two or more fire and rescue authorities created by order under section 4A.

3 Consultation on proposal

3 (1) Before submitting a section 4A proposal to the Secretary of State, a relevant police and crime commissioner must—

(a) consult each relevant local authority about the proposal,

(b) consult people in the commissioner's police area about the proposal,

(c) consult each of the following about the proposal—

(i) persons appearing to the commissioner to represent employees who may be affected by the proposal;

(ii) persons appearing to the commissioner to represent members of a police force who may be so affected, and

(d) publish, in such manner as the commissioner thinks appropriate, the commissioner's response to the representations made or views expressed in response to those consultations.

(2) Each consultation under sub-paragraph (1) is to be carried out in such manner as the relevant police and crime commissioner thinks appropriate.

4 Provision of representations to Secretary of State

4 (1) Sub-paragraphs (2) to (4) apply if, in response to a consultation by a relevant police and crime commissioner under paragraph 3(1)(a), a relevant local authority indicates that it does not support a section 4A proposal.

(2) The commissioner must, in submitting the proposal to the Secretary of State, provide the Secretary of State with—

(a) copies of each document provided by the commissioner for the purposes of paragraph 3,

(b) copies of each representation made by a relevant local authority in response,

(c) a summary of the views expressed by people in the commissioner's police area about the proposal,

(d) a summary of the views expressed about the proposal by persons consulted under paragraph 3(1)(c), and

(e) the commissioner's response to those representations and views.

(3) The Secretary of State must—

(a) obtain an independent assessment of the proposal, and

(b) have regard to that assessment and to the material provided to the Secretary of State under sub-paragraph (2) in deciding whether to make an order under section 4A in response to the proposal.

(4) The Secretary of State must publish the independent assessment—

(a) as soon as is reasonably practicable after making a determination in response to the proposal, and

(b) in such manner as the Secretary of State thinks appropriate.

5 Decision by Secretary of State

5 (1) Subject to sub-paragraphs (2) and (3), the Secretary of State may, in making an order under section 4A, give effect to the proposal for the order with such modifications as the Secretary of State thinks appropriate.

(2) If paragraph 1(2) applies to the proposal, the Secretary of State may not in response to the proposal make an order under section 4A which is not combined with an order under section 4H.

(3) Before making an order which gives effect to the proposal for the order with modifications, the Secretary of State must consult the following on the modifications—

(a) the relevant police and crime commissioner;

(b) each relevant local authority.

6 Interpretation

6 (1) In this Schedule "section 4A proposal" has the meaning given by paragraph 1(1).

(2) In this Schedule "relevant police and crime commissioner", in relation to a section 4A proposal, means a police and crime commissioner—

(a) whose police area is the same as, or contains all of, the area of the fire and rescue authority proposed to be created by the order, or

(b) all or part of whose police area falls within the area of that fire and rescue authority.

(3) Any changes to the police areas contained in the proposal are to be disregarded in determining who is a relevant police and crime commissioner for the purposes of sub-paragraph (2).

(4) If there is more than one relevant police and crime commissioner in relation to a section 4A proposal, references in this Schedule to the relevant police and crime commissioner are to all of those police and crime commissioners acting jointly.

(5) In this Schedule "relevant fire and rescue authority", in relation to a section 4A proposal prepared by a police and crime commissioner, means a fire and rescue authority—

(a) whose area is the same as, or contains all of, the police area of the police and crime commissioner, or

(b) all or part of whose area falls within the police area of the police and crime commissioner.

(6) In this Schedule "relevant local authority", in relation to a section 4A proposal, means a local authority—

(a) whose area is the same as, or contains all of, the area of the fire and rescue authority proposed to be created by the order, or

(b) all or part of whose area falls within the area of that fire and rescue authority.

(7) In sub-paragraph (6) "local authority" means—

(a) a county council,

(b) a district council for an area for which there is no county council,

(c) the Council of the Isles of Scilly, or

(d) a combined authority established under section 103 of the Local Democracy, Economic Development and Construction Act 2009 which exercises the functions of a fire and rescue authority by virtue of section 105 or 105A of that Act.

7 Application of this Schedule to certain orders under section 4H

7 (1) This paragraph makes provision about the application of this Schedule to an order under section 4H which is not combined, or proposed to be combined, with an order under section 4A (a "section 4H order").

(2) Subject as follows, this Schedule applies to a section 4H order as it applies to an order under section 4A.

(3) The following provisions of this Schedule do not apply in relation to a section 4H order—

(a) paragraph 1(2);
(b) paragraph 5(2);
(c) paragraph 6.

(4) In the application of this Schedule to a section 4H order—

(a) "relevant police and crime commissioner" means the police and crime commissioner for the police area—
(i) which corresponds to the area of the fire and rescue authority to which the order relates, or
(ii) within which the area of that fire and rescue authority falls;

(b) "relevant fire and rescue authority" means that fire and rescue authority, and

(c) "relevant local authority" means a local authority (within the meaning of paragraph 6(7))—
(i) whose area is the same as, or contains all of, the area of that fire and rescue authority, or
(ii) all or part of whose area falls within the area of that fire and rescue authority.

SCHEDULE A2 Section 4M(1)

APPLICATION OF LEGISLATION RELATING TO POLICE AND CRIME COMMISSIONERS

1 Introductory

1 (1) This Schedule makes provision about the application of certain enactments relating to police and crime commissioners to a relevant fire and rescue authority.

(2) In this Schedule—

"relevant chief constable", in relation to a relevant fire and rescue authority, means the chief constable of a police force (if any) to whom functions of the authority have been delegated under provision made under section 4H;

"relevant fire and rescue authority" means a fire and rescue authority created by an order under section 4A;

"relevant police and crime panel", in relation to a relevant fire and rescue authority, means the police and crime panel for the police area—

(a) which corresponds to the area of the fire and rescue authority, or

(b) within which the area of the fire and rescue authority falls.

(3) In this Schedule "fire and rescue plan" means a document which—

(a) is prepared and published by a relevant fire and rescue authority in accordance with the Fire and Rescue National Framework, and

(b) sets out the authority's priorities and objectives, for the period covered by the document, in connection with the discharge of the authority's functions.

(4) In this Schedule "fire and rescue statement" means a document which—

(a) is prepared and published by a relevant fire and rescue authority in accordance with the Fire and Rescue National Framework, and

(b) contains a statement of the way in which the authority has had regard, in the period covered by the document, to the Framework and to any fire and rescue plan prepared by the authority for that period.

2 Arrangements for obtaining the views of the community

2 (1) Subsections (1), (1B), (2), (5A) and (5B) of section 96 of the Police Act 1996 (arrangements for obtaining the views of the community on policing) apply in relation to a relevant fire and rescue authority as they apply in relation to an elected local policing body, subject to sub-paragraph (2).

(2) As applied by sub-paragraph (1), those subsections have effect as if—

(a) the reference in subsection (1) to each police area were to each area of a relevant fire and rescue authority,

(b) in that subsection, for paragraphs (a) and (b) and the words following those paragraphs there were substituted "the views of people in that area about fire and rescue services",

(c) in subsections (1B) and (5A) the references to a police area listed in Schedule 1 to that Act were to the area of a relevant fire and rescue authority,

(d) the reference in subsection (2) to the police area were to the area of the relevant fire and rescue authority, and

(e) the reference in that subsection to the chief officer of police for that police area were to the relevant chief constable.

3 Scrutiny of fire and rescue plan

3 (1) Subsections (6) to (12) of section 5 of the Police Reform and Social Responsibility Act 2011 (scrutiny of police and crime plans) apply in relation to a relevant fire and rescue authority as they apply in relation to an elected local policing body, subject to sub-paragraph (2).

(2) As applied by sub-paragraph (1), those subsections have effect as if—

(a) references to a police and crime plan were to a fire and rescue plan,

(b) references to the relevant chief constable (within the meaning of that section) were to the relevant chief constable (within the meaning of this Schedule),

(c) references to the relevant police and crime panel (within the meaning of that Act) were to the relevant police and crime panel (within the meaning of this Schedule),

(d) in subsection (9), paragraph (b)(ii) and the words following that paragraph were omitted, and

(e) in subsection (10)(a) the words from "and to each" to "relevant police area" were omitted.

4 Information for public

4 (1) Section 11 of the Police Reform and Social Responsibility Act 2011 (information for public etc) applies in relation to a relevant fire and rescue authority as it applies in relation to an elected local policing body, subject to sub-paragraph (2).

(2) As applied by sub-paragraph (1), that section has effect as if—

(a) references to the relevant chief officer of police were to the relevant chief constable, and

(b) references to the chief officer's functions were to the relevant chief constable's fire and rescue functions.

5 Scrutiny of fire and rescue statement

5 (1) Subsections (2) to (5) of section 12 of the Police Reform and Social Responsibility Act 2011 (annual reports) apply in relation to a relevant fire and rescue authority as they apply in relation to an elected local policing body, subject to sub-paragraph (2).

(2) As applied by sub-paragraph (1), those subsections have effect as if—

(a) references to an annual report were to a fire and rescue statement, and

(b) references to the relevant police and crime panel (within the meaning of that Act) were to the relevant police and crime panel (within the meaning of this Schedule).

6 Information for police and crime panels

6 (1) Section 13 of the Police Reform and Social Responsibility Act 2011 (information for police and crime panels) applies in relation to a relevant fire and rescue authority as it applies in relation to an elected local policing body, subject to sub-paragraph (2).

(2) As applied by sub-paragraph (1), that section has effect as if—

(a) references to the relevant police and crime panel (within the meaning of that Act) were to the relevant police and crime panel (within the meaning of this Schedule), and

(b) in subsection (2), paragraphs (a) to (c) were omitted.

7 Duties when carrying out functions

7 (1) Subsections (1), (2) and (4) to (7) of section 17 of the Police Reform and Social Responsibility Act 2011 (duties when carrying out functions) apply in relation to a relevant fire and rescue authority as they apply in relation to an elected local policing body, subject to sub-paragraph (2).

(2) As applied by sub-paragraph (1), those subsections have effect as if—

(a) the reference in subsection (1) to policing in an elected local policing body's area were to fire and rescue services in the relevant fire and rescue authority's area,

(b) the reference in subsection (2) to the relevant police and crime panel (within the meaning of that Act) were to the relevant police and crime panel (within the meaning of this Schedule),

(c) the reference in that subsection to any report or recommendations made by the panel on the annual report for the previous financial year were to any report or recommendations made by the panel with respect to the discharge of the relevant fire and rescue authority's functions, and

(d) the reference in subsection (7) to elected local policing bodies were to relevant fire and rescue authorities.

8 Powers of police and crime panels

8 (1) Subsections (2) to (9) and (11) of section 28 of the Police Reform and Social Responsibility Act 2011 (police and crime panels outside London) apply in relation to a relevant fire and rescue authority as they apply in relation to a police and crime commissioner, subject to sub-paragraph (2).

(2) As applied by sub-paragraph (1), those subsections have effect as if—

(a) references to the police and crime panel or a police and crime panel were to the relevant police and crime panel,

(b) the references in subsection (3) to the draft police and crime plan were to the draft fire and rescue plan,

(c) the references in subsection (4) to an annual report were to a fire and rescue statement,

(d) the references in subsections (5) and (6) to Schedules 1 and 5 were to those Schedules as applied by this Schedule,

(e) the references in those subsections to Schedule 8 were omitted, and

(f) the second reference in subsection (8) to the police area were to the area of the relevant fire and rescue authority.

9 Power to require attendance and information

9 (1) Section 29 of the Police Reform and Social Responsibility Act 2011 (power to require attendance and information) applies in relation to a relevant fire and rescue authority as it applies in relation to a police and crime commissioner, subject to sub-paragraph (2).

(2) As applied by sub-paragraph (1), that section has effect as if—

(a) references to the police and crime panel or a police and crime panel were to the relevant police and crime panel, and

(b) the reference in subsection (6) to the relevant chief constable (within the meaning of that section) were to the relevant chief constable (within the meaning of this Schedule).

10 Conduct of fire and rescue authority

10 Section 31 of the Police Reform and Social Responsibility Act 2011 (conduct of police and crime commissioner etc) applies in relation to a holder of the office of relevant fire and rescue authority as it applies in relation to a holder of the office of police and crime commissioner.

11 Scrutiny of appointment of chief finance officer

11 (1) Paragraphs 9(1)(b) and (2) and 10 to 12 of Schedule 1 to the Police Reform and Social Responsibility Act 2011 (scrutiny of appointment of chief finance officer) apply in relation to a relevant fire and rescue authority as they apply in relation to a police and crime commissioner, subject to sub-paragraph (2).

(2) As applied by sub-paragraph (1), those paragraphs have effect as if—

(a) the references in paragraph 9 to the relevant police and crime panel (within the meaning of that Act) were to the relevant police and crime panel (within the meaning of this Schedule),

(b) the reference in paragraph 9(1)(b) to the commissioner's chief finance officer were to the relevant fire and rescue authority's chief finance officer within the meaning of section 4D of this Act,

(c) the references in paragraphs 10, 11 and 12 to the police and crime panel or a police crime panel were to the relevant police and crime panel, and

(d) paragraph 10(9) defined "relevant post-election period" as the period that—

(i) begins with the day of the poll at an ordinary election under section 50 of the Police Reform and Social

Responsibility Act 2011 of the police and crime commissioner for the relevant police area, and

(ii) ends with the day on which the person elected as that police and crime commissioner delivers a declaration of acceptance of office under section 70 of that Act.

(3) In sub-paragraph (2)(d)(i) "the relevant police area" means the police area—

(a) which corresponds to the area of the relevant fire and rescue authority, or

(b) within which the area of the relevant fire and rescue authority falls.

12 Scrutiny of precepts

12 (1) Schedule 5 to the Police Reform and Social Responsibility Act 2011 (issuing precepts) applies in relation to a relevant fire and rescue authority as it applies in relation to a police and crime commissioner, subject to sub-paragraph (2).

(2) As applied by sub-paragraph (1), that Schedule has effect as if references to the relevant police and crime panel (within the meaning of that Act) or to the police and crime panel were to the relevant police and crime panel (within the meaning of this Schedule).

13 Regulations about complaints and conduct matters

13 (1) Schedule 7 to the Police Reform and Social Responsibility Act 2011 (regulations about complaints and conduct matters) applies in relation to a holder of the office of relevant fire and rescue authority as it applies in relation to a holder of the office of police and crime commissioner, subject to sub-paragraph (2).

(2) As applied by sub-paragraph (1), that Schedule has effect as if references to police and crime panels were to relevant police and crime panels."

PART 2

AMENDMENTS TO OTHER ACTS

Fire Services Act 1947 (c. 41)

14 In section 26 of the Fire Services Act 1947 (firefighters' pension scheme) (as continued in force by order under section 36 of the Fire and Rescue Services Act 2004) after subsection (5) insert—

"(5A) References in this section to employment as a member of a fire brigade or on duties connected with the provision of fire services include employment by the chief constable of the police force for a police area as a result of—

(a) a transfer to the chief constable under a scheme made under section 4I(1) of the Fire and Rescue Services Act 2004, or

(b) an appointment by the chief constable under section 4I(4) of that Act.

(5B) References in this section to a fire authority include the chief constable of the police force for a police area who employs persons as mentioned in subsection (5A)."

Landlord and Tenant Act 1954 (c. 56)

15 In section 69(1) of the Landlord and Tenant Act 1954 (interpretation) in the definition of "local authority" for "or a combined authority established under section 103 of that Act" substitute ", a combined authority established under section 103 of that Act or a fire and rescue authority created by an order under section 4A of the Fire and Rescue Services Act 2004".

Local Government Act 1966 (c. 42)

16 In section 11 of the Local Government Act 1966 (grants for certain expenditure due to ethnic minority population) in subsection (2) (bodies to which the section applies) after "This section shall apply to" insert "a fire and rescue authority created by an order under section 4A of the Fire and Rescue Services Act 2004,".

Leasehold Reform Act 1967 (c. 88)

17 The Leasehold Reform Act 1967 is amended as follows.

18 In section 28 (retention or resumption of land required for public purposes) in subsection (5)(a) (application to local authorities) after "any combined authority established under section 103 of that Act," insert "any fire and rescue authority created by an order under section 4A of the Fire and Rescue Services Act 2004,".

19 In Schedule 4A (exclusion of certain shared ownership leases) in paragraph 2(2) (leases granted by certain local authorities: bodies to which the exclusion applies) after paragraph (b) insert—

"(ba) a fire and rescue authority created by an order under section 4A of the Fire and Rescue Services Act 2004;".

Local Government Grants (Social Need) Act 1969 (c. 2)

20 In section 1 of the Local Government Grants (Social Need) Act 1969 (grants for special social needs) in subsection (3) (meaning of "local authority") after "shall also include" insert "a fire and rescue authority created by an order under section 4A of the Fire and Rescue Services Act 2004,".

Employers' Liability (Compulsory Insurance) Act 1969 (c. 57)

21 In section 3(2)(b) of the Employers' Liability (Compulsory Insurance) Act 1969 (employers exempted from insurance: employers to which the exemption applies) after "a combined authority established under section 103 of that Act," insert "a fire and rescue authority created by an order under section 4A of the Fire and Rescue Services Act 2004,".

Local Authorities (Goods and Services) Act 1970 (c. 39)

22 In section 1 of the Local Authorities (Goods and Services) Act 1970 (supply of goods and services by local authorities) in subsection (4) (interpretation) after "any combined authority established under section 103 of that Act," insert "any fire and rescue authority created by an order under section 4A of the Fire and Rescue Services Act 2004,".

Local Government Act 1972 (c. 70)

23 The Local Government Act 1972 is amended as follows.

24 In section 120 (acquisition of land by agreement) after subsection (3A) insert—

"(3B) A fire and rescue authority created by an order under section 4A of the Fire and Rescue Services Act 2004 is to be treated as a principal council for the purposes of this section (apart from subsection (1)(b))."

25 In section 138C(1) (application of provisions about religious etc observance and involvement with religious etc events) after paragraph (p) insert—

"(pa) a fire and rescue authority created by an order under section 4A of that Act, but only for the purposes of section 138B;".

26 In section 222 (power of local authority to prosecute or defend legal proceedings) in subsection (2) (application to bodies other than local authorities) after "the Common Council" insert "and a fire and rescue authority created by an order under section 4A of the Fire and Rescue Services Act 2004".

27 In section 223 (appearance of local authorities in legal proceedings) in subsection (2) (application to bodies other than local authorities) after "a combined authority," insert "a fire and rescue authority created by an order under section 4A of the Fire and Rescue Services Act 2004,".

28 In section 229 (photographic copies of documents) in subsection (8) (meaning of "local authority") after "a combined authority," insert "a fire and rescue authority created by an order under section 4A of the Fire and Rescue Services Act 2004,".

29 In section 231 (service of notices on local authorities, etc) in subsection (4) (meaning of "local authority") after "a combined authority," insert "a fire and rescue authority created by an order under section 4A of the Fire and Rescue Services Act 2004,".

30 In section 232 (public notices) in subsection (1A) (meaning of "local authority") after "a combined authority," insert "a fire and rescue authority created by an order under section 4A of the Fire and Rescue Services Act 2004,".

31 In section 233 (service of notices by local authorities) in subsection (11) (meaning of "local authority") after "a combined authority," insert "a fire and rescue authority created by an order under section 4A of the Fire and Rescue Services Act 2004,".

32 In section 234 (authentication of documents) in subsection (4) (meaning of "local authority") after "a combined authority," insert "a fire and rescue authority created by an order under section 4A of the Fire and Rescue Services Act 2004,".

Employment Agencies Act 1973 (c. 35)

33 In section 13(7) of the Employment Agencies Act 1973 (activities to which the Act does not apply) after paragraph (fh) insert—

"(fi) the exercise by a fire and rescue authority created by an order under section 4A of the Fire and Rescue Services Act 2004 of any of its functions;".

Local Government Act 1974 (c. 7)

34 In section 25(1) of the Local Government Act 1974 (authorities subject to investigation) after paragraph (bg) insert—

"(bh) a fire and rescue authority created by an order under section 4A of that Act;".

Health and Safety at Work etc Act 1974 (c. 37)

35 In section 28(6) of the Health and Safety at Work etc Act 1974 (restrictions on disclosure of information: meaning of local authority) after "a combined authority established under section 103 of that Act" insert ", a fire and rescue authority created by an order under section 4A of the Fire and Rescue Services Act 2004".

Local Government (Miscellaneous Provisions) Act 1976 (c. 57)

36 In section 44(1) of the Local Government (Miscellaneous Provisions) Act 1976 (interpretation of Part 1) in paragraph (a) of the definition of "local authority" after "a combined authority established under section 103 of that Act" insert ", a fire and rescue authority created by an order under section 4A of the Fire and Rescue Services Act 2004".

Rent (Agriculture) Act 1976 (c. 80)

37 In section 5(3) of the Rent (Agriculture) Act 1976 (tenancies which are not statutory tenancies) after paragraph (bbb) insert—

"(bbc) a fire and rescue authority created by an order under section 4A of the Fire and Rescue Services Act 2004;".

Rent Act 1977 (c. 42)

38 In section 14(1) of the Rent Act 1977 (tenancies which are not protected tenancies) after paragraph (cc) insert—

"(cd) a fire and rescue authority created by an order under section 4A of the Fire and Rescue Services Act 2004;".

Protection from Eviction Act 1977 (c. 43)

39 In section 3A(8)(a) of the Protection from Eviction Act 1977 (excluded tenancies and licences: licences to occupy local authority etc hostels) after "the Inner London Education Authority," insert "a fire and rescue authority created by an order under section 4A of the Fire and Rescue Services Act 2004,".

Local Government, Planning and Land Act 1980 (c. 65)

40 The Local Government, Planning and Land Act 1980 is amended as follows.

41 In section 99 (disposal of land at direction of Secretary of State - supplementary) in subsection (4) (authorities who may make representations about directions) after paragraph (dbb) insert—

"(dbc) a fire and rescue authority created by an order under section 4A of the Fire and Rescue Services Act 2004;".

42 In Schedule 16 (bodies to whom Part 10 applies) after paragraph 5BC insert—

"5BD A fire and rescue authority created by an order under section 4A of the Fire and Rescue Services Act 2004."

Acquisition of Land Act 1981 (c. 67)

43 In section 17(4) of the Acquisition of Land Act 1981 (local authority and statutory undertakers' land: interpretation) in paragraph (a) of the definition of "local authority" after "the Common Council of the City of London," insert "a fire and rescue authority created by an order under section 4A of the Fire and Rescue Services Act 2004,".

Local Government (Miscellaneous Provisions) Act 1982 (c. 30)

44 The Local Government (Miscellaneous Provisions) Act 1982 is amended as follows.

45 In section 33 (enforceability by local authorities of certain covenants relating to land) in subsection (9)(a) (meaning of "principal council") after "the London Residuary Body," insert "a fire and rescue authority created by an order under section 4A of the Fire and Rescue Services Act 2004,".

46 In section 41 (lost and uncollected property) in subsection (13) (interpretation) in the definition of "local authority" after paragraph (ezb) insert—

"(ezc) a fire and rescue authority created by an order under section 4A of the Fire and Rescue Services Act 2004;".

47 In section 45 (arrangements under Employment and Training Act 1973) in subsection (2) (local authorities to which section applies) after paragraph (c) (but before the "and" at the end of that paragraph) insert—

"(ca) a fire and rescue authority created by an order under section 4A of the Fire and Rescue Services Act 2004;".

County Courts Act 1984 (c. 28)

48 In section 60(3) of the County Courts Act 1984 (right of audience of local authority: interpretation) in the definition of "local authority" after "a combined authority established under section 103 of that Act," insert "a fire and rescue authority created by an order under section 4A of the Fire and Rescue Services Act 2004,".

Housing Act 1985 (c. 68)

49 In section 4(1)(e) of the Housing Act 1985 (other descriptions of authority: local authorities) after "a combined authority" in both places insert ", a fire and rescue authority created by an order under section 4A of the Fire and Rescue Services Act 2004".

Landlord and Tenant Act 1985 (c.70)

50 In section 38 of the Landlord and Tenant Act 1985 (minor definitions) in the definition of "local authority" after "a combined authority established under section 103 of that Act" insert ", a fire and rescue authority created by an order under section 4A of the Fire and Rescue Services Act 2004".

Local Government Act 1986 (c. 10)

51 The Local Government Act 1986 is amended as follows.

52 In section 6(2)(a) (meaning of "local authority" for the purposes of Part 2) after the entry relating to a combined authority established under section 103 of the Local Democracy, Economic Development and Construction Act 2009 insert—

"a fire and rescue authority created by an order under section 4A of the Fire and Rescue Services Act 2004,".

53 In section 9(1)(a) (meaning of "local authority" for the purposes of Part 3) after the entry relating to a combined authority established under section 103 of the Local Democracy, Economic Development and Construction Act 2009 insert—

"a fire and rescue authority created by an order under section 4A of the Fire and Rescue Services Act 2004,".

Landlord and Tenant Act 1987 (c.31)

54 In section 58(1) of the Landlord and Tenant Act 1987 (exempt landlords) in paragraph (a) (local authorities) after "the Common Council of the City of London," insert "a fire and rescue authority created by an order under section 4A of the Fire and Rescue Services Act 2004,".

Local Government Act 1988 (c. 9)

55 In Schedule 2 to the Local Government Act 1988 (public supply or works contracts: the public authorities) in the entry relating to a fire and rescue authority constituted by a scheme under section 2 of the Fire and Rescue Services Act 2004 and other fire and rescue authorities, after "applies" insert ", a fire and rescue authority created by an order under section 4A of that Act".

Housing Act 1988 (c. 50)

56 The Housing Act 1988 is amended as follows.

57 In section 74(8) (transfer of land etc to housing action trusts: meaning of "local authority") after paragraph (fb) insert—

"(fc) a fire and rescue authority created by an order under section 4A of the Fire and Rescue Services Act 2004;".

58 In Part 1 of Schedule 1 (tenancies which cannot be assured tenancies) in paragraph 12(2) (local authority tenancies: meaning of "local authority") after paragraph (e) insert—

"(ea) a fire and rescue authority created by an order under section 4A of the Fire and Rescue Services Act 2004;".

Road Traffic Act 1988 (c. 52)

59 In section 144(2)(a)(i) of the Road Traffic Act 1988 (exceptions from the requirement for third party insurance) after "the Inner London Education Authority," insert "a fire and rescue authority created by an order under section 4A of the Fire and Rescue Services Act 2004,".

Local Government and Housing Act 1989 (c. 42)

60 The Local Government and Housing Act 1989 is amended as follows.

61 In section 1(9) (meaning of politically restricted post under a local authority) at the end insert ", and every member of staff of a fire and rescue authority created by an order under section 4A of the Fire and Rescue Services Act 2004."

62 (1) Section 4 (designation and reports of head of paid service) is amended as follows.

(2) In subsection (4) after paragraph (a) insert—

"(aa) in the case of a fire and rescue authority created by an order under section 4A of the Fire and Rescue Services Act 2004, to the authority and to the police and crime panel for the police area—

(i) which corresponds to the authority's area, or

(ii) within which the area of the authority falls;".

(3) After subsection (5A) insert—

"(5B) It shall be the duty of a fire and rescue authority created by an order under section 4A of the Fire and Rescue Services Act 2004 to consider any report under this section by the head of the authority's paid service and to do so no later than three months after the authority is sent a copy of the report."

(4) In subsection (6)(a) for "and an elected local policing body" substitute ", an elected local policing body and a fire and rescue authority created by an order under section 4A of the Fire and Rescue Services Act 2004".

63 (1) Section 5 (designation and reports of monitoring officer) is amended as follows.

(2) In subsection (3) after the second paragraph (a) insert—

"(aa) in the case of a fire and rescue authority created by an order under section 4A of the Fire and Rescue Services Act 2004, to the authority and to the police and crime panel for the police area—

(i) which corresponds to the authority's area, or

(ii) within which the area of the authority falls;".

(3) In subsection (5)(a) after sub-paragraph (i) insert—

"(ia) in the case of a fire and rescue authority created by an order under section 4A of the Fire and Rescue Services Act 2004, no later than three months after the authority is sent a copy of the report;".

(4) In subsection (8)—

(a) in the definition of "chief finance officer" after "Schedule 1 to the Police Reform and Social Responsibility Act 2011" insert ", section 4D(4) of the Fire and Rescue Services Act 2004", and

(b) in paragraph (a) of the definition of "relevant authority" for "and an elected local policing body" substitute ", an elected local policing body and a fire and rescue authority created by an order under section 4A of the Fire and Rescue Services Act 2004".

64 In section 21 (interpretation of Part 1) after subsection (1) insert—

"(1A) In section 7 references to a local authority include a fire and rescue authority created by an order under section 4A of the Fire and Rescue Services Act 2004.

(1B) In the application of section 1(1) to a fire and rescue authority created by an order under section 4A of the Fire and Rescue Services Act 2004 by virtue of subsection (1A) the reference to being or remaining a member of a local authority is to be read as a reference to becoming or remaining such an authority."

65 In section 152(2) (meaning of "relevant authority" for the purposes of sections 150 and 151) after paragraph (f) insert—

"(fa) a fire and rescue authority created by an order under section 4A of that Act;".

66 In section 155(4) (emergency financial assistance to local authorities: meaning of "local authority") after paragraph (h) insert—

"(ha) a fire and rescue authority created by an order under section 4A of that Act;".

67 Until the coming into force of the repeal of section 67 of the Local Government and Housing Act 1989 (application of provisions about companies in which local authorities have interests) by the Local Government and Public Involvement in Health Act 2007, subsection (3) of that section has effect as if after paragraph (h) there were inserted—

"(ha) a fire and rescue authority created by an order under section 4A of that Act;".

Town and Country Planning Act 1990 (c. 8)

68 The Town and Country Planning Act 1990 is amended as follows.

69 In section 252 (procedures for highways orders) in the definition of "local authority" in subsection (12) after "a combined authority established under section 103 of that Act," insert "a fire and rescue authority created by an order under section 4A of the Fire and Rescue Services Act 2004,".

70 In Schedule 14 (procedure for footpaths and bridleway orders) in paragraph 1(3) (meaning of "council") for "or a combined authority established under section 103 of that Act" substitute ", a combined authority established under section 103 of that Act or a fire and rescue authority created by an order under section 4A of the Fire and Rescue Services Act 2004".

Local Government Finance Act 1992 (c. 14)

71 (1) The Local Government Finance Act 1992 is amended as follows.

(2) In section 39(1) (major precepting authorities) after paragraph (da) insert—

"(db) a fire and rescue authority created by an order under section 4A of that Act;".

(3) In section 65(3) (duty of relevant authority to consult ratepayers: meaning of "relevant authority") after "apart from a police and crime commissioner" insert "or a fire and rescue authority created by an order under section 4A of the Fire and Rescue Services Act 2004.".

Local Government (Overseas Assistance) Act 1993 (c. 25)

72 In section 1 of the Local Government (Overseas Assistance) Act 1993 (power to provide advice and assistance) in subsection (10) (other bodies) after paragraph (a) insert—

"(aa) a fire and rescue authority created by an order under section 4A of that Act;".

Deregulation and Contracting Out Act 1994 (c. 40)

73 The Deregulation and Contracting Out Act 1994 is amended as follows.

74 In section 70(1ZB) (functions of local authorities: application to certain fire and rescue authorities) after "applies" insert "or a fire and rescue authority created by an order under section 4A of that Act".

75 In section 79A (local authorities in England) after paragraph (n) insert—

"(na) a fire and rescue authority created by an order under section 4A of that Act;".

Police Act 1996 (c. 16)

76 In section 63 of the Police Act 1996 (Police Advisory Board for England and Wales), at the end insert—

"(4) Section 4K of the Fire and Rescue Services Act 2004 also imposes a requirement on the Secretary of State to consult the Police Advisory Board for England and Wales."

Crime and Disorder Act 1998 (c. 37)

77 The Crime and Disorder Act 1998 is amended as follows.

78 In section 5(5) (authorities responsible for strategies: interpretation) in the definition of "fire and rescue authority" after paragraph (a) insert—

"(aa) a fire and rescue authority created by an order under section 4A of that Act;".

79 In section 17(2) (duty to consider crime and disorder implications: authorities to which duty applies) after the entry relating to a fire and rescue authority constituted by a scheme under section 2 of the Fire and Rescue Services Act 2004 or a scheme to which section 4 of that Act applies insert—

"a fire and rescue authority created by an order under section 4A of that Act;".

80 In section 115(2) (disclosure of information: meaning of relevant authority) after paragraph (i) insert—

"(ia) a fire and rescue authority created by an order under section 4A of that Act;".

Freedom of Information Act 2000 (c. 36)

81 In Part 2 of Schedule 1 to the Freedom of Information Act 2000 (public authorities: local government) after paragraph 14 insert—

"14A A fire and rescue authority created by an order under section 4A of that Act."

Police Reform Act 2002 (c. 30)

82 In section 38 of the Police Reform Act 2002 (police powers for civilian staff) after subsection (11) insert—

"(11A) In the case of a police force maintained for a police area in England in accordance with section 2 of the Police Act 1996, the following are also relevant employees for the purposes of this section—

(a) any member of staff transferred to the chief constable of the police force under a scheme made under section 4I(1) of the Fire and Rescue Services Act 2004 (transfer of property, rights and liabilities to chief constable to whom fire functions of a fire and rescue authority may be delegated);

(b) any member of staff appointed by that chief constable under section 4I(4) of that Act (appointment of staff by chief constable to whom fire functions of a fire and rescue authority may be delegated)."

Local Government Act 2003 (c. 26)

83 (1) The Local Government Act 2003 is amended as follows.

(2) In section 23(1) (local authorities to which the provisions about capital finance etc and accounts apply) after paragraph (m) insert—

"(ma) a fire and rescue authority created by an order under section 4A of that Act;".

(3) In section 33(1) (expenditure grant: interpretation) after paragraph (l) insert—

"(la) a fire and rescue authority created by an order under section 4A of that Act;".

(4) In section 95(7) (power to trade in function-related activities through a company: interpretation) in the definition of "relevant authority" after paragraph (ab) insert—

"(ac) a fire and rescue authority created by an order under section 4A of the Fire and Rescue Services Act 2004;".

(5) In section 97(11) (power to modify enactments in connection with charging or trading: interpretation) in the definition of "relevant authority" after paragraph (aa) insert—

"(ab) a fire and rescue authority created by an order under section 4A of the Fire and Rescue Services Act 2004;".

Local Government and Public Involvement in Health Act 2007 (c. 28)

84 In section 104 of the Local Government and Public Involvement in Health Act 2007 (partner authorities) in subsection (5) (meaning of "fire and rescue authority") after paragraph (a) insert—

"(aa) a fire and rescue authority created by an order under section 4A of that Act;".

Equality Act 2010 (c. 15)

85 In Part 1 of Schedule 19 to the Equality Act 2010 (public authorities) after the entry relating to a fire and rescue authority constituted by a scheme under section 2 of the Fire and Rescue Services Act 2004 or a scheme to which section 4 of that Act applies insert—

"A fire and rescue authority created by an order under section 4A of that Act."

Police Reform and Social Responsibility Act 2011 (c. 13)

86 The Police Reform and Social Responsibility Act 2011 is amended as follows.

87 (1) Section 1 (police and crime commissioners) is amended as follows.

(2) In subsection (3) for "The" substitute "Unless subsection (3B) applies, the".

(3) After subsection (3) insert—

"(3A) Subsection (3B) applies if the person who is the police and crime commissioner for a police area is also the fire and rescue authority for the area which corresponds to, or an area which falls within, the police area.

(3B) In that case the name of the police and crime commissioner is "the Police, Fire and Crime Commissioner for" with the addition of the name of the police area."

88 In section 5 (police and crime commissioner to issue police and crime plan) after subsection (5) insert—

"(5A) Subsections (5B) to (5E) apply to a police and crime commissioner for a police area—

(a) which corresponds to the area of a fire and rescue authority created by an order under section 4A, or

(b) within which the area of such a fire and rescue authority falls.

(5B) Subject to subsection (5E), in issuing or varying a police and crime plan, the police and crime commissioner must have regard to—

(a) the current Fire and Rescue National Framework prepared under section 21 of the Fire and Rescue Services Act 2004, and

(b) the last document prepared and published by the fire and rescue authority in accordance with that Framework which sets out the authority's priorities and objectives, for the period covered by the document, in connection with the discharge of the authority's functions.

(5C) A police and crime plan which the police and crime commissioner is required to prepare may be prepared jointly by the commissioner and the fire and rescue authority.

(5D) If the police and crime commissioner and the fire and rescue authority prepare a joint police and crime plan, the plan must also set out the fire and rescue authority's priorities and objectives, for the period of the plan, in connection with the discharge of the authority's functions.

(5E) Subsection (5B)(b) does not apply to a joint police and crime plan."

89 In section 28 (police and crime panels outside London) after subsection (1) insert—

"(1A) Subsection (1B) applies if the person who is the police and crime commissioner for a police area is also the fire and rescue authority for the area which corresponds to, or an area which falls within, the police area.

(1B) The police and crime panel for the police area is to be known as "the Police, Fire and Crime Panel"."

90 In section 66 (disqualification from election or holding office as police and crime commissioner: other grounds) after subsection (9) insert—

"(10) Subsection (11) applies to the police and crime commissioner for a police area if, by virtue of an order under section 4A of the Fire and Rescue Services Act 2004, the person who is for the time being the commissioner for that area is also the fire rescue authority for an area which corresponds to or falls within the police area.

(11) A person is disqualified from being elected as, or being, that police and crime commissioner if the person is employed by—

(a) a fire and rescue authority within section 1(2) or (3) of the Fire and Rescue Services Act 2004,

(b) a fire and rescue authority constituted by a scheme under section 2 of that Act or a scheme to which section 4 of that Act relates, or

(c) a fire and rescue authority created by an order under section 4A of that Act."

91 In Schedule 1 (police and crime commissioners) in paragraph 2 (salary etc) after sub-paragraph (3) insert—

"(4) Where the person who is the police and crime commissioner for a police area is also a fire and rescue authority created by an order under section 4A of the Fire and Rescue Services Act 2004, a determination under this paragraph in relation to that person may, in particular, take account of the fact that the person also exercises functions as that fire and rescue authority."

92 (1) Schedule 6 (police and crime panels) is amended as follows.

(2) In paragraph 4(6) (functions of panels) at the end insert "or by, or by virtue of, the Fire and Rescue Services Act 2004."

(3) In paragraph 22 (co-opted members of police and crime panels)—

(a) the existing paragraph becomes sub-paragraph (1), and

(b) at the end of that sub-paragraph insert—

"(2) Sub-paragraph (3) applies (as well as sub-paragraph (1)) in relation to a police and crime panel for a police area which, under or by virtue of the Fire and Rescue Services Act 2004, exercises functions in relation to a fire and rescue authority.

(3) A person may not be a co-opted member of the panel if the person is—

(a) a member of staff of the fire and rescue authority, or

(b) if an order under section 4H of that Act is in force in relation to that authority, a member of staff of the chief constable of the police force for the police area who has been—

(i) transferred to the chief constable under a scheme made under subsection 4I(1) of that Act, or

(ii) appointed by the chief constable under section 4I(4) of that Act."

(4) In paragraph 27 (exercise of special functions) after sub-paragraph (2) insert—

"(3) The references in sub-paragraph (2) to section 28(3) and (4) and Schedule 5 include those provisions as applied in relation to a fire and rescue authority by virtue of Schedule A2 to the Fire and Rescue Services Act 2004."

(5) After paragraph 32 insert—

"32A Duty to produce panel with fire and rescue expertise

32A (1) Sub-paragraph (2) applies in relation to a police and crime panel for a police area if—

(a) a fire and rescue authority is created by an order under section 4A of the Fire and Rescue Services Act 2004, and

(b) the area of the fire and rescue authority is the same as, or falls within, the police area.

(2) Each person listed in sub-paragraph (3)—

(a) must consider whether the person could exercise a function conferred on the person by or by virtue of this Schedule to enable the fire and rescue expertise objective to be met or to contribute to that objective being met, and

(b) if the person considers that the person could exercise such a function to that end, must do so.

(3) Those persons are—

(a) the panel,

(b) a relevant local authority, and

(c) the Secretary of State.

(4) The "fire and rescue expertise objective" referred to in this paragraph is the objective that members of the panel (when taken together) have the skills, knowledge and experience necessary for the panel effectively to discharge its functions in relation to the fire and rescue authority."

93 In Schedule 8 (appointment, suspension and removal of senior police officers) in paragraph 2 (no appointment until end of confirmation process)—

(a) in sub-paragraph (1A) for "A person" substitute insert "Subject to sub-paragraph (1AA), a person", and

(b) after sub-paragraph (1A) insert—

"(1AA) Where, under an order under section 4H of the Fire and Rescue Services Act 2004, functions of a fire and rescue authority are delegated to the chief constable of the police force for a police area, a person is eligible for appointment as that chief constable if the person—

(a) has experience at a senior level in the provision of services provided under the Fire and Rescue Services Act 2004, and

(b) has undertaken training in relation to policing matters of a kind that is specified by the College of Policing for the purposes of this paragraph."

Localism Act 2011 (c. 20)

94 (1) The Localism Act 2011 is amended as follows.

(2) In section 41(3) (power of fire and rescue authority to appoint officers and employees to be subject to pay policy statement) after "43(1)(i)" insert "or (j)".

(3) In section 43(1) (meaning of "relevant authority" for purposes of provisions on pay accountability)—

(a) omit the "or" at the end of paragraph (h), and

(b) at the end of paragraph (i) insert ", or

(j) in relation only to sections 38, 40 and 41 and this section, a fire and rescue authority created by an order under section 4A of that Act."

Public Service Pensions Act 2013 (c. 25)

95 In Schedule 1 to the Public Service Pensions Act 2013 (persons in public service: definitions) in paragraph 6 (fire and rescue workers) for the "or" at end of paragraph (a) substitute—

"(aa) the chief constable of the police force for a police area having been—

(i) transferred to the chief constable under a scheme made under section 4I(1) of the Fire and Rescue Services Act 2004, or

(ii) appointed by the chief constable under section 4I(4) of that Act, or".

Energy Act 2013 (c. 32)

96 In Part 3 of Schedule 9 to the Energy Act 2013 (protected information: permitted disclosures and restrictions on use) in paragraph 14(3) (local authorities and water authorities: interpretation) in the definition of "local authority" after paragraph (d) insert—

"(da) a fire and rescue authority created by an order under section 4A of the Fire and Rescue Services Act 2004;".

Local Audit and Accountability Act 2014 (c. 2)

97 (1) The Local Audit and Accountability Act 2014 is amended as follows.

(2) In Schedule 2 (relevant authorities) after paragraph 22 insert—

"22A A fire and rescue authority created by an order under section 4A of the Fire and Rescue Services Act 2004."

(3) In Schedule 7 (reports and recommendations by local auditor) in paragraph 5(7) (duty of certain authorities to consider report or recommendation) for "or the Mayor's Office for Policing and Crime" substitute ", the Mayor's Office for Policing and Crime or a fire and rescue authority created by an order under section 4A of the Fire and Rescue Services Act 2004".

SCHEDULE 2

Section 9

THE LONDON FIRE COMMISSIONER

PART 1

AMENDMENTS TO THE GREATER LONDON AUTHORITY ACT 1999

1 The Greater London Authority Act 1999 is amended as follows.

2 In section 21 (disqualification from being the Mayor or an Assembly member) after subsection (1) insert—

"(1A) Subsection (1)(a) does not prevent a person appointed under section 67(1)(b) as the Deputy Mayor for Fire, or appointed under section 67(1)(b) and designated as the Deputy Mayor for Fire, from being elected as or being an Assembly member."

3 In section 31(1) (limits of the Authority's general power) for paragraph (c) substitute—

"(c) the London Fire Commissioner."

4 (1) Section 45 (the Mayor's periodic report to the Assembly) is amended as follows.

(2) In subsection (6) omit "except as provided by subsection (7) below."

(3) Omit subsections (7) and (8).

5 (1) Section 60A (confirmation hearings etc for certain appointments by the Mayor) is amended as follows.

(2) In subsection (3) (offices to which section 60A applies)—

(a) before the entry for the chairman or deputy chairman of Transport for London insert—

"London Fire Commissioner (see section 327A);

person appointed by the Mayor under section 67(1)(b) as the Deputy Mayor for Fire;", and

(b) omit the entry for the chairman of the London Fire and Emergency Planning Authority.

(3) After subsection (4) insert—

"(4A) This section also applies in any case where the Mayor proposes to designate as the Deputy Mayor for Fire a person appointed under section 67(1)(b).

(4B) References in section 327H and Schedule 4A to appointment of a person as the Deputy Mayor for Fire (however expressed) include such a designation."

6 (1) Section 61 (power to require attendance at Assembly meetings) is amended as follows.

(2) In subsection (11) omit ", except as provided by subsection (12) below,".

(3) Omit subsections (12) and (13).

7 In section 67(1)(b) (power of Mayor to appoint ten members of staff in addition to the Mayor's political advisers) for "ten" substitute "eleven".

8 In section 68 (disqualification and political restriction) after subsection (3) insert—

"(3A) Subsections (1) and (2) above do not prevent a person appointed under section 67(1)(b) as the Deputy Mayor for Fire, or appointed under section 67(1)(b) and designated as the Deputy Mayor for Fire, from becoming or remaining a member of the Assembly or any other local authority within the meaning of sections 1, 2 and 3A of the Local Government and Housing Act 1989."

9 In section 70 (terms and conditions of employment) after subsection (7) insert—

"(7A) Subsection (3) does not prevent—

(a) a person appointed under section 67(1)(b) as the Deputy Mayor for Fire, or

(b) a person appointed under section 67(1)(b) and designated as the Deputy Mayor for Fire,

from being required to perform any work or services as an Assembly member."

10 After Part 6 insert—

"**PART 6A**

THE LONDON FIRE COMMISSIONER

327A The London Fire Commissioner

327A 327A The London Fire Commissioner

(1) There is to be a London Fire Commissioner.

(2) The London Fire Commissioner is a corporation sole.

(3) The Mayor is to appoint the London Fire Commissioner.

(4) The London Fire Commissioner has—

(a) the functions of the fire and rescue authority for Greater London under the Fire and Rescue Services Act 2004, and

(b) the other functions conferred on the Commissioner by or by virtue of any other enactment.

(5) The London Fire Commissioner must secure that the London Fire and Rescue Service is efficient and effective.

(6) In subsection (5) "the London Fire and Rescue Service" means the personnel, services and equipment secured by the London Fire Commissioner for the purposes of the carrying out of the Commissioner's functions under—

(a) section 6 of the Fire and Rescue Services Act 2004 (fire safety),

(b) section 7 of that Act (fire-fighting),

(c) section 8 of that Act (road traffic accidents),

(d) any order under section 9 of that Act (emergencies) which applies to the Commissioner, or

(e) any other provision of or made under an enactment which confers functions on a fire and rescue authority.

(7) The Mayor must hold the London Fire Commissioner to account for the exercise of the Commissioner's functions.

(8) Schedule 27A makes further provision about the London Fire Commissioner.

327B Disqualification for appointment as London Fire Commissioner

327B 327B Disqualification for appointment as London Fire Commissioner

(1) A person may not be appointed as the London Fire Commissioner unless the person has reached the age of 18.

(2) A person is disqualified from being appointed as, or being, the London Fire Commissioner if the person is a member of the Assembly or a London borough council.

(3) A person is disqualified from being appointed as, or being, the London Fire Commissioner if—

(a) the person is the subject of—

(i) a debt relief restrictions order under paragraph 1 of Schedule 4ZB to the Insolvency Act 1986,

(ii) an interim debt relief restrictions order under paragraph 5 of that Schedule,

(iii) a bankruptcy restrictions order under paragraph 1 of Schedule 4A to that Act, or

(iv) a bankruptcy restrictions interim order under paragraph 5 of that Schedule,

(b) a debt relief restrictions undertaking has effect in respect of the person under paragraph 7 of Schedule 4ZB to that Act,

(c) the person has been convicted in the United Kingdom, the Channel Islands or the Isle of Man of any imprisonable offence (whether or not sentenced to a term of imprisonment in respect of the offence), or

(d) the person is incapable of being elected as a member of the House of Commons, or is required to vacate a seat in the House of Commons, under Part 3 of the Representation of the People Act 1983 (consequences of corrupt or illegal practices).

(4) For the purposes of subsection (3)(c) "an imprisonable offence" means an offence—

(a) for which a person who has reached the age of 18 may be sentenced to a term of imprisonment, or

(b) for which, in the case of such a person, the sentence is fixed by law as life imprisonment.

(5) For the purposes of subsection (3)(c) a person is to be treated as having been convicted—

(a) on the expiry of the ordinary period allowed for an appeal or application in respect of the conviction, or

(b) if an appeal or application is made in respect of the conviction, when the appeal or application is finally disposed of or abandoned or fails by reason of non-prosecution.

327C Suspension and removal of London Fire Commissioner

327C 327C Suspension and removal of London Fire Commissioner

(1) The Mayor may with the approval of the Secretary of State suspend the London Fire Commissioner from duty.

(2) If the Mayor suspends the London Fire Commissioner from duty, the Mayor must notify the Secretary of State of the suspension.

(3) The Mayor may, subject to subsections (5) and (6), and with the approval of the Secretary of State, call upon the London Fire Commissioner to resign or retire.

(4) The London Fire Commissioner must resign or retire if called upon to do so in accordance with subsection (3).

(5) Before calling upon the London Fire Commissioner to resign or retire, the Mayor must—

(a) give the Commissioner a written explanation of the reasons why the Mayor is proposing to call for the Commissioner's resignation or retirement,

(b) give the Commissioner the opportunity to make written representations about the proposal to call for the Commissioner's resignation or retirement, and

(c) consider any written representations made by the Commissioner.

(6) The Mayor must comply with subsection (5) before seeking the approval of the Secretary of State to call upon the London Fire Commissioner to resign or retire.

327D Directions etc by the Mayor

327D 327D Directions etc by the Mayor

(1) The Mayor may issue to the London Fire Commissioner—

(a) guidance as to the manner in which the Commissioner is to exercise the Commissioner's functions,

(b) general directions as to the manner in which the Commissioner is to exercise the Commissioner's functions, or

(c) specific directions as to the exercise of the Commissioner's functions.

(2) Directions issued by the Mayor under subsection (1)(c) above may include a direction not to exercise a power specified in the direction.

(3) The guidance or directions which may be issued by the Mayor under subsection (1) above include guidance or directions as to the manner in which the London Fire Commissioner—

(a) is to perform any of the Commissioner's duties, or

(b) is to conduct any legal proceedings.

(4) In exercising any power conferred by this section, the Mayor must have regard to—

(a) the Fire and Rescue National Framework, and

(b) fire safety enforcement guidance.

(5) In this section—

"the Fire and Rescue National Framework" means the Fire and Rescue National Framework prepared under section 21 of the Fire and Rescue Services Act 2004;

"fire safety enforcement guidance" means guidance under article 26 (enforcement) of the Regulatory Reform (Fire Safety) Order 2005 (SI 2005/1541) given by the Secretary of State to the London Fire Commissioner in the Commissioner's capacity as an enforcing authority for the purposes of that Order.

327E Directions to the Mayor by the Secretary of State

327E 327E Directions to the Mayor by the Secretary of State

(1) This section applies if the Secretary of State thinks that any guidance or directions ("the inconsistent guidance or directions") issued under section 327D by the Mayor are inconsistent with—

(a) the Fire and Rescue National Framework, or

(b) fire safety enforcement guidance.

(2) In order to remove the inconsistency, the Secretary of State may direct the Mayor—

(a) to make such revisions of the inconsistent guidance or directions as may be specified by the Secretary of State in the direction, or

(b) if the inconsistency arises from a specific direction under section 327D(1)(c) above, to revoke the direction.

(3) Any direction given by the Secretary of State under subsection (2) above must specify or otherwise identify the inconsistency in question.

(4) The Mayor must comply with any direction under subsection (2) above.

(5) In this section "the Fire and Rescue National Framework" and "fire safety enforcement guidance" have the same meanings as in section 327D.

327F The Deputy Mayor for Fire

327F 327F The Deputy Mayor for Fire

(1) The Mayor may arrange for the Deputy Mayor for Fire to exercise any function of the Mayor relating to fire and rescue.

(2) In this Part "the Deputy Mayor for Fire" means—

(a) a person who has been appointed by the Mayor under section 67(1)(b) as the Deputy Mayor for Fire, or

(b) a person who has been appointed by the Mayor under section 67(1)(b) and designated by the Mayor as the Deputy Mayor for Fire.

(3) In subsection (1) the reference to the functions of the Mayor relating to fire and rescue are to the Mayor's functions under—

(a) section 327A(7) (duty to hold London Fire Commissioner to account), and

(b) section 327D(1) (power to give guidance and directions to the London Fire Commissioner).

(4) Section 327E applies in relation to the exercise of functions under section 327D(1) by the Deputy Mayor for Fire as it applies in relation to their exercise by the Mayor.

327G Scrutiny of documents prepared by London Fire Commissioner

327G 327G Scrutiny of documents prepared by London Fire Commissioner

(1) This section applies to a document which is prepared and published by the London Fire Commissioner in accordance with the Fire and Rescue National Framework and which—

(a) sets out the Commissioner's priorities and objectives, for the period covered by the document, in connection with the discharge of the Commissioner's functions, or

(b) contains a statement of the way in which the Commissioner has had regard, in the period covered by the document, to the Framework and to any document within paragraph (a) prepared by the Commissioner for that period.

(2) The Commissioner must, before publishing the document or any revision to it, send a copy of the document or revision in draft to the Mayor and the Assembly.

(3) The Commissioner may not publish the document or any revision to it unless—

(a) the Assembly has had an opportunity to review the draft document or revision, and make a report on it to the Mayor, under section 327I(1), and

(b) the Mayor has approved the draft document or revision.

(4) In this section "the Fire and Rescue National Framework" has the same meaning as in section 327D.

327H The Assembly fire and emergency committee

327H 327H The Assembly fire and emergency committee

(1) The Assembly must arrange for the functions referred to in subsection (2) to be discharged on its behalf by a particular committee of the Assembly ("the fire and emergency committee").

(2) Those functions ("the fire and emergency committee functions") are—

(a) the functions conferred on the Assembly by section 327I, and

(b) the functions conferred on the Assembly by section 60A and Schedule 4A in relation to the appointment of the London Fire Commissioner and the Deputy Mayor for Fire.

(3) The Assembly may not arrange for the fire and emergency committee functions to be discharged on its behalf otherwise than in accordance with subsection (1).

(4) The Assembly may not arrange for any of its other functions to be discharged by the fire and emergency committee.

(5) The special scrutiny functions may only be exercised at a meeting of the whole committee; but that is without prejudice to rules of procedure about the quorum of a meeting of the whole committee.

(6) Any provision made by or by virtue of an enactment which applies to committees of the Assembly, apart from the excluded provisions, applies to the fire and emergency committee as if the fire and emergency committee functions were to be discharged by the committee by virtue of arrangements under section 54(1)(a).

(7) In subsection (6) "the excluded provisions" means—

(a) section 54(5), so far as it provides for the Assembly to retain power to exercise functions delegated to a committee, and

(b) section 55 (Assembly committees and sub-committees).

(8) Any provision made by or by virtue of an enactment which confers, or relates to, the fire and emergency committee functions is to be read with the appropriate modifications; in particular—

(a) references to the Assembly are to be read as references to the fire and emergency committee, and

(b) references to proceedings of the Assembly are to be read as references to proceedings of the fire and emergency committee.

(9) For the purposes of subsection (8), references to the fire and emergency committee include references to a sub-committee or member (if any) by whom functions are to be discharged in accordance with section 54(3).

(10) The following provisions apply to the fire and emergency committee—

(a) the number of members of the committee, and their term of office, are to be fixed by the Assembly;

(b) persons who are not members of the Assembly may be members of the committee.

(11) The following provisions apply to any sub-committee by which fire and emergency committee functions are to be discharged—

(a) the number of members of the sub-committee, and their term of office, are to be fixed by the fire and emergency committee;

(b) persons who are not members of the Assembly may be members of the sub-committee.

(12) The fire and emergency committee functions must be exercised with a view to supporting the effective exercise of the functions of the London Fire Commissioner.

(13) In this section "special scrutiny functions" means the functions conferred—

(a) by section 327I(1), or

(b) by section 60A and Schedule 4A in relation to the appointment of the London Fire Commissioner and the Deputy Mayor for Fire.

327I Functions to be discharged by the fire and emergency committee

327I 327I Functions to be discharged by the fire and emergency committee

(1) The Assembly must—

(a) review any draft document or revision given to the Assembly by the London Fire Commissioner under section 327G(2), and

(b) make a report or recommendations on the draft document or revision to the Mayor.

(2) The Assembly must keep under review the exercise of the functions of the London Fire Commissioner, insofar as the Assembly is not otherwise required to do so by the other provisions of this section or by Schedule 4A.

(3) For the purposes of subsection (2), the powers of the Assembly include, in particular, power to investigate, and prepare reports about—

(a) any actions and decisions of the London Fire Commissioner,

(b) any actions and decisions of an officer of the London Fire Commissioner,

(c) matters relating to the functions of the London Fire Commissioner,

(d) matters in relation to which the functions of the London Fire Commissioner are exercisable, or

(e) any other matters which the Assembly considers to be of importance to fire and rescue services in Greater London.

(4) The Assembly may investigate, and prepare reports about, the actions and decisions of the Deputy Mayor for Fire.

(5) The Assembly may submit proposals to the London Fire Commissioner.

(6) The Assembly may require a person referred to in subsection (7)—

(a) to attend proceedings of the Assembly for the purpose of giving evidence, or

(b) to produce to the Assembly documents in the person's possession or under the person's control.

(7) Those persons are—

(a) the Deputy Mayor for Fire,

(b) the London Fire Commissioner,

(c) any officer of the London Fire Commissioner,

(d) any person who has within the 8 years prior to the date of the requirement to be imposed under subsection (6) been the Deputy Mayor for Fire or the London Fire Commissioner.

(8) Nothing in subsection (6) requires an officer of the London Fire Commissioner to give any evidence, or produce any document, which discloses advice given to the London Fire Commissioner by that officer.

(9) The following provisions apply (with appropriate modifications) to a requirement under subsection (6) as they apply to a requirement under section 61(1)—

(a) section 61(14) (meaning of document etc);

(b) section 62(3) to (6) (procedure for requiring attendance);

(c) section 63 (restriction of information);

(d) section 64 (failure to attend proceedings);

(e) section 65 (openness)."

11 (1) Omit Part 7 (the London Fire and Emergency Planning Authority).

(2) The repeal of section 328 in that Part by sub-paragraph (1) does not affect the continued operation of subsections (5) to (7) of that section, and subsection (9) of that section so far as applying to those subsections.

(3) In the application of those subsections by virtue of sub-paragraph (2), references in those subsections to the Fire etc Authority are to be read as references to the London Fire Commissioner.

12 In section 419(1) (bodies to be treated as local authorities for the purposes of enactments relating to taxation) for paragraph (c) substitute—

"(c) the London Fire Commissioner,".

13 (1) Section 424(1) (interpretation) is amended as follows.

(2) Omit the definition of "the Fire etc Authority".

(3) In the definition of "functional body" for paragraph (d) substitute—

"(d) the London Fire Commissioner;".

14 (1) Schedule 4A (confirmation hearings etc for certain appointments) is amended as follows.

(2) In paragraph 1 after sub-paragraph (7) insert—

"(8) Paragraph 9 does not apply in relation to—

(a) the appointment of a person as the London Fire Commissioner, or

(b) the appointment of a person as the Deputy Mayor for Fire under section 67(1)(b),

(but see section 327H).

(9) Paragraph 11 applies to—

(a) the appointment of a person as the London Fire Commissioner, and

(b) the appointment of a person as the Deputy Mayor for Fire under section 67(1)(b) if the candidate is not a member of the Assembly.

(10) Paragraphs 2, 4 and 5 are subject to paragraph 11."

(3) After paragraph 10 insert—

"11 (1) The Assembly may veto—

(a) the appointment of the candidate as the London Fire Commissioner, or

(b) the appointment of the candidate as the Deputy Mayor for Fire if the candidate is not a member of the Assembly.

(2) The exercise of that power of veto in relation to an appointment is not valid unless the Assembly—

(a) has held a confirmation meeting in relation to the appointment before the exercise of the power; and

(b) notifies the Mayor of the veto within the period of 3 weeks described in paragraph 4(3).

(3) If the Assembly vetoes the appointment of the candidate, the Mayor must not appoint the candidate.

(4) References in this Schedule to the Assembly vetoing the appointment of a candidate are references to the Assembly making a decision, by the required majority, that the candidate should not be appointed—

(a) as the London Fire Commissioner, or

(b) as the Deputy Mayor for Fire.

(5) For that purpose, the Assembly makes that decision by the required majority if at least two-thirds of the votes given in making that decision are votes in favour of making that decision."

15 After Schedule 27 insert—

"SCHEDULE 27A

Section 327A

THE LONDON FIRE COMMISSIONER

1 Appointment and tenure of office

1 (1) The terms and conditions on which the London Fire Commissioner is appointed are to be determined by the Mayor.

(2) A person holds and vacates office as the London Fire Commissioner in accordance with the terms and conditions of the person's appointment.

(3) Sub-paragraph (2) is subject to section 327C (suspension and removal of London Fire Commissioner).

2 Remuneration

2 (1) The person who is the London Fire Commissioner is to be paid such remuneration, allowances and gratuities as may be provided for under the terms and conditions of the Commissioner's appointment.

(2) In sub-paragraph (1) "allowances", in relation to the London Fire Commissioner, means allowances in respect of expenses incurred by the person in the performance of the Commissioner's functions.

(3) There is to be paid—

(a) a pension to, or in respect of, a person who has been the London Fire Commissioner, or

(b) amounts for or towards the provision of a pension to, or in respect of, such a person,

in accordance with the terms and conditions of the Commissioner's appointment.

(4) Payments under this paragraph are to be made by the London Fire Commissioner.

(5) In determining the London Fire Commissioner's terms and conditions relating to these matters, the Mayor must have regard to the financial resources of the Commissioner.

3 The Deputy London Fire Commissioner

3 (1) The London Fire Commissioner may exercise the power in section 112 of the Local Government Act 1972 (appointment of staff) to appoint a Deputy London Fire Commissioner.

(2) The Deputy London Fire Commissioner may exercise any or all of the powers and duties of the London Fire Commissioner—

(a) during any absence, incapacity or suspension from duty of the Commissioner,

(b) during any vacancy in the office of Commissioner, or

(c) at any other time, with the consent of the Commissioner.

(3) The Deputy London Fire Commissioner may not act under sub-paragraph (2)(a) or (b) for a continuous period of three months or more without the consent of the Mayor.

4 Damages and costs in legal proceedings

4 (1) The following amounts must be paid by the London Fire Commissioner—

(a) any damages or costs awarded against the Commissioner in any proceedings brought against the Commissioner in respect of the acts or omissions of an officer employed by the Commissioner;

(b) any costs incurred by the Commissioner in any such proceedings so far as not recovered by the Commissioner in the proceedings;

(c) any sum required in connection with the settlement of any claim made against the Commissioner in respect of the acts or omissions of an officer employed by the Commissioner, if the settlement is approved by the Mayor.

(2) The London Fire Commissioner may, in such cases and to such extent as appears to the Commissioner to be appropriate, pay—

(a) any damages or costs awarded against an officer employed by the Commissioner in proceedings for any unlawful conduct of that officer,

(b) any costs incurred and not recovered by such an officer in such proceedings, and

(c) any sum required in connection with the settlement of a claim that has or might have given rise to such proceedings."

16 Omit Schedule 28 (the London Fire and Emergency Planning Authority).

17 Omit Schedule 29 (amendments relating to the London Fire and Emergency Planning Authority).

PART 2

AMENDMENTS TO OTHER ACTS

Essex County Council Act 1952 (c. l)

18 In section 80 of the Essex County Council Act 1952 (precautions against fire) for "the London Fire and Emergency Planning Authority" substitute "the London Fire Commissioner".

Landlord and Tenant Act 1954 (c. 56)

19 In section 69(1) of the Landlord and Tenant Act 1954 (interpretation) in the definition of "local authority" for ", the London Fire and Emergency Planning Authority" substitute ", the London Fire Commissioner".

Local Government (Records) Act 1962 (c. 56)

20 The Local Government (Records) Act 1962 is amended as follows.

21 In section 2 (acquisition and deposit of records) in subsection (6) (bodies to which section 2 applies) for "to the London Fire and Emergency Planning Authority," substitute "to the London Fire Commissioner,".

22 In section 8(1) (interpretation) in the definition of "local authority" for "the London Fire and Emergency Planning Authority," substitute "the London Fire Commissioner,".

London Government Act 1963 (c. 33)

23 The London Government Act 1963 is amended as follows.

24 In section 5(3) (delegation of functions in Greater London) for "the London Fire and Emergency Planning Authority" substitute "the London Fire Commissioner".

25 In section 75 (compensation for injury to or death of officers) in subsection (4) (application to London Fire and Emergency Planning Authority) for "the London Fire and Emergency Planning Authority" substitute "the London Fire Commissioner".

Local Government Act 1966 (c. 42)

26 In section 11 of the Local Government Act 1966 (grants for certain expenditure due to ethnic minority population) in subsection (2) (bodies to which the section applies) for "the London Fire and Emergency Planning Authority" substitute "the London Fire Commissioner".

Leasehold Reform Act 1967 (c. 88)

27 The Leasehold Reform Act 1967 is amended as follows.

28 In section 28 (retention or resumption of land required for public purposes) in subsection (5)(a) (application to local authorities) for "the London Fire and Emergency Planning Authority," substitute "the London Fire Commissioner,".

29 In Schedule 4A (exclusion of certain shared ownership leases) in paragraph 2(2) (leases granted by certain local authorities: bodies to which the exclusion applies) for paragraph (bb) substitute—

"(bb) the London Fire Commissioner;".

Local Government Grants (Social Need) Act 1969 (c. 2)

30 In section 1 of the Local Government Grants (Social Need) Act 1969 (grants for special social needs) in subsection (3) (meaning of "local authority") for "the London Fire and Emergency Planning Authority" substitute "the London Fire Commissioner".

Employers' Liability (Compulsory Insurance) Act 1969 (c. 57)

31 In section 3(2)(b) of the Employers' Liability (Compulsory Insurance) Act 1969 (employers exempted from insurance: employers to which the exemption applies) for "the London Fire and Emergency Planning Authority," substitute "the London Fire Commissioner,".

Greater London Council (General Powers) Act 1969 (c. lii)

32 In section 30(ii) of the Greater London Council (General Powers) Act 1969 (savings for London Fire and Emergency Planning Authority) for "the London Fire and Emergency Planning Authority" substitute "the London Fire Commissioner".

Local Authorities (Goods and Services) Act 1970 (c. 39)

33 In section 1 of the Local Authorities (Goods and Services) Act 1970 (supply of goods and services by local authorities) in subsection (4) (interpretation) in the definition of "local authority" for "the London Fire and Emergency Planning Authority" substitute "the London Fire Commissioner".

Pensions (Increase) Act 1971 (c. 56)

34 In Schedule 3 to the Pensions (Increase) Act 1971 (further administrative, incidental and consequential provisions) in paragraph 6(1)(a) (meaning of "local authority") for sub-paragraph (ib) substitute—

"(ib) the London Fire Commissioner;".

Local Government Act 1972 (c. 70)

35 The Local Government Act 1972 is amended as follows.

36 In section 70 (restriction on promotion of Bills for changing local government areas etc) for subsection (2) substitute—

"(2) Subsection (1) above shall have effect as if the reference to a joint authority included a reference to the London Fire Commissioner."

37 (1) Section 100J (application of provisions about access to meetings and documents) is amended as follows.

(2) In subsection (1) (bodies to which provisions about access to meetings and documents apply) omit paragraph (bb).

(3) In subsection (2) omit ", (bb)".

(4) In subsection (3) omit "(bb),".

(5) Omit subsection (4A).

38 (1) Section 101 (arrangements for discharge of functions by local authorities) is amended as follows.

(2) In subsection (13) omit "the London Fire and Emergency Planning Authority,".

(3) After subsection (13) insert—

"(13A) In this section "local authority" includes the London Fire Commissioner; but nothing in this section authorises functions of the Commissioner to be discharged by a committee or sub-committee of the Commissioner."

39 In section 104 (disqualification for membership of committees and joint committees) omit subsection (5) (application to the London Fire and Emergency Planning Authority).

40 In section 138 (powers of principal councils with respect to emergencies or disasters) in subsection (5) (power of London Fire and Emergency Planning Authority to incur expenditure in connection with planning by principal councils) for "the London Fire and Emergency Planning Authority" substitute "the London Fire Commissioner".

41 In section 138C(1) (other authorities to which provisions about prayer and other religious observance apply) for paragraph (d) substitute—

"(d) the London Fire Commissioner but only for the purposes of section 138B;".

42 In section 142 (provision of information etc relating to matters affecting local government) for subsection (4) substitute—

"(4) This section shall have effect as if any reference to a local authority included a reference to the London Fire Commissioner."

43 (1) Section 146A (application of miscellaneous provisions about local authorities to other authorities) is amended as follows.

(2) In subsection (1)—

(a) for "or (1ZE)" substitute ", (1ZE) or (1ZF)", and

(b) for "the London Fire and Emergency Planning Authority" substitute "the London Fire Commissioner".

(3) In subsection (1ZC) for "the London Fire and Emergency Planning Authority" substitute "the London Fire Commissioner".

(4) After subsection (1ZE) insert—

"(1ZF) The London Fire Commissioner is not to be treated as a local authority for the purposes of section 135."

44 In section 175 (allowances for attending conferences and meetings) in subsection (3B) (application to the London Fire and Emergency Planning Authority etc) for "the London Fire and Emergency Planning Authority, an economic prosperity board, a combined authority or" substitute "an economic prosperity board, a combined authority or".

45 In section 176 (payment of expenses of official and courtesy visits) in subsection (3) (application to the London Fire and Emergency Planning Authority etc)—

(a) after "board," insert "and", and

(b) omit "and the London Fire and Emergency Planning Authority".

46 In section 222 (power of local authority to prosecute or defend legal proceedings) in subsection (2) (application to the London Fire and Emergency Planning Authority etc) for "and the London Fire and Emergency Planning Authority" substitute "and the London Fire Commissioner".

47 For section 244A substitute—

"244A Application of this Part to the London Fire Commissioner

"244A Application of this Part to the London Fire Commissioner

This Part shall have effect as if any reference to a joint authority included a reference to the London Fire Commissioner."

Employment Agencies Act 1973 (c. 35)

48 In section 13(7) of the Employment Agencies Act 1973 (activities to which the Act does not apply) for paragraph (fh) substitute—

"(fh) the exercise by the London Fire Commissioner of any of the Commissioner's functions;".

Local Government Act 1974 (c. 7)

49 In section 25(1) of the Local Government Act 1974 (authorities subject to investigation) for paragraph (cza) substitute—

"(cza) the London Fire Commissioner;".

Health and Safety at Work etc Act 1974 (c. 37)

50 In section 28(6) of the Health and Safety at Work etc Act 1974 (restrictions on disclosure of information: meaning of local authority) for "and the London Fire and Emergency Planning Authority" substitute "and the London Fire Commissioner".

Local Government (Miscellaneous Provisions) Act 1976 (c. 57)

51 In section 44(1) of the Local Government (Miscellaneous Provisions) Act 1976 (interpretation of Part 1) in the definition of "local authority"—

(a) in paragraph (a) for "and the London Fire and Emergency Planning Authority" substitute "and the London Fire Commissioner", and

(b) in paragraph (c) for "the London Fire and Emergency Planning Authority" substitute "the London Fire Commissioner".

Rent (Agriculture) Act 1976 (c. 80)

52 In section 5(3) of the Rent (Agriculture) Act 1976 (tenancies which are not statutory tenancies) for paragraph (bbb) substitute—

"(bbb) the London Fire Commissioner;".

Rent Act 1977 (c. 42)

53 In section 14(1) of the Rent Act 1977 (tenancies which are not protected tenancies) for paragraph (cc) substitute—

"(cc) the London Fire Commissioner;".

London Hydraulic Power Act 1977 (c. xi)

54 In section 3(3)(b) of the London Hydraulic Power Act 1977 (notice of intention to use new pipeline) for "the London Fire and Emergency Planning Authority" substitute "the London Fire Commissioner".

Protection from Eviction Act 1977 (c. 43)

55 In section 3A(8)(a) of the Protection from Eviction Act 1977 (excluded tenancies and licences: licences to occupy local authority etc hostels) for "the London Fire and Emergency Planning Authority," substitute "the London Fire Commissioner,".

Local Government, Planning and Land Act 1980 (c. 65)

56 The Local Government, Planning and Land Act 1980 is amended as follows.

57 In section 2 (duty of authorities to publish information) in subsection (1) (authorities to which the duty applies) for paragraph (kb) substitute—

"(kb) the London Fire Commissioner;".

58 In section 98 (disposal of land at direction of Secretary of State) in subsection (8A) (authorities to which provisions as to associated bodies apply) for paragraph (f) substitute—

"(f) the London Fire Commissioner."

59 In section 99 (disposal of land at direction of Secretary of State - supplementary) in subsection (4) (authorities who may make representations about directions) for paragraph (dbb) substitute—

"(dbb) the London Fire Commissioner;"

60 In section 100 (interpretation and extent of Part 10) in subsection (1)(a) (meaning of "subsidiary") for ", the London Fire and Emergency Planning Authority" substitute ", the London Fire Commissioner".

61 In Schedule 16 (bodies to whom Part 10 applies) for paragraph 5BB substitute—

"5BB The London Fire Commissioner."

Acquisition of Land Act 1981 (c. 67)

62 The Acquisition of Land Act 1981 is amended as follows.

63 In section 7(1) (interpretation) in the definition of "local authority" for paragraph (a1) substitute—

"(a1) the London Fire Commissioner;".

64 In section 17(4) (local authority and statutory undertakers' land: interpretation) in paragraph (a) of the definition of "local authority" for "the London Fire and Emergency Planning Authority," substitute "the London Fire Commissioner,".

Local Government (Miscellaneous Provisions) Act 1982 (c. 30)

65 The Local Government (Miscellaneous Provisions) Act 1982 is amended as follows.

66 In section 33 (enforceability by local authorities of certain covenants relating to land) in subsection (9)(a) (meaning of "principal council") for "the London Fire and Emergency Planning Authority," substitute "the London Fire Commissioner,".

67 In section 41 (lost and uncollected property) in subsection (13) (interpretation) in the definition of "local authority" for paragraph (f) substitute—

"(f) the London Fire Commissioner;".

68 In section 45 (arrangements under Employment and Training Act 1973) in subsection (2) (local authorities to which section applies) for paragraph (d) substitute—

"(d) the London Fire Commissioner."

County Courts Act 1984 (c. 28)

69 In section 60(3) of the County Courts Act 1984 (right of audience of local authority: interpretation) in the definition of "local authority" for "the London Fire and Emergency Planning Authority" substitute "the London Fire Commissioner".

Local Government Act 1985 (c. 51)

70 The Local Government Act 1985 is amended as follows.

71 In section 72 (accounts and audit) in subsection (5) for paragraph (a) substitute—

"(a) the London Fire Commissioner;".

72 In Schedule 11 (police and fire services) in paragraph 2(4) (references to the Metropolitan Board of Works in the Metropolitan Fire Brigade Act 1985 to be

construed as references to the London Fire and Emergency Planning Authority) for "the London Fire and Emergency Planning Authority" substitute "the London Fire Commissioner".

Housing Act 1985 (c. 68)

73 In section 4(1)(e) of the Housing Act 1985 (other descriptions of authority: local authorities) for "and the London Fire and Emergency Planning Authority" in both places substitute "and the London Fire Commissioner".

Housing Associations Act 1985 (c.69)

74 In section 106(1) of the Housing Associations Act 1985 (minor definitions - general) in the definition of "local authority"—

(a) for ", a combined authority established under section 103 of that Act" substitute "and a combined authority established under section 103 of that Act",

(b) omit "and the London Fire and Emergency Planning Authority", and

(c) omit "the London Fire and Emergency Planning Authority," (in the second place).

Landlord and Tenant Act 1985 (c.70)

75 In section 38 of the Landlord and Tenant Act 1985 (minor definitions) in the definition of "local authority" for "and the London Fire and Emergency Planning Authority" substitute "and the London Fire Commissioner".

Local Government Act 1986 (c. 10)

76 The Local Government Act 1986 is amended as follows.

77 In section 6(2)(a) (meaning of "local authority" for the purposes of Part 2) for the entry relating to the London Fire and Emergency Planning Authority substitute—

"the London Fire Commissioner,".

78 In section 9(1)(a) (meaning of "local authority" for the purposes of Part 3) for the entry relating to the London Fire and Emergency Planning Authority substitute—

"the London Fire Commissioner,".

Landlord and Tenant Act 1987 (c.31)

79 In section 58(1) of the Landlord and Tenant Act 1987 (exempt landlords) in paragraph (a) (local authorities) for "the London Fire and Emergency Planning Authority," substitute "the London Fire Commissioner,".

Local Government Act 1988 (c. 9)

80 In Schedule 2 to the Local Government Act 1988 (public supply or works contracts: the public authorities) for the entry relating to the London Fire and Emergency Planning Authority substitute—

"The London Fire Commissioner."

Housing Act 1988 (c. 50)

81 The Housing Act 1988 is amended as follows.

82 In section 74(8) (transfer of land etc to housing action trusts: meaning of "local authority") for paragraph (g) substitute—

"(g) the London Fire Commissioner."

83 In Part 1 of Schedule 1 (tenancies which cannot be assured tenancies) in paragraph 12(2) (local authority tenancies: meaning of "local authority") for paragraph (ee) substitute—

"(ee) the London Fire Commissioner;".

Road Traffic Act 1988 (c. 52)

84 In section 144(2)(a)(i) of the Road Traffic Act 1988 (exceptions from the requirement for third party insurance) for "the London Fire and Emergency Planning Authority," substitute "the London Fire Commissioner,".

Local Government and Housing Act 1989 (c. 42)

85 The Local Government and Housing Act 1989 is amended as follows.

86 In section 1(9) (meaning of politically restricted post under a local authority) for "and every member of staff of a fire and rescue authority created by an order under section 4A of the Fire and Rescue Services Act 2004" (as inserted by paragraph 61 of Schedule 1) substitute "every member of staff of a fire and rescue authority created by an order under section 4A of the Fire and Rescue Services Act 2004 and every member of staff of the London Fire Commissioner".

87 (1) Section 4 (designation and reports of head of paid service) is amended as follows.

(2) In subsection (4) after paragraph (aa) (as inserted by paragraph 62(2) of Schedule 1) insert—

"(ab) in the case of the London Fire Commissioner, to the Commissioner;".

(3) After subsection (5B) (as inserted by paragraph 62(3) of Schedule 1) insert—

"(5C) It shall be the duty of the London Fire Commissioner to consider any report under this section by the head of the Commissioner's paid service and to do so no later than three months after the Commissioner is sent a copy of the report."

(4) In subsection (6)(a) for "and a fire and rescue authority created by an order under section 4A of the Fire and Rescue Services Act 2004" (as inserted by paragraph 62(4) of Schedule 1) substitute ", a fire and rescue authority created by an order under section 4A of the Fire and Rescue Services Act 2004 and the London Fire Commissioner".

88 (1) Section 5 (designation and reports of monitoring officer) is amended as follows.

(2) In subsection (3) after paragraph (aa) (as inserted by paragraph 63(2) of Schedule 1) insert—

"(ab) in the case of the London Fire Commissioner, to the Commissioner;".

(3) In subsection (5)(a) after sub-paragraph (ia) (as inserted by paragraph 63(3) of Schedule 1) insert—

"(ib) in the case of the London Fire Commissioner, no later than three months after the Commissioner is sent a copy of the report;".

(4) In subsection (8) in paragraph (a) of the definition of "relevant authority" for "and a fire and rescue authority created by an order under section 4A of the Fire and Rescue Services Act 2004" (as inserted by paragraph 63(4) of Schedule 1) substitute ", a fire and rescue authority created by an order under section 4A of the Fire and Rescue Services Act 2004 and the London Fire Commissioner".

89 (1) Section 21 (interpretation of Part 1) is amended as follows.

(2) In subsection (1)(i) omit "or the London Fire and Emergency Planning Authority".

(3) After subsection (1B) (as inserted by paragraph 64 of Schedule 1) insert—

"(1C) In the following provisions of this Part references to a local authority include the London Fire Commissioner—

(a) section 7 (all staff to be appointed on merit), and

(b) section 10 (limit on paid leave for local authority duties).

(1D) In the application of section 1(1) to the London Fire Commissioner by virtue of subsection (1C) the reference to being or remaining a member of a local authority is to be read as a reference to becoming or remaining the London Fire Commissioner."

90 In section 152(2) (meaning of "relevant authority" for the purposes of sections 150 and 151) for paragraph (n) substitute—

"(n) the London Fire Commissioner."

91 In section 155(1A) (emergency financial assistance to local authorities: expenditure treated as incurred by Greater London Authority) for paragraph (a) substitute—

"(a) the London Fire Commissioner,".

Town and Country Planning Act 1990 (c. 8)

92 The Town and Country Planning Act 1990 is amended as follows.

93 In section 252 (procedures for highways orders) in the definition of "local authority" in subsection (12) for "the London Fire and Emergency Planning Authority," substitute "the London Fire Commissioner,".

94 In section 336(1) (interpretation) in the definition of "local authority" for paragraph (ab) substitute—

"(ab) the London Fire Commissioner;".

95 In Schedule 14 (procedure for footpaths and bridleways orders) in paragraph 1(3) (meaning of "council" in provisions about notices) for ", the London Fire and Emergency Planning Authority," substitute ", the London Fire Commissioner,".

London Local Authorities Act 1991 (c. xiii)

96 The London Local Authorities Act 1991 is amended as follows.

97 In section 7 (licensing of special treatment premises: duty to notify London Fire and Emergency Planning Authority of application) for "the London Fire and Emergency Planning Authority" in each place substitute "the London Fire Commissioner".

98 In section 15(1) (powers of entry) for "the London Fire and Emergency Planning Authority" substitute "the London Fire Commissioner".

Local Government (Overseas Assistance) Act 1993 (c. 25)

99 In section 1 of the Local Government (Overseas Assistance) Act 1993 (power to provide advice and assistance) in subsection (10) (other bodies) for paragraph (dd) substitute—

"(dd) the London Fire Commissioner;"

London Local Authorities Act 1995 (c. x)

100 In section 2 of the London Local Authorities Act 1995 (interpretation) in paragraph (b) of the definition of "the fire and rescue authority" for "the London Fire and Emergency Planning Authority" substitute "the London Fire Commissioner".

Housing Grants, Construction and Regeneration Act 1996 (c. 53)

101 In section 3(2) of the Housing Grants, Construction and Regeneration Act 1996 (persons ineligible for grant) for paragraph (k) substitute—

"(k) the London Fire Commissioner."

Channel Tunnel Rail Link Act 1996 (c. 61)

102 In Schedule 3 to the Channel Tunnel Rail Link Act 1996 (highways) in paragraph 2(11) (definition of local authority) for "the London Fire and Emergency Planning Authority," substitute "the London Fire Commissioner,".

Crime and Disorder Act 1998 (c. 37)

103 The Crime and Disorder Act 1998 is amended as follows.

104 In section 5(5) (authorities responsible for strategies: interpretation) in the definition of "fire and rescue authority" for paragraph (c) substitute—

"(c) the London Fire Commissioner."

105 In section 17(2) (duty to consider crime and disorder implications: authorities to which duty applies) for the entry relating to the London Fire and Emergency Planning Authority substitute—

"the London Fire Commissioner;".

106 In section 115(2) (disclosure of information: meaning of relevant authority) for paragraph (h) substitute—

"(h) the London Fire Commissioner;".

Local Government Act 1999 (c. 27)

107 In section 1(1) of the Local Government Act 1999 (best value authorities) for paragraph (f) substitute—

"(f) the London Fire Commissioner;".

Freedom of Information Act 2000 (c. 36)

108 In Part 2 of Schedule 1 to the Freedom of Information Act 2000 (public authorities: local government) for paragraph 20 substitute—

"20 The London Fire Commissioner."

Courts Act 2003 (c. 39)

109 (1) Section 41 of the Courts Act 2003 (disqualification of lay justices who are members of local authorities) is amended as follows.

(2) In subsection (6) for paragraph (d) substitute—

"(d) the London Fire Commissioner,".

(3) After subsection (6) insert—

"(7) In the application of this section to the London Fire Commissioner, the reference in subsection (1) to a member of the local authority is to the person who is for the time being the Commissioner."

Fire and Rescue Services Act 2004 (c. 21)

110 The Fire and Rescue Services Act 2004 is amended as follows.

111 In section 1(2) (fire and rescue authorities in England) in paragraph (c) for "London Fire and Emergency Planning Authority" substitute "London Fire Commissioner".

112 In section 5A(3) (powers of certain fire and rescue authorities: authorities to which the section applies) for paragraph (b) substitute—

"(b) the London Fire Commissioner,".

113 In section 5B (boundaries of power under section 5A) after subsection (5) insert—

"(5A) Section 5A(1) does not authorise the London Fire Commissioner to enter into a contract to which this subsection applies without the consent of the Mayor of London.

(5B) Subsection (5A) applies to a contract if—

(a) the Mayor of London has notified the London Fire Commissioner that the Commissioner requires the Mayor's consent before entering into a contract of a kind specified in the notification, and

(b) the contract is of that kind."

Local Government and Public Involvement in Health Act 2007 (c. 28)

114 In section 104 of the Local Government and Public Involvement in Health Act 2007 (partner authorities) in subsection (5) (meaning of "fire and rescue authority") for paragraph (c) substitute—

"(c) the London Fire Commissioner."

Crossrail Act 2008 (c. 18)

115 In Schedule 3 to the Crossrail Act 2008 (stopping-up of highways) in paragraph 2(11) (local authorities which must be notified of proposed stopping-up) for paragraph (c) substitute—

"(c) the London Fire Commissioner,".

Equality Act 2010 (c. 15)

116 In Part 1 of Schedule 19 to the Equality Act 2010 (public authorities) for the entry relating to the London Fire and Emergency Planning Authority substitute—

"The London Fire Commissioner,".

Police Reform and Social Responsibility Act 2011 (c. 13)

117 In section 66 of the Police Reform and Social Responsibility Act 2011 (disqualification from election or holding office as police and crime commissioner: other grounds) after subsection (11) (as inserted by paragraph 90 of Schedule 1) insert—

"(12) A person is disqualified from being elected as, or being, police and crime commissioner if the person—

(a) is the London Fire Commissioner, or

(b) is a member of the staff of the London Fire Commissioner."

Localism Act 2011 (c. 20)

118 The Localism Act 2011 is amended as follows.

119 In section 27 (duty to promote and maintain high standards of conduct) in subsection (6) (meaning of "relevant authority") omit paragraph (g) (the London Fire and Emergency Planning Authority).

120 In section 43(1) (meaning of "relevant authority" for purposes of provisions on pay accountability) for paragraph (g) substitute—

"(g) in relation only to sections 38, 40 and 41 and this section, the London Fire Commissioner,".

Energy Act 2013 (c. 32)

121 In Part 3 of Schedule 9 to the Energy Act 2013 (protected information: permitted disclosures and restrictions on use) in paragraph 14(3) (local authorities and water authorities: interpretation) in the definition of "local authority" for paragraph (e) substitute—

"(e) the London Fire Commissioner,".

Local Audit and Accountability Act 2014 (c. 2)

122 (1) The Local Audit and Accountability Act 2014 is amended as follows.

(2) In section 40 (access to local government meetings and documents) in subsection (6) (bodies to which provisions apply) for paragraph (f) substitute—

"(f) the London Fire Commissioner,".

(3) In Schedule 7 (reports and recommendations by local auditor) in paragraph 5(7) (duty of certain authorities to consider report or recommendation) (as amended by paragraph 97 of Schedule 1) for "or a fire and rescue authority created by an order under section 4A of the Fire and Rescue Services Act 2004" substitute ", a fire and

rescue authority created by an order under section 4A of the Fire and Rescue Services Act 2004 or the London Fire Commissioner".

Consequential repeals

123 In consequence of the amendments made by this Schedule the following provisions are repealed—

(a) sections 25, 26 and 27 of the Greater London Authority Act 2007;

(b) paragraph 8(6) of Schedule 3 to the Local Government and Public Involvement in Health Act 2007.

SCHEDULE 3

Section 11

SCHEDULE TO BE INSERTED AS SCHEDULE A3 TO THE FIRE AND RESCUE SERVICES ACT 2004

"SCHEDULE A3

Section 28

ENGLISH INSPECTORS

1 Interpretation

1 (1) This paragraph applies for the purposes of this Schedule.

(2) References to an English inspector are to an inspector appointed under section 28(A1).

(3) References to the inspection function are to the function conferred on the English inspectors by section 28(A3).

(4) References to a person providing services to a fire and rescue authority are to a person providing services, in pursuance of contractual arrangements (but without being employed by a fire and rescue authority), to assist the fire and rescue authority in relation to the exercise of its functions.

(5) "Public authority" includes any person certain of whose functions are functions of a public nature.

2 Delegation

2 An English inspector may arrange for the inspection function to be exercised (to such extent as the inspector may determine) by another public authority on behalf of the inspector.

3 Working with Her Majesty's Inspectors of Constabulary

3 An English inspector, when exercising the inspection function, must co-operate with Her Majesty's Inspectors of Constabulary.

4 An English inspector may act jointly with Her Majesty's Inspectors of Constabulary where it is appropriate to do so for the efficient and effective exercise of the inspection function.

5 Assistance for other public authorities

5 (1) The chief fire and rescue inspector for England may, if he or she thinks it appropriate to do so, provide assistance to any other public authority for the purpose of the exercise by that authority of its functions.

(2) The chief fire and rescue inspector for England may do anything he or she thinks appropriate to facilitate the carrying out of an inspection under section 10 of the Local Government Act 1999 (inspection of best value authorities).

(3) Anything done under this paragraph may be done on such terms (including terms as to payment) as the chief fire and rescue inspector for England thinks fit.

6 Powers of English inspectors to obtain information etc

6 (1) An English inspector may serve on a relevant person a notice requiring the person—

(a) to provide the inspector with any information or documents that the inspector reasonably requires for the purpose of the exercise of the inspection function;

(b) to produce or deliver up to the inspector any evidence or other things that the inspector reasonably requires for that purpose.

This is subject to sub-paragraphs (6) to (8).

(2) In sub-paragraph (1), "relevant person" means—

(a) a fire and rescue authority in England;

(b) an employee of a fire and rescue authority in England;

(c) a person providing services to a fire and rescue authority in England;

(d) an employee of a person providing services to a fire and rescue authority in England;

(e) any other person who is, by virtue of any enactment, carrying out any of the activities of a fire and rescue authority in England.

(3) A notice under this paragraph must—

(a) specify or describe the information, documents, evidence or other things that are required by the inspector;

(b) specify the period within which the information, documents, evidence or other things must be provided, produced or delivered up.

(4) A notice under this paragraph may specify the form and manner in which any information, documents, evidence or other things are to be provided, produced or delivered up.

(5) An English inspector may cancel a notice under this paragraph by written notice to the person on whom it was served.

(6) A notice under this paragraph must not be used to obtain information, or any document or other thing, from a person if—

(a) the information, or the document or other thing, was obtained by that person (directly or indirectly) from a body or other entity mentioned in sub-paragraph (7), or

(b) the information, or the document or other thing, relates to a body or other entity mentioned in that sub-paragraph.

(7) The bodies and other entities referred to in sub-paragraph (6) are—

(a) the Security Service,

(b) the Secret Intelligence Service,

(c) the Government Communications Headquarters, or

(d) any part of Her Majesty's forces, or of the Ministry of Defence, which engages in intelligence activities.

(8) A notice under this paragraph must not require a person—

(a) to provide information that might incriminate the person;

(b) to provide an item subject to legal privilege within the meaning of the Police and Criminal Evidence Act 1984 (see section 10 of that Act).

(9) In this paragraph—

"document" means anything in which information of any description is recorded;

"English inspector" includes—

(a) a person appointed under section 28(A5) as an assistant inspector or other officer;

(b) a person authorised by an English inspector to act on behalf of the inspector for the purposes of this paragraph.

7 Powers of English inspectors to obtain access to premises

7 (1) An English inspector may serve on a person a notice requiring the person to allow the inspector access, which the inspector reasonably requires for the purpose of the exercise of the inspection function, to—

(a) premises that are occupied (wholly or partly) for the purposes of—

(i) a fire and rescue authority in England,

(ii) a person providing services to a fire and rescue authority in England, or

(iii) any other person who is, by virtue of any enactment, carrying out any of the activities of a fire and rescue authority in England, and

(b) documents and other things on those premises.

(2) A notice under this paragraph must—

(a) specify or describe the premises to which the inspector requires access;

(b) specify the time when access is required (which may be immediately after the service of the notice).

(3) Where there are reasonable grounds for not allowing the inspector to have access to the premises at the time specified under sub-paragraph (2)(b), the requirement under this paragraph has effect as a requirement to secure that access is allowed to the inspector at the earliest practicable time specified by the inspector after there cease to be such grounds.

(4) An English inspector may cancel a notice under this paragraph by written notice to the person on whom it was served.

(5) In this paragraph "document" and "English inspector" have the same meanings as in paragraph 6 (and, for that purpose, the reference in paragraph (b) of the definition

of "English inspector" in paragraph 6(9) to paragraph 6 is to be read as a reference to this paragraph).

8 Failure to comply with notice under paragraph 6 or 7

8 (1) If a person who has received a notice under paragraph 6 or 7—

(a) fails or refuses without reasonable excuse to do what is required by the notice, or

(b) (in the case of a notice under paragraph 6) knowingly or recklessly provides information in response to the notice that is false in a material respect,

the chief fire and rescue inspector for England may certify in writing to the High Court that the person has failed to comply with the notice.

(2) The High Court may then inquire into the matter and, after hearing any witness who may be produced against or on behalf of the person, and after hearing any statement offered in defence, deal with the person as if the person had committed a contempt of court.

9 Sensitive information: restriction on further disclosure

9 (1) Where an English inspector, in exercise of the inspection function, receives information within sub-paragraph (2), the inspector must not disclose the information, or the fact that it has been received, unless the relevant authority consents to the disclosure.

(2) The information is—

(a) intelligence service information;

(b) information obtained from a government department which, at the time it is provided to the inspector, is identified by the department as information the disclosure of which may, in the opinion of the relevant authority—

(i) cause damage to national security, international relations or the economic interests of the United Kingdom or any part of the United Kingdom, or

(ii) jeopardise the safety of any person.

(3) Where an English inspector discloses to another person information within sub-paragraph (2) that the inspector received in exercise of the inspection function, or the fact that the inspector has received such information in exercise of the inspection function, the other person must not disclose that information or that fact unless the relevant authority consents to the disclosure.

(4) A prohibition on disclosure in sub-paragraph (1) or (3) does not apply to disclosure by one English inspector to another.

(5) In this paragraph—

"English inspector" includes—

(a) a person appointed under section 28(A5) as an assistant inspector or other officer;

(b) a person authorised by an English inspector to act on behalf of the inspector for the purposes of paragraph 6 or 7;

"government department" means a department of Her Majesty's Government but does not include—

(a) the Security Service,
(b) the Secret Intelligence Service, or
(c) the Government Communications Headquarters ("GCHQ");

"intelligence service information" means information that was obtained (directly or indirectly) from or that relates to—

(a) the Security Service,
(b) the Secret Intelligence Service,
(c) GCHQ, or
(d) any part of Her Majesty's forces, or of the Ministry of Defence, which engages in intelligence activities;

"Minister of the Crown" includes the Treasury;

"relevant authority" means—

(a) in the case of intelligence service information obtained (directly or indirectly) from or relating to the Security Service, the Director-General of the Security Service;
(b) in the case of intelligence service information obtained (directly or indirectly) from or relating to the Secret Intelligence Service, the Chief of the Secret Intelligence Service;
(c) in the case of intelligence service information obtained (directly or indirectly) from or relating to GCHQ, the Director of GCHQ;
(d) in the case of intelligence service information obtained (directly or indirectly) from or relating to Her Majesty's forces or the Ministry of Defence, the Secretary of State;
(e) in the case of information within sub-paragraph (2)(b)—
    (i) the Secretary of State, or
    (ii) the Minister of the Crown in charge of the government department from which the information was obtained (if that Minister is not a Secretary of State).

10 Provision of intelligence service information to English inspectors

10 (1) A person who provides information that is intelligence service information to an English inspector exercising the inspection function must—

(a) make the inspector aware that the information is intelligence service information, and
(b) provide the inspector with such additional information as will enable the inspector to identify the relevant authority in relation to the information.

(2) In this paragraph, "English inspector", "intelligence service information" and "relevant authority" have the same meaning as in paragraph 9."

SCHEDULE 4

Section 14

AMENDMENTS CONSEQUENTIAL ON THE AMENDED DEFINITION OF POLICE COMPLAINT

1 The Police Reform Act 2002 is amended as follows.

2 In section 10 (general functions of the Independent Police Complaints Commission), in subsection (2)—

(a) in paragraph (a), for "made about the conduct of persons serving with the police" substitute "(within the meaning given by section 12)";

(b) in paragraph (b), for "such persons" substitute "persons serving with the police".

3 (1) Section 16 (payment for assistance with investigations) is amended as follows.

(2) In subsection (2)(a)—

(a) before sub-paragraph (i) insert—

"(ai) an investigation of a complaint where the complainant expressed dissatisfaction with the other force,";

(b) in sub-paragraph (i), after "investigation" insert "of a recordable conduct matter".

(3) In subsection (2)(b)—

(a) before sub-paragraph (i) insert—

"(ai) an investigation of a complaint where the complainant expressed dissatisfaction with a force other than that force,";

(b) in sub-paragraph (i), after "investigation" insert "of a recordable conduct matter".

4 In section 21 (duty to provide information for other persons), in subsection (2), in the words before paragraph (a), for "complaint or" substitute "complaint that relates to conduct of a person serving with the police or a".

5 In section 23 (regulations), in subsection (2)(a), in the words before sub-paragraph (i), for "against any person" substitute "that relates to conduct of a person serving with the police".

6 (1) Section 29 (interpretation of Part 2) is amended as follows.

(2) In subsection (1), in the definition of "appropriate authority"—

(a) omit "and" at the end of paragraph (a);

(b) after paragraph (a) insert—

"(aa) in relation to any other complaint, means the chief officer of the police force with which dissatisfaction is expressed by the complainant; and";

(3) In subsection (1), in the definition of "person complained against", after "a complaint" insert "that relates to conduct of a person serving with the police".

(4) In subsection (2), for paragraphs (a) and (b) substitute—

"(a) to the person by whom the complaint or purported complaint was made, or

(b) in a case where the complaint or purported complaint was made on behalf of someone else, to the person on whose behalf it was made;".

(5) After subsection (4) insert—

"(4A) In this Part references, in relation to anything purporting to be a complaint other than a complaint about any conduct, to a member of the public include references to any person falling within subsection (3)(a) to (d) other than a person who is—

(a) a member of the police force with which dissatisfaction is expressed,

(b) a civilian employee of that police force,

(c) a special constable who is under the direction and control of the chief officer of that police force, or

(d) where dissatisfaction is expressed with the City of London police force, an employee of the Common Council of the City of London who is under the direction and control of the chief officer of that force."

7 (1) Part 1 of Schedule 3 (handling of complaints) is amended as follows.

(2) In paragraph 1(6), omit "any conduct that is".

(3) In paragraph 4(1)(a), after "conduct" insert "or other matter".

(4) In paragraph 4(6)(b), at the end insert "(if any)".

(5) In paragraph 5(3)(b), at the end insert "(if any)".

8 (1) Part 3 of Schedule 3 (investigations and subsequent proceedings) is amended as follows.

(2) In paragraph 23(2A), after "a person" insert "(if any)".

(3) In paragraph 24(2A), after "a person" insert "(if any)".

(4) In paragraph 25(10)(d), at the end insert "(if any)".

SCHEDULE 5

Section 16

COMPLAINTS, CONDUCT MATTERS AND DSI MATTERS: PROCEDURE

PART 1

RECORDING AND REFERENCE OF COMPLAINTS

1 Part 1 of Schedule 3 to the Police Reform Act 2002 (handling of complaints) is amended as follows.

2 (1) Paragraph 2 (initial handling and recording of complaints) is amended as follows.

(2) In sub-paragraph (6), in the words following paragraph (c), for "record the complaint" substitute "contact the complainant and seek the complainant's views on how the complaint should be handled".

(3) After sub-paragraph (6) insert—

"(6A) A local policing body or chief officer that is subject to the duty in sub-paragraph (6) in relation to a complaint must record the complaint if—

(a) at any time the complainant indicates a wish for the complaint to be recorded, or

(b) the local policing body or chief officer determines that the complaint is to be handled in accordance with this Schedule.

(6B) The local policing body or chief officer must determine that a complaint is to be handled in accordance with this Schedule if—

(a) the complaint is one alleging that the conduct or other matter complained of has resulted in death or serious injury,

(b) the complaint is one alleging that there has been conduct by a person serving with the police which (if proved) might constitute the commission of a criminal offence or justify the bringing of disciplinary proceedings,

(c) the conduct or other matter complained of (if proved) might have involved the infringement of a person's rights under Article 2 or 3 of the Convention (within the meaning of the Human Rights Act 1998), or

(d) the complaint is of a description specified for the purposes of paragraph 4(1)(b) in regulations made by the Secretary of State.

(6C) Where a local policing body or chief officer determines (for the purposes of sub-paragraph (6A)) that a complaint is to be handled otherwise than in accordance with this Schedule, the local policing body or chief officer must handle the complaint in such other manner as the local policing body or chief officer considers appropriate with a view to resolving the complaint to the complainant's satisfaction.

(The duty in this sub-paragraph ceases to apply if the complaint is recorded in accordance with sub-paragraph (6A)(a).)

(6D) Where a local policing body or chief officer records a complaint under sub-paragraph (6A), or determines that a complaint is to be handled otherwise than in accordance with this Schedule, the local policing body or chief officer must notify the complainant of the recording of the complaint or (as the case may be) of the determination."

(4) For sub-paragraph (7) substitute—

"(7) Nothing in this paragraph shall require the taking of any action in relation to a complaint if the complaint has been withdrawn."

(5) Omit sub-paragraph (8).

(6) At the end insert—

"(9) If a local policing body or chief officer decides that it or (as the case may be) he is not required to comply with any of sub-paragraphs (2), (3) and (6) to (6C) on the basis of a determination that what purports to be a complaint is not a complaint, the local policing body or chief officer must notify the complainant of the determination and the grounds on which it was made.

(10) If a local policing body or chief officer determines that part of what has been received (whether directly or by virtue of a notification under this paragraph) is a complaint and part is not, the local policing body or chief officer must proceed under this paragraph as if those two parts had been separately received."

3 Omit paragraph 3 (failures to notify or record a complaint) and the italic heading before that paragraph.

4 (1) Paragraph 4 (reference of complaints to the Commission) is amended as follows.

(2) In sub-paragraph (6)(b), for "a possible future investigation of the complaint" substitute "an investigation of the complaint (whether an existing investigation or a possible future one)".

(3) After sub-paragraph (6) insert—

"(6A) A local policing body which refers a complaint to the Commission under sub-paragraph (3) shall also give a notification of the making of the reference to the appropriate authority."

(4) Omit sub-paragraph (8).

(5) At the end insert—

"(9) The appropriate authority must record any complaint that is referred to the Commission under this paragraph that has not already been recorded."

PART 2

HANDLING OF COMPLAINTS

5 Part 1 of Schedule 3 to the Police Reform Act 2002 (handling of complaints) is further amended as follows.

6 (1) Paragraph 6 (handling of complaints by the appropriate authority) is amended as follows.

(2) In sub-paragraph (2), omit the "or" at the end of paragraph (a) and omit paragraph (b).

(3) After sub-paragraph (2) insert—

"(2A) The appropriate authority must handle the complaint in such reasonable and proportionate manner as the authority determines.

(2B) An appropriate authority may handle a complaint in accordance with sub-paragraph (2A) by (amongst other things)—

(a) making arrangements for the complaint to be investigated by the authority on its own behalf;

(b) notifying the complainant that no further action is to be taken in relation to the complaint.

(2C) The appropriate authority must comply with its duty under sub-paragraph (2A) by making arrangements for the complaint to be investigated by the authority on its own behalf if at any time it appears to the authority from the complaint, or from the authority's handling of the complaint to that point, that there is an indication that—

(a) a person serving with the police may have committed a criminal offence or behaved in a manner that would justify the bringing of disciplinary proceedings, or

(b) there may have been the infringement of a person's rights under Article 2 or 3 of the Convention (within the meaning of the Human Rights Act 1998).

(2D) The Secretary of State may by regulations provide for the duty in sub-paragraph (2C) to be subject to exceptions.

(2E) A statement made by any person for the purposes of the handling of any complaint in accordance with sub-paragraph (2A) otherwise than by the appropriate authority making arrangements for the complaint to be investigated by the authority on its own behalf is not admissible in any subsequent criminal, civil or disciplinary proceedings except to the extent that it consists of an admission relating to a matter that has not been subjected to such handling."

(4) Omit sub-paragraphs (3) to (11).

7 Omit paragraph 7 (disapplication of requirements of Schedule) and the italic heading before that paragraph.

8 Omit paragraph 8 (local resolution of complaints) and the italic heading before that paragraph.

PART 3

INVESTIGATIONS AND SUBSEQUENT PROCEEDINGS

9 Schedule 3 to the Police Reform Act 2002 (handling of complaints and conduct matters etc) is further amended as follows.

10 (1) Paragraph 5 (duties of Commission on references under paragraph 4: complaints) is amended as follows.

(2) After sub-paragraph (1) insert—

"(1A) The Secretary of State may by regulations provide that the Commission must determine that it is necessary for complaints referred to it that relate to the conduct of a chief officer or the Deputy Commissioner of Police of the Metropolis to be investigated.

(1B) Regulations under sub-paragraph (1A) may provide that the duty on the Commission applies only in relation to complaints relating to the conduct of a chief officer or the Deputy Commissioner of Police of the Metropolis that are of a description specified in the regulations.

(1C) Regulations under sub-paragraph (1A) may also provide that, where the Commission is required by the regulations to determine that it is necessary for a complaint to be investigated, paragraph 15 is to apply in relation to the complaint as if sub-paragraphs (4)(a), (4A) and (5A)(b) were omitted."

(3) In sub-paragraph (2), for the words from ", it may" to the end of the sub-paragraph substitute "—

(a) in a case where the complaint is already being investigated by the appropriate authority on its own behalf (and notwithstanding the Commission's determination), the Commission must refer the complaint back to the appropriate authority for the investigation to be completed, and

(b) in any other case, the Commission may, if it thinks fit, refer the complaint back to the appropriate authority to be dealt with by that authority in accordance with paragraph 6."

(4) In sub-paragraph (3)(b), for "a possible future investigation of the complaint" substitute "an investigation of the complaint (whether an existing investigation or a possible future one)".

11 In paragraph 6 (handling of complaints by the appropriate authority), in sub-paragraph (2)(a), for "5" substitute "5(2)(b)".

12 In paragraph 13 (reference of conduct matters to the Commission), in sub-paragraph (6)(b), for "a possible future investigation of that matter" substitute "an investigation of that matter (whether an existing investigation or a possible future one)".

13 (1) Paragraph 14 (duties of Commission on references under paragraph 13: recordable conduct matters) is amended as follows.

(2) After sub-paragraph (1) insert—

"(1A) The Secretary of State may by regulations provide that the Commission must determine that it is necessary for recordable conduct matters referred to it that relate to the conduct of a chief officer or the Deputy Commissioner of Police of the Metropolis to be investigated.

(1B) Regulations under sub-paragraph (1A) may provide that the duty on the Commission applies only in relation to recordable conduct matters relating to the conduct of a chief officer or the Deputy Commissioner of Police of the Metropolis that are of a description specified in the regulations.

(1C) Regulations under sub-paragraph (1A) may also provide that, where the Commission is required by the regulations to determine that it is necessary for a recordable conduct matter to be investigated, paragraph 15 is to apply in relation to the matter as if sub-paragraphs (4)(a), (4A) and (5A)(b) were omitted."

(3) In sub-paragraph (2), for the words from ", it may" to the end of the sub-paragraph substitute "—

(a) in a case where the recordable conduct matter is already being investigated by the appropriate authority on its own behalf (and notwithstanding the Commission's determination), the Commission must refer the matter back to the appropriate authority for the investigation to be completed, and

(b) in any other case, the Commission may, if it thinks fit, refer the matter back to the appropriate authority to be dealt with by that authority in such manner (if any) as that authority may determine."

(4) In sub-paragraph (3)(b), for "a possible future investigation of that matter" substitute "an investigation of that matter (whether an existing investigation or a possible future one)".

14 (1) Paragraph 14D (duties of Commission on references under paragraph 14C: DSI matters) is amended as follows.

(2) After sub-paragraph (1) insert—

"(1A) The Secretary of State may by regulations provide that the Commission must determine that it is necessary for DSI matters referred to it in relation to which the relevant officer is a chief officer or the Deputy Commissioner of Police of the Metropolis to be investigated.

(1B) Regulations under sub-paragraph (1A) may provide that the duty on the Commission applies only in relation to DSI matters in relation to which the relevant officer is a chief officer or the Deputy Commissioner of Police of the Metropolis that are of a description specified in the regulations.

(1C) Regulations under sub-paragraph (1A) may also provide that, where the Commission is required by the regulations to determine that it is necessary for a DSI matter to be investigated, paragraph 15 is to apply in relation to the matter as if sub-paragraphs (4)(a), (4A) and (5A)(b) were omitted."

(3) In sub-paragraph (2), for the words from ", it may" to the end of the sub-paragraph substitute "—

(a) in a case where the DSI matter is already being investigated by the appropriate authority on its own behalf (and notwithstanding the Commission's determination), the Commission must refer the matter back to the appropriate authority for the investigation to be completed, and

(b) in any other case, the Commission may, if it thinks fit, refer the matter back to the appropriate authority to be dealt with by that authority in such manner (if any) as that authority may determine."

15 (1) Paragraph 15 (power of the Commission to determine the form of an investigation) is amended as follows.

(2) In sub-paragraph (1)(b), after "determines" insert "under paragraph 5(1), 14(1) or 14D(1)".

(3) After sub-paragraph (1) insert—

"(1A) This paragraph also applies where the Commission determines under paragraph 6A(5)(a) that it is necessary for a complaint to be investigated."

(4) Omit sub-paragraph (3).

(5) In sub-paragraph (4)—

(a) omit paragraph (b);

(b) in paragraph (c), for "management" substitute "direction".

(6) After sub-paragraph (4) insert—

"(4A) In making a determination under sub-paragraph (2) the Commission must first determine whether, having regard to the seriousness of the case and the public interest, it is appropriate for the investigation to take the form of an investigation by the appropriate authority on its own behalf and if it is the Commission must determine that the investigation is to take that form.

(4B) Where, in accordance with sub-paragraph (4A), the Commission determines that it is not appropriate for the investigation to take the form of an investigation by the appropriate authority on its own behalf, the Commission must determine that the investigation is to take the form of an investigation by the Commission unless sub-paragraph (4C) applies.

(4C) This sub-paragraph applies where the Commission determines that it would be more appropriate for the investigation to take the form of an investigation by the appropriate authority under the direction of the Commission, in which case the Commission must determine that the investigation is to take that form."

(7) For sub-paragraph (5) substitute—

"(5) Where the Commission determines under sub-paragraph (4C) or (5B) that an investigation is to take the form of an investigation by the appropriate authority under the direction of the Commission, the Commission must keep under review whether that form of investigation continues to be the most appropriate form of investigation.

(5A) If, on such a review, the Commission determines that—

(a) it would be more appropriate for the investigation to take the form of an investigation by the Commission, the Commission must make a further determination under this paragraph (to replace the earlier one) that the investigation is instead to take that form;

(b) having regard to the seriousness of the case and the public interest, it would be more appropriate for the investigation to take the form of an investigation by the appropriate authority on its own behalf, the Commission may make a further determination under this paragraph (to replace the earlier one) that the investigation is instead to take that form.

(5B) Subject to sub-paragraph (5A), if at any time the Commission determines that, were it to apply sub-paragraphs (4A) to (4C) again, the form of the investigation would be different, the Commission may make a further determination under this paragraph (to replace the earlier one) such that the investigation takes that different form."

(8) In sub-paragraph (8), at the end insert "and of its reasons for making the determination".

(9) After sub-paragraph (8) insert—

"(9) The Commission shall also notify the following of any determination that it makes under this paragraph in relation to a particular complaint, recordable conduct matter or DSI matter and of its reasons for making the determination—

(a) every person entitled to be kept properly informed in relation to the complaint or matter under section 21;

(b) where the determination is made in relation to a complaint, the complainant;

(c) the person to whose conduct the investigation will relate.

(10) The duty imposed by sub-paragraph (9) on the Commission in relation to a complaint, recordable conduct matter or DSI matter shall have effect subject to such exceptions as may be provided for by regulations made by the Secretary of State.

(11) Subsections (6) to (8) of section 20 apply for the purposes of sub-paragraph (10) as they apply for the purposes of that section."

16 (1) Paragraph 16 (investigations by the appropriate authority on its own behalf) is amended as follows.

(2) Before sub-paragraph (1) insert—

"(A1) This paragraph applies if the appropriate authority, acting in accordance with paragraph 6(2A) or in response to a recommendation under paragraph 6A(6)(b), is to make arrangements for a complaint to be investigated by the appropriate authority on its own behalf."

(3) In sub-paragraph (1)—

(a) in the words before paragraph (a), after "paragraph" insert "also";

(b) omit paragraph (a) and the "or" following it.

17 Omit paragraph 17 (investigations supervised by the Commission) and the italic heading before that paragraph.

18 In the italic heading before paragraph 18, for "managed" substitute "directed".

19 (1) Paragraph 18 (investigations managed by the Commission) is amended as follows.

(2) In sub-paragraph (1), for "manage" substitute "direct".

(3) For sub-paragraph (2) substitute—

"(2) On being given notice of that determination, the appropriate authority shall, if it has not already done so, appoint—

(a) a person serving with the police (whether under the direction and control of the chief officer of police of the relevant force or of the chief officer of another force), or

(b) a National Crime Agency officer,

to investigate the complaint or matter.

(2A) The Commission may require that no appointment is made under sub-paragraph (2) unless it has given notice to the appropriate authority that it approves the person whom that authority proposes to appoint.

(2B) Where at any time the Commission is not satisfied with the person investigating, the Commission may require the appropriate authority, as soon as reasonably practicable after being required to do so—

(a) to select another person falling within sub-paragraph (2)(a) or (b) to investigate the complaint or matter, and

(b) to notify the Commission of the person selected.

(2C) Sub-paragraph (2B) applies whether the person investigating was appointed—

(a) before the appropriate authority was given notice of the Commission's determination that it should direct the investigation by the appropriate authority,

(b) under sub-paragraph (2) (including where the appointment was approved by the Commission in accordance with sub-paragraph (2A)), or

(c) under sub-paragraph (2D)(a).

(2D) Where a selection made in pursuance of a requirement under sub-paragraph (2B) has been notified to the Commission—

(a) the appropriate authority shall appoint that person to investigate the complaint or matter if, but only if, the Commission notifies the authority that it approves the appointment of that person;

(b) if the Commission notifies the authority that it does not approve the appointment of that person, the appropriate authority must make another selection in accordance with sub-paragraph (2B).

(2E) A person appointed under this paragraph to investigate any complaint or conduct matter—

(a) in the case of an investigation relating to any conduct of a chief officer, must not be a person under that chief officer's direction and control, and

(b) in the case of an investigation relating to any conduct of the Commissioner of Police of the Metropolis or of the Deputy Commissioner of Police of the Metropolis, must be a person nominated by the Secretary of State for appointment under this paragraph (and approved for appointment in accordance with sub-paragraph (2A) (if required) or (2D)(a)).

(2F) A person appointed under this paragraph to investigate any DSI matter—

(a) in relation to which the relevant officer is a chief officer, must not be a person under that chief officer's direction and control, and

(b) in relation to which the relevant officer is the Commissioner of Police of the Metropolis or the Deputy Commissioner of Police of the Metropolis, must be a person nominated by the Secretary of State for appointment under this paragraph (and approved for appointment in accordance with sub-paragraph (2A) (if required) or (2D)(a))."

(4) After sub-paragraph (3) insert—

"(4) The person appointed to investigate the complaint or matter shall keep the Commission informed of the progress of the investigation."

20 In paragraph 19 (investigations by the Commission itself), in sub-paragraph (7), omit paragraph (aa) and the "or" following it.

21 For paragraphs 19A to 19E (special procedure where investigation relates to police officer or special constable) substitute—

"19A (1) This paragraph applies to an investigation where condition A, B or C is satisfied.

(2) Condition A is that—

(a) the investigation is an investigation of a complaint, and

(b) during the course of the investigation it appears to the person investigating that there is an indication that a member of a police force, or a special constable, to whose conduct the investigation relates may have committed a criminal offence or behaved in a manner which would justify the bringing of disciplinary proceedings.

(3) Condition B is that—

(a) the investigation is an investigation of a complaint being carried out by a person appointed under paragraph 18, and

(b) during the course of the investigation the Commission determines that there is an indication that a member of a police force, or a special constable, to whose conduct the investigation relates may have committed a criminal offence or behaved in a manner which would justify the bringing of disciplinary proceedings.

(4) Condition C is that—

(a) the investigation is an investigation of a recordable conduct matter, and

(b) the investigation relates to the conduct of a member of a police force or a special constable.

(5) Where this paragraph applies to an investigation the person investigating must proceed with the investigation in accordance with regulations made by the Secretary of State under this sub-paragraph.

(6) Regulations under sub-paragraph (5) may (amongst other things) make provision—

(a) as to the procedure to be followed in connection with any interview of the person concerned, including provision requiring the person concerned to attend an interview;

(b) requiring the person investigating to supply information to the appropriate authority.

(7) In this paragraph "the person concerned"—

(a) in relation to an investigation of a complaint, means the person in respect of whom it appears to the person investigating that there is the indication mentioned in sub-paragraph (2)(b) or (as the case may be) the person in respect of whom the Commission determines that there is the indication mentioned in sub-paragraph (3)(b);

(b) in relation to an investigation of a recordable conduct matter, means the person to whose conduct the investigation relates."

22 (1) Paragraph 19F (interview of persons serving with the police etc during certain investigations) is amended as follows.

(2) In sub-paragraph (2)—

(a) in paragraph (a), for ", and" substitute "other than, in the case of an investigation to which paragraph 19A applies, a serving officer who is the person concerned in relation to the investigation (within the meaning of paragraph 19A).";

(b) omit paragraph (b).

(3) In sub-paragraph (7)—

(a) omit the "or" at the end of paragraph (a);

(b) after paragraph (a) insert—

"(aa) a body required by section 26BA to enter into an agreement with the Commission, or".

23 For paragraphs 20A to 20I (accelerated procedure in special cases) substitute—

"20A (1) This paragraph applies where—

(a) at any time before the completion of an investigation of a complaint or recordable conduct matter, the person investigating believes that the appropriate authority would, on consideration of the matter, be likely to consider that the conditions in sub-paragraph (2) are satisfied, or

(b) at any time before the completion of an investigation of a complaint or recordable conduct matter being carried out by a person appointed under paragraph 18, the Commission determines that the appropriate authority would, on consideration of the matter, be likely to consider that the conditions in sub-paragraph (2) are satisfied.

(2) The conditions in this sub-paragraph are that—

(a) there is sufficient evidence, in the form of written statements or other documents, to establish on the balance of probabilities that conduct to which the investigation relates constitutes gross misconduct, and

(b) it is in the public interest for the person whose conduct it is to cease to be a member of a police force, or to be a special constable, without delay.

(3) Where this paragraph applies the person investigating, the appropriate authority and the Commission must proceed in accordance with regulations made by the Secretary of State.

(4) Regulations under sub-paragraph (3) may (amongst other things) make provision—

(a) for the person investigating to continue the investigation (whether to its full extent or to such lesser extent as is provided) or to stop investigating;

(b) for the person investigating to submit a report on the investigation to a point before its completion (not being a report under paragraph 22);

(c) for the conduct to which the investigation relates to be certified for the purposes of paragraph 20(1)(a)."

24 Omit paragraph 21 (power to discontinue an investigation) and the italic heading before that paragraph.

25 (1) Paragraph 21A (procedure where conduct matter is revealed during investigation of DSI matter) is amended as follows.

(2) After sub-paragraph (2) insert—

"(2A) If during the course of an investigation of a DSI matter being carried out by a person appointed under paragraph 18 the Commission determines (without there having been a submission under sub-paragraph (1)) that there is an indication that a person serving with the police ("the person whose conduct is in question") may have—

(a) committed a criminal offence, or

(b) behaved in a manner which would justify the bringing of disciplinary proceedings, it shall notify the appropriate authority in relation to the DSI matter and (if different) the appropriate authority in relation to the person whose conduct is in question of its determination."

(3) In sub-paragraph (5)(a), after "(2)" insert "or (2A)".

26 (1) Paragraph 23 (action by the Commission in response to an investigation report under paragraph 22) is amended as follows.

(2) After sub-paragraph (5) insert—

"(5A) On receipt of the report, the Commission shall also—

(a) seek the views of the appropriate authority on—

(i) whether any person to whose conduct the investigation related has a case to answer in respect of misconduct or gross misconduct or has no case to answer,

(ii) whether or not any such person's performance is unsatisfactory, and

(iii) the other matters (if any) dealt with in the report (but not on whether the conditions in sub-paragraphs (2A) and (2B) are satisfied in respect of the report),

(b) having considered the views (if any) of the appropriate authority, make a determination as to—

(i) the matters described in paragraph (a)(i) and (ii), and

(ii) whether or not disciplinary proceedings should be brought against any person to whose conduct the investigation related and, if so, what form the disciplinary proceedings should take,

(c) having considered the views (if any) of the appropriate authority and if the Commission considers it appropriate to do so, make a determination as to any matter dealt with in the report, being a determination other than one that it is required to make under sub-paragraph (2)(b) or paragraph (b) of this sub-paragraph,

(d) notify the appropriate authority of its determination under paragraph (b) and any determination under paragraph (c),

(e) where the Commission determines that disciplinary proceedings of a form specified in the determination should be brought against a person, direct the appropriate authority to bring those proceedings, and

(f) direct the appropriate authority to determine what action (if any) the appropriate authority will in its discretion take, not being action involving the bringing of disciplinary proceedings, in respect of the matters dealt with in the report and having regard to the Commission's determination under paragraph (b) and any determination under paragraph (c).

(5B) The appropriate authority must comply with a direction given under sub-paragraph (5A)(e) and must secure that the proceedings, once brought, are proceeded with to a proper conclusion.

(5C) The Commission may at any time withdraw a direction given under sub-paragraph (5A)(e); and sub-paragraph (5B) shall not impose any obligation in relation to any time after the withdrawal of the direction.

(5D) The appropriate authority must keep the Commission informed of the action it takes in response to a direction given under sub-paragraph (5A)(e).

(5E) The appropriate authority must comply with the direction given under sub-paragraph (5A)(f) and must notify the Commission of the determination it makes.

(5F) On receipt of the report, where it is a report of an investigation of a complaint, the Commission may also make a recommendation under paragraph 28ZA."

(3) Omit sub-paragraphs (6) to (8).

27 (1) Paragraph 24 (action by the appropriate authority in response to an investigation report under paragraph 22) is amended as follows.

(2) In sub-paragraph (6)—

(a) after paragraph (a) insert—

"(aa) if it considers it appropriate to do so, make a determination as to any matter dealt with in the report, being a determination other than one that it is required to make by sub-paragraph (2)(a) or paragraph (a) of this sub-paragraph, and";

(b) for paragraph (b) substitute—

"(b) determine what action (if any), in addition to the action mentioned in paragraph (a)(ii), the authority will in its discretion take in respect of the matters dealt with in the report."

(3) After sub-paragraph (6) insert—

"(6A) Where the report is a report of an investigation of a complaint and the appropriate authority is a local policing body, the appropriate authority may also, on receipt of the report, make a recommendation under paragraph 28ZA."

28 In paragraph 24A (final reports on investigations: other DSI matters), at the end insert —

"(5) On receipt of the report, the Commission shall also, if it considers it appropriate to do so, make a determination as to any matter dealt with in the report, being a determination other than one that it is required to make under sub-paragraph (4) or that the appropriate authority may be required to make by virtue of paragraph 24C(3)."

PART 4

REVIEWS

29 Schedule 3 to the Police Reform Act 2002 (handling of complaints and conduct matters etc) is further amended as follows.

30 In paragraph 4 (reference of complaints to the Commission), after sub-paragraph (5) insert—

"(5A) The power of an appropriate authority to refer a complaint to the Commission under sub-paragraph (2) is also exercisable after a complaint has been handled in accordance with this Schedule if a recommendation is made under paragraph 6A(6)(a) or 25(4E)(b) (recommendation on a review)."

31 After paragraph 6 insert—

"6A Reviews relating to complaints dealt with other than by investigation

6A (1) This paragraph applies where a complaint is handled by the appropriate authority in accordance with paragraph 6(2A) otherwise than by the authority making arrangements for the complaint to be investigated by the authority on its own behalf.

(2) The complainant has the right to apply to the relevant review body for a review of the outcome of the complaint.

(3) The relevant review body must notify the following of an application for a review under sub-paragraph (2)—

(a) the appropriate authority,

(b) every person entitled to be kept properly informed in relation to the complaint under section 21, and

(c) the person complained against (if any).

(4) On a review applied for under sub-paragraph (2), the relevant review body must determine whether the outcome is a reasonable and proportionate outcome.

(5) Where the Commission is the relevant review body and the Commission finds that the outcome is not a reasonable and proportionate outcome, the Commission may—

(a) determine that it is necessary for the complaint to be investigated;

(b) make a recommendation under paragraph 28ZA.

(6) Where a local policing body is the relevant review body and the local policing body finds that the outcome is not a reasonable and proportionate outcome, the local policing body may—

(a) where the complaint has not previously been referred to the Commission under paragraph 4, make a recommendation to the appropriate authority that it refer the complaint to the Commission under sub-paragraph (2) of that paragraph;

(b) make a recommendation to the appropriate authority that it make arrangements for the complaint to be investigated by the authority on its own behalf;

(c) make a recommendation under paragraph 28ZA.

(7) The Secretary of State may by regulations make further provision about recommendations under sub-paragraph (6)(a) or (b).

(8) The regulations may (amongst other things) authorise the local policing body making the recommendation to require a response to the recommendation.

(9) The relevant review body must give notification of the outcome of a review under this paragraph and of its reasons for the determination made under sub-paragraph (4)—

(a) to the appropriate authority,

(b) to the complainant,

(c) to every person entitled to be kept properly informed in relation to the complaint under section 21, and

(d) except in a case where it appears to the relevant review body that to do so might prejudice any investigation of the complaint, to the person complained against (if any).

(10) In this paragraph references to the outcome of a complaint do not include the outcome of any criminal or disciplinary proceedings brought in relation to any matter which was the subject of the complaint."

32 Omit paragraph 8A (appeals relating to complaints dealt with other than by investigation) and the italic heading before that paragraph.

33 In the italic heading before paragraph 25, for "Appeals" substitute "Reviews".

34 (1) Paragraph 25 (appeals with respect to an investigation) is amended as follows.

(2) After sub-paragraph (1) insert—

"(1A) But this paragraph does not apply where the person investigating submitted a report on the investigation under provision made by virtue of paragraph 20A(4)(b) and did not (as a result of provision made by virtue of paragraph 20A(4)(a)) submit a further report under paragraph 22(2).

(1B) Where this paragraph applies, the complainant has the right to apply to the relevant review body for a review of the outcome of the complaint.

(1C) The relevant review body must notify the following of an application for a review under sub-paragraph (1B)—

(a) the appropriate authority,

(b) every person entitled to be kept properly informed in relation to the complaint under section 21, and

(c) the person complained against (if any)."

(3) Omit sub-paragraphs (2) to (3).

(4) For sub-paragraph (4) substitute—

"(4) Where the relevant review body so requires on the making of an application for a review under sub-paragraph (1B), the appropriate authority must provide the relevant review body with—

(a) a copy of the report of the investigation, and

(b) such information concerning the authority's determinations under paragraph 24 as is described in a notification given by the relevant review body to the authority."

(5) After sub-paragraph (4) insert—

"(4A) On a review applied for under sub-paragraph (1B), the relevant review body must determine whether the outcome of the complaint is a reasonable and proportionate outcome.

(4B) In making a determination under sub-paragraph (4A), the relevant review body may review the findings of the investigation.

(4C) Where the Commission is the relevant review body and the Commission finds that the outcome is not a reasonable and proportionate outcome, the Commission may—

(a) make its own findings (in place of, or in addition to, findings of the investigation);

(b) direct that the complaint be re-investigated;

(c) make a recommendation to the appropriate authority in respect of any person serving with the police—

(i) that the person has a case to answer in respect of misconduct or gross misconduct or has no case to answer in relation to the person's conduct to which the investigation related;

(ii) that the person's performance is, or is not, unsatisfactory;

(iii) that disciplinary proceedings of the form specified in the recommendation are brought against the person in respect of the person's conduct, efficiency or effectiveness to which the investigation related;

(iv) that any disciplinary proceedings brought against that person are modified so as to deal with such aspects of that conduct, efficiency or effectiveness as may be so specified;

(d) make a recommendation under paragraph 28ZA.

(4D) Where the Commission makes a recommendation under sub-paragraph (4C)(c)—

(a) the appropriate authority must notify the Commission whether it accepts the recommendation and (if it does) set out in the notification the steps that it is proposing to take to give effect to it, and

(b) sub-paragraphs (4) to (8) and (9)(b) of paragraph 27 apply in relation to the recommendation as if it had been made under that paragraph.

(4E) Where a local policing body is the relevant review body and the local policing body finds that the outcome is not a reasonable and proportionate outcome, the local policing body may—

(a) make a recommendation to the appropriate authority that the complaint be re-investigated by the authority on its own behalf;

(b) where the complaint has not previously been referred to the Commission under paragraph 4, make a recommendation to the appropriate authority that it refer the complaint to the Commission under sub-paragraph (2) of that paragraph;

(c) make a recommendation to the appropriate authority in respect of any person serving with the police—

(i) that the person has a case to answer in respect of misconduct or gross misconduct or has no case to answer in relation to the person's conduct to which the investigation related;

(ii) that the person's performance is, or is not, unsatisfactory;

(iii) that disciplinary proceedings of the form specified in the recommendation are brought against the person in respect of the person's conduct, efficiency or effectiveness to which the investigation related;

(iv) that any disciplinary proceedings brought against that person are modified so as to deal with such aspects of that conduct, efficiency or effectiveness as may be so specified;

(d) make a recommendation under paragraph 28ZA.

(4F) Sub-paragraph (4G) applies where, on a review applied for under sub-paragraph (1B), the relevant review body determines that the report of the investigation indicates that a criminal offence may have been committed by a person (if any) to whose conduct the investigation related and that—

(a) the circumstances are such that, in the opinion of the relevant review body, it is appropriate for the matters dealt with in the report to be considered by the Director of Public Prosecutions, or

(b) any matters dealt with in the report fall within any category of matters prescribed for the purposes of paragraph 24(2B)(b).

(4G) Where this sub-paragraph applies—

(a) if the Commission is the relevant review body, the Commission must notify the Director of Public Prosecutions of the determination under sub-paragraph (4F) and send the Director a copy of the report;

(b) if a local policing body is the relevant review body, the local policing body must make a recommendation to the appropriate authority that the appropriate authority—

(i) notify the Director of Public Prosecutions of the determination under sub-paragraph (4F), and

(ii) send the Director a copy of the report.

(4H) The Secretary of State may by regulations make further provision about recommendations under sub-paragraph (4E)(a), (b) or (c) or (4G)(b).

(4I) The regulations may (amongst other things) authorise the local policing body making the recommendation to require a response to the recommendation.

(4J) Where this paragraph applies because the person investigating submitted a report on the investigation under provision made by virtue of paragraph 20A(4)(b) ("the first report") and a further report under paragraph 22(2), the references in sub-paragraphs (4B) and (4C)(a) to the findings of the investigation do not include a reference to findings on the first report."

(6) Omit sub-paragraphs (5) to (9A).

(7) In sub-paragraph (10)—

(a) in the words before paragraph (a)—
   (i) for "appeal" substitute "review";
   (ii) for "any determination" substitute "the outcome of a review";
   (iii) after "paragraph" insert "and of its reasons for the determination made under sub-paragraph (4A)";

(b) in paragraph (a), omit "(unless it is the relevant appeal body)";

(c) in paragraph (d)—
   (i) for "appeal" substitute "review";
   (ii) omit "proposed review or".

(8) Omit sub-paragraph (11).

(9) In sub-paragraph (13)—

(a) in paragraph (a), for "appeals under this paragraph are to be brought" substitute "applications under sub-paragraph (1B) are to be made";

(b) in paragraph (b), for "appeal must be brought" substitute "application must be made";

(c) for paragraph (c) substitute—

"(c) for the procedure to be followed by the relevant review body when carrying out a review applied for under sub-paragraph (1B)."

(10) After sub-paragraph (13) insert—

"(14) In this paragraph references in relation to an investigation to the outcome of the complaint do not include the outcome of any criminal or disciplinary proceedings brought in relation to any matter which was the subject of the investigation."

35 After paragraph 25 insert—

"25A Information for complainant about disciplinary recommendations

25A (1) This paragraph applies where, on the review of the outcome of a complaint under paragraph 25, the Commission makes a recommendation under sub-paragraph (4C)(c) of that paragraph.

(2) Where the appropriate authority notifies the Commission under paragraph 25(4D)(a) that the recommendation has been accepted, the Commission must notify the complainant and every person entitled to be kept properly informed in relation to the complaint under section 21 of that fact and of the steps that have been, or are to be taken, by the appropriate authority to give effect to it.

(3) Where the appropriate authority—

(a) notifies the Commission under paragraph 25(4D)(a) that it does not (either in whole or in part) accept the recommendation, or

(b) fails to take steps to give full effect to the recommendation,

the Commission must determine what, if any, further steps to take under paragraph 27 as applied by paragraph 25(4D)(b).

(4) The Commission must notify the complainant and every person entitled to be kept properly informed in relation to the complaint under section 21—

(a) of any determination under sub-paragraph (3) not to take further steps, and

(b) where the Commission determines under that sub-paragraph that it will take further steps, of the outcome of the taking of those steps."

36 For the italic heading before paragraph 26, substitute "Re-investigations following a review".

37 (1) Paragraph 26 (reviews and re-investigations following an appeal) is amended as follows.

(2) Omit sub-paragraph (1).

(3) In sub-paragraph (2), omit "or sub-paragraph (1)".

(4) In sub-paragraph (3), for "(3)" substitute "(4)".

(5) After sub-paragraph (3) insert—

"(3A) Where, following a recommendation under paragraph 25(4E)(a) in relation to a complaint, the appropriate authority determines that it is appropriate for it to re-investigate the complaint on its own behalf, sub-paragraphs (3) to (5) of paragraph 16 shall apply in relation to the re-investigation as they apply in relation to an investigation to which paragraph 16 applies."

(6) In sub-paragraph (4)—

(a) for "25(8)" substitute "25(4C)(b)";

(b) omit "or sub-paragraph (1) of this paragraph";

(c) before "as they apply" insert "and any re-investigation of the type described in sub-paragraph (3A) of this paragraph".

(7) After sub-paragraph (4) insert—

"(4A) Where the Commission determines under sub-paragraph (2) that the re-investigation should take the form of an investigation by the appropriate authority on its own behalf, the Commission may also give the appropriate authority such directions as to the handling of the matter in future as the Commission thinks fit."

(8) For sub-paragraph (5) substitute—

"(5) The Commission shall notify the appropriate authority of any determination that it makes under this paragraph and of its reasons for making the determination.

(5A) The Commission shall also notify the following of any determination that it makes under this paragraph and of its reasons for making the determination—

(a) the complainant;

(b) every person entitled to be kept properly informed in relation to the complaint under section 21;

(c) the person complained against (if any).

(5B) The duty imposed by sub-paragraph (5A) on the Commission shall have effect subject to such exceptions as may be provided for by regulations made by the Secretary of State.

(5C) Subsections (6) to (8) of section 20 apply for the purposes of sub-paragraph (5B) as they apply for the purposes of that section."

(9) Omit sub-paragraph (6).

38 In the italic heading before paragraph 30—

(a) for "Appeals" substitute "Reviews";

(b) for "appeal" substitute "review".

39 (1) Paragraph 30 (appeals: the relevant appeal body) is amended as follows.

(2) In sub-paragraph (1)—

(a) in the words before paragraph (a)—

(i) for "appeal", in the first place it occurs, substitute "review";

(ii) for "an appeal" substitute "a review";

(b) in paragraph (a), after "in a case where" insert "a local policing body is the appropriate authority in relation to the relevant complaint or";

(c) for paragraph (b) substitute—

"(b) the local policing body which is the relevant local policing body in relation to the relevant complaint, in any other case."

(3) For sub-paragraph (2) substitute—

"(2) In this paragraph and paragraphs 31 and 32—

"relevant complaint", in relation to a review, means the complaint to which the review relates;

"relevant local policing body", in relation to a relevant complaint where a chief officer is the appropriate authority in relation to the complaint, means the local policing body for the area of the police force of which the chief officer is a member;

"review" means a review applied for under paragraph 6A(2) or 25(1B)."

40 For paragraph 31 (appeal made to the Commission in error) substitute—

"31 (1) This paragraph applies in a case where—

(a) an application for a review is made to the Commission, and

(b) a local policing body is the relevant review body in relation to the review.

(2) The Commission must—

(a) forward the application to the local policing body, and

(b) notify the person who applied for the review—

(i) that the local policing body is the relevant review body, and

(ii) the application has been forwarded.

(3) The application is to be taken to have been—

(a) made to the local policing body, and

(b) so made at the time when it is forwarded to the local policing body."

41 For paragraph 32 (appeal made to appropriate authority in error) substitute—

"32 (1) This paragraph applies in a case where—

(a) an application for a review is made to a local policing body, and

(b) the Commission is the relevant review body in relation to the review.

(2) The local policing body must—

(a) forward the application to the Commission, and

(b) notify the person who applied for the review—

(i) that the Commission is the relevant review body, and

(ii) the application has been forwarded.

(3) The application is to be taken to have been—

(a) made to the Commission, and

(b) so made at the time when it is forwarded to the Commission."

42 In section 15 of the Police Reform Act 2002 (general duties of local policing bodies, chief officers and inspectors)—

(a) in subsection (4) (duty to provide the Commission with assistance), at the end insert "or any review under paragraph 25 of Schedule 3";

(b) in subsection (6)—

(i) in paragraph (a), after "investigation" insert "or review (as the case may be)";

(ii) omit the "and" at the end of paragraph (a);

(iii) in paragraph (b), at the beginning insert "in the case of an investigation,";

(iv) at the end of paragraph (b) insert "and

(c) in the case of a review applied for under paragraph 25(1B) of Schedule 3 in respect of an investigation, irrespective of who had the person appointed to carry out the investigation under his direction and control;".

43 In section 16 of the Police Reform Act 2002 (payment for assistance with investigations)—

(a) in subsection (1)(b), for "in such a connection to the Commission." substitute "to the Commission in connection with an investigation under this Part or a review under paragraph 25 of Schedule 3.";

(b) in subsection (2)(b)—

(i) in the words before sub-paragraph (i), for "in such a connection by a police force ("the assisting force") to the Commission" substitute "by a police force ("the assisting force") to the Commission in connection with an investigation under this Part or a review under paragraph 25 of Schedule 3";

(ii) omit the "or" at the end of sub-paragraph (i);

(iii) after sub-paragraph (ii) insert “, or

(iii) a review under paragraph 25 of Schedule 3 of the outcome of a complaint where the complainant expressed dissatisfaction with a force other than that force.”

44 In section 18 of the Police Reform Act 2002 (inspections of police premises on behalf of the Commission), in subsection (2), after paragraph (b) insert—

“(c) the purposes of any review by the Commission under paragraph 25 of Schedule 3.”

PART 5

RECOMMENDATIONS BY THE COMMISSION AND LOCAL POLICING BODIES

45 In Part 3 of Schedule 3 to the Police Reform Act 2002, after paragraph 28 insert—

“28ZA Recommendations by the Commission or a local policing body

28ZA (1) A recommendation under this paragraph (for the purposes of paragraphs 6A, 23, 24 and 25) is a recommendation of a kind described in regulations made by the Secretary of State which is made with a view to remedying the dissatisfaction expressed by the complainant concerned.

(2) A recommendation of a kind described in regulations under subsection (1) may (amongst other things) be a recommendation that compensation be paid.

(3) The reference in subsection (1) to the complainant concerned—

(a) in relation to a recommendation made by virtue of paragraph 6A(5)(b) or (6)(c), is a reference to the complainant who applied under paragraph 6A(2) for the review;

(b) in relation to a recommendation made by virtue of paragraph 23(5F) or 24(6A), is a reference to the complainant whose complaint, having been investigated, resulted in the submission of the report under paragraph 22;

(c) in relation to a recommendation made by virtue of paragraph 25(4C)(d) or (4E)(d), is a reference to the complainant who applied under paragraph 25(1B) for the review.

(4) The Secretary of State may by regulations make further provision about recommendations under this paragraph.

(5) The regulations may (amongst other things)—

(a) specify the persons to whom recommendations under this paragraph may be made;

(b) authorise the person making a recommendation under this paragraph (whether the Commission or a local policing body) to require a response to the recommendation;

(c) require the person making a recommendation under this paragraph to send a copy of the recommendation, and any response to it, to any prescribed person or person of a prescribed description."

46 In consequence of the insertion of paragraph 28ZA, in paragraph 28A of Schedule 3 to the Police Reform Act 2002, after sub-paragraph (3) insert—

"(3A) Where this paragraph applies—

(a) by virtue of sub-paragraph (1)(a) or (b) and the report is a report of an investigation of a complaint, or

(b) by virtue of sub-paragraph (2),

a recommendation made under sub-paragraph (3) may not be a recommendation of a kind described in regulations made under paragraph 28ZA(1)."

PART 6

CONSEQUENTIAL AMENDMENTS

47 In the Police Reform Act 2002—

(a) in section 15—

(i) in subsection (3)(a), omit ", 17";

(ii) in subsection (5), in the words after paragraph (c), omit ", 17";

(b) in section 18(2)(b)—

(i) omit "supervision or";

(ii) for "management" substitute "direction";

(c) in section 20—

(i) in subsection (1)(b), for "management" substitute "direction";

(ii) in subsection (2), omit the "or" at the end of paragraph (a) and omit paragraph (b);

(d) in section 21—

(i) in subsection (6)(b), for "management" substitute "direction";

(ii) in subsection (7), omit the "or" at the end of paragraph (a) and omit paragraph (b);

(e) in section 22—

(i) omit subsection (5)(c);

(ii) omit subsection (5)(f);

(f) in section 23—

(i) in subsection (2)(i)—

(a) omit "supervision or";

(b) for "management" substitute "direction";

(ii) omit subsection (2)(m);

(g) in section 29—

(i) in subsection (1), omit the definition of "local resolution";

(ii) in subsection (6)—

(a) omit "under the supervision of the Commission,";

(b) for "management" substitute "direction";

(c) omit "17,";

(h) in Schedule 3—

(i) in paragraph 19F(1)(a), for "management" substitute "direction";

(ii) in paragraph 20(1), for paragraph (a) substitute—

"(a) the conduct to which the investigation relates has been certified in accordance with regulations under paragraph 20A, or";

(iii) in paragraph 20, omit sub-paragraph (2);

(iv) in paragraph 21A(3), omit "or 17";

(v) in paragraph 21A(6)(a), for "15(5)" substitute "15(5A) or (5B)";

(vi) in paragraph 22(3), omit "17 or";

(vii) in paragraph 22(7) and (8), for "within paragraph 19C(1)(a) or (b)" substitute "to which paragraph 19A applies";

(viii) in paragraph 23(1)(a), for "management" substitute "direction";

(ix) in paragraph 23(13), after "21A(2)" insert ", (2A)";

(x) in paragraph 24(1), omit the "or" at the end of paragraph (a) and omit paragraph (b);

(xi) in paragraph 24(2), omit "or (as the case may be) of the copy";

(xii) omit paragraph 24(5A) to (5C);

(xiii) in paragraph 24(6), omit "or (as the case may be) copy";

(xiv) in paragraph 24(11), after "21A(2)" insert ", (2A)";

(xv) in paragraph 24A(1), after "21A(2)" insert ", (2A)";

(xvi) in paragraph 24B(3)(a), for "15(5)" substitute "15(5A) or (5B)";

(xvii) in paragraph 25(1), omit the "or" at the end of paragraph (a) and omit paragraph (b);

(xviii) omit paragraph 27(1)(b) and (3);

(xix) in paragraph 27(9)(a), for "(1)(b) or (c)" substitute "(1)(c)";

(xx) omit paragraph 28;

(xxi) in paragraph 28A(1)(a)—

(a) omit "supervised or";

(b) for "managed" substitute "directed";

(xxii) in paragraph 28A(2), in the words before paragraph (a), for "an appeal" substitute "a review";

(xxiii) in paragraph 28A(2)(a)—

(a) for "8A" substitute "6A";

(b) for "appeal" substitute "review";

(xxiv) in paragraph 28A(2)(b) and (3), for "appeal" substitute "review";

(xxv) in paragraph 28A(4)(b), for "an appeal" substitute "a review";

(xxvi) in paragraph 29, omit the definition of "direction and control matter".

48 In the Serious Organised Crime and Police Act 2005—

(a) in Schedule 11, omit paragraphs 3 and 4;

(b) in Schedule 12, omit paragraphs 15, 16(3) and 19.

49 In the Police and Justice Act 2006, in Part 7 of Schedule 1, omit paragraph 89(4).

50 In the Criminal Justice and Immigration Act 2008, in Schedule 23, omit paragraphs 5 to 10, 14(5), 13(5) and (6), 17 and 18(3).

51 In the Police Reform and Social Responsibility Act 2011—

(a) in Schedule 14, omit paragraphs 8(5), 9(2), 10, 13, 14(2), (4) and (5), 16, 17, 18, 19 and 20(3) to (11) and (13);

(b) in Schedule 16, omit paragraph 300(4).

52 In the Police (Complaints and Conduct) Act 2012, omit section 1(3).

53 In the Crime and Courts Act 2013, in Part 2 of Schedule 6, omit paragraph 17(3).

54 In the Anti-social Behaviour, Crime and Policing Act 2014, in Part 3 of Schedule 11, omit paragraph 95(2) to (5).

SCHEDULE 6

Section 28

SCHEDULE TO BE INSERTED AS SCHEDULE 3A TO THE POLICE REFORM ACT 2002

"SCHEDULE 3A

Section 29D(5)

WHISTLE-BLOWING INVESTIGATIONS: PROCEDURE

1 Designation of persons to take part in investigation

1 (1) Paragraph 19(1), (2) and (4) to (8) of Schedule 3 (investigations under that Schedule by the Commission itself), and any order made under paragraph 19(4) of that Schedule, apply where the Commission decides to carry out an investigation under section 29D(1) as they apply where the Commission has determined to investigate, or is required to investigate, a complaint, recordable conduct matter or DSI matter under that Schedule.

(2) In the case of an investigation under section 29D(1) relating to any conduct of the Commissioner of Police of the Metropolis or the Deputy Commissioner of Police of the Metropolis, the person designated under paragraph 19(2) of Schedule 3 (as applied by sub-paragraph (1)) must be the person nominated by the Secretary of State for that purpose.

2 Protection of anonymity

2 (1) The person in charge of an investigation under section 29D(1), and any other person designated for the purposes of the investigation by virtue of paragraph 1, may not disclose the identity of the whistle-blower or information that might (whether alone or with other information) tend to reveal that identity.

(2) Sub-paragraph (1) does not apply to the extent that—

(a) the whistle-blower consents to the disclosure of his or her identity or (as the case may be) to the disclosure of information that might tend to reveal it, or

(b) the disclosure is authorised by regulations made by the Secretary of State under section 29J.

(3) The person in charge of an investigation under section 29D(1) must take all reasonable steps to ensure that, where the identity of the whistle-blower, or information that might tend to reveal that identity, is disclosed for the purposes of the investigation (whether with the consent of the whistle-blower or in accordance with regulations under section 29J), it is not further disclosed without the consent of the person in charge.

(4) For the purpose of the duty under sub-paragraph (3), the person in charge may impose such requirements on persons to whom the identity of the whistle-blower, or information that might tend to reveal that identity, is disclosed as are specified in regulations made by the Secretary of State for the purpose of this paragraph.

3 Powers to obtain information etc

3 Paragraphs 19ZA to 19ZC of Schedule 3 apply in relation to an investigation under section 29D(1) as they apply in relation to an investigation under paragraph 19 of that Schedule.

4 Procedure where conduct matter is revealed during investigation

4 (1) If, during the course of an investigation under section 29D(1), it appears to the person in charge that there is an indication that a person serving with the police ("the person whose conduct is in question") may have—

(a) committed a criminal offence, or

(b) behaved in a manner which would justify the bringing of disciplinary proceedings,

the person in charge must make a submission to that effect to the Commission.

(2) If, after considering the submission, the Commission determines that there is such an indication, it must—

(a) notify the appropriate authority in relation to the person whose conduct is in question of its determination, and

(b) send to it a copy of the submission under sub-paragraph (1).

(3) Where the appropriate authority in relation to the person whose conduct is in question is notified under sub-paragraph (2), it must record the matter under paragraph 11 of Schedule 3 to this Act as a conduct matter.

(4) Where a matter is, in accordance with sub-paragraph (3), recorded under paragraph 11 of Schedule 3 as a conduct matter—

(a) the person in charge of the investigation under section 29D(1) must (subject to any determination made by the Commission under paragraph 15(5B) of Schedule 3) continue the investigation as if appointed or designated to investigate the conduct matter, and

(b) the other provisions of Schedule 3 apply in relation to that matter accordingly (subject to regulations under sub-paragraph (5)).

(5) The Secretary of State may by regulations make provision modifying Schedule 3 in relation to an investigation of a matter that, in accordance with sub-paragraph (3), is recorded under paragraph 11 of that Schedule as a conduct matter but only for the purpose of making provision for the protection of the anonymity of whistle-blowers.

5 Procedure where DSI matter is revealed during investigation

5 (1) If, during the course of an investigation under section 29D(1), it appears to the person in charge that the matter may be a DSI matter, the person must make a submission to that effect to the Commission.

(2) If, after considering the submission, the Commission determines the matter is a DSI matter, it must—

(a) notify the appropriate authority in relation to the DSI matter, and

(b) send to it a copy of the submission under sub-paragraph (1).

(3) Where the appropriate authority in relation to the DSI matter is notified under sub-paragraph (2), it must record the matter under paragraph 14A of Schedule 3 to this Act as a DSI matter.

(4) Where a matter is, in accordance with sub-paragraph (3), recorded under paragraph 14A of Schedule 3 as a DSI matter—

(a) the person in charge of the investigation under section 29D(1) must (subject to any determination made by the Commission under paragraph 15(5B) of Schedule 3) continue the investigation as if appointed or designated to investigate the DSI matter, and

(b) the other provisions of Schedule 3 apply in relation to that matter accordingly (subject to regulations under sub-paragraph (5)).

(5) The Secretary of State may by regulations make provision modifying Schedule 3 in relation to an investigation that, in accordance with sub-paragraph (3), is recorded under paragraph 14A of that Schedule as a DSI matter but only for the purpose of making provision for the protection of the anonymity of whistle-blowers.

(6) In this paragraph, references to the appropriate authority in relation to a DSI matter have the same meaning as in Part 2 (see section 29).

6 Conclusion of investigation

6 (1) When an investigation under section 29D(1) is concluded, the person in charge of the investigation must submit a report on it to the Commission.

(2) The Commission—

(a) must send a copy of the report to the whistle-blower, and

(b) may, with the consent of the whistle-blower, send a copy of the report to the appropriate authority.

(3) The Secretary of State may by regulations make provision for circumstances in which the duty under sub-paragraph (2)(a) does not apply.

(4) The power conferred by sub-paragraph (3) may be exercised only to the extent that the Secretary of State considers necessary for any of the permitted non-disclosure purposes.

(5) The Secretary of State may also by regulations make provision for circumstances in which (despite sub-paragraph (2)(b)) a copy of the report may be sent to the appropriate authority without the consent of the whistle-blower.

(6) The power conferred by sub-paragraph (5) may be exercised only to the extent that the Secretary of State considers necessary for any of the permitted disclosure purposes.

(7) Where the Commission would contravene section 21A by sending a copy of a report in its entirety to the whistle-blower or to the appropriate authority, the Commission may comply with its duty under sub-paragraph (2)(a) or (as the case may be) may

exercise its power under sub-paragraph (2)(b) (or under regulations under sub-paragraph (5)) by sending instead a copy of the report after having removed or obscured the information which it is prohibited from disclosing by section 21A.

(8) In this paragraph—

(a) "the permitted non-disclosure purposes" has the same meaning as in section 29I;

(b) "the permitted disclosure purposes" has the same meaning as in section 29J.

7 Power of Commission to make recommendations

7 (1) On receipt of a report under paragraph 6, the Commission may make a recommendation in relation to any matter dealt with in it.

(2) The Secretary of State may by regulations make further provision about recommendations under this paragraph.

(3) The regulations may (amongst other things)—

(a) describe the kinds of recommendations that the Commission may make under this paragraph;

(b) specify the persons to whom the recommendations may be made;

(c) authorise the Commission to require a response to a recommendation made under this paragraph."

SCHEDULE 7

Section 29

DISCIPLINARY PROCEEDINGS: FORMER MEMBERS OF MOD POLICE, BRITISH TRANSPORT POLICE AND CIVIL NUCLEAR CONSTABULARY

Ministry of Defence Police Act 1987 (c. 4)

1 The Ministry of Defence Police Act 1987 is amended as follows.

2 (1) Section 3A (regulations relating to disciplinary matters) is amended as follows.

(2) After subsection (1A) insert—

"(1B) Regulations under this section may provide for the procedures that are established by or under regulations made by virtue of subsection (1A) to apply (with or without modifications) in respect of the conduct, efficiency or effectiveness of any person where—

(a) an allegation relating to the conduct, efficiency or effectiveness of the person comes to the attention of the chief constable of the Ministry of Defence Police, the Ministry of Defence Police Committee, the Independent Police Complaints Commission, the Police Investigations and Review Commissioner or the Police Ombudsman for Northern Ireland,

(b) at the time of the alleged misconduct, inefficiency or ineffectiveness the person was a member of the Ministry of Defence Police, and

(c) condition A, B or C is satisfied in relation to the person.

(1C) Condition A is that the person ceases to be a member of the Ministry of Defence Police after the allegation first comes to the attention of a person mentioned in subsection (1B)(a).

(1D) Condition B is that the person had ceased to be a member of the Ministry of Defence Police before the allegation first came to the attention of a person mentioned in subsection (1B)(a) but the period between the person having ceased to be a member of the Ministry of Defence Police and the allegation first coming to the attention of a person mentioned in subsection (1B)(a) does not exceed the period specified in regulations under this section.

(1E) Condition C is that—

(a) the person had ceased to be a member of the Ministry of Defence Police before the allegation first came to the attention of a person mentioned in subsection (1B)(a),

(b) the period between the person having ceased to be a member of the Ministry of Defence Police and the allegation first coming to the attention of a person mentioned in subsection (1B)(a) exceeds the period specified for the purposes of condition B, and

(c) the alleged misconduct, inefficiency or ineffectiveness is such that, if proved, the person could have been dealt with by dismissal if the person had still been a member of the Ministry of Defence Police.

(1F) Regulations made by virtue of subsection (1B) as they apply in a case where condition C is satisfied in relation to a person must provide that disciplinary proceedings may be taken against the person in respect of the alleged misconduct, inefficiency or ineffectiveness only if the Independent Police Complaints Commission determines that taking such proceedings would be reasonable and proportionate having regard to—

(a) the seriousness of the alleged misconduct, inefficiency or ineffectiveness,

(b) the impact of the allegation on public confidence in the police, and

(c) the public interest.

(1G) Regulations made by virtue of subsection (1B) may make provision about matters to be taken into account by the Independent Police Complaints Commission for the purposes of subsection (1F)(a) to (c).

(1H) Regulations made by virtue of subsection (1B) must provide that disciplinary proceedings which are not the first disciplinary proceedings to be taken against the person in respect of the alleged misconduct, inefficiency or ineffectiveness may be taken only if they result from a re-investigation of the allegation (whether carried out under regulations under this section or by virtue of section 26 of the Police Reform Act 2002) that begins within the period specified in the regulations.

The period specified must begin with the date when the person ceased to be a member of the Ministry of Defence Police."

(3) In subsection (2), for "The regulations" substitute "Regulations under this section".

3 In section 4 (representation etc at disciplinary proceedings), in subsection (4)—

(a) in the definition of "the officer concerned", after "member" insert "or, as the case may be, the former member";

(b) in the definition of "relevant authority"—

(i) after paragraph (a) insert—

"(aa) where the officer concerned is a former member of the Ministry of Defence Police who immediately before ceasing to be such a member was not a senior officer, the chief constable for the Ministry of Defence Police;";

(ii) after paragraph (b) insert—

"(c) where the officer concerned is a former member of the Ministry of Defence Police who immediately before ceasing to be such a member was a senior officer, the Ministry of Defence Police Committee;".

4 In section 4A (appeals against dismissal etc), in subsection (1)(a), after "member" insert ", or former member,".

5 Regulations made in pursuance of section 3A(1B) of the Ministry of Defence Police Act 1987 (as inserted by paragraph 2)—

(a) may not make provision in relation to a person who ceases to be a member of the Ministry of Defence Police before the coming into force of paragraph 2 of this Schedule;

(b) may make provision in relation to a person who ceases to be a member of the Ministry of Defence Police after the coming into force of paragraph 2 of this Schedule even though the alleged misconduct, inefficiency or ineffectiveness occurred at a time before the coming into force of that paragraph, but only if the alleged misconduct, inefficiency or ineffectiveness is such that, if proved, there could be a finding in relation to the person in disciplinary proceedings that the person would have been dismissed if the person had still been a member of the Ministry of Defence Police.

Railways and Transport Safety Act 2003 (c. 20)

6 The Railways and Transport Safety Act 2003 is amended as follows.

7 In section 36 (police regulations: general), after subsection (1) insert—

"(1A) To the extent that subsection (1) concerns regulations made in pursuance of section 50(3A) of the Police Act 1996, or matters that could be dealt with by such regulations, the reference in subsection (1) to constables or other persons employed in the service of the Police Force includes former constables and other persons formerly employed in the service of the Police Force."

8 In section 37 (police regulations: special constables), after subsection (1) insert—

"(1ZA) To the extent that subsection (1) concerns regulations made in pursuance of section 51(2B) of the Police Act 1996, or matters that could be dealt with by such regulations, the reference in subsection (1) to special constables of the Police Force includes former special constables of the Police Force."

9 In section 42 (police regulations by Secretary of State), in subsection (3)—

(a) after "50(3)" insert "or (3A)";

(b) after "51(2A)" insert "or (2B)".

10 Regulations made under section 36, 37 or 42 of the Railways and Transport Safety Act 2003 that make provision that applies regulations made in pursuance of section 50(3A) or 51(2B) of the Police Act 1996, or that deals with matters that could be dealt with by such regulations, in relation to former constables, and former special constables, of the British Transport Police Force and other persons formerly employed in the service of the British Transport Police Force—

(a) may not make provision that would not be permitted in relation to former members of a police force and former special constables by section 29(7)(a);

(b) may make provision that would be permitted in relation to former members of a police force and former special constables by section 29(7)(b).

Energy Act 2004 (c. 20)

11 The Energy Act 2004 is amended as follows.

12 In section 58 (government, administration and conditions of service of Civil Nuclear Constabulary), in subsection (1)(a), after "members" insert "or former members".

13 (1) In Schedule 13 (directions by Secretary of State about Civil Nuclear Constabulary), paragraph 3 (government, administration and conditions of service) is amended as follows.

(2) After sub-paragraph (2) insert—

"(2A) To the extent that sub-paragraph (2) concerns provision that may be made in pursuance of section 50(3A) of the Police Act 1996, the reference in sub-paragraph (1) to members of the Constabulary includes former members."

14 Provision made by the Civil Nuclear Police Authority that relates to former members of the Civil Nuclear Constabulary and matters which are the subject of regulations made in pursuance of section 50(3A) of the Police Act 1996—

(a) may not be provision that would not be permitted in relation to former members of a police force and former special constables by section 29(7)(a);

(b) may be provision that would be permitted in relation to former members of a police force and former special constables by section 29(7)(b).

SCHEDULE 8

Section 30

PART TO BE INSERTED AS PART 4A OF THE POLICE ACT 1996

"PART 4A

POLICE BARRED LIST AND POLICE ADVISORY LIST

Police barred list

88A Duty to report dismissals etc to College of Policing

88A 88A Duty to report dismissals etc to College of Policing

(1) The relevant authority must report a person to the College of Policing where—

(a) the person ceases to be a member of a police force or a special constable by virtue of being dismissed at proceedings conducted under regulations made in pursuance of section 50(3) or 51(2A);

(b) the person is a former member of a police force or a former special constable and there is a finding in relation to the person in disciplinary proceedings that the person would have been dismissed if the person had still been a member of a police force or a special constable;

(c) the person ceases to be a civilian police employee by virtue of being dismissed and the reason, or one of the reasons, for the dismissal relates to conduct, efficiency or effectiveness;

(d) the person is a former civilian police employee and there is a finding in relation to the person in disciplinary proceedings that the person would have been dismissed if the person had still been such an employee.

(2) A report under subsection (1)—

(a) must be made within such period as is specified in regulations made by the Secretary of State;

(b) must include such information as is so specified.

(3) In this section "relevant authority" means—

(a) in relation to a person falling within subsection (1)(a), other than a person who was a chief officer of police immediately before being dismissed, the chief officer of police of the police force of which the person was a member, or for which the person was appointed as a special constable, at that time;

(b) in relation to a person falling within subsection (1)(a) who was a chief officer of police immediately before being dismissed, the local policing body for the police force of which the person was a member at that time;

(c) in relation to a person falling within subsection (1)(b), other than a former chief officer of police, the chief officer of police of the police force of which the person was last a member or for which the person was last appointed as a special constable;

(d) in relation to a person falling within subsection (1)(b) who is a former chief officer of police, the local policing body for the police force of which the person was last a member;

(e) in relation to a person falling within subsection (1)(c), the chief officer of police under whose direction and control the person was immediately before being dismissed;

(f) in relation to a person falling within subsection (1)(d), the chief officer of police under whose direction and control the person was immediately before ceasing to be a civilian police employee.

(4) In this section "disciplinary proceedings" means—

(a) in relation to a former member of a police force or a former special constable, proceedings conducted under regulations made in pursuance of section 50(3A) or 51(2B);

(b) in relation to a former civilian police employee, any proceedings that are identified as disciplinary proceedings in relation to such a person by regulations made by the Secretary of State.

(5) For the purposes of this section, a person is a civilian police employee if the person is—

(a) a member of the civilian staff of a police force, including the metropolitan police force (within the meaning of Part 1 of the Police Reform and Social Responsibility Act 2011), or

(b) a person employed by the Common Council of the City of London in its capacity as police authority who is under the direction and control of the Commissioner of Police for the City of London.

(6) A person is dismissed for the purposes of subsection (1)(c) if the circumstances in which the person ceases to be a civilian police employee amount to dismissal within the meaning of Part 10 of the Employment Rights Act 1996 (see section 95 of that Act).

(7) Regulations under this section may make different provision for different cases and circumstances.

(8) A statutory instrument containing regulations under this section is subject to annulment in pursuance of a resolution of either House of Parliament.

88B Duty to maintain police barred list

88B 88B Duty to maintain police barred list

(1) The College of Policing must maintain a list of persons who are reported to the College under section 88A.

(2) The list maintained under subsection (1) is to be known as the police barred list.

(3) The police barred list must include such information in relation to a person reported to the College of Policing under section 88A as is specified in regulations made by the Secretary of State.

(4) Regulations under this section—

(a) may make different provision for different cases and circumstances;

(b) may confer a discretion on the College of Policing.

(5) A statutory instrument containing regulations under this section is subject to annulment in pursuance of a resolution of either House of Parliament.

88C Effect of inclusion in police barred list

88C 88C Effect of inclusion in police barred list

(1) A person who is included in the police barred list is a barred person for the purposes of this section and sections 88D and 88E.

(2) Before employing or appointing any person, a person mentioned in subsection (5) must check with the College of Policing whether the proposed employee or proposed appointee (as the case may be) is a barred person.

(3) A person mentioned in subsection (5) may not employ a barred person or otherwise appoint a barred person to any position.

(4) For the purposes of subsections (2) and (3) a person who is to be seconded to work for a person mentioned in subsection (5), and who will not be employed by that person, is to be regarded as being appointed by that person.

(5) The persons referred to in subsections (2) to (4) are—

  (a) a chief officer of police;

  (b) a local policing body;

  (c) the chief inspector of constabulary;

  (d) the Independent Police Complaints Commission;

  (e) a person specified in regulations made by the Secretary of State.

(6) A person may be specified in regulations under subsection (5)(e) only if the person has relevant public functions.

(7) In this section and sections 88D and 88E "relevant public functions" means functions of a public nature exercisable in, or in relation to, England and Wales that relate to policing or law enforcement.

(8) A statutory instrument containing regulations under subsection (5)(e) may not be made unless a draft of the instrument has been laid before and approved by a resolution of each House of Parliament.

88D Application of section 88C to persons with mixed functions

88D 88D Application of section 88C to persons with mixed functions

(1) If a person to be specified in regulations under section 88C(5)(e) has both relevant public functions and other functions, the person may be so specified as follows (but not otherwise)—

  (a) in relation to the exercise of the person's relevant public functions, or

  (b) in relation to the exercise of such of those relevant public functions as are of a description specified in the regulations.

(2) In this section—

  (a) a person who is specified in regulations under section 88C(5)(e) is referred to as a specified person, and

  (b) in relation to that person, the functions in relation to the exercise of which the person is specified are referred to as specified functions.

(3) In relation to a specified person—

(a) the duties in section 88C(2) and (3) apply only to the extent that the proposed employee or proposed appointee (as the case may be) will be involved in the exercise of specified functions;

(b) the additional duties in subsections (4) and (5) of this section apply where the specified person is proposing to arrange for an existing employee or existing appointee to become involved in the exercise of specified functions (not having previously been so involved).

(4) Before making the arrangement, the specified person must check with the College of Policing whether the existing employee or existing appointee (as the case may be) is a barred person.

(5) The specified person may not arrange for an existing employee or existing appointee who is a barred person to become involved in the exercise of specified functions.

(6) For the purposes of subsections (3) to (5) a person who is seconded to work for a specified person is to be regarded as an existing appointee of that person (if not an existing employee of that person).

88E Prohibition on contractors using barred persons

88E 88E Prohibition on contractors using barred persons

(1) A person mentioned in section 88C(5) may not enter into a contract for the provision of services if the terms of the contract would permit a barred person to be involved in the exercise of relevant public functions.

(2) A local policing body may not enter into a contract for the provision of services to a chief officer of police if the terms of the contract would permit a barred person to be involved in the exercise of relevant public functions.

(3) Subsection (1) applies in relation to a person specified in regulations under section 88C(5)(e) as described in section 88D(1)(b) as if the reference in subsection (1) to relevant public functions were a reference to those relevant public functions in relation to the exercise of which the person is specified.

88F Removal from police barred list

88F 88F Removal from police barred list

(1) This section applies where a relevant authority reports a person to the College of Policing under section 88A and—

(a) in relation to a person reported by virtue of section 88A(1)(a), the person is reinstated as a member of a police force or a special constable (as the case may be) at proceedings conducted under rules made under section 85;

(b) in relation to a person reported by virtue of section 88A(1)(b), the finding that the person would have been dismissed is set aside at proceedings conducted under rules made under section 85;

(c) in relation to a person reported by virtue of section 88A(1)(c), the dismissal is found to have been an unfair dismissal—

(i) following a complaint under section 111 of the Employment Rights Act 1996, and

(ii) whether by an employment tribunal or on appeal;

(d) in relation to a person reported by virtue of section 88A(1)(d), the finding that the person would have been dismissed is set aside at proceedings that are identified as appeal proceedings by regulations made by the Secretary of State.

(2) Where this section applies, the relevant authority must make a further report to the College of Policing in relation to the person.

(3) A report under subsection (2)—

(a) must be made within such period as is specified in regulations made by the Secretary of State;

(b) must include such information as is so specified.

(4) On receipt of a report under subsection (2) in relation to a person the College of Policing must remove the person from the police barred list.

(5) The Secretary of State may by regulations make provision in connection with the removal of a person from the police barred list otherwise than under subsection (4).

(6) Regulations under subsection (5) may confer functions on the College of Policing including functions which involve the exercise of a discretion.

(7) "Relevant authority" has the same meaning in this section as it has in section 88A.

(8) Regulations under this section may make different provision for different cases and circumstances.

(9) A statutory instrument containing regulations under this section is subject to annulment in pursuance of a resolution of either House of Parliament.

88G Publication of information in police barred list

88G 88G Publication of information in police barred list

(1) This section applies to a person who—

(a) is included in the police barred list, and

(b) is of a description specified in regulations made by the Secretary of State.

(2) The College of Policing must (in accordance with subsection (3)) publish such information included in the police barred list in relation to a person to whom this section applies as is specified in regulations made by the Secretary of State.

(3) Information published under subsection (2) must—

(a) be published in such manner as the College of Policing considers appropriate,

(b) be published within such period following its inclusion in the police barred list as is specified in regulations made by the Secretary of State,

(c) remain published by the College for a period of 5 years beginning with the date on which it is first published, and

(d) cease to be published by the College at the end of that period.

(4) The Secretary of State may by regulations provide for the duty in subsection (2) to be subject to exceptions.

(5) Regulations under subsection (4) may (amongst other things) make provision which has the effect that—

(a) information is never published;

(b) information ceases to be published by the College of Policing before the end of the period referred to in subsection (3)(c).

(6) Regulations which make provision of the type described in subsection (5)(b) may confer functions on the College of Policing including functions which involve the exercise of a discretion.

(7) Regulations under this section may make different provision for different cases and circumstances.

(8) A statutory instrument containing regulations under this section is subject to annulment in pursuance of a resolution of either House of Parliament.

88H Power to disclose information in police barred list

88H 88H Power to disclose information in police barred list

The College of Policing may, if it considers it to be in the public interest to do so, disclose to any person information included in the police barred list which relates to a particular person who is included in the police barred list.

Police advisory list

88I Duty to report resignations and retirements to College of Policing

88I 88I Duty to report resignations and retirements to College of Policing

(1) The relevant authority must report a person to the College of Policing where—

(a) the person ceases to be a person serving with the police by resigning or retiring after a relevant allegation about the person comes to the attention of the relevant authority but before disciplinary proceedings in respect of the allegation are brought or, if brought, before they are concluded;

(b) the person is a former member of a police force or a former special constable and a relevant allegation about the person comes to the attention of the relevant authority after the person having ceased to be a member of a police force or a special constable (as the case may be) by resigning or retiring.

(2) But the duty in subsection (1)(a) does not apply if, before the person resigns or retires, it is determined that no disciplinary proceedings will be brought against the person in respect of the allegation.

(3) A report under subsection (1)—

(a) must be made within such period as is specified in regulations made by the Secretary of State;

(b) must include such information as is so specified.

(4) In this section "relevant authority" means—

(a) in relation to a person who was a member of a police force, other than a chief officer of police, immediately before resigning or retiring, the chief officer of police of that police force;

(b) in relation to a person who was a chief officer of police immediately before resigning or retiring, the local policing body for the police force of which the person was a member at that time;

(c) in relation to a person who was a special constable immediately before resigning or retiring, the chief officer of police of the police force for which the person was appointed as a special constable immediately before resigning or retiring;

(d) in relation to a person who was a civilian police employee immediately before resigning or retiring, the chief officer of police under whose direction and control the person was at that time.

(5) For the purposes of this section a person is serving with the police if the person is—

(a) a member of a police force,

(b) a special constable, or

(c) a civilian police employee (within the meaning of section 88A).

(6) For the purposes of this section an allegation about a person is a relevant allegation if—

(a) it relates to the conduct, efficiency or effectiveness of the person, and

(b) the allegation (if proved) is of a type that might have resulted in the person being dismissed as described in section 88A(1)(a) or (c) if the person had not resigned or retired.

(7) Regulations under this section may make different provision for different cases and circumstances.

(8) A statutory instrument containing regulations under this section is subject to annulment in pursuance of a resolution of either House of Parliament.

88J Duty to maintain police advisory list

88J 88J Duty to maintain police advisory list

(1) The College of Policing must maintain a list of persons who are reported to the College under section 88I.

(2) The list maintained under subsection (1) is to be known as the police advisory list.

(3) The police advisory list must include such information in relation to a person reported to the College of Policing under section 88I as is specified in regulations made by the Secretary of State.

(4) Regulations under this section—

(a) may make different provision for different cases and circumstances;

(b) may confer a discretion on the College of Policing.

(5) A statutory instrument containing regulations under this section is subject to annulment in pursuance of a resolution of either House of Parliament.

88K Effect of inclusion in police advisory list

88K 88K Effect of inclusion in police advisory list

(1) Before employing or appointing any person, a person mentioned in subsection (3) must check with the College of Policing whether the proposed employee or proposed appointee (as the case may be) is included in the police advisory list.

(2) For the purposes of subsection (1) a person who is to be seconded to work for a person mentioned in subsection (3), and who will not be employed by that person, is to be regarded as being appointed by that person.

(3) The persons referred to in subsections (1) and (2) are—

(a) a chief officer of police;

(b) a local policing body;

(c) the chief inspector of constabulary;

(d) the Independent Police Complaints Commission;

(e) a person specified in regulations made by the Secretary of State for the purposes of section 88C(5)(e).

(4) In this section—

(a) a person who is specified in regulations under section 88C(5)(e) is referred to as a specified person, and

(b) in relation to that person, the functions in relation to the exercise of which the person is specified are referred to as specified functions.

(5) In relation to a specified person—

(a) the duty in subsection (1) applies only to the extent that the proposed employee or proposed appointee (as the case may be) will be involved in the exercise of specified functions;

(b) the additional duty in subsection (6) applies where the specified person is proposing to arrange for an existing employee or existing appointee to become involved in the exercise of specified functions (not having previously been so involved).

(6) Before making the arrangement, the specified person must check with the College of Policing whether the existing employee or existing appointee (as the case may be) is included in the police advisory list.

(7) For the purposes of subsections (5) and (6) a person who is seconded to work for a specified person is to be regarded as an existing appointee of that person (if not an existing employee of that person).

88L Removal from police advisory list

88L 88L Removal from police advisory list

(1) Subsection (2) applies where a relevant authority reports a person to the College of Policing under section 88I(1)(a) or (b) and—

(a) it is determined that no disciplinary proceedings will be brought against the person,

(b) the disciplinary proceedings brought against the person are withdrawn, or

(c) the disciplinary proceedings brought against the person are concluded without there being a finding that the person would have been dismissed if the person had still been a person serving with the police.

(2) Where this subsection applies, the relevant authority must make a further report to the College of Policing in relation to the person.

(3) A report under subsection (2)—

(a) must be made within such period as is specified in regulations made by the Secretary of State;

(b) must include such information as is so specified.

(4) On receipt of a report under subsection (2) in relation to a person the College of Policing must remove the person from the police advisory list.

(5) The College of Policing must remove a person from the police advisory list if the person becomes included in the police barred list by virtue of section 88A(1)(b) or (d).

(6) The Secretary of State may by regulations make provision in connection with the removal from the police advisory list (otherwise than under subsection (4) or (5)) of a person who, immediately before resigning or retiring, was a member of a police force or a special constable.

(7) The Secretary of State must by regulations make provision in connection with the removal from the police advisory list (otherwise than under subsection (4) or (5)) of a person who, immediately before resigning or retiring, was a civilian police employee.

(8) Regulations under subsection (6) or (7) may confer functions on the College of Policing including functions which involve the exercise of a discretion.

(9) In this section—

"civilian police employee" has the same meaning as in section 88A;

"disciplinary proceedings" has the same meaning as in section 88A;

"person serving with the police" has the same meaning as in section 88I;

"relevant authority" has the same meaning as in section 88I.

(10) Regulations under this section may make different provision for different cases and circumstances.

(11) A statutory instrument containing regulations under this section is subject to annulment in pursuance of a resolution of either House of Parliament.

88M Power to disclose information in police advisory list

88M 88M Power to disclose information in police advisory list

The College of Policing may, if it considers it to be in the public interest to do so, disclose to any person information included in the police advisory list which relates to a particular person who is included in the police advisory list."

SCHEDULE 9

Section 33

INDEPENDENT OFFICE FOR POLICE CONDUCT

PART 1

AMENDMENTS TO SCHEDULE 2 TO THE POLICE REFORM ACT 2002

Introductory

1 Schedule 2 to the Police Reform Act 2002 is amended in accordance with this Part of this Schedule (see also paragraph 55 below for further minor and consequential amendments).

Director General

2 (1) Paragraph 1 (chairman) is amended as follows.

(2) For sub-paragraph (1) substitute—

"(1) The Director General holds office in accordance with the terms of his or her appointment.

(1A) A person who holds office as Director General must not be an employee of the Office (but may have been such an employee before appointment as the Director General)."

(3) In sub-paragraph (2) for "chairman of the Commission" substitute "Director General".

(4) In sub-paragraph (3)—

(a) for "chairman of the Commission" substitute "Director General";

(b) for "chairman" substitute "Director General".

(5) In sub-paragraph (4)—

(a) for "chairman of the Commission" substitute "Director General";

(b) for "chairman" substitute "Director General".

(6) In sub-paragraph (5) for "chairman" substitute "Director General".

Appointment etc of members

3 After paragraph 1 insert—

"1A Appointment of members

1A (1) The non-executive members of the Office are to be appointed by the Secretary of State.

(2) A person who is a non-executive member must not be an employee of the Office (but may have been such an employee before appointment as a non-executive member).

1B (1) The employee members of the Office are to be appointed from the staff of the Office by the non-executive members.

(2) If the non-executive members propose to appoint an employee member, the Director General must recommend a person to the non-executive members for appointment.

(3) The Director General may also recommend a person to the non-executive members for appointment as an employee member without any proposal having been made under sub-paragraph (2).

(4) On a recommendation of a person for appointment under sub-paragraph (2) or (3), the non-executive members may—

(a) appoint the person, or

(b) reject the recommendation.

(5) If the non-executive members reject a recommendation they may require the Director General to recommend another person for appointment (in which case this sub-paragraph applies again and so on until somebody is appointed)."

4 (1) Paragraph 2 (ordinary members of the Commission) is amended as follows.

(2) In sub-paragraph (1) for "an ordinary" substitute "a non-executive".

(3) Omit sub-paragraph (2).

(4) In sub-paragraph (3) for "an ordinary" substitute "a non-executive".

(5) In sub-paragraph (4)—

(a) for "an ordinary", in both places, substitute "a non-executive";

(b) for "five" substitute "three".

(6) In sub-paragraph (5)—

(a) for "An ordinary" substitute "A non-executive";

(b) for "his office as a member of the Commission" substitute "from being a non-executive member of the Office".

(7) In sub-paragraph (6)—

(a) for "an ordinary" substitute "a non-executive";

(b) omit paragraph (b).

(8) Omit sub-paragraph (8).

5 After paragraph 2 insert—

"2A Terms of appointment etc: employee members

2A (1) A person holds office as an employee member in accordance with the terms of his or her appointment (subject to the provisions of this Schedule).

(2) Those terms may not include arrangements in relation to remuneration.

(3) An appointment as an employee member may be full-time or part-time.

(4) The appointment of an employee member terminates—

(a) if the terms of the member's appointment provides for it to expire at the end of a period, at the end of that period, and

(b) in any event, when the member ceases to be an employee of the Office.

(5) An employee member may resign by giving written notice to the non-executive members.

(6) The non-executive members may terminate the appointment of an employee member by giving the member written notice if they are satisfied that any of the grounds mentioned in paragraph 2(6)(a) to (g) apply in relation to the employee member."

6 Omit paragraph 3 (deputy chairmen) (including the italic heading before that paragraph).

7 Omit paragraph 5 (chief executive) (including the italic heading before that paragraph).

Vacancy or incapacity in office of Director General

8 After paragraph 3 insert—

"3A Director General: vacancy or incapacity

3A (1) This paragraph applies if—

(a) the office of Director General is vacant, or

(b) it appears to the Office that the ability of the Director General to carry out the Director General's functions is seriously impaired because of ill health (whether mental or physical).

(2) The Office may, with the agreement of the Secretary of State, authorise an employee of the Office to carry out the functions of the Director General during the vacancy or period of ill health.

(3) A person who falls within section 9(3) may not be authorised under this paragraph to carry out the functions of the Director General.

(4) A person who has been sentenced to a term of imprisonment of three months or more may not, at any time in the five years following the day of sentence, be authorised under this paragraph to carry out the functions of the Director General.

(5) Paragraph 1(6) applies for the purposes of sub-paragraph (4).

(6) Authorisation of a person under this paragraph ceases to have effect—

(a) at the end of the vacancy or period of ill health,

(b) on the Office revoking the authorisation for any reason, or

(c) on the Secretary of State withdrawing agreement to the authorisation for any reason."

Remuneration arrangements

9 (1) Paragraph 4 (remuneration, pensions etc of members) is amended as follows.

(2) In sub-paragraph (1), for the words from "the chairman" to the end substitute "the Director General as the Secretary of State may determine".

(3) In sub-paragraph (2)—

(a) in paragraph (a), for "chairman, deputy chairman or member of the Commission" substitute "Director General";

(b) in the words after paragraph (b) for "Commission" substitute "Office".

(4) After sub-paragraph (2) insert—

"(3) The Secretary of State may make remuneration arrangements in relation to non-executive members of the Office.

(4) Remuneration arrangements under sub-paragraph (3)—

(a) may make provision for a salary, allowances and other benefits but not for a pension, and

(b) may include a formula or other mechanism for adjusting one or more of those elements from time to time.

(5) Amounts payable by virtue of sub-paragraph (4) are to be paid by the Office."

Staff

10 (1) Paragraph 6 (staff) is amended as follows.

(2) For sub-paragraph (1) substitute—

"(1) The Office may appoint staff."

(3) In sub-paragraph (2) for "Commission", in both places, substitute "Office".

(4) In sub-paragraph (3)—

(a) for "Commission" substitute "Office";

(b) after "staffing" insert "(including arrangements in relation to terms and conditions and management of staff)";

(c) for "it" substitute "the Director General".

(5) In sub-paragraph (4)—

(a) for "Commission", in the first place, substitute "Office";

(b) for "Commission", in the second place, substitute "Director General".

(6) After sub-paragraph (4) insert—

"(4A) The powers under this paragraph are exercisable only by the Director General acting on behalf of the Office (subject to the power under paragraph 6A(1))."

(7) In sub-paragraph (5) for "by the Commission of its" substitute "of the".

Delegation of functions

11 After paragraph 6 insert—

"6A Delegation of functions

6A (1) The Director General may authorise a person within sub-paragraph (2) to exercise on the Director General's behalf a function of the Director General.

(2) The persons within this sub-paragraph are—

(a) employee members of the Office;

(b) employees of the Office appointed under paragraph 6;

(c) seconded constables within the meaning of paragraph 8.

(3) The reference in sub-paragraph (1) to a function of the Director General is to any function that the Director General has under this Act or any other enactment.

(4) A person ("A") who is authorised under sub-paragraph (1) to exercise a function may authorise another person within sub-paragraph (2) to exercise that function (but only so far as permitted to do so by the authorisation given to A).

(5) An authorisation under this paragraph may provide for a function to which it relates to be exercisable—

(a) either to its full extent or to the extent specified in the authorisation;

(b) either generally or in cases, circumstances or areas so specified;

(c) either unconditionally or subject to conditions so specified.

(6) Provision under sub-paragraph (5) may (in particular) include provision for restricted persons not to exercise designated functions.

(7) For the purposes of sub-paragraph (6)—

(a) "designated functions" are any functions of the Director General that are designated by the Director General for the purposes of this paragraph (and such functions may in particular be designated by reference to the position or seniority of members of staff);

(b) "restricted persons" are, subject to any determination made under sub-paragraph (8), persons who fall within section 9(3).

(8) The Director General may, in such circumstances as the Director General considers appropriate, determine that persons are not to be treated as restricted persons so far as relating to the exercise of designated functions (whether generally or in respect of particular functions specified in the determination).

(9) The Director General must publish a statement of policy about how the Director General proposes to exercise the powers conferred by sub-paragraphs (7)(a) and (8).

(10) The statement must in particular draw attention to any restrictions on the carrying out of functions imposed by virtue of their designation under sub-paragraph (7)(a) and explain the reasons for imposing them.

(11) The exercise of the powers conferred by sub-paragraphs (7)(a) and (8) is subject to any regulations under section 23(1) of the kind mentioned in section 23(2)(g) (regulations limiting persons who may be appointed to carry out investigations etc).

(12) An authorisation under this paragraph does not prevent the Director General from exercising the function to which the authorisation relates.

(13) Anything done or omitted to be done by or in relation to a person authorised under this paragraph in, or in connection with, the exercise or purported exercise of the function to which the authorisation relates is to be treated for all purposes as done or omitted to be done by or in relation to the Director General.

(14) Sub-paragraph (13) does not apply for the purposes of any criminal proceedings brought in respect of anything done or omitted to be done by the authorised person."

Protection from personal liability

12 After paragraph 7 insert—

"7A Liability for acts of the Director General

7A (1) A person holding office as the Director General has no personal liability for an act or omission done by the person in the exercise of the Director General's functions unless it is shown to have been done otherwise than in good faith.

(2) The Office is liable in respect of unlawful conduct of the Director General in the carrying out, or purported carrying out, of the Director General's functions in the same way as an employer is liable in respect of any unlawful conduct of employees in the course of their employment.

(3) Accordingly, the Office is to be treated, in the case of any such unlawful conduct which is a tort, as a joint tortfeasor."

Regional offices

13 For paragraph 9 (power of Commission to set up regional offices) substitute—

"9 (1) The Office may set up regional offices in places in England and Wales.

(2) But the power under sub-paragraph (1) is exercisable only by the Director General acting on behalf of the Office (subject to the power in paragraph 6A(1)).

(3) The power under sub-paragraph (1) may be exercised—

(a) only with the consent of the Secretary of State, and

(b) only if it appears to the Director General necessary to do so for the purpose of ensuring that the functions of the Director General, or those of the Office, are carried out efficiently and effectively."

Proceedings

14 In paragraph 10 (proceedings), after sub-paragraph (1) insert—

"(1A) But the arrangements must include provision for—

(a) the quorum for meetings to be met only if a majority of members present are non-executive members of the Office, and

(b) an audit committee of the Office to be established to perform such monitoring, reviewing and other functions as are appropriate.

(1B) The arrangements must secure that the audit committee consists only of non-executive members of the Office."

PART 2

MINOR AND CONSEQUENTIAL AMENDMENTS TO THE POLICE REFORM ACT 2002

15 The Police Reform Act 2002 is amended in accordance with this Part of this Schedule.

16 For the italic heading before section 9, substitute "The Independent Office for Police Conduct".

17 (1) Section 10 (general functions of the Commission) is amended as follows.

(2) In subsection (1)(a) omit "itself".

(3) In subsection (1)(e) for "its" substitute "the Director General's".

(4) In subsection (1)(f) for "it" substitute "the Director General".

(5) In subsection (3) for "it" substitute "the Director General".

(6) In subsection (3A) (as inserted by this Act), for "it" substitute "the Director General".

(7) In subsection (3B) (as inserted by this Act), for "it" substitute "the Director General".

(8) In subsection (4), in paragraph (a)—

(a) for "it", in both places, substitute "the Director General";

(b) for "its" substitute "the Director General's".

(9) In subsection (6)—

(a) for "it" substitute "the Director General";

(b) for "its" substitute "the Director General's".

(10) In subsection (7)—

(a) for "it", in both places, substitute "the Director General";

(b) for "its", in both places, substitute "the Director General's".

18 (1) Section 11 (reports to the Secretary of State) is amended as follows.

(2) In subsection (1)—

(a) for "its", in the first place it occurs, substitute "the Office's";

(b) for "Commission shall" substitute "Director General and the Office must jointly";

(c) for "its", in the second place it occurs, substitute "their".

(3) For subsection (2) substitute—

"(2) The Secretary of State may also require reports to be made (at any time)—

(a) by the Director General about the carrying out of the Director General's functions,

(b) by the Office about the carrying out of the Office's functions, or

(c) jointly by the Director General and the Office about the carrying out of their functions."

(4) After subsection (2) insert—

"(2A) The Director General may, from time to time, make such other reports to the Secretary of State as the Director General considers appropriate for drawing the Secretary of State's attention to matters which—

(a) have come to the Director General's notice, and

(b) are matters which the Director General considers should be drawn to the attention of the Secretary of State by reason of their gravity or of other exceptional circumstances."

(5) In subsection (3)—

(a) for "Commission" substitute "Office";

(b) for "Commission's" substitute "Office's".

(6) After subsection (3) insert—

"(3A) The Director General and the Office may jointly make reports under subsections (2A) and (3)."

(7) In subsection (4)—

(a) for "Commission" substitute "Director General";

(b) for "it", in both places, substitute "the Director General";

(c) for "its" substitute "the Director General's".

(8) In subsection (6) for "Commission" substitute "Office".

(9) After subsection (6) insert—

"(6A) The Director General must send a copy of every report under subsection (2A) —

(a) to any local policing body that appears to the Director General to be concerned, and

(b) to the chief officer of police of any police force that appears to the Director General to be concerned."

(10) In subsection (7) for "Commission", in both places, substitute "Office".

(11) In subsection (8)—

(a) after "subsection" insert "(2A) or";

(b) for "Commission" substitute "Director General or the Office (as the case may be)".

(12) In subsection (9)—

(a) after "subsection" insert "(2A) or";

(b) for "Commission" substitute "Director General or the Office (as the case may be)".

(13) In subsection (10) for "Commission" substitute "Director General".

(14) In subsection (11)—

(a) for "Commission", in each place, substitute "Director General";

(b) for "it" substitute "the Director General";

(c) for "(3)" substitute "(2A)".

(15) After subsection (11) insert—

"(12) The Office must send a copy of every report made or prepared by it under subsection (3) to such of the persons (in addition to those specified in the preceding subsections) who—

(a) are referred to in the report, or

(b) appear to the Office otherwise to have a particular interest in its contents,

as the Office thinks fit.

(13) Where a report under subsection (2A) or (3) is prepared jointly by virtue of subsection (3A), a duty under this section to send a copy of the report to any person is met if either the Director General or the Office sends a copy to that person."

19 In section 12 (complaints, matters and persons to which Part 2 applies), in subsection (6)(a) for "Commission" substitute "Director General".

20 (1) Section 13B (power of the Commission to require re-investigation) (as inserted by this Act) is amended as follows.

(2) For "Commission", in each place (including the heading), substitute "Director General".

(3) In subsection (1)—

(a) for "it", in both places, substitute "the Director General";

(b) in paragraph (b), before "under" insert "(or, in the case of an investigation carried out under paragraph 19 of Schedule 3 by the Director General personally, is otherwise completed by the Director General)".

(4) In subsection (2) for "it" substitute "the Director General".

(5) In subsection (3) for "it" substitute "the Director General".

(6) In subsection (10)—

(a) for "it" substitute "the Director General";

(b) for "its" substitute "the Director General's".

(7) In subsection (11)—

(a) for "it" substitute "the Director General";

(b) for "its" substitute "the Director General's".

21 (1) Section 15 (general duties of local policing bodies, chief officers and inspectors) is amended as follows.

(2) In subsection (3), in the words after paragraph (c) after "Director General" insert "of the Agency".

(3) In subsection (4)—

(a) for "Commission", in each place, substitute "Director General";

(b) for "Commission's" substitute "Office's".

22 (1) Section 16 (payment for assistance with investigations) is amended as follows.

(2) For "Commission", in each place except as mentioned in sub-paragraph (3), substitute "Director General".

(3) In subsection (4), for "the Commission", in the second place where it occurs, substitute "Office".

(4) In subsection (5)(b), after "Director General" insert "of that Agency".

23 (1) Section 17 (provision of information to the Commission) is amended as follows.

(2) For "Commission", in each place (including the heading), substitute "Director General".

(3) In subsection (2)—

(a) for "it" substitute "the Director General";

(b) for "its" substitute "the Director General's".

24 (1) Section 18 (inspections of police premises on behalf of the Commission) is amended as follows.

(2) For "Commission", in each place (including the heading and provisions inserted by amendments made by this Act), substitute "Director General".

(3) In subsection (2)(b), for "its" substitute "the Director General's".

25 (1) Section 19 (use of investigatory powers by or on behalf of the Commission) is amended as follows.

(2) In the heading, for "Commission" substitute "Director General".

(3) In subsection (1), for "Commission's" substitute "Director General's".

26 (1) Section 20 (duty to keep complainant informed) is amended as follows.

(2) For "Commission", in each place (including provisions inserted by amendments made by this Act), substitute "Director General".

(3) In subsection (1)(b) for "its" substitute "the Director General's".

(4) In subsection (3) for "it", where it occurs after "as", substitute "the Director General".

(5) In subsection (8A) (as inserted by this Act)—

(a) for "its" substitute "their";

(b) after "submitted", in the first place it occurs, insert "(or finalised)";

(c) after "submitted", in the second place it occurs, insert "(or completed)".

(6) In subsection (9) for "its" substitute "their".

27 (1) Section 21 (duty to provide information for other persons) is amended as follows.

(2) For "Commission", in each place (including provisions inserted by amendments made by this Act), substitute "Director General".

(3) In subsection (6)(b) for "its" substitute "the Director General's".

(4) In subsection (8) for "it", where it occurs after "as", substitute "the Director General".

(5) In subsection (11A) (as inserted by this Act)—

(a) for "its" substitute "their";

(b) after "submitted", in the first place it occurs, insert "(or finalised)";

(c) after "submitted", in the second place it occurs, insert "(or completed)".

28 In section 21A (restriction on disclosure of sensitive information) (as inserted by this Act), for "Commission", in each place, substitute "Director General".

29 In section 21B (provision of sensitive information to the Commission and certain investigators) (as inserted by this Act), for "Commission", in each place (including the heading), substitute "Director General".

30 (1) Section 22 (power of the Commission to issue guidance) is amended as follows.

(2) For "Commission", in each place (including the heading), substitute "Director General".

(3) In subsection (3)(c) for "it" substitute "the Director General".

31 (1) Section 23 (regulations) is amended as follows.

(2) For "Commission", in each place, substitute "Director General".

(3) In subsection (2)(i) for "its" substitute "the Director General".

(4) In subsection (2)(o) for "it" substitute "the Director General or the Office".

32 In section 24 (consultation on regulations), for paragraph (a) substitute—

"(a) the Office;

(aa) the Director General;".

33 In section 26 (forces maintained otherwise than by local policing bodies), for "Commission", in each place, substitute "Director General".

34 In section 26BA (College of Policing), for "Commission", in both places, substitute "Director General".

35 (1) Section 26C (the National Crime Agency) is amended as follows.

(2) In subsection (1)—

(a) for "Independent Police Complaints Commission" substitute "Director General";

(b) before "and other" insert "of the National Crime Agency".

(3) In subsection (2) for "Independent Police Complaints Commission" substitute "the Office or in respect of its Director General".

(4) In subsection (4) for "Independent Police Complaints Commission", in both places, substitute "Director General".

(5) In subsection (5)—

(a) for "Independent Police Complaints Commission" substitute "Director General";

(b) for "Commission's", in both places, substitute "Director General's";

(c) for "Commission" substitute "Director General".

(6) In subsection (6) for "Independent Police Complaints Commissioner" substitute "Director General".

(7) In subsection (9) after "Director General" insert "of the National Crime Agency".

36 (1) Section 26D (labour abuse prevention officers) is amended as follows.

(2) For "Commission", in each place other than in subsection (2), substitute "Director General".

(3) In subsection (2)(b) for "Commission" substitute "Office or in respect of the Director General".

(4) In subsection (4), for "Commission's", in both places, substitute "Director General's".

37 (1) Section 27 (conduct of the Commission's staff) is amended as follows.

(2) For "Commission's", in each place (including the heading), substitute "Office's".

(3) In subsection (4) for "Commission" substitute "Office and the Director General".

38 (1) Omit section 28 (transitional arrangements in connection with establishing Commission etc).

(2) The repeal of section 28 does not affect an order made under that section before its repeal or the power under that section to revoke or amend any such order.

39 (1) Section 28A (application of Part 2 to old cases) is amended as follows.

(2) For "Commission", in each place other than in subsection (3) of that section, substitute "Director General".

(3) In subsection (1), for "it" substitute "the Director General".

(4) In subsection (4), for "it" substitute "the Director General".

40 (1) Section 29 (interpretation of Part 2) is amended as follows.

(2) In subsection (1)—

(a) omit the definition of "the Commission";

(b) after the definition of "death or serious injury matter" insert—

> ""the Director General" means (unless otherwise specified) the Director General of the Office;";

(c) before the definition of "person complained against" insert—

> ""the Office" means the Independent Office for Police Conduct;".

(3) In subsection (6)—

(a) for "Commission", in each place, substitute "Director General";

(b) omit "itself".

41 In section 29C (regulations about super-complaints) (as inserted by this Act), in subsection (3) for "Independent Police Complaints Commission", in both places, substitute "Director General of the Independent Office for Police Conduct".

42 (1) Section 29D (power to investigate concerns raised by whistle-blowers) (as inserted by this Act) is amended as follows.

(2) For "Commission", in each place, substitute "Director General".

(3) In subsection (1) for "it" substitute "the Director General".

43 (1) Section 29E (Commission's powers and duties where it decides not to investigate) (as inserted by this Act) is amended as follows.

(2) For "Commission", in each place, substitute "Director General".

(3) In the heading—

(a) for "Commission's" substitute "Director General's";

(b) for "where it decides" substitute "on decision".

44 (1) Section 29F (special provision for "conduct matters") (as inserted by this Act) is amended as follows.

(2) For "Commission", in each place, substitute "Director General".

(3) In subsection (2)—

(a) or "it", in both places, substitute "the Director General";

(b) for "its" substitute "the".

45 (1) Section 29G (special provision for "DSI matters") (as inserted by this Act) is amended as follows.

(2) For "Commission", in each place, substitute "Director General".

(3) In subsection (2), for "it", in both places, substitute "the Director General".

46 (1) Section 29H (Commission's powers and duties where whistle-blower is deceased) (as inserted by this Act) is amended as follows.

(2) For "Commission", in each place, substitute "Director General".

(3) In the heading for "Commission's" substitute "Director General's".

(4) In subsection (1) for "it" substitute "the Director General".

47 In section 29I (duty to keep whistle-blowers informed) (as inserted by this Act), in subsection (1)—

(a) for "Commission" substitute "Director General";

(b) for "it" substitute "the Director General".

48 In section 29J (protection of anonymity of whistle-blowers) (as inserted by this Act) for "Commission", in both places, substitute "Director General".

49 In section 29K (other restrictions on disclosure of information) (as inserted by this Act), for "Commission", in both places, substitute "Director General".

50 In section 29L (application of provisions of Part 2) (as inserted by this Act), for "Commission", in each place, substitute "Director General".

51 In section 29M (regulation-making powers: consultation) (as inserted by this Act), for "Commission" substitute "Director General".

52 In section 29N (interpretation) (as inserted by this Act), in subsection (1)—
(a) omit the definition of "the Commission";
(b) after the definition of "conduct" insert—
""the Director General" means the Director General of the Independent Office for Police Conduct;".

53 In section 36 (conduct of disciplinary proceedings), in subsection (1)(a) for "Independent Police Complaints Commission" substitute "Director General of the Independent Office for Police Conduct".

54 In section 105 (powers of Secretary of State to make orders and regulations), in subsection (5) for "Independent Police Complaints Commission" substitute "Director General of the Independent Office for Police Conduct".

55 (1) Schedule 2 (the Independent Police Complaints Commission) is amended as follows.

(2) For the title to the Schedule substitute "The Independent Office for Police Conduct".

(3) For the italic heading before paragraph 1 substitute "Director General".

(4) For the italic heading before paragraph 2 substitute "Terms of appointment etc: non-executive members".

(5) In paragraph 7—
(a) for "Commission", in each place, substitute "Office";
(b) for "chairman or as a deputy chairman of the Commission" substitute "Director General";
(c) omit "or as a member of it".

(6) In paragraph 8—
(a) for "Commission", in both places, substitute "Office";
(b) for "Commission's", in both places, substitute "Office's".

(7) In the heading before paragraph 9 omit "of Commission".

(8) In paragraph 10—
(a) for "Commission", in each place, substitute "Office";
(b) for "Commission's", in each place, substitute "Office's";
(c) in sub-paragraph (5)(c) omit "by the chief executive or".

(9) In paragraph 11—
(a) for "Commission", in each place, substitute "Office";
(b) in paragraph (a) for "chairman, a deputy chairman" substitute "Director General";
(c) in paragraph (b) for "chairman" substitute "Director General".

(10) In the italic heading before paragraph 12, for "Commission's" substitute "Office's".

(11) In paragraph 12—
(a) in the words before paragraph (a), for "Commission" substitute "Office";
(b) in paragraph (a) for "Commission" substitute "Office";
(c) in paragraph (b) for "Commission" substitute "Director General".

(12) In paragraph 13 for "Commission" substitute "Office".

(13) In paragraph 14—

(a) for "Commission" substitute "Office";

(b) in paragraph (b) for "by it in the carrying out of its functions" substitute "in the carrying out of its or the Director General's functions".

(14) In the italic heading before paragraph 15, for "Commission" substitute "Office".

(15) In paragraph 15(1)—

(a) for "Commission" substitute "Office";

(b) after "its" insert "or the Director General's".

(16) In paragraph 16 for "Commission" substitute "Office".

(17) In paragraph 17 for "Commission", in each place, substitute "Office".

(18) In the italic heading before paragraph 18, for "Commission" substitute "Office".

(19) In paragraph 18 for "Commission", in both places, substitute "Office".

56 (1) Schedule 3 is amended as follows.

(2) For "Commission", in each place where it occurs, substitute "Director General".

(3) For "Commission's", in each place where it occurs, substitute "Director General's".

(4) For "it", in each place where it occurs and is used as a pronoun in place of "the Commission", substitute "the Director General".

(5) For "its", in each place where it occurs and is used to mean "the Commission's", substitute "the Director General's".

(6) The amendments made by virtue of sub-paragraphs (2) to (5)—

(a) include amendments of provisions of Schedule 3 that are inserted, or otherwise amended, by other provisions of this Act (whether or not those other provisions come into force before or after the coming into force of this paragraph);

(b) do not apply if otherwise provided by another provision of this paragraph.

(7) In paragraph 19 (investigations by the Commission itself)—

(a) in the heading omit "itself";

(b) in sub-paragraph (1) omit "itself";

(c) for sub-paragraph (2) substitute—

"(2) The Director General must designate both—

(a) a person to take charge of the investigation, and

(b) such members of the Office's staff as are required by the Director General to assist the person designated to take charge of the investigation.

(2A) The person designated under sub-paragraph (2) to take charge of an investigation must be—

(a) the Director General acting personally, or

(b) a person who is authorised to exercise the function of taking charge of the investigation on behalf of the Director General by virtue of paragraph 6A of Schedule 2 (delegation of Director General's functions).";

(d) in sub-paragraph (4) for "member of the Commission's staff" substitute "person";

(e) in sub-paragraph (5) for "member of the Commission's staff" substitute "person designated under sub-paragraph (2)";

(f) in sub-paragraph (6) for "members of the Commission's staff" substitute "persons";

(g) in sub-paragraph (6A) for "member of the Commission's staff" substitute "the Director General or a member of the Office's staff".

(8) In paragraph 19ZH (further provision about things retained under paragraph 19ZG) (as inserted by this Act)—

(a) in sub-paragraph (2) for "Commission's" substitute "Office's";

(b) in sub-paragraph (4)(a) for "Commission's" substitute "Office's".

(9) In paragraph 19A (as substituted by this Act), in sub-paragraphs (2)(b) and (7)(a) after "investigating" insert "or, in the case of an investigation by a designated person under paragraph 19, the Director General,".

(10) In paragraph 19F (interview of persons serving with police etc during certain investigations), in sub-paragraph (1)(b) for "the Commission itself" substitute "a person designated under paragraph 19 (investigations by Director General)".

(11) In paragraph 20 (restrictions on proceedings pending conclusion of investigation), in sub-paragraph (1)(b) at the end insert "or, where under paragraph 19 the Director General has personally carried out the investigation, a report has been completed by the Director General".

(12) In paragraph 20A (as substituted by this Act)—

(a) in sub-paragraph (1)(a) after "investigating" insert "or, in the case of an investigation by a designated person under paragraph 19, the Director General,";

(b) in sub-paragraph (3) after "and" insert "(where the person investigating is not also the Director General carrying out an investigation under paragraph 19 personally)";

(c) in sub-paragraph (4)(b) after "investigation" insert "or, where the investigation is carried out under paragraph 19 by the Director General personally, finalise one,".

(13) In paragraph 21A (procedure where conduct matter is revealed during investigation of DSI matter)—

(a) in sub-paragraph (1), omit "or designated under paragraph 19";

(b) after sub-paragraph (2A) (as inserted by this Act), insert—

"(2B) If during the course of an investigation of a DSI matter being carried out by a person designated under paragraph 19 the Director General determines that there is an indication that a person serving with the police ("the person whose conduct is in question") may have—

(a) committed a criminal offence, or

(b) behaved in a manner which would justify the bringing of disciplinary proceedings,

the Director General must proceed under sub-paragraph (2C).

(2C) The Director General must—

(a) prepare a record of the determination,

(b) notify the appropriate authority in relation to the DSI matter and (if different) the appropriate authority in relation to the person whose conduct is in question of the determination, and

(c) send to it (or each of them) a copy of the record of the determination prepared under paragraph (a).";

(c) in sub-paragraph (5), after paragraph (a) insert—

"(aa) is notified of a determination by the Director General under sub-paragraph (2C),".

(14) In paragraph 22 (final reports on investigations: complaints, conduct matters and certain DSI matters)—

(a) for sub-paragraph (5) substitute—

"(5) A person designated under paragraph 19 as the person in charge of an investigation must—

(a) submit a report on the investigation to the Director General, or

(b) where the person in charge of the investigation is the Director General acting personally, complete a report on the investigation.";

(b) in sub-paragraph (6) after "submitting" insert "or, in the case of an investigation under paragraph 19 by the Director General personally, completing";

(c) in sub-paragraph (8) after "submitted" insert "or, in the case of an investigation under paragraph 19 by the Director General personally, completed".

(15) In the italic heading before paragraph 23 (action by the Commission in response to investigation reports), for "response" substitute "relation".

(16) In paragraph 23—

(a) in sub-paragraph (1)(b) before "under" insert ", or is otherwise completed,";

(b) in sub-paragraph (1A) (as inserted by this Act), after "submission" insert "or completion";

(c) in each of the following places, after "receipt of the report" insert "(or on its completion by the Director General)"—

(i) sub-paragraph (2);

(ii) sub-paragraph (5A) (as inserted by this Act);

(iii) sub-paragraph (5F) (as inserted by this Act);

(iv) in sub-paragraph (13), before "or (4)" insert ", (2B)".

(17) In paragraph 24 (action by appropriate authority in response to an investigation report), in sub-paragraph (11) before "or (4)" insert ", (2B)".

(18) In paragraph 24A (final reports on investigations: other DSI matters)—

(a) in sub-paragraph (1), before "or (4)" insert ", (2B)";

(b) after sub-paragraph (2) insert—

"(2A) Sub-paragraph (2)(a) does not apply where the person investigating is the Director General carrying out an investigation personally under paragraph 19, but the Director General must complete a report on the investigation.";

(c) in sub-paragraph (3) for "this paragraph" substitute "sub-paragraph (2) or completing one under sub-paragraph (2A)";

(d) in sub-paragraph (4) after "receipt of the report" insert "(or on its completion by the Director General)";

(e) in sub-paragraph (5) (as inserted by this Act) after "receipt of the report" insert "(or on its completion by the Director General)";

(f) in sub-paragraph (6) (as inserted by this Act)—

(i) after "sub-paragraph (2)" insert "or completed under sub-paragraph (2A)";

(ii) after "submission" insert "or completion".

(19) In the italic heading before paragraph 24B (action by the Commission in response to an investigation report under paragraph 24A), for "response" substitute "relation".

(20) In paragraph 28ZA (recommendations by the Commission or a local policing body) (as inserted by this Act), in sub-paragraph (3)(b), after "submission" insert "or completion".

(21) In paragraph 28A (recommendations by the Commission)—

(a) in sub-paragraph (1)—

(i) after "received a report" insert "(or otherwise completed one in relation to an investigation carried out under paragraph 19 by the Director General personally)";

(ii) in paragraph (b) for "Commission itself" substitute "or on behalf of the Director General";

(iii) in paragraph (c) after "24A(2)" insert "or (2A)";

(b) in sub-paragraph (4)(a) after "receipt" insert "or completion".

(22) In paragraph 28B (response to recommendation), in sub-paragraph (12) (as inserted by this Act) after "received a report on" insert "(or otherwise completed one on in relation to an investigation carried out under paragraph 19 by the Director General personally)".

57 (1) Schedule 3 is further amended as follows (but an amendment made by sub-paragraph (2), (3), (4) or (5) applies only if this Schedule comes into force before the coming into force of paragraph 21, 23, 24 or 26 (as the case may be) of Schedule 5 to this Act).

(2) In paragraph 19B (assessment of seriousness of conduct under investigation), in sub-paragraph (1) after "investigating" insert "or, in the case of an investigation by a designated person under paragraph 19, the Director General,".

(3) In paragraph 20A (accelerated procedure in special cases)—

(a) in sub-paragraph (1)—

(i) for "his" substitute "an";

(ii) after "conduct matter" insert "or, in the case of an investigation by a designated person under paragraph 19, the Director General,";

(iii) for "he" substitute "the person investigating";

(b) in sub-paragraph (3) for "his belief" substitute "the belief referred to in sub-paragraph (1)".

(4) In paragraph 21 (power to discontinue an investigation), in sub-paragraph (4)(b) omit "itself".

(5) In paragraph 23 (action by the Commission in response to an investigation report), in sub-paragraph (6) after "receipt of the report" insert "(or on its completion by the Director General)".

58 (1) Schedule 3A (whistle-blowing investigations: procedure) (as inserted by this Act) is amended as follows.

(2) For "Commission", in each place, substitute "Director General".

(3) In paragraph 1(1)—

(a) after ", (2)" insert ", (2A)";

(b) omit "itself".

(4) In paragraph 4(1)—

(a) in the words before paragraph (a), for "it appears to the person in charge" substitute "the Director General determines";

(b) for the words after paragraph (b) substitute "the Director General must proceed under sub-paragraph (2)".

(5) For paragraph 4(2) substitute—

"(2) The Director General must—

(a) prepare a record of the determination,

(b) notify the appropriate authority in relation to the person whose conduct is in question of the determination, and

(c) send to it a copy of the record of the determination prepared under paragraph (a)."

(6) In paragraph 5(1)—

(a) for "it appears to the person in charge" substitute "the Director General determines";

(b) for "the person must make a submission to that effect to the Commission" substitute "the Director General must proceed under sub-paragraph (2)".

(7) For paragraph 5(2) substitute—

"The Director General must—

(a) prepare a record of the determination,

(b) notify the appropriate authority in relation to the DSI matter, and

(c) send to it a copy of the determination prepared under paragraph (a)."

(8) After paragraph 6(1) insert—

"(1A) Sub-paragraph (1) does not apply where the person in charge of the investigation is the Director General acting personally, but the Director General must complete a report on the investigation."

(9) In paragraph 6(2)(a) for "the report" substitute "a report submitted under sub-paragraph (1) or completed under sub-paragraph (1A)".

(10) In paragraph 7(1) after "paragraph 6" insert "(1) or on its completion by the Director General under paragraph 6(1A)".

PART 3

OTHER MINOR AND CONSEQUENTIAL AMENDMENTS

Superannuation Act 1972 (c. 11)

59 In Schedule 1 to the Superannuation Act 1972—

- (a) in the list of entries under the heading "Royal Commissions and other Commissions", omit the entry relating to the Independent Police Complaints Commission;
- (b) in the list of entries under the heading "Other Bodies", insert at the appropriate place—

  "The Independent Office for Police Conduct.";
- (c) in the list of entries under the heading "Offices", omit the entries relating to—
  - (i) the Chairman of the Independent Police Complaints Commission;
  - (ii) the Commissioners of the Independent Police Complaints Commission;
  - (iii) the Deputy Chairman of the Independent Police Complaints Commission.

House of Commons Disqualification Act 1975 (c. 24)

60 In Part 2 of Schedule 1 to the House of Commons Disqualification Act 1975 (bodies of which all members are disqualified), omit the entry relating to the Independent Police Complaints Commission and insert at the appropriate place—

"The Independent Office for Police Conduct."

Northern Ireland Assembly Disqualification Act 1975 (c. 25)

61 In Part 2 of Schedule 1 to the Northern Ireland Assembly Disqualification Act 1975 (bodies of which all members are disqualified), omit the entry relating to the Independent Police Complaints Commission and insert at the appropriate place—

"The Independent Office for Police Conduct."

Police Pensions Act 1976 (c. 35)

62 In section 11 of the Police Pensions Act 1976 (interpretation), in subsection (2A)(ba) for "Independent Police Complaints Commission" substitute "Independent Office for Police Conduct".

Ministry of Defence Police Act 1987 (c. 4)

63 (1) The Ministry of Defence Police Act 1987 is amended as follows.

(2) In section 3A (regulations relating to disciplinary matters), in subsections (1B)(a), (1F) and (1G) (as inserted by this Act) for "Independent Police Complaints Commission" substitute "Director General of the Independent Office for Police Conduct".

(3) In section 4 (representation etc at disciplinary proceedings), in subsection (5)(a) for "Independent Police Complaints Commission" substitute "Independent Office for Police Conduct".

Aviation and Maritime Security Act 1990 (c. 31)

64 In section 22 of the Aviation and Maritime Security Act 1990 (power to require harbour authorities to promote searches in harbour areas), in subsection (4)(b)(i) for "Independent Police Complaints Commission" substitute "Director General of the Independent Office for Police Conduct".

Police Act 1996 (c. 16)

65 (1) The Police Act 1996 is amended as follows.

(2) In the following provisions, for "Independent Police Complaints Commission" substitute "Director General of the Independent Office for Police Conduct"—

(a) section 50(3A)(a), (3E) and (3F) (regulation of police forces) (as inserted by this Act);

(b) section 51(2B)(a), (2F) and (2G) (regulations for special constables) (as inserted by this Act);

(c) section 87(1) (guidance concerning disciplinary proceedings etc) (as amended by this Act).

(3) In the following provisions, for "Independent Police Complaints Commission" substitute "Independent Office for Police Conduct"—

(a) section 84(5) (representation etc at disciplinary and other proceedings);

(b) section 88C(5)(d) (effect of inclusion in police barred list) (as inserted by this Act);

(c) section 88K(3)(d) (effect of inclusion in police advisory list) (as inserted by this Act).

(4) In section 54(2D) (appointment and functions of inspectors of constabulary)—

(a) in paragraph (a)—

(i) for "Independent Police Complaints Commission" substitute "Director General of the Independent Office for Police Conduct ("the Director General")";

(ii) for "that Commission" substitute "the Director General";

(b) in paragraph (b)—

(i) for "that Commission", in both places, substitute "the Director General";

(ii) for "its" substitute "his or her".

Freedom of Information Act 2000 (c. 36)

66 In Part 6 of Schedule 1 to the Freedom of Information Act 2000 (other public bodies and offices: general) omit the entry relating to the Independent Police Complaints Commission and insert at the appropriate place—

> "The Director General of the Independent Office for Police Conduct."
>
> "The Independent Office for Police Conduct."

Fire and Rescue Services Act 2004 (c. 21)

67 In section 4K of the Fire and Rescue Services Act 2004 (as inserted by this Act), in subsection (5)(b) for "Independent Police Complaints Commission" substitute "Director General of the Independent Office for Police Conduct".

Commissioners for Revenue and Customs Act 2005 (c. 11)

68 (1) The Commissions for Revenue and Customs Act 2005 is amended as follows.

(2) In section 18 (confidentiality), in subsection (2)(g)—

- (a) for "Independent Police Complaints Commission" substitute "Director General of the Independent Office for Police Conduct";
- (b) for "its" substitute "the Director General's".

(3) In section 28 (complaints and misconduct: England and Wales)—

- (a) in subsection (1), for "Independent Police Complaints Commission" substitute "Director General of the Independent Office for Police Conduct ("the Director General")";
- (b) in subsection (2)—
  - (i) for "Independent Police Complaints Commission", in both places, substitute "Director General";
  - (ii) for "its" substitute "the Director General's";
- (c) in subsection (3) for "Independent Police Complaints Commission" substitute "Director General";
- (d) in subsection (4) for "Independent Police Complaints Commission", in both places, substitute "Director General".

(4) In section 29 (confidentiality etc), in subsection (3)—

- (a) in the words before paragraph (a), for "Independent Police Complaints Commission" substitute "Director General of the Independent Office for Police Conduct";
- (b) for "its" substitute "the Director General's";
- (c) in paragraph (a), for "Commission" substitute "Director General";
- (d) in paragraph (b), for "Commission" substitute "Director General".

Police and Justice Act 2006 (c. 48)

69 (1) In section 41 of the Police and Justice Act 2006 (immigration and asylum enforcement functions and customs functions: complaints and misconduct)—

- (a) in subsection (1) for "Independent Police Complaints Commission" substitute "Director General of the Independent Office for Police Conduct ("the Director General")";

(b) in subsection (2A) for "Independent Police Complaints Commission" substitute "Director General";

(c) in subsection (3) for "Independent Police Complaints Commission" substitute "Director General";

(d) in subsection (4)(b), for "Independent Police Complaints Commission" substitute "Director General";

(e) in subsection (5) for "Independent Police Complaints Commission" substitute "Director General";

(f) in subsection (6) for "Independent Police Complaints Commission", in both places, substitute "Director General".

(2) In the italic heading before that section for "Independent Police Complaints Commission" substitute "Director General of the Independent Office for Police Conduct".

Local Democracy, Economic Development and Construction Act 2009 (c. 20)

70 In section 107EE of the Local Democracy, Economic Development and Construction Act 2009 (section 107EA orders: complaints and conduct matters etc) (as inserted by this Act), in subsection (5)(b) for "Independent Police Complaints Commission" substitute "Director General of the Independent Office for Police Conduct".

Coroners and Justice Act 2009 (c. 25)

71 In section 47 of the Coroners and Justice Act 2009 (meaning of "interested person") —

(a) in subsection (2)(k) for "Independent Police Complaints Commission" substitute "Director General of the Independent Office for Police Conduct";

(b) in subsection (5) for "Independent Police Complaints Commission" substitute "Director General of the Independent Office for Police Conduct".

Equality Act 2010 (c. 15)

72 In Part 1 of Schedule 19 to the Equality Act 2010 (public authorities: general), under the heading "Police" omit the entry relating to the Independent Police Complaints Commission and insert at the appropriate place—

"The Director General of the Independent Office for Police Conduct."

"The Independent Office for Police Conduct."

Police Reform and Social Responsibility Act 2011 (c. 13)

73 (1) The Police Reform and Social Responsibility Act 2011 is amended as follows.

(2) In section 65 (disqualification from election or holding office as police and crime commissioner: police grounds), for "Independent Police Complaints Commission" substitute "Independent Office for Police Conduct".

(3) In Schedule 7 (regulations about complaints and conduct matters), for "Independent Police Complaints Commission", in each place, substitute "Director General of the Independent Office for Police Conduct."

Investigatory Powers Act 2016

74 (1) The Investigatory Powers Act 2016 is amended as follows.

(2) In section 58 (section 57: meaning of "excepted disclosure"), in subsection (4)(c)—

(a) for "the Independent Police Complaints Commission" substitute "the Director General of the Independent Office for Police Conduct";

(b) for "its functions" substitute "the Director General's functions".

(3) In section 106 (power to issue warrants to law enforcement officers), in subsection (11)—

(a) for "the chairman, or a deputy chairman, of the Independent Police Complaints Commission" substitute "the Director General of the Independent Office for Police Conduct";

(b) omit "by the Commission".

(4) In section 107 (restriction on issue of warrants to certain law enforcement officers), in subsection (2), for paragraph (h) substitute—

"(h) the Director General of the Independent Office for Police Conduct;".

(5) In section 133 (section 132: meaning of "excepted disclosure"), in subsection (3)(b) —

(a) for "the Independent Police Complaints Commission" substitute "the Director General of the Independent Office for Police Conduct";

(b) for "its functions" substitute "the Director General's functions".

(6) In Schedule 4 (relevant public authorities and designated senior officers), in Part 1—

(a) omit the entry relating to the Independent Police Complaints Commission;

(b) after the entry relating to the Office of Communications insert—

"Independent Office for Police Conduct	Director or an equivalent grade	All	(b) and (i)"

(7) In Schedule 6 (issue of warrants under section 106 etc. table), in the entry relating to the chairman, or a deputy chairman, of the Independent Police Complaints Commission, for the first two columns substitute—

"The Director General of the Independent Office for Police Conduct.	A person falling within paragraph 6A(2) of Schedule 2 to the Police Reform Act 2002 who is designated by the Director General for the purpose."

SCHEDULE 10

Section 38

SCHEDULE TO BE INSERTED AS SCHEDULE 3B TO THE POLICE REFORM ACT 2002

"SCHEDULE 3B

Section 38(6B)(a) and (6D)

DESIGNATIONS UNDER SECTION 38

PART 1

EXCLUDED POWERS AND DUTIES OF CONSTABLES

1 Any power or duty of a constable to make an arrest.

2 Any power or duty of a constable to stop and search an individual or a vehicle or other thing.

3 The power of a constable, under section 36(4) of the Police and Criminal Evidence Act 1984, to perform the functions of a custody officer at a designated police station if a custody officer is not readily available to perform them.

4 Any power that is exercisable only by a constable of a particular rank.

5 Any power of a constable under—

(a) the Terrorism Act 2000;

(b) the Terrorism Act 2006;

(c) the Counter-Terrorism Act 2008;

(d) the Terrorism Prevention and Investigation Measures Act 2011;

(e) the Counter-Terrorism and Security Act 2015.

6 Any power of a constable under the Official Secrets Acts 1911 to 1989.

7 The power of a constable to make an application on behalf of the Commissioner of Police of the Metropolis under section 19 or 21 of the Investigatory Powers Act 2016 (applications for warrants under Chapter 1 of Part 2 of that Act).

PART 2

APPLICATION OF LEGISLATION

8 (1) Where a power or duty of a constable is conferred or imposed on a person designated under section 38—

(a) a reference to a constable (however expressed) in legislation relating to the power or duty includes a reference to the person designated under section 38;

(b) a reference in legislation to anything done in the exercise or purported exercise of the power, or in the performance or purported performance of the duty, includes a reference to anything done in the exercise or purported exercise of the power, or the performance or purported performance of the duty, by the person designated under section 38.

(2) The Secretary of State may by regulations make provision for legislation relating to a power or duty of a constable specified in the regulations to apply in relation

to a person designated under section 38 in a way that modifies or supplements the effect of sub-paragraph (1).

(3) In this paragraph, "legislation" means any provision of—

(a) an Act;

(b) subordinate legislation within the meaning of the Interpretation Act 1978;

(c) a Measure or Act of the National Assembly for Wales or an instrument made under a Measure or Act of that Assembly."

SCHEDULE 11

Section 38

SCHEDULE TO BE INSERTED AS SCHEDULE 3C TO THE POLICE REFORM ACT 2002

"SCHEDULE 3C

Section 38(6B)(b)

DESIGNATIONS UNDER SECTION 38: ADDITIONAL POWERS AND DUTIES

1 Introduction

1 (1) The designation of a person under section 38 as a community support officer or a community support volunteer may provide for any of paragraphs 2 to 11 to apply to the community support officer or the community support volunteer.

(2) The designation may provide for any such paragraph to apply—

(a) to its full extent, or

(b) only in cases or circumstances described in the designation.

(3) Where the designation provides for any of those paragraphs to apply—

(a) the community support officer or community support volunteer has any power or duty described in the paragraph as a power or duty of a community support officer or community support volunteer (subject to provision included in the designation under sub-paragraph (2)(b) or section 38(7A)), and

(b) any provision made by the paragraph in connection with the exercise of the power or the performance of the duty applies in relation to the exercise of the power or the performance of the duty by the community support officer or community support volunteer.

(4) In this Schedule—

"CSO" means a person designated by a chief officer of police as a community support officer under section 38;

"CSV" means a person designated by a chief officer of police as a community support volunteer under section 38;

"the relevant police area", in relation to a CSO or CSV, means the police area for which the police force in question is maintained.

(5) Expressions used in this Schedule and in the 1984 Act have the same meanings in this Schedule as in that Act.

2 Powers to issue fixed penalty notices

2 (1) A CSO or CSV has the power of an authorised officer of a litter authority to give a notice under section 88 of the Environmental Protection Act 1990 (fixed penalty notices in respect of litter) in relation to an individual whom the CSO or CSV has reason to believe has committed an offence under section 87 of that Act at a place within the relevant police area.

(2) A CSO or CSV has the power of an authorised officer of a local authority to give a notice under section 43(1) of the Anti-social Behaviour Act 2003 (penalty notices in respect of graffiti or fly-posting) in relation to an individual whom the CSO or CSV has reason to believe has committed an offence that is a relevant offence for the purposes of section 43(1) at a place within the relevant police area.

(3) A CSO or CSV designated under section 38 by the Commissioner of Police of the Metropolis has the power of an authorised officer of a borough council to give a notice under section 15 of the London Local Authorities Act 2004 in relation to an individual whom the CSO or CSV has reason to believe has committed an offence under section 38(1) of the London Local Authorities Act 1990.

(4) A CSO or CSV designated under section 38 by the Commissioner of Police for the City of London has the power of an authorised officer of a borough council to give a notice under section 15 of the London Local Authorities Act 2004 in relation to an individual whom the CSO or CSV has reason to believe has committed an offence under section 27(1) of the City of Westminster Act 1999 (unlicensed street trading).

(5) A CSO or CSV has the power of an authorised officer of an authority to give a notice under section 237A of the Local Government Act 1972 or under section 12 of the Local Government Byelaws (Wales) Act 2012 (fixed penalty notices in relation to offences against certain byelaws) in relation to an individual whom the CSO or CSV has reason to believe has committed an offence against a listed byelaw at a place within the relevant police area.

(6) A byelaw is a "listed byelaw" for the purposes of sub-paragraph (5) if, at the time the CSO or CSV gives the notice—

(a) it is a byelaw to which section 237A of the Local Government Act 1972 or to which section 12 of the Local Government Byelaws (Wales) Act 2012 (fixed penalty notices in relation to offences against certain byelaws) applies, and

(b) the chief officer of police for the relevant police area and the authority that made the byelaw have agreed to include it in a list of byelaws kept for the purposes of sub-paragraph (5).

(7) The chief officer of police for the relevant police area must publish the list of byelaws kept for the purposes of sub-paragraph (5) in such a way as to bring it to the attention of members of the public in localities where the byelaws in the list apply.

(8) The list of byelaws kept for the purposes of sub-paragraph (5) may be amended from time to time by agreement between the chief officer of police and the authority, by adding byelaws to it or removing byelaws from it.

(9) Where the list of byelaws is amended, the amended list must be published by the chief officer as mentioned in sub-paragraph (7).

3 Powers to require names and addresses

3 (1) A CSO or CSV may require a person to give his or her name and address if the CSO or CSV has reason to believe that—

(a) the person has committed a relevant offence in the relevant police area, or

(b) the person has committed a relevant licensing offence (whether or not in the relevant police area).

(2) A person who fails to comply with a requirement under sub-paragraph (1) is guilty of an offence and liable on summary conviction to a fine not exceeding level 3 on the standard scale.

(3) In this paragraph, "relevant offence" means any of the following offences—

(a) an offence in respect of which the CSO or CSV is authorised to give a penalty notice (whether in consequence of paragraph 2 of this Schedule or in consequence of provision included in his or her designation in reliance on section 38(6B)(a));

(b) an offence under section 3 or 4 of the Vagrancy Act 1824;

(c) an offence committed in a specified park which by virtue of section 2 of the Parks Regulation (Amendment) Act 1926 is an offence against the Parks Regulation Act 1872;

(d) an offence under section 39 of the Anti-social Behaviour, Crime and Policing Act 2014;

(e) an offence under a listed byelaw;

(f) an offence the commission of which appears to the CSO or CSV to have caused—

(i) injury, alarm or distress to any other person, or

(ii) the loss of, or any damage to, any other person's property.

(4) In this paragraph, "relevant licensing offence" means an offence under any of the following provisions of the Licensing Act 2003—

(a) section 141 (otherwise than by virtue of subsection (2)(c) or (3) of that section);

(b) section 142;

(c) section 146(1);

(d) section 149(1)(a), (3)(a) or (4)(a);

(e) section 150(1);

(f) section 150(2) (otherwise than by virtue of subsection (3)(b) of that section);

(g) section 152(1) (excluding paragraph (b)).

(5) A byelaw is a "listed byelaw" for the purposes of sub-paragraph (3)(e) if, at the time the CSO or CSV requires a person to give his or her name and address—

(a) it is a byelaw which has been made by a relevant body with authority to make byelaws for any place within the relevant police area, and

(b) it is included in the list of byelaws published for the purposes of this paragraph by the chief officer of police for the relevant police area.

(6) A byelaw may be included in the list of byelaws published for the purposes of this paragraph only if the chief officer of police and the relevant body which made the byelaw agree that it should be included.

(7) The chief officer of police for the relevant police area must publish the list in such a way as to bring it to the attention of members of the public in localities where the byelaws in the list apply.

(8) The list of byelaws published for the purposes of this paragraph may be amended from time to time by agreement between the chief officer of police and the relevant body, by adding byelaws to it or removing byelaws from it.

(9) Where the list of byelaws is amended, the amended list must be published by the chief officer as mentioned in sub-paragraph (8).

(10) In sub-paragraphs (5), (6) and (8), "relevant body" means—

- (a) in England, a county council, a district council, a London borough council or a parish council;
- (b) in Wales, a county council, a county borough council or a community council;
- (c) the Greater London Authority;
- (d) Transport for London;
- (e) an Integrated Transport Authority for an integrated transport area in England;
- (f) a combined authority established under section 103 of the Local Democracy, Economic Development and Construction Act 2009;
- (g) a body specified in regulations made by the Secretary of State.

(11) Regulations under sub-paragraph (10)(g) may provide, in relation to any body specified in the regulations, that the agreement mentioned in sub-paragraph (6) or (8) is to be made between the chief officer and the Secretary of State (rather than between the chief officer and the relevant body).

(12) In the case of a relevant offence that is an offence under a listed byelaw (see sub-paragraphs (3)(e) and (5)), the power to impose a requirement under sub-paragraph (1) is exercisable only in a place to which the byelaw relates.

(13) In its application in relation to an offence in respect of which the CSO or CSV is authorised to give a penalty notice under section 444A of the Education Act 1996 (penalty notice in respect of failure to secure regular attendance at school of registered pupil), sub-paragraph (1)(a) of this paragraph has effect as if the words "in the relevant police area" were omitted.

(14) In this paragraph, "specified park" has the same meaning as in section 162 of the Serious Organised Crime and Police Act 2005.

4 Powers to search for and seize alcohol and tobacco

4 (1) A CSO or CSV may search a person for alcohol or a container for alcohol if—

- (a) the CSO or CSV has (in consequence of provision included in his or her designation in reliance on section 38(6B)(a)) imposed a requirement on a person to surrender alcohol or a container for alcohol under section 63(2) of the Anti-social Behaviour, Crime and Policing Act 2014 or under section 1 of the Confiscation of Alcohol (Young Persons) Act 1997,
- (b) the person has failed to comply with the requirement, and
- (c) the CSO or CSV reasonably believes that the person has alcohol or a container for alcohol in his or her possession.

(2) A CSO or CSV may search a person for tobacco or cigarette papers where—

(a) the CSO or CSV has (in consequence of provision included in his or her designation in reliance on section 38(6B)(a)) sought to seize the tobacco or cigarette papers under section 7(3) of the Children and Young Persons Act 1933 (seizure of tobacco from young persons),

(b) the person from whom the CSO or CSV sought to seize the item has failed to surrender it, and

(c) the CSO or CSV reasonably believes that the person has it in his or her possession.

(3) The power to search under sub-paragraph (1) or (2)—

(a) is to do so only to the extent that is reasonably required for the purpose of discovering whatever the CSO or CSV is searching for, and

(b) does not authorise the CSO or CSV to require a person to remove any of his or her clothing in public other than an outer coat, jacket or gloves.

(4) A person who without reasonable excuse fails to consent to being searched in the exercise of a power under this paragraph is guilty of an offence and is liable, on summary conviction, to a fine not exceeding level 3 on the standard scale.

(5) A CSO or CSV who proposes to exercise a power to search a person under sub-paragraph (1) or (2) must inform him or her that failing without reasonable excuse to consent to being searched is an offence.

(6) If the person in question fails to consent to being searched, the CSO or CSV may require him or her to give the CSO or CSV his or her name and address.

(7) If on searching the person the CSO or CSV discovers what he or she is searching for, the CSO or CSV may seize it and dispose of it.

5 Powers to seize and detain: controlled drugs

5 (1) A CSO or CSV may exercise the powers conferred by sub-paragraph (2) or (3) in the relevant police area.

(2) If the CSO or CSV—

(a) finds a controlled drug in a person's possession (whether or not the CSO or CSV finds it in the course of searching the person in the exercise of a power or duty conferred or imposed by his or her designation under section 38), and

(b) reasonably believes that it is unlawful for the person to be in possession of it,

the CSO or CSV may seize it and retain it.

(3) If the CSO or CSV—

(a) either—

(i) finds a controlled drug in a person's possession (as mentioned in sub-paragraph (2)(a)), or

(ii) reasonably believes that a person is in possession of a controlled drug, and

(b) reasonably believes that it is unlawful for the person to be in possession of it, the CSO or CSV may require the person to give the CSO or CSV his or her name and address.

(4) If, in exercise of the power conferred by sub-paragraph (2), the CSO or CSV seizes and retains a controlled drug, the CSO or CSV must—

(a) if the person from whom it was seized maintains that he or she was lawfully in possession of it, tell the person where inquiries about its recovery may be made, and

(b) comply with a constable's instructions about what to do with it.

(5) A person who fails to comply with a requirement imposed under sub-paragraph (3) is guilty of an offence and liable, on summary conviction, to a fine not exceeding level 3 on the standard scale.

(6) In this paragraph, "controlled drug" has the same meaning as in the Misuse of Drugs Act 1971.

6 Powers to seize and detain: psychoactive substances

6 (1) A CSO or CSV may exercise the powers conferred by sub-paragraph (2) or (3) in the relevant police area.

(2) If the CSO or CSV—

(a) finds a psychoactive substance in a person's possession (whether or not the CSO or CSV finds it in the course of searching the person in the exercise of a power or duty conferred or imposed by his or her designation under section 38), and

(b) reasonably believes that it is unlawful for the person to be in possession of it,

the CSO or CSV may seize it and retain it.

(3) If the CSO or CSV—

(a) either—

(i) finds a psychoactive substance in a person's possession (as mentioned in sub-paragraph (2)(a)), or

(ii) reasonably believes that a person is in possession of a psychoactive substance, and

(b) reasonably believes that it is unlawful for the person to be in possession of it,

the CSO or CSV may require the person to give the CSO or CSV his or her name and address.

(4) If, in exercise of the power conferred by sub-paragraph (2), the CSO or CSV seizes and retains a psychoactive substance, the CSO or CSV must—

(a) if the person from whom it was seized maintains that he or she was lawfully in possession of it—

(i) tell the person where inquiries about its recovery may be made, and

(ii) explain the effect of sections 49 to 51 and 53 of the Psychoactive Substances Act 2016 (retention and disposal of items), and

(b) comply with a constable's instructions about what to do with it.

(5) Any substance seized in exercise of the power conferred by sub-paragraph (2) is to be treated for the purposes of sections 49 to 53 of the Psychoactive Substances Act 2016 as if it had been seized by a police or customs officer under section 36 of that Act.

Section 50 of that Act applies in relation to any such substance as if the reference in subsection (1)(b) to the police or customs officer who seized it were a reference to the CSO or CSV who seized it.

(6) A person who fails to comply with a requirement imposed under sub-paragraph (3) is guilty of an offence and liable, on summary conviction, to a fine not exceeding level 3 on the standard scale.

(7) In this paragraph, "police or customs officer" and "psychoactive substance" have the same meaning as in the Psychoactive Substances Act 2016.

7 Powers to detain pending arrival of a constable etc

7 (1) A CSO or CSV may require a person to wait with the CSO or CSV, for a period not exceeding 30 minutes, for the arrival of a constable where—

- (a) the CSO or CSV has required the person to give his or her name and address (whether in consequence of paragraph 3, 4(6), 5(3) or 6(3) or in consequence of provision included in his or her designation in reliance on section 38(6B)(a)), and
- (b) either—
  - (i) the person has failed to comply with the requirement, or
  - (ii) the CSO or CSV has reasonable grounds for suspecting that the person has given a name or address that is false or inaccurate.

(2) Sub-paragraph (1) does not apply if the requirement to give a name and address was imposed in connection with a relevant licensing offence mentioned in paragraph 3(4)(a), (c) or (f) which the CSO or CSV believes to have been committed on licensed premises (within the meaning of the Licensing Act 2003).

(3) A CSO or CSV may require a person to wait with the CSO or CSV, for a period not exceeding 30 minutes, for the arrival of a constable where—

- (a) the CSO or CSV has reason to believe that the person is committing an offence under section 3 or 4 of the Vagrancy Act 1824,
- (b) the CSO or CSV requires the person to stop doing whatever gives rise to that belief, and
- (c) the person fails to stop as required.

(4) A person who has been required under sub-paragraph (1) or (3) to wait with a CSO or CSV may, if requested to do so, elect that (instead of waiting) he or she will accompany the CSO or CSV to a police station in the relevant police area.

(5) Where the person does not elect to accompany the CSO or CSV to the police station, and the constable arrives within the period of 30 minutes, the CSO or CSV is under a duty to remain with the person and the constable until the CSO or CSV has transferred control of the person to the constable.

(6) Where the person does elect to accompany the CSO or CSV to the police station—

(a) the CSO or CSV is under a duty to remain at the police station until the CSO or CSV has transferred control of the person to the custody officer there,

(b) until control is transferred, the CSO or CSV is treated for all purposes as having the person in his or her lawful custody, and

(c) for so long as the CSO or CSV remains at the police station or in its immediate vicinity (whether before control of the person is transferred or afterwards), the CSO or CSV is under a duty to prevent the person's escape and to assist in keeping the person under control.

(7) A person who—

(a) makes off while subject to a requirement under sub-paragraph (1) or (3), or

(b) makes off while accompanying a CSO or CSV to a police station in accordance with an election under sub-paragraph (4),

is guilty of an offence and liable, on summary conviction, to a fine not exceeding level 3 on the standard scale.

8 Powers to search etc individuals detained under paragraph 7

8 (1) A CSO or CSV may exercise the powers set out in sub-paragraphs (2) and (3) in relation to a person whom the CSO or CSV has required to wait for the arrival of a constable under paragraph 7(1) or (3) (whether or not that person makes an election under paragraph 7(4)).

(2) If the CSO or CSV has reasonable grounds for believing that the person may present a danger to himself or herself or to others, the CSO or CSV may search the person.

(3) If the CSO or CSV has reasonable grounds for believing that the person may have concealed on him or her anything which might be used to assist in escaping from lawful custody, the CSO or CSV may search the person for that thing.

(4) The power conferred by sub-paragraph (2) or (3)—

(a) does not authorise a CSO or CSV to require a person to remove any of his or her clothing in public other than an outer coat, jacket or gloves;

(b) does authorise a search of a person's mouth.

(5) A CSO or CSV searching a person under sub-paragraph (2) may seize and retain anything that is found, if the CSO or CSV has reasonable grounds for believing that the person searched might use it to cause physical injury to himself or herself or to any other person.

(6) A CSO or CSV searching a person under sub-paragraph (3) may seize and retain anything that is found, other than an item subject to legal privilege, if the CSO or CSV has reasonable grounds for believing that the person might use it to assist in escaping from lawful custody.

(7) If a CSO or CSV seizes or retains anything under sub-paragraph (5) or (6), the CSO or CSV must—

(a) tell the person from whom it was seized where inquiries about its recovery may be made, and

(b) comply with a constable's instructions about what to do with it.

9 Persons detained under paragraph 7: park trading offences

9 (1) If a CSO or CSV reasonably suspects that a person required to wait for the arrival of a constable under paragraph 7(1) has committed a park trading offence, the CSO or CSV may take possession of anything of a non-perishable nature which—

(a) the person has in his or her possession or under his control, and

(b) the CSO or CSV reasonably believes to have been used in the commission of the offence.

(2) The CSO or CSV may retain possession of the thing in question for a period not exceeding 30 minutes unless the person makes an election under paragraph 7(4), in which case the CSO or CSV may retain possession of the thing in question until he or she is able to transfer control of it to a constable.

(3) In this paragraph "park trading offence" means an offence committed in a specified park which is a park trading offence for the purposes of the Royal Parks (Trading) Act 2000.

(4) In sub-paragraph (3), "specified park" has the same meaning as in section 162 of the Serious Organised Crime and Police Act 2005.

10 Road traffic

10 A CSO or CSV has in the relevant police area the powers conferred on persons designated by regulations under section 99 of the Road Traffic Regulation Act 1984 (removal of abandoned vehicles).

11 Power to use reasonable force

11 A CSO or CSV has power to use reasonable force—

(a) to prevent a person whom the CSO or CSV has required under paragraph 7(1) or (3) to wait for a constable from making off, or to keep the person under control, at any time while the person is subject to the requirement;

(b) where such a person elects under paragraph 7(4) to accompany a CSO or CSV to a police station, to prevent the person from making off, or to keep the person under control, while the person is accompanying the CSO or CSV to the police station;

(c) where a CSO or CSV is fulfilling a duty imposed under paragraph 7(5) or (6), to prevent the person from making off (or escaping) and to keep him or her under control;

(d) where a CSO or CSV is exercising a power conferred by paragraph 8."

SCHEDULE 12

Section 45

POWERS OF CIVILIAN STAFF AND VOLUNTEERS: FURTHER AMENDMENTS

PART 1

AMENDMENTS OF THE POLICE REFORM ACT 2002

1 (1) Section 38B (police powers for civilian employees under collaboration agreements) is amended as follows.

(2) In subsection (1)(a), after "civilian employee of" insert ", or a police volunteer with,".

(3) In subsection (2), for "one or more of the descriptions specified in section 38(2)" substitute "either or both of the descriptions specified in section 38(1) (if C is a civilian employee of the assisting force) or section 38(1A) (if C is a police volunteer with the assisting force)".

(4) In subsection (3), for "section 38(2)" substitute "section 38(1) or (as the case may be) section 38(1A)".

(5) In subsection (10)—

(a) for "civilian employees of the assisting force" substitute "persons designated under section 38 by the chief officer of police of the assisting force";

(b) for "section 23B" substitute "section 23AA".

2 (1) Section 42 (supplementary provisions relating to designations and accreditations) is amended as follows.

(2) Omit subsections (A1) to (C1) and (1A).

(3) In subsection (2A), for "investigating officer", in each place where it occurs, substitute "policing support officer or policing support volunteer".

(4) In subsection (2B), for ""investigating officer" means a person designated as an investigating officer" substitute ""policing support officer" and "policing support volunteer" mean (respectively) a person designated as a policing support officer or (as the case may be) a policing support volunteer".

(5) After subsection (7A) insert—

"(7B) For the purposes of determining liability for the unlawful conduct of police volunteers designated under section 38, conduct by such a volunteer in reliance or purported reliance on a designation under that section is to be taken to be conduct by that person in the course of employment by the chief officer of police by whom the designation is made; and, in the case of a tort, that chief officer is to be treated as a joint tortfeasor accordingly.

(7C) For the purposes of determining liability for the unlawful conduct of police volunteers designated under section 38, conduct by such a volunteer in reliance or purported reliance on a designation under section 38B is to be taken to be conduct by that person in the course of employment by the chief officer of police by whom the designation under section 38 is made; and, in the case of a tort, that chief officer is to be treated as a joint tortfeasor accordingly."

3 Omit section 45 (code of practice relating to chief officers' powers under Chapter 1).

4 In section 105 (powers of Secretary of State to make orders and regulations), in subsection (3)(b)—

(a) for "any order that is" substitute "any order or regulations that are";

(b) after "section 19(3)," insert "38(9C),";

(c) omit ", 38A(4)";

(d) omit "or paragraph 15A(2) of Schedule 4".

5 (1) Schedule 4 is amended as follows.

(2) For the heading to the Schedule substitute "Powers exercisable by contracted-out staff".

(3) Omit Parts 1 and 2.

(4) In Part 5, in paragraph 36—

(a) in sub-paragraph (1)(a), for "section 38 or 39" substitute "section 39";

(b) omit sub-paragraphs (2) and (2A);

(c) in sub-paragraph (3), for "section 38 or 39" substitute "section 39";

(d) omit sub-paragraph (3A).

PART 2

OTHER AMENDMENTS

6 (1) Schedule 1 to the Representation of the People Act 1983 (parliamentary election rules) is amended as follows.

(2) In paragraph 31(2)—

(a) after "community support officer" insert "or community support volunteer";

(b) in the words in brackets, after "employees" insert "or volunteers".

(3) In paragraph 32(5)—

(a) after "community support officer" insert "or community support volunteer";

(b) in the words in brackets, after "employees" insert "or volunteers".

7 (1) The Police and Criminal Evidence Act 1984 is amended as follows.

(2) In section 55 (intimate searches), in subsection (17), in the definition of "appropriate officer", omit paragraph (b).

(3) In section 64A (photographing of suspects etc), in subsection (1B)—

(a) in paragraph (c), for "with a community support officer under paragraph 2(3) or (3B) of Schedule 4" substitute "with a community support officer or a community support volunteer under paragraph 7 of Schedule 3B";

(b) for paragraph (e) substitute—

"(e) given a fixed penalty notice by a community support officer or community support volunteer who is authorised to give the notice by virtue of his or her designation under section 38 of the Police Reform Act 2002;".

(4) In section 67 (codes of practice - supplementary), in subsection (9A)(a), in the words in brackets, after "civilian staff" insert "and volunteers".

8 In the Road Traffic Act 1988, in section 144 (exceptions from requirement of third-party insurance or security), in subsection (2)(b), after "in its capacity as a police authority," insert "by a police volunteer designated under section 38 of the Police Reform Act 2002,".

9 In the Road Traffic Offenders Act 1988, in section 79 (statements by constables), in subsection (2), after "civilian police employee" insert ", or by a police volunteer designated under section 38 of the Police Reform Act 2002,".

10 (1) The Police Act 1996 is amended as follows.

(2) In section 23AA (force collaboration provision about civilian employees)—

(a) in subsection (1), for "designated civilian employees of one police force" substitute "persons designated under section 38 of the Police Reform Act 2002 ("designated persons") by the chief officer of one police force";

(b) in subsection (2), for "designated civilian employees" (in both places where it occurs) substitute "designated persons";

(c) in subsection (3)—

(i) for "designated civilian employees" substitute "designated persons";

(ii) for "those employees" substitute "those persons";

(d) in subsection (4), for "designated civilian employees" substitute "designated persons";

(e) in subsection (5) —

(i) in the opening words, for "civilian employees of the assisting force" substitute "persons designated under section 38 of the Police Reform Act 2002 by the chief officer of the assisting force";

(ii) in each of paragraphs (a) to (c), for "civilian employees" substitute "designated persons";

(f) in subsection (6), omit the definition of "designated";

(g) in that subsection, in the definition of "relevant section 38 designation"—

(i) for "designated civilian employee" substitute "designated person";

(ii) for "the employee" substitute "the person".

(3) In section 23I(7) (collaboration agreements: definition)—

(a) omit the "and" at the end of paragraph (a);

(b) at the end of paragraph (b), insert "and

(c) references to persons who are under the direction and control of the chief officer of police by virtue of being volunteers with the force;".

11 In the Crime and Disorder Act 1998, in section 66H (interpretation of Chapter 1), in paragraph (c), for "an investigating officer" substitute "a policing support officer or a policing support volunteer".

12 In the Representation of the People Act 2000, in Schedule 4 (absent voters in Great Britain), in paragraph 2(5ZA)—

(a) after "community support officer" insert "or community support volunteer";

(b) in the words in brackets, after "employees" insert "or volunteers".

13 In the Terrorism Act 2000, in section 47AE (effect of code), in subsection (5), omit "paragraph 15 of Schedule 4 to the Police Reform Act 2002 or".

14 In the Private Security Industry Act 2001, in Schedule 2 (activities liable to control under the Act), in paragraph 2, for sub-paragraph (7)(f) substitute—

"(f) activities of a person designated under section 38 of the Police Reform Act 2002 (police powers for civilian staff and volunteers) which are carried out by virtue of the designation;".

15 In the Anti-social Behaviour Act 2003 omit the following—

(a) section 23(3) and (4);

(b) section 46(1);

(c) section 89(3) and (4).

16 (1) The Criminal Justice Act 2003 is amended as follows.

(2) In section 27 (interpretation), in the definition of "investigating officer", for "an investigating officer" substitute "a policing support officer or a policing support volunteer".

(3) In Schedule 1, omit paragraphs 17 to 19.

17 (1) Section 28 of the Railways and Transport Safety Act 2003 (exercise of powers by civilians) is amended as follows.

(2) In subsection (1)—

(a) in paragraph (a), in the words in brackets, at the end insert "and volunteers";

(b) omit paragraph (aa);

(c) omit paragraph (d);

(d) omit the "and" after paragraph (f);

(e) after paragraph (f) insert—

"(fa) Schedule 3B (designations under section 38),

(fb) Schedule 3C (designations under section 38: additional powers and duties), and";

(f) in paragraph (g), in the words in brackets, for "civilians" substitute "contracted-out staff".

(3) In subsection (2)—

(a) omit paragraph (e);

(b) in paragraph (f), for "Schedule 4" substitute "Schedules 3C and 4".

18 In the Serious Organised Crime and Police Act 2005—

(a) omit section 122(3);

(b) in Schedule 8, omit paragraphs 1 to 15;

(c) in Schedule 9, omit paragraphs 2 to 6;

(d) in Schedule 13, omit paragraph 13.

19 In the Violent Crime Reduction Act 2006, omit section 24(6).

20 In the Education and Inspections Act 2006, omit the following—

(a) section 107(2) and (3);

(b) section 108(7).

21 (1) The Police and Justice Act 2006 is amended as follows.

(2) Omit sections 7 and 8.

(3) In section 9, omit "makes amendments consequential on section 7 (standard powers and duties of community support officers), and".

(4) In Schedule 5, omit paragraphs 2(3) and (4), 3 and 5(2) to (9).

(5) In Schedule 14, omit paragraph 48.

22 In the Local Government and Public Involvement in Health Act 2007—

(a) omit section 133(2);

(b) in Schedule 6, omit paragraph 4(1).

23 In the UK Borders Act 2007, omit section 47.

24 In the Local Transport Act 2008, in Schedule 4, omit paragraph 65.

25 In the Local Democracy, Economic Development and Construction Act 2009, in Schedule 6, omit paragraph 116.

26 In the Policing and Crime Act 2009, in Schedule 7, omit paragraph 125(3)(b).

27 In the Police Reform and Social Responsibility Act 2011, in Schedule 16, omit paragraphs 292(3), 293, 298 and 303.

28 In the Protection of Freedoms Act 2012, in Schedule 9, omit paragraph 30.

29 In the Legal Aid, Sentencing and Punishment of Offenders Act 2012, in Schedule 23, omit paragraph 14(3).

30 In the Local Government Byelaws (Wales) Act 2012 (anaw 2), omit section 17(2).

31 In the Anti-social Behaviour, Crime and Policing Act 2014, omit the following—

(a) section 40;

(b) section 53(5) and (6);

(c) section 69;

(d) section 152 and Schedule 10;

(e) in Schedule 11, paragraph 32.

32 In the Psychoactive Substances Act 2016, in Schedule 5, omit paragraph 3.

PART 3

MINOR CORRECTING AMENDMENTS

33 (1) The Police Reform Act 2002 is amended as follows.

(2) In section 50 (persons acting in an anti-social manner), in subsection (1), for "has been acting, or is acting, in an anti-social manner" substitute "has engaged, or is engaging, in anti-social behaviour".

(3) In consequence of the amendment made by sub-paragraph (2), in the heading of the section, for "acting in an anti-social manner" substitute "engaging in anti-social behaviour".

(4) In Schedule 5, in paragraph 3, the existing text becomes sub-paragraph (1).

(5) In that sub-paragraph, for the words from "to have been acting" to "(anti-social behaviour orders))" substitute "to have been engaging, or to be engaging, in anti-social behaviour".

(6) After that sub-paragraph insert—

"(2) In sub-paragraph (1), "anti-social behaviour" has the meaning given by section 2 of the Anti-social Behaviour, Crime and Policing Act 2014 (ignoring subsection (2) of that section)."

(7) In consequence of the amendment made by sub-paragraph (5), in the italic heading before paragraph 3, for "acting in an anti-social manner" substitute "engaging in anti-social behaviour".

SCHEDULE 13

Section 46

ABOLITION OF OFFICE OF TRAFFIC WARDEN

Chronically Sick and Disabled Persons Act 1970 (c.44)

1 In section 21 of the Chronically Sick and Disabled Persons Act 1970 (badges for display on motor vehicles used by disabled persons), in subsection (4BB), omit paragraph (a).

Aviation Security Act 1982 (c.36)

2 In section 29 of the Aviation Security Act 1982 (control of road traffic at relevant aerodromes), in subsection (2)—

(a) at the beginning insert "In the application of this Part to Scotland and Northern Ireland,";

(b) in paragraph (a), for the words from "the chief officer of police" to "(in any other case)" substitute "the police authority".

Road Traffic Offenders Act 1988 (c.53)

3 In Schedule 2 to the Road Traffic Offenders Act 1988 (prosecution and punishment of offences), in Part 1, in the fifth column of the entry relating to section 35 of the Road Traffic Act 1988, for "traffic officer or traffic warden" substitute "or traffic officer".

Greater London Authority Act 1999 (c.29)

4 In the Greater London Authority Act 1999, omit section 290 (exercise by traffic wardens of functions of parking attendants).

Police Reform Act 2002 (c.30)

5 In the Police Reform Act 2002, omit section 44 (removal of restriction on powers conferred on traffic wardens).

Police Reform and Social Responsibility Act 2011 (c.13)

6 In Schedule 16 to the Police Reform and Social Responsibility Act 2011 (minor and consequential amendments), omit paragraphs 166(2) and 167(3).

SCHEDULE 14

Section 51

REMOVAL OF REFERENCES TO ACPO

Replacement of definition of ACPO with definition of NPCC

1 (1) Section 101(1) of the Police Act 1996 is amended as follows.

(2) Omit the definition of "the Association of Chief Police Officers".

(3) After the definition of "national or international functions" insert—

> ""the National Police Chiefs' Council" means the body called the National Police Chiefs' Council which was established in accordance with a collaboration agreement under section 22A above entered into on 1 April 2015;".

Repeal of references to ACPO

2 (1) The Police Reform Act 2002 is amended as follows.

(2) Omit section 96.

(3) In section 106 omit the definition of "the Association of Chief Police Officers".

3 (1) The Police and Justice Act 2006 is amended as follows.

(2) In the heading of section 6 for "and ACPO" substitute "and body representing chief officers of police".

(3) Schedule 4 is amended as follows—

- (a) omit paragraph 2;
- (b) omit paragraph 6;
- (c) omit paragraph 8;
- (d) omit paragraph 17;
- (e) omit paragraph 18.

Substitution of references to NPCC for references to ACPO

4 In each of the provisions listed in paragraph 5 for "the Association of Chief Police Officers of England, Wales and Northern Ireland" substitute "the National Police Chiefs' Council".

5 The provisions mentioned in paragraph 4 are—

- (a) section 67(4)(b) of the Police and Criminal Evidence Act 1984;
- (b) section 21A(4)(za) of the Criminal Procedure and Investigations Act 1996;
- (c) section 6(2)(b) of the Police and Justice Act 2006.

6 In each of the provisions listed in paragraph 7 for "the Association of Chief Police Officers" substitute "the National Police Chiefs' Council".

7 The provisions mentioned in paragraph 6 are—

(a) section 42B(2)(b) of the Firearms Act 1968;

(b) section 18B(2)(b) of the Firearms (Amendment) Act 1988;

(c) sections 40B(2)(b), 42A(2)(b), 53(2)(b), 53B(3)(c), 53B(6)(b) and 57(4)(b) of the Police Act 1996;

(d) section 35A(2)(b) of the Firearms (Amendment) Act 1997;

(e) sections 22(3)(b), 24(c), 38A(3)(b), 43(9)(a), 45(3)(f) and 51(7)(b) of the Police Reform Act 2002;

(f) section 70(2)(j) of the Courts Act 2003;

(g) section 31(3)(a) of the Crime and Security Act 2010;

(h) sections 29(5)(b) and 33(8)(b) of the Protection of Freedoms Act 2012.

SCHEDULE 15

Section 116(2)

SCHEDULE TO BE INSERTED AS SCHEDULE 7A TO THE CRIMINAL JUSTICE AND PUBLIC ORDER ACT 1994

"SCHEDULE 7A

Section 137B

OFFENCES SPECIFIED FOR THE PURPOSES OF SECTION 137A

PART 1

OFFENCES UNDER THE LAW OF ENGLAND AND WALES

1 Any of the following offences at common law—

(a) false imprisonment;

(b) kidnapping;

(c) indecent exposure;

(d) cheating in relation to the public revenue.

2 An offence under any of the following provisions of the Offences against the Person Act 1861—

(a) section 20 (inflicting bodily injury);

(b) section 24 (administering poison etc with intent);

(c) section 27 (exposing child whereby life is endangered etc);

(d) section 31 (setting spring-guns etc with intent);

(e) section 37 (assaulting an officer etc on account of his preserving wreck);

(f) section 47 (assault occasioning actual bodily harm).

3 (1) An offence under any of the following provisions of the Sexual Offences Act 1956 —

(a) section 10 (incest by a man);

(b) section 11 (incest by a woman);

(c) section 30 (man living on the earnings of prostitution);

(d) section 31 (woman exercising control over a prostitute);

(e) section 33A (keeping a brothel used for prostitution).

(2) An offence under section 12 of that Act (buggery), other than an offence committed by a person where the other person involved in the conduct constituting the offence consented to it and was aged 16 or over.

(3) An offence under section 13 of that Act (indecency between men), where the offence was committed by a man aged 21 or over and the other person involved in the conduct constituting the offence was under the age of 16.

4 An offence under section 4 of the Criminal Law Act 1967 (assisting offenders).

5 An offence under section 5 of the Sexual Offences Act 1967 (living on the earnings of male prostitution).

6 An offence under any of the following provisions of the Firearms Act 1968—

(a) section 1(1) (possession etc of firearms or ammunition without certificate);

(b) section 2(1) (possession etc of shot gun without certificate);

(c) section 3(1) (manufacturing, selling etc firearms or ammunition by way of trade or business without being registered as a firearms dealer).

7 An offence under section 106A of the Taxes Management Act 1970 (fraudulent evasion of income tax).

8 (1) An offence under section 50(2) or (3) of the Customs and Excise Management Act 1979 (improper importation of goods), other than an offence mentioned in subsection (5B) of that section.

(2) An offence under section 68(2) of that Act (exportation of prohibited or restricted goods).

(3) An offence under section 170 of that Act (fraudulent evasion of duty etc), other than an offence mentioned in subsection (4B) of that section.

9 An offence under section 4 of the Aviation Security Act 1982 (offences in relation to certain dangerous articles).

10 An offence under section 127 of the Mental Health Act 1983 (ill-treatment of patients).

11 An offence under either of the following provisions of the Child Abduction Act 1984—

(a) section 1 (abduction of child by parent etc);

(b) section 2 (abduction of child by other persons).

12 An offence under section 1 of the Prohibition of Female Circumcision Act 1985 (prohibition of female circumcision).

13 An offence under either of the following provisions of the Public Order Act 1986—

(a) section 2 (violent disorder);

(b) section 3 (affray).

14 An offence under section 160 of the Criminal Justice Act 1988 (possession of indecent photograph of a child).

15 An offence under section 2 of the Computer Misuse Act 1990 (unauthorised access with intent to commit or facilitate commission of further offences).

16 An offence under section 72(1), (3) or (8) of the Value Added Tax Act 1994 (fraudulent evasion of VAT etc).

17 An offence under either of the following provisions of the Protection from Harassment Act 1997—

(a) section 4 (putting people in fear of violence);

(b) section 4A (stalking involving fear of violence or serious alarm or distress).

18 An offence under section 29(1)(a) or (b) of the Crime and Disorder Act 1998 (certain racially or religiously aggravated assaults).

19 An offence under section 38B of the Terrorism Act 2000 (information about acts of terrorism).

20 An offence under section 3 of the Sexual Offences (Amendment) Act 2000 (sexual activity with a person aged under 18 in abuse of a position of trust).

21 An offence under section 35 of the Tax Credits Act 2002 (tax credit fraud).

22 (1) An offence under any of the following provisions of the Sexual Offences Act 2003—

(a) section 13 (child sex offences committed by children or young persons);

(b) section 16 (abuse of position of trust: sexual activity with a child);

(c) section 17 (abuse of position of trust: causing or inciting a child to engage in sexual activity);

(d) section 18 (abuse of position of trust: sexual activity in the presence of a child);

(e) section 19 (abuse of position of trust: causing a child to watch a sexual act);

(f) section 40 (care workers: sexual activity in the presence of a person with a mental disorder);

(g) section 41 (care workers: causing a person with a mental disorder to watch a sexual act);

(h) section 52 (causing or inciting prostitution for gain);

(i) section 53 (controlling prostitution for gain).

(2) An offence under section 25 or 26 of that Act (family child sex offences) where the offence is committed by a person under the age of 18.

(3) An offence under section 47 of that Act (paying for sexual services of a child), where the offence is committed against a person aged 16 or over.

23 An offence under either of the following provisions of the Terrorism Act 2006—

(a) section 1 (encouragement of terrorism);

(b) section 2 (dissemination of terrorist publications).

24 An offence under section 45 of the Serious Crime Act 2015 (participating in activities of organised crime group).

25 An offence under section 68 of the Policing and Crime Act 2017 (breach of pre-charge bail conditions relating to travel).

PART 2

OFFENCES UNDER THE LAW OF SCOTLAND

26 Any of the following offences at common law—

(a) culpable homicide;
(b) treason;
(c) rape;
(d) assault, where the assault results in serious injury or endangers life;
(e) assault with intent to rape or ravish;
(f) indecent assault;
(g) abduction with intent to rape;
(h) public indecency;
(i) clandestine injury to women;
(j) lewd, indecent or libidinous behaviour or practices;
(k) sodomy, other than an offence committed by a person where the other person involved in the conduct constituting the offence consented to it and was aged 16 or over;
(l) abduction;
(m) mobbing;
(n) fire-raising;
(o) robbery;
(p) fraud;
(q) extortion;
(r) embezzlement;
(s) theft;
(t) threats;
(u) attempting to pervert the course of justice.

27 An offence under any of the following provisions of the Firearms Act 1968—

(a) section 1(1) (possession etc of firearms or ammunition without certificate);
(b) section 2(1) (possession etc of shot gun without certificate);
(c) section 3(1) (manufacturing, selling etc firearms or ammunition by way of trade or business without being registered as a firearms dealer).

28 An offence under section 106A of the Taxes Management Act 1970 (fraudulent evasion of income tax).

29 (1) An offence under section 50(2) or (3) of the Customs and Excise Management Act 1979 (improper importation of goods), other than an offence mentioned in subsection (5B) of that section.

(2) An offence under section 68(2) of that Act (exportation of prohibited or restricted goods).

(3) An offence under section 170 of that Act (fraudulent evasion of duty etc), other than an offence mentioned in subsection (4B) of that section.

30 An offence under section 4 of the Aviation Security Act 1982 (offences in relation to certain dangerous articles).

31 An offence under either of the following provisions of the Civic Government (Scotland) Act 1982—

(a) section 51(2) (publication etc of obscene material);

(b) section 52 (taking, distributing etc indecent photographs of children).

32 An offence under section 6 of the Child Abduction Act 1984 (parent etc. taking or sending a child out of the United Kingdom).

33 An offence under section 1 of the Prohibition of Female Circumcision Act 1985 (prohibition of female circumcision).

34 An offence under section 2 of the Computer Misuse Act 1990 (unauthorised access with intent to commit or facilitate commission of further offences).

35 An offence under section 72(1), (3) or (8) of the Value Added Tax Act 1994 (fraudulent evasion of VAT etc).

36 An offence under any of the following provisions of the Criminal Law (Consolidation) (Scotland) Act 1995—

(a) section 7 (procuring prostitution etc);

(b) section 8(3) (unlawful detention of women and girls);

(c) section 10 (parents etc encouraging girls under 16 to engage in prostitution etc);

(d) section 11(1)(b) (males soliciting etc for immoral purposes).

37 An offence under section 38B of the Terrorism Act 2000 (information about acts of terrorism).

38 An offence under section 35 of the Tax Credits Act 2002 (tax credit fraud).

39 An offence under section 313 of the Mental Health (Care and Treatment) (Scotland) Act 2003 (persons providing care services: sexual offences).

40 An offence under either of the following provisions of the Terrorism Act 2006—

(a) section 1 (encouragement of terrorism);

(b) section 2 (dissemination of terrorist publications).

41 Any of the following offences under the Sexual Offences (Scotland) Act 2009—

(a) section 8 (sexual exposure);

(b) section 9 (voyeurism);

(c) section 11 (administering a substance for sexual purposes);

(d) section 32 (causing an older child to be present during a sexual activity);

(e) section 33 (causing an older child to look at a sexual image);

(f) section 34(1) (communicating indecently with an older child);

(g) section 34(2) (causing an older child to see or hear an indecent communication);

(h) section 35 (sexual exposure to an older child);

(i) section 36 (voyeurism towards an older child);

(j) section 42 (sexual abuse of trust);

(k) section 46 (sexual abuse of trust of a mentally disordered person).

42 An offence under either of the following provisions of the Criminal Justice and Licensing (Scotland) Act 2010—

(a) section 38 (threatening or abusive behaviour);

(b) section 39 (stalking).

43 An offence under section 2 of the Abusive Behaviour and Sexual Harm (Scotland) Act 2016 (disclosing etc an intimate photograph or film).

PART 3

OFFENCES UNDER THE LAW OF NORTHERN IRELAND

44 Any of the following offences at common law—

(a) false imprisonment;
(b) kidnapping;
(c) riot;
(d) affray;
(e) indecent exposure;
(f) cheating in relation to the public revenue.

45 An offence under any of the following provisions of the Offences against the Person Act 1861—

(a) section 20 (inflicting bodily injury);
(b) section 24 (administering poison etc with intent);
(c) section 27 (exposing child whereby life is endangered etc);
(d) section 31 (setting spring-guns etc with intent);
(e) section 37 (assaulting an officer etc on account of his preserving wreck);
(f) section 47 (assault occasioning actual bodily harm).

46 An offence under section 11 of the Criminal Law Amendment Act 1885 (indecency between men), where the offence was committed by a man aged 21 or over and the other person involved in the conduct constituting the offence was under the age of 16.

47 An offence under either of the following provisions of the Punishment of Incest Act 1908—

(a) section 1 (incest by a man);
(b) section 2 (incest by a woman).

48 An offence under section 4 of the Criminal Law Act (Northern Ireland) 1967 (assisting offenders).

49 An offence under section 106A of the Taxes Management Act 1970 (fraudulent evasion of income tax).

50 (1) An offence under section 50(2) or (3) of the Customs and Excise Management Act 1979 (improper importation of goods), other than an offence mentioned in subsection (5B) of that section.

(2) An offence under section 68(2) of that Act (exportation of prohibited or restricted goods).

(3) An offence under section 170 of that Act (fraudulent evasion of duty etc), other than an offence mentioned in subsection (4B) of that section.

51 An offence under section 4 of the Aviation Security Act 1982 (offences in relation to certain dangerous articles).

52 An offence under Article 8 of the Homosexual Offences (Northern Ireland) Order 1982 (S.I. 1982/1536 (N.I. 19)) (living on the earnings of male prostitution).

53 An offence under section 1 of the Prohibition of Female Circumcision Act 1985 (prohibition of female circumcision).

54 An offence under either of the following provisions of the Child Abduction (Northern Ireland) Order 1985 (S.I. 1985/1638 (N.I. 17))—

(a) Article 3 (abduction of child by parent etc);
(b) Article 4 (abduction of child by other persons).

55 An offence under Article 121 of the Mental Health (Northern Ireland) Order 1986 (S.I. 1986/595 (N.I. 4)) (ill-treatment of patients).

56 An offence under Article 15 of the Criminal Justice (Evidence, Etc.) (Northern Ireland) Order 1988 (S.I. 1988/1847 (N.I. 17)) (possession of indecent photograph of a child).

57 An offence under section 2 of the Computer Misuse Act 1990 (unauthorised access with intent to commit or facilitate commission of further offences).

58 An offence under section 72(1), (3) or (8) of the Value Added Tax Act 1994 (fraudulent evasion of VAT etc).

59 An offence under Article 6 of the Protection from Harassment (Northern Ireland) Order 1997 (S.I. 1997/1180 (N.I. 9)) (putting people in fear of violence).

60 An offence under section 38B of the Terrorism Act 2000 (information about acts of terrorism).

61 An offence under section 3 of the Sexual Offences (Amendment) Act 2000 (sexual activity with a person aged under 18 in abuse of a position of trust).

62 An offence under section 35 of the Tax Credits Act 2002 (tax credit fraud).

63 An offence under section 53 of the Sexual Offences Act 2003 (controlling prostitution for gain).

64 An offence under any of the following provisions of the Firearms (Northern Ireland) Order 2004 (S.I. 2004/702 (N.I. 3))—

(a) Article 3(1)(b) (possession etc of firearms other than handguns without certificate);
(b) Article 3(2) (possession etc of ammunition without certificate);
(c) Article 24(1) (manufacturing, selling etc firearms or ammunition by way of trade or business without being registered as a firearms dealer).

65 An offence under either of the following provisions of the Terrorism Act 2006—

(a) section 1 (encouragement of terrorism);
(b) section 2 (dissemination of terrorist publications).

66 (1) An offence under any of the following provisions of the Sexual Offences (Northern Ireland) Order 2008 (S.I. 2008/1769 (N.I. 2))—

(a) Article 20 (child sex offences committed by children or young persons);
(b) Article 23 (abuse of position of trust: sexual activity with a child);
(c) Article 24 (abuse of position of trust: causing or inciting a child to engage in sexual activity);
(d) Article 25 (abuse of position of trust: sexual activity in the presence of a child);
(e) Article 51 (care workers: sexual activity with a person with a mental disorder);

(f) Article 53 (care workers: sexual activity in the presence of a person with a mental disorder);

(g) Article 62 (causing or inciting prostitution for gain);

(h) Article 63 (controlling prostitution for gain);

(i) Article 64 (keeping a brothel used for prostitution).

(2) An offence under Article 32 or 33 of that Order (family child sex offences) where the offence is committed by a person under the age of 18.

(3) An offence under Article 37 of that Order (paying for sexual services of a child), where the offence is committed against a person aged 16 or over.

67 An offence under section 68 of the Policing and Crime Act 2017 (breach of pre-charge bail conditions relating to travel)."

SCHEDULE 16

Section 116(3)

SCHEDULE TO BE INSERTED AS SCHEDULE 7B TO THE CRIMINAL JUSTICE AND PUBLIC ORDER ACT 1994

"SCHEDULE 7B

Section 137D

RIGHTS OF PERSONS ARRESTED UNDER SECTION 137A: MODIFICATIONS

PART 1

ARRESTS IN RESPECT OF OFFENCES COMMITTED IN ENGLAND AND WALES

1 (1) This Part sets out the modifications mentioned in section 137D(2), that is, modifications of the provisions which apply in relation to persons arrested under section 137A in respect of a specified offence committed in England and Wales.

(2) Except as expressly provided by this Part, a reference to a constable in any of those provisions is to be read as a reference to a constable of the arresting force.

(3) In this Part, references to the arresting force and the investigating force have the same meaning as in section 137C (see subsection (8) of that section).

2 (1) Section 56 of the Police and Criminal Evidence Act 1984 (right to have someone informed when arrested) is modified as follows.

(2) Subsection (1) is to be read as if (instead of referring to the case where a person has been arrested and is being held in custody in a police station or other premises) it referred to the case where a person has been arrested under section 137A and is being detained under section 137C.

(3) Subsection (2)(a) does not apply.

(4) Subsection (2)(b) is to be read as if (instead of referring to an officer of at least the rank of inspector) it referred—

(a) in relation to delay during the period of 24 hours beginning with the time of the arrest under section 137A, to an officer of the investigating force of at least the rank of inspector;

(b) in relation to delay during any remaining period for which the person may be detained under section 137C, to an officer of the investigating force of a rank above that of inspector.

(5) Subsection (3) does not apply.

(6) The reference in subsection (5)(a) to an indictable offence is to be read as a reference to an offence that is an indictable offence under the law of England and Wales.

(7) Subsection (5A)(a) is to be read as if (instead of referring to the person detained for the indictable offence) it referred to the person detained under section 137C.

(8) Subsection (6)(b) is to be read as if (instead of referring to a person's custody record) it referred to the record made by the arresting force in relation to the person's arrest under section 137A and detention under section 137C.

(9) Subsection (8) is to be read as if (instead of referring to a person detained at a police station or other premises) it referred to a person detained under section 137C.

3 (1) Section 58 of the Police and Criminal Evidence Act 1984 (access to legal advice) is modified as follows.

(2) Subsection (1) is to be read as if (instead of referring to a person held in custody in a police station or other premises) it referred to a person detained under section 137C.

(3) Subsections (2) and (9)(b) are to be read as if (instead of referring to a person's custody record) they referred to the record made by the arresting force in relation to the person's arrest under section 137A and detention under section 137C.

(4) Subsections (3) and (5) do not apply.

(5) Subsection (6)(a) does not apply.

(6) The reference in subsection (6)(b) to an officer of at least the rank of superintendent is to be read as a reference to an officer of at least that rank in the investigating force.

(7) The reference in subsection (8)(a) to an indictable offence is to be read as a reference to an indictable offence under the law of England and Wales.

(8) Subsection (8A)(a) is to be read as if (instead of referring to the person detained for the indictable offence) it referred to the person detained under section 137C.

4 (1) Section 34 of the Children and Young Persons Act 1933 (attendance at court of parent of child or young person charged with an offence, etc) is modified as follows.

(2) Subsection (2) is to be read as if (instead of referring to the case where a child or young person is in police detention) it referred to the case where a child or young person is being detained under section 137C.

(3) Subsection (3) is to be read as if (in addition to the information mentioned in paragraphs (a) to (c)) it also mentioned the information set out in section 137D(1)(a) and (b).

(4) The reference in subsection (9) to a child's or young person's rights under section 56 of the Police and Criminal Evidence Act 1984 is to be read as a reference to that section as modified by this Schedule.

PART 2

ARRESTS IN RESPECT OF OFFENCES COMMITTED IN SCOTLAND

5 (1) This Part sets out the modifications mentioned in section 137D(3), that is, modifications of the provisions which apply in relation to persons arrested under section 137A in respect of a specified offence committed in Scotland.

(2) Except as expressly provided by this Part, a reference to a constable in any of those provisions is to be read as a reference to a constable of the arresting force.

(3) A reference to a person in police custody in any of those provisions is to be read as a reference to a person detained under section 137C.

(4) In this Part, references to the arresting force and the investigating force have the same meaning as in section 137C (see subsection (8) of that section).

6 (1) Section 38 of the Criminal Justice (Scotland) Act 2016 (right to have intimation sent to other person) is modified as follows.

(2) Subsection (6) applies as if (instead of the provision made by that subsection) it defined "an appropriate constable" as being—

(a) in relation to delay during the period of 24 hours beginning with the time of the arrest under section 137A, an officer of the investigating force of at least the rank of inspector who has not been involved in the investigation in connection with which the arrest was made;

(b) in relation to delay during any remaining period for which a person may be detained under section 137C, an officer of the investigating force of a rank above that of inspector who has not been involved in the investigation in connection with which the arrest was made.

7 (1) Section 40 of that Act (right of under 18s to have access to another person) is modified as follows.

(2) Subsection (5) applies as if (instead of the provision made by that subsection) it provided for a decision to refuse or restrict access to a person under subsection (1) or (2) to be taken only by—

(a) in the case of a decision to refuse or restrict access during the period of 24 hours beginning with the time of the arrest under section 137A, an officer of the investigating force of at least the rank of inspector who has not been involved in the investigation in connection with which the arrest was made;

(b) in the case of a decision to refuse or restrict access during any remaining period for which a person may be detained under section 137C, an officer of the investigating force of a rank above that of inspector who has not been involved in the investigation in connection with which the arrest was made.

8 (1) Section 41 of that Act (social work involvement in relation to under 18s) is modified as follows.

(2) Subsection (6) applies as if (instead of the provision made by that subsection) it provided for a decision to refuse or restrict access to a person under subsection (4)(b) to be taken only by—

(a) in the case of a decision to refuse or restrict access during the period of 24 hours beginning with the time of the arrest under section 137A, an officer of the investigating force of at least the rank of inspector who has not been involved in the investigation in connection with which the arrest was made;

(b) in the case of a decision to refuse or restrict access during any remaining period for which a person may be detained under section 137C, an officer of the investigating force of a rank above that of inspector who has not been involved in the investigation in connection with which the arrest was made.

9 (1) Section 42 of that Act (support for vulnerable persons) is modified as follows.

(2) Subsection (5)(b)(ii) is to be read as if (instead of referring to a person appointed as a member of police staff under section 26(1) of the Police and Fire Reform (Scotland) Act 2012) it referred to a person who performs a function which is equivalent to a function performed at a police station in Scotland by a person appointed as a member of police staff under section 26(1) of that Act.

10 (1) Section 43 of that Act (right to have intimation sent to solicitor) is modified as follows.

(2) Subsection (1) is to be read as if the list of matters of which a person has a right to have intimation sent to a solicitor—

(a) did not include paragraph (d), but

(b) did include the matters mentioned in section 137D(1)(a) and (b).

11 (1) Section 44 of that Act (right to consultation with solicitor) is modified as follows.

(2) Subsection (3) applies as if (instead of the provision made by that subsection) it provided for a decision to delay the exercise of the right under subsection (1) to be taken only by—

(a) in the case of a delay during the period of 24 hours beginning with the time of the arrest under section 137A, an officer of the investigating force of at least the rank of inspector who has not been involved in the investigation in connection with which the arrest was made;

(b) in the case of a delay during any remaining period for which a person may be detained under section 137C, an officer of the investigating force of a rank above that of inspector who has not been involved in the investigation in connection with which the arrest was made.

12 (1) Section 51 of that Act (duty to consider child's wellbeing) is modified as follows.

(2) Subsection (1) is to be read as if it did not include paragraphs (a), (c) and (d).

Part 3

Arrests in respect of offences committed in Northern Ireland

13 (1) This Part sets out the modifications mentioned in section 137D(4), that is, modifications of the provisions which apply in relation to persons arrested under section 137A in respect of a specified offence committed in Northern Ireland.

(2) Except as expressly provided by this Part, a reference to a constable in any of those provisions is to be read as a reference to a constable of the arresting force.

(3) In this Part, references to the arresting force and the investigating force have the same meaning as in section 137C (see subsection (8) of that section).

14 (1) Article 57 of the Police and Criminal Evidence (Northern Ireland) Order 1989 (right to have someone informed when arrested) is modified as follows.

(2) Paragraph (1) is to be read as if (instead of referring to the case where a person has been arrested and is being held in custody in a police station or other premises) it referred to the case where a person has been arrested under section 137A and is being detained under section 137C.

(3) Paragraph (2)(a) does not apply.

(4) Paragraph (2)(b) is to be read as if (instead of referring to an officer of at least the rank of inspector) it referred—

(a) in relation to delay during the period of 24 hours beginning with the time of the arrest under section 137A, to an officer of the investigating force of at least the rank of inspector;

(b) in relation to delay during any remaining period for which the person may be detained under section 137C, to an officer of the investigating force of a rank above that of inspector.

(5) Paragraph (3) does not apply.

(6) The reference in paragraph (5)(a) to an indictable offence is to be read as a reference to an offence that is an indictable offence under the law of Northern Ireland.

(7) Paragraph (5A)(a) is to be read as if (instead of referring to the person detained for the indictable offence) it referred to the person detained under section 137C.

(8) Paragraph (6)(b) is to be read as if (instead of referring to a person's custody record) it referred to the record made by the arresting force in relation to the person's arrest under section 137A and detention under section 137C.

(9) Paragraph (8) is to be read as if (instead of referring to a person detained at a police station or other premises) it referred to a person detained under section 137C.

15 (1) Article 59 of the Police and Criminal Evidence (Northern Ireland) Order 1989 (access to legal advice) is modified as follows.

(2) Paragraph (1) is to be read as if (instead of referring to a person held in custody in a police station or other premises) it referred to a person detained under section 137C.

(3) Paragraphs (2) and (9)(b) are to be read as if (instead of referring to a person's custody record) they referred to the record made by the arresting force in relation to the person's arrest under section 137A and detention under section 137C.

(4) Paragraphs (3) and (5) do not apply.

(5) Paragraph (6)(a) does not apply.

(6) The reference in paragraph (6)(b) to an officer of at least the rank of superintendent is to be read as a reference to an officer of at least that rank in the investigating force.

(7) The reference in paragraph (8)(a) to an indictable offence is to be read as a reference to an indictable offence under the law of Northern Ireland.

(8) Paragraph (8A)(a) is to be read as if (instead of referring to the person detained for the indictable offence) it referred to the person detained under section 137C.

16 (1) Article 10 of the Criminal Justice (Children) (Northern Ireland) Order 1998 (duty to inform person responsible for welfare of child in police detention) is modified as follows.

(2) Paragraph (1) is to be read as if (instead of referring to the case where a child is in police detention) it referred to the case where a child is being detained under section 137C.

(3) That paragraph is also to be read as if (in addition to the information mentioned in sub-paragraphs (a) to (c)) it also mentioned the information set out in section 137D(1)(a) and (b).

(4) The reference in paragraph (6) to a child's rights under Article 57 of the Police and Criminal Evidence (Northern Ireland) Order 1989 is to be read as a reference to that Article as modified by this Schedule."

SCHEDULE 17

Section 119

CROSS-BORDER ENFORCEMENT: MINOR AND CONSEQUENTIAL AMENDMENTS

PART 1

AMENDMENTS OF PART 10 OF THE CRIMINAL JUSTICE AND PUBLIC ORDER ACT 1994

1 Part 10 of the Criminal Justice and Public Order Act 1994 (cross-border enforcement) is amended in accordance with paragraphs 2 to 8.

Powers of constables of PSNI etc under section 137

2 (1) Section 137 (cross-border powers of arrest etc.) is amended as follows.

(2) In subsection (3), for "the conditions applicable to this subsection are satisfied" substitute "the condition applicable to this subsection is satisfied".

(3) For subsection (6) substitute—

"(6) The condition applicable to subsection (3) above is that it appears to the constable that it would have been lawful for him to have exercised the powers had the suspected person been in Northern Ireland."

(4) In subsection (9), omit the definition of "arrestable offence".

3 In section 138 (powers of arrest: supplementary provisions), omit subsections (3) to (5).

Powers to search premises under section 139

4 (1) Section 139 (search powers available on arrests under sections 136 and 137) is amended as follows.

(2) In the heading, for "sections 136 and 137" substitute "sections 136, 137 and 137A".

(3) For subsection (1) substitute—

"(1) The powers conferred by subsections (2) and (3) are available to a constable in relation to—

(a) a person arrested under section 136(1), (2)(b) or (3)(a);

(b) a person arrested under section 137(1) or (3);

(c) a person arrested under section 137A in respect of a specified offence committed in England and Wales or Northern Ireland."

(4) Omit subsection (3)(b).

(5) After subsection (3) insert—

"(3A) The powers conferred by subsection (3B) are available to a constable in relation to—

(a) a person arrested under section 136(1) or (3)(a) in the execution of a warrant issued in England and Wales in respect of an offence that is an indictable offence in England and Wales;

(b) a person arrested under section 136(1) or (2)(b) in the execution of a warrant issued in Northern Ireland in respect of an offence that is an indictable offence in Northern Ireland;

(c) a person arrested under section 137(1) in respect of an offence that is an indictable offence in England and Wales;

(d) a person arrested under section 137(3) in respect of an offence that is an indictable offence in Northern Ireland;

(e) a person arrested under section 137A(2) or (4) in respect of a specified offence committed in England and Wales;

(f) a person arrested under section 137A(1) or (2) in respect of a specified offence committed in Northern Ireland.

(3B) The constable may enter and search any premises in which the person was when arrested or immediately before he was arrested for evidence relating to the offence."

(6) In subsection (4), after "subsection (3)" insert "or (3B)".

(7) In subsection (7)—

(a) for "subsection (3)(b)" substitute "subsection (3B)";

(b) for "that paragraph" substitute "that subsection".

(8) In subsection (8), for "subsection (3)(b)" substitute "subsection (3B)".

(9) After subsection (10) insert—

"(10A) Where a constable of a police force in England and Wales searches premises in the exercise of the power conferred by subsection (3B) or where a constable of the British Transport Police searches premises in England and Wales in the exercise of that power—

(a) the constable has the same powers as the constable would have under section 19 of the Police and Criminal Evidence Act 1984 if the search had taken place under section 32(2)(b) of that Act, and

(b) sections 21 and 22 of that Act apply in relation to anything seized in the exercise of the powers conferred by paragraph (a) above.

(10B) Where a constable of a police force in Northern Ireland searches premises in the exercise of the power conferred by subsection (3B)—

(a) the constable has the same powers as the constable would have under Article 21 of the Police and Criminal Evidence (Northern Ireland)

Order 1989 (S.I. 1989/1341 (N.I.12)) if the search had taken place under Article 34(2)(b) of that Order, and

(b) Articles 23 and 24 of that Order apply in relation to anything seized in the exercise of the powers conferred by paragraph (a) above.

(10C) Where a constable of a police force in Scotland searches premises in the exercise of the power conferred by subsection (3B), or where a constable of the British Transport Police searches premises in Scotland in the exercise of that power, the constable has the same powers of seizure and retention as the constable would have if the search had taken place in the exercise of a power of the constable (by virtue of any rule of law) in relation to a person arrested and charged with an offence by the constable in Scotland."

(10) In subsection (12)—

(a) in the definition of "premises", at the end of paragraph (b) (before the "and") insert—

"(ba) any renewable energy installation;";

(b) omit the "and" after that definition;

(c) in the definition of "offshore installation" for "section 1 of the Mineral Workings (Offshore Installations) Act 1971" substitute "section 44 of the Petroleum Act 1998";

(d) at the end of the subsection insert "; and

renewable energy installation" has the same meaning as in Chapter 2 of Part 2 of the Energy Act 2004 (see section 104 of that Act)."

Reciprocal powers of arrest - minor correction

5 In section 140 (reciprocal powers of arrest)—

(a) in subsection (1), for the words in brackets substitute "(arrest without warrant)";

(b) in subsection (5), for the words in the second set of brackets substitute "(arrest without warrant)".

References to the British Transport Commission Act 1949 - updating

6 In each of the following places, for references to "section 53 of the British Transport Commission Act 1949" substitute "section 24 of the Railways and Transport Safety Act 2003"—

(a) section 136(1) and (2);

(b) section 137(2A);

(c) section 140(6A).

Other amendments

7 (1) Section 136 (execution of warrants) is amended as follows.

(2) After subsection (4) insert—

"(4A) The following provisions apply in relation to the execution under this section by a constable of a warrant issued in England and Wales or Northern Ireland—

(a) where the warrant is executed under subsection (1), the constable has the same powers of entry and search for the purpose of executing the warrant as a constable of a police force in Scotland would have if the warrant had been issued in Scotland;

(b) where the warrant is executed under subsection (2)(b) or (3)(a), the constable has the powers of entry and search conferred by section 137E;

(c) where the warrant is executed under subsection (1), (2)(b) or (3)(a), the constable has the powers conferred by section 139 in relation to the arrested person;

(d) the constable may use reasonable force, if necessary, in arresting the person or in exercising the powers conferred by sections 137E and 139."

(3) In subsection (5), omit paragraph (a).

8 (1) Section 137 (cross-border powers of arrest etc.) is amended as follows.

(2) After subsection (7) insert—

"(7A) The following provisions apply in relation to an arrest under this section by a constable under subsection (1) or (3)—

(a) where the arrest is under subsection (1) in Northern Ireland or under subsection (3) in England and Wales, the constable has the powers of entry and search conferred by section 137E;

(b) where the arrest is under subsection (1) or (3) in Scotland, the constable has the same powers of entry and search for the purpose of the arrest as a constable of a police force in Scotland would have if there were reasonable grounds for suspecting that the offence had been committed or attempted in Scotland;

(c) the constable has the powers conferred by section 139 in relation to the arrested person;

(d) the constable may use reasonable force, if necessary, in arresting the person or in exercising the powers conferred by sections 137E and 139."

(3) In subsection (8), omit paragraph (a).

PART 2

AMENDMENTS OF OTHER LEGISLATION

Finance Act 2007 (c.11)

9 (1) Section 87 of the Finance Act 2007 (cross-border exercise of powers) is amended as follows.

(2) After subsection (2) insert—

"(2A) In the application of section 137C where a person is arrested under section 137A by an officer of Revenue and Customs in respect of a specified offence that is being investigated by an officer of Revenue and Customs—

(a) subsection (2)(b) is to be read as if (instead of requiring the detention to be authorised by both an officer of at least the rank of inspector in the arresting force and an officer of at least the rank of inspector in the investigating force) it required the detention to be authorised by an officer of Revenue and Customs of at least the grade equivalent to the rank of inspector;

(b) subsection (2)(c) is to be read as if (instead of requiring the detention to be authorised by both an officer of a rank above that of inspector in the arresting force and an officer of a rank above that of inspector in the investigating force) it required the detention to be authorised by an officer of Revenue and Customs of a grade above that equivalent to the rank of inspector;

(c) subsection (3) is omitted;

(d) in subsections (4) and (5), the reference to an officer of the investigating force is to be read as a reference to an officer of Revenue and Customs;

(e) in subsection (6), the reference to an appropriate officer in the investigating force is to be read as a reference to an appropriate officer of Revenue and Customs (as defined by subsection (7));

(f) subsection (6)(a) is omitted;

(g) in subsection (7)(b), the reference to an officer of at least the rank of inspector is to be read as a reference to an officer of Revenue and Customs of at least the equivalent grade;

(h) in subsection (7)(c), the reference to an officer of a rank above that of inspector is to be read as a reference to an officer of Revenue and Customs of above the equivalent grade;

(i) subsections (8) to (10) are omitted.

(2B) Where section 137C applies in accordance with subsection (2A), Schedule 7B applies with the following modifications—

(a) any reference to a constable in the arresting force is to be read as a reference to an officer of Revenue and Customs;

(b) any reference to an officer of at least, or above, a particular rank in the investigating force is to be read as a reference to an officer of Revenue and Customs of at least, or above, the equivalent grade;

(c) any reference to the arresting force or to the investigating force (otherwise than in relation to a description of officer in the force) is to be read as a reference to officers of Revenue and Customs;

(d) instead of the modification made by paragraph 9, section 42 of the Criminal Justice (Scotland) Act 2016 is to be read as if the references in subsections (1)(c)(ii) and (3)(b) to the police were references to officers of Revenue and Customs;

(e) the Schedule is to be read as if it also provided for references in the provisions applied by section 137D(2)(d), (3)(d) and (4)(d) to a police station to include references to an office of Revenue and Customs.

(2C) In the application of section 137C where a person is arrested under section 137A by an officer of Revenue and Customs in respect of a specified offence other than one that is being investigated by an officer of Revenue and Customs—

(a) any reference to an officer of at least, or above, the rank of inspector in the arresting force is to be read as a reference to an officer of Revenue and Customs of at least, or above, the equivalent grade;

(b) the reference in subsection (6)(a) to the arresting force is to be read as a reference to any officer of Revenue and Customs.

(2D) Where section 137C applies in accordance with subsection (2C), Schedule 7B applies with the following modifications—

(a) any reference to a constable in the arresting force is to be read as a reference to an officer of Revenue and Customs;

(b) any reference to the arresting force (otherwise than in relation to a description of officer in the force) is to be read as a reference to officers of Revenue and Customs;

(c) instead of the modification made by paragraph 9, section 42 of the Criminal Justice (Scotland) Act 2016 is to be read as if the references in subsections (1)(c)(ii) and (3)(b) to the police were references to officers of Revenue and Customs;

(d) the Schedule is to be read as if it also provided for references in the provisions applied by section 137D(2)(d), (3)(d) and (4)(d) to a police station to include references to an office of Revenue and Customs."

Crime and Courts Act 2013 (c.22)

10 (1) In Schedule 21 to the Crime and Courts Act 2013 (powers of immigration officers), Part 2 (modification of applied enactments) is amended as follows.

(2) In paragraph 41, for "Paragraphs 42 and 43" substitute "Paragraphs 42 to 43".

(3) After paragraph 42 insert—

"42A (1) This paragraph has effect in relation to the application of section 137C of the 1994 Act where a person is arrested under section 137A by an immigration officer in respect of a specified offence that is being investigated by an immigration officer.

(2) Subsection (2)(b) is to be read as if (instead of requiring the detention to be authorised by both an officer of at least the rank of inspector in the arresting force and an officer of at least the rank of inspector in the investigating force) it required the detention to be authorised by an immigration officer of at least the grade equivalent to the rank of inspector.

(3) Subsection (2)(c) is to be read as if (instead of requiring the detention to be authorised by both an officer of a rank above that of inspector in the arresting force and an officer of a rank above that of inspector in the investigating force) it required the detention to be authorised by an immigration officer of a grade above that equivalent to the rank of inspector.

(4) Subsection (3) is omitted.

(5) In subsections (4) and (5), the reference to an officer of the investigating force is to be read as a reference to an officer of Revenue and Customs.

(6) In subsection (6), the reference to an appropriate officer in the investigating force is to be read as a reference to an appropriate immigration officer (as defined by subsection (7)).

(7) Subsection (6)(a) is omitted.

(8) In subsection (7)—

(a) in paragraph (b), the reference to an officer of at least the rank of inspector is a reference to an immigration officer of at least the equivalent grade;

(b) in paragraph (c), the reference to an officer of a rank above that of inspector is to be read as a reference to an immigration officer of above the equivalent grade.

(9) Subsections (8) to (10) are omitted.

42B (1) Where section 137C applies in accordance with paragraph 42A, Schedule 7B applies with the following modifications.

(2) Any reference to a constable in the arresting force is to be read as a reference to an immigration officer.

(3) Any reference to an officer of at least, or above, the rank of inspector in the investigating force is to be read as a reference to an immigration officer who is at least, or above, the equivalent grade.

(4) Any reference to the arresting force or to the investigating force (otherwise than in relation to a description of officer in the force) is to be read as a reference to immigration officers.

(5) Instead of the modification made by paragraph 9, section 42 of the Criminal Justice (Scotland) Act 2016 is to be read as if the references in subsections (1)(c)(ii) and (3)(b) to the police were references to immigration officers.

42C (1) This paragraph has effect in relation to the application of section 137C of the 1994 Act where a person is arrested under section 137A by an immigration officer in respect of a specified offence other than one that is being investigated by an immigration officer.

(2) Any reference to an officer of at least, or above, the rank of inspector in the arresting force is to be read as a reference to an immigration officer of at least, or above, the equivalent grade.

(3) The reference in subsection (6)(a) to the arresting force is to be read as a reference to any immigration officer.

42D (1) Where section 137C applies in accordance with paragraph 42C, Schedule 7B applies with the following modifications.

(2) Any reference to a constable in the arresting force is to be read as a reference to an immigration officer.

(3) Any reference to the arresting force (otherwise than in relation to a description of officer in the force) is to be read as a reference to immigration officers.

(4) Instead of the modification made by paragraph 9, section 42 of the Criminal Justice (Scotland) Act 2016 is to be read as if the references in subsections (1)(c)(ii) and (3)(b) to the police were references to immigration officers."

SCHEDULE 18

Section 142

LATE NIGHT LEVY REQUIREMENTS

1 Chapter 2 of Part 2 of the Police Reform and Social Responsibility Act 2011 (late night levy) is amended as follows.

2 (1) Section 126 ("relevant late night authorisation" and related definitions) is amended as follows.

(2) In subsection (2)—

(a) for ""Relevant late night authorisation"" substitute ""Relevant late night alcohol authorisation"";

(b) after "licensing authority" insert ", a late night levy requirement";

(c) at the end of paragraph (b) insert "(whether or not it also authorises the provision of late night refreshment at a time or times during such a period)".

(3) After subsection (2) insert—

"(2A) Relevant late night refreshment authorisation", in relation to a licensing authority, a late night levy requirement and a levy year, means a premises licence which—

(a) is granted by the authority,

(b) authorises the provision of late night refreshment at a time or times during the late night supply period on one or more days in the related payment year, and

(c) does not also authorise the supply of alcohol at a time or times during any such period."

(4) After subsection (3) insert—

"(3A) Where a licensing authority decides under section 125(2) to apply a late night levy requirement in respect of both relevant late night alcohol authorisations and relevant late night refreshment authorisations, the licensing authority may determine under section 132(1)—

(a) a single late night levy period that is to apply in respect of both kinds of authorisations, or

(b) two late night levy periods, one of which is to apply in respect of relevant late night alcohol authorisations and the other of which is to apply in respect of relevant late night refreshment authorisations."

(5) In subsection (5), for "The late night supply period" substitute "A late night supply period".

(6) In subsection (8)—

(a) for "the late night levy requirement" substitute "a late night levy requirement";

(b) omit “in its area”.

3 (1) Section 127 (liability to pay late night levy) is amended as follows.

(2) In subsection (1)—

(a) for “the late night levy requirement” substitute “a late night levy requirement”;

(b) after “the area” insert “or part of the area”;

(c) for “a relevant late night authorisation” substitute “a late night authorisation to which the requirement relates”.

(3) In subsection (2), for “a relevant late night authorisation” substitute “a late night authorisation to which the requirement relates”.

(4) After subsection (2) insert—

“(2A) In addition, if the requirement relates to a late night authorisation that is a relevant late night refreshment authorisation, the holder of the authorisation is not liable to pay the late night levy for a levy year if only hot drinks are supplied (or held out for supply) in reliance on the authorisation during the levy year.”

(5) In subsection (3), for “in its area” substitute “in relation to the late night levy requirement”.

4 (1) Section 128 (amount of late night levy) is amended as follows.

(2) In subsection (1) after “For” insert “any levy requirement and”.

(3) In subsection (2), for “a relevant late night authorisation” substitute “a late night authorisation to which a late night levy requirement relates”.

(4) In subsection (3)—

(a) after “in relation to” insert “a late night levy requirement and”;

(b) for “in its area” substitute “in relation to the late night levy requirement”.

(5) In subsection (4)—

(a) for “the late night levy” substitute “a late night levy”;

(b) after “the same” insert “, in respect of all late night levy requirements”;

(c) for “the levy” substitute “a levy”;

(d) omit “for the levy year”.

5 (1) Section 129 (payment and administration of the levy) is amended as follows.

(2) In subsection (1), in the closing words, for “the late night levy” substitute “a late night levy”.

(3) In subsection (2)—

(a) for “the levy” substitute “a levy”;

(b) for “relevant late night authorisations” substitute “a late night authorisation to which a late night levy requirement relates”.

(4) In subsection (4)—

(a) in paragraph (a), for “a relevant late night authorisation” substitute “a late night authorisation to which a late night levy requirement relates”;

(b) in paragraph (b), for "a relevant late night authorisation" substitute "a late night authorisation to which a late night levy requirement relates";

(c) in paragraph (c), for "the relevant late night authorisation" substitute "a relevant late night alcohol authorisation to which a late night levy requirement relates";

(d) in the closing words, for "the levy year" substitute "the levy year in question".

(5) In subsection (5), for "the late night levy" substitute "a late night levy".

(6) In subsection (6), in the closing words, for "the late night levy" (in both places where it occurs) substitute "a late night levy".

6 (1) Section 130 (net amount of levy payments) is amended as follows.

(2) In subsection (1), after "In this Chapter" insert ", in relation to a late night levy requirement,".

(3) In subsection (3), for "the late night levy requirement" substitute "a late night levy requirement".

(4) In subsection (5), in the opening words, at the beginning insert "In relation to a late night levy requirement,".

7 (1) Section 131 (application of net amount of levy payments) is amended as follows.

(2) In subsection (1), at the beginning insert "In relation to a late night levy requirement,".

(3) After subsection (4) insert—

"(4A) The licensing authority must publish information as to how it applies the remainder of the net amount mentioned in subsection (2)(b).

(4B) The information must be published at least once in each calendar year during which any part of the remainder is applied.

(4C) It is for the licensing authority to determine the manner in which the information is published."

(4) In subsection (6)(b), for "in respect of the levy" substitute "in respect of a levy".

8 (1) Section 132 (introduction of late night levy requirement) is amended as follows.

(2) In subsection (1)—

(a) in the opening words, for "the late night levy requirement" substitute "a late night levy requirement";

(b) in those words, omit "in its area";

(c) in paragraph (b)—

(i) in sub-paragraph (i), after "period" insert "or periods (as to which see section 126(3A))";

(ii) in sub-paragraph (ii), omit "in its area";

(iii) in sub-paragraph (iii), omit "in its area".

9 (1) Section 133 (amendment of late night levy requirement) is amended as follows.

(2) In subsection (1)—

(a) in the opening words, for the words from the beginning to "section 125," substitute "Where, in consequence of a decision by a licensing authority under section 125, a late night levy requirement applies,"

(b) in paragraph (a), omit "in the area";

(c) in paragraph (c), for "in the area" substitute "in relation to the late night levy requirement".

(3) After subsection (1) insert—

"(1A) Where the late night levy requirement is in respect of both relevant late night alcohol authorisations and relevant late night refreshment authorisations, the power conferred by subsection (1)(b) includes—

(a) where a single late night levy period applies, power to decide that two late night levy periods are to apply instead;

(b) where two late night levy periods apply, power to decide that a single late night levy period is to apply instead."

(4) In subsection (4)—

(a) in paragraph (b), omit "in the area of a licensing authority";

(b) in that paragraph, after "relevant decision" insert "by a licensing authority";

(c) in the closing words, omit "in its area".

10 (1) Section 134 (introduction or variation of late night levy requirement: procedure) is amended as follows.

(2) In subsection (1)—

(a) in paragraph (a), for "the late night levy requirement" substitute "a late night levy requirement";

(b) in that paragraph, omit "in the area of the licensing authority";

(c) in paragraph (b), for "the late night levy requirement" substitute "a late night levy requirement";

(d) in that paragraph omit "in the area of the licensing authority".

(3) In subsection (2)—

(a) in paragraph (a)(iii), for "relevant late night authorisations" substitute "late night authorisations to which the levy requirement in question relates or would relate";

(b) in paragraph (c)(i), for "so as to cease to be a relevant late night authorisation before the beginning of the first levy year" substitute "so that it is not a late night authorisation to which the levy requirement relates at the beginning of the first levy year".

(4) In subsection (3)—

(a) for "the late night levy requirement" substitute "a late night levy requirement";

(b) omit "to the area of a licensing authority".

(5) In subsection (4)—

(a) for "the late night levy requirement" substitute "a late night levy requirement";

(b) omit "in its area".

(6) Omit subsection (5).

11 (1) Section 135 (permitted exemption and reduction categories) is amended as follows.

(2) In subsection (1)—

(a) in paragraph (a), for "relevant late night authorisations" substitute "relevant late night alcohol authorisations or relevant late night refreshment authorisations";

(b) in that paragraph, for "the requirement to pay the late night levy is not to apply" substitute "no requirement to pay a late night levy is to apply";

(c) in paragraph (b), for "relevant late night authorisations" substitute "relevant late night alcohol authorisations or relevant late night refreshment authorisations";

(d) in that paragraph, for "the levy" substitute "a levy".

(3) In subsection (2), omit "in its area".

(4) In subsection (4)—

(a) in paragraph (a), for "the levy" substitute "a levy";

(b) in paragraph (b), for "the levy" substitute "a levy";

(c) in the closing words—

(i) for "the late night levy" substitute "a late night levy";

(ii) after "the same" insert ", in respect of all late night levy requirements,";

(iii) for "relevant late night authorisations" substitute "relevant late night alcohol authorisations or relevant late night refreshment authorisations";

(iv) omit "for a levy year".

12 After section 136 insert—

"136A Late night levy: requests by relevant local policing bodies

"136A "136A Late night levy: requests by relevant local policing bodies

(1) The relevant local policing body in relation to a licensing authority may request the licensing authority to make a proposal for a decision under section 125(2) that a late night levy requirement of a kind described in the request is to apply.

(2) In deciding whether to make a request, the relevant local policing body must consider the matters mentioned in section 125(3).

(3) A request must be accompanied by any evidence the relevant local policing body has in support of its request.

(4) In deciding how to respond to the request, the licensing authority must consider the matters mentioned in section 125(3).

(5) The licensing authority must publish—

(a) the request, including the evidence accompanying it, and

(b) its response to the request.

(6) The response must include reasons, including an explanation of the outcome of the authority's consideration of the matters mentioned in section 125(3).

(7) It is for the licensing authority to determine the manner in which it publishes the request and its response under subsection (4)."

13 (1) Section 137 (interpretation) is amended as follows.

(2) For "“the late night levy requirement”" substitute "“a late night levy requirement”".

(3) At the appropriate place insert—

"“late night refreshment” has the same meaning as in the Licensing Act 2003 (see Schedule 2 to that Act);".

(4) In the definition of "levy year"—

(a) for "the late night levy requirement" substitute "a late night levy requirement";

(b) omit "in the area of the authority".

(5) In the definition of "payment year", for "a relevant late night authorisation" substitute "a late night authorisation to which a late night levy requirement relates".

SCHEDULE 19

Section 157(5)

AMENDMENTS WHERE NCA IS PARTY TO POLICE COLLABORATION AGREEMENT

Police Act 1997 (c. 50)

1 (1) Section 93 of the Police Act 1997 (authorisations to interfere with property etc) is amended as follows.

(2) In subsection (1B), after "National Crime Agency officer" insert "giving an authorisation on an application made by virtue of subsection (3)(b)(i)".

(3) In subsection (3)—

(a) omit "or" at the end of paragraph (za)(i);

(b) in paragraph (za)(ii) for "section 23(1)" substitute "section 22A";

(c) at the end of paragraph (za)(ii) insert "or

(iii) in a case where the chief officer of police of the authorising force has made an agreement under that section with the Director General of the National Crime Agency, by a National Crime Agency officer (but see subsection (3AA));";

(d) in paragraph (b)—

(i) for "subsection (5)(f), by" substitute "subsection (5)(f)—

(i) by";

(ii) at the end insert "or

(ii) in a case where the Director General of the National Crime Agency has made an agreement under section 22A of the Police Act 1996 with the chief officer of police of one or more police forces, by a member of a collaborative force;".

(4) After subsection (3A) insert—

"(3AA) A National Crime Agency officer may make an application by virtue of subsection (3)(za)(iii) only if permitted by the terms of the agreement mentioned in that provision to make applications for authorisations under this section to the authorising officer of the authorising force.

(3AB) For the purposes of subsection (3)(b), a police force is a collaborative force if—

(a) its chief officer of police is a party to the agreement mentioned in that provision, and

(b) its members are permitted by the terms of the agreement to make applications for authorisations under this section to the authorising officer mentioned in that provision.

Paragraph (b) of subsection (3A) applies for the purposes of this subsection."

(5) In subsection (6)—

(a) after paragraph (aa) insert—

"(ab) in relation to a person within any of those paragraphs to whom an application is made by virtue of subsection (3)(za)(iii), means the area in England and Wales for which—

(i) the person's police force is maintained, or

(ii) any other police force whose chief officer of police is a party to the agreement mentioned in subsection (3)(za)(iii) is maintained,

and which is specified in relation to NCA officers in the agreement mentioned in that provision;";

(b) after paragraph (cb) insert—

"(cba) in relation to a person within subsection (5)(f) to whom an application is made by virtue of subsection (3)(b)(ii), means the area in England and Wales—

(i) for which any collaborative force (within the meaning of subsection (3AB)) is maintained, and

(ii) which is specified in relation to members of that force in the agreement mentioned in subsection (3)(b)(ii);".

Regulation of Investigatory Powers Act 2000 (c. 23)

2 The Regulation of Investigatory Powers Act 2000 is amended as follows.

3 (1) Section 29 (authorisation of covert human intelligence sources) is amended as follows.

(2) For subsection (2A) substitute—

"(2A) For the meaning of "relevant collaborative unit" in subsection (2)(c)(i), see section 29A."

(3) In subsection (4A), at the end of paragraph (a) insert "(see section 29A for the meaning of "qualifying person")".

(4) Omit subsection (7A).

(5) Omit subsection (10).

4 After section 29 insert—

"29A Section 29: supplementary provision in relation to relevant collaborative units

"29A Section 29: supplementary provision in relation to relevant collaborative units

(1) For the purposes of section 29(2)(c)(i), a "relevant collaborative unit" is a unit that falls within subsection (2) or (3).

(2) A unit falls within this subsection if—

(a) it consists of two or more police forces whose chief officers of police have made an agreement under section 22A of the Police Act 1996, and

(b) the agreement relates to the discharge by persons holding offices, ranks or positions with any of the forces of functions in connection with the conduct or use of the covert human intelligence source concerned.

(3) A unit falls within this subsection if—

(a) it consists of one or more police forces and the National Crime Agency,

(b) it is in place by virtue of an agreement made under section 22A of the Police Act 1996, and

(c) the agreement relates to the discharge by persons holding offices, ranks or positions within any such force, or by persons who are National Crime Agency officers, of functions in connection with the conduct or use of the covert human intelligence source concerned.

(4) In the case of a relevant collaborative unit that falls within subsection (2), a person is a "qualifying person" for the purposes of section 29(4A) if—

(a) the person holds an office, rank or position with a police force whose chief officer of police is a party to the agreement mentioned in subsection (2)(a) above, and

(b) the person is permitted by the terms of the agreement to have the responsibility mentioned in section 29(4A)(a) or (c) or the general oversight mentioned in section 29(4A)(b).

(5) In the case of a relevant collaborative unit that falls within subsection (3), a person is a qualifying person for the purposes of section 29(4A) if—

(a) the person—

(i) is a National Crime Agency officer, or

(ii) holds an office, rank or position with a police force whose chief officer of police is a party to the agreement mentioned in subsection (3)(b) above, and

(b) the person is permitted by the terms of the agreement to have the responsibility mentioned in section 29(4A)(a) or (c) or the general oversight mentioned in section 29(4A)(b).

(6) For the purposes of this section references to a police force are to the following—

(a) any police force maintained under section 2 of the Police Act 1996 (police forces in England and Wales outside London),

(b) the metropolitan police force, and

(c) the City of London police force."

5 (1) Section 33 (rules for grant of authorisations) is amended as follows.

(2) In subsection (1), after "(1ZB)" insert "and section 33A".

(3) In subsection (1ZA), for "23(1)" substitute "22A".

(4) In subsection (1A), at the end insert "(subject to section 33A)".

(5) In subsection (3), after "(3ZB)" insert "and section 33A".

(6) In subsection (3ZA), in paragraph (a) for "23(1)" substitute "22A".

(7) In subsection (3A), at the end insert "(subject to section 33A)".

6 After section 33 insert—

"33A Section 33: further provision in cases where NCA is party to collaboration agreement

"33A Section 33: further provision in cases where NCA is party to collaboration agreement

(1) This section applies where the Director General of the National Crime Agency has made a collaboration agreement with the chief officer of police of one or more police forces (a "collaborative police force").

(2) A person who is a designated person for the purposes of section 28 or 29 by reference to an office, rank or position with a collaborative police force may grant an authorisation under that section on an application made by a National Crime Agency officer.

(3) A person who is a designated person for the purposes of section 28 or 29 by reference to their position as a National Crime Agency officer may grant an authorisation under that section on an application made by a member of a collaborative police force.

(4) Authorisations may be granted to persons by virtue of subsection (2) or (3) only if such persons are permitted under the terms of the collaboration agreement to make applications for authorisations under section 28 or 29 to a person who is a designated person for the purposes of that section—

(a) in the case of authorisations granted by virtue of subsection (2), by reference to an office, rank or position with the collaborative police force concerned, or

(b) in the case of authorisations granted by virtue of subsection (3), by reference to the person's position as a National Crime Agency officer.

(5) A person who is a senior authorising officer by reference to a collaborative police force may grant an authorisation for the carrying out of intrusive surveillance on an application made by a National Crime Agency officer.

(6) The Director General of the National Crime Agency, or a person designated for the purposes of section 32(6)(k) by that Director General, may grant an authorisation for the carrying out of intrusive surveillance on an application made by a member of a collaborative police force.

(7) Authorisations may be granted to persons by virtue of subsection (5) or (6) only if such persons are permitted under the terms of the collaboration agreement to make applications for authorisations for the carrying out of intrusive surveillance to a person who—

(a) in the case of authorisations granted by virtue of subsection (5), is a senior authorising officer by reference to the collaborative police force concerned, or

(b) in the case of authorisations granted by virtue of subsection (6), is the Director General of the National Crime Agency or a person designated for the purposes of section 32(6)(k) by that Director General.

(8) In the case of an application made by virtue of subsection (5) or (6) for the carrying out of intrusive surveillance in relation to any residential premises, authorisation may be granted only in relation to premises in the area which is—

(a) the area of operation of a collaborative police force, and

(b) specified in relation to members of that force in the collaboration agreement.

(9) For the purposes of this section the area of operation of a collaborative police force is the area for which that force is maintained.

(10) In this section—

"collaboration agreement" means an agreement made under section 22A of the Police Act 1996;

"collaborative police force" has the meaning given by subsection (1);

"police force" has the meaning given by section 33(5A)."

Adapted and published by GRANGIS under the OGL Licence 3.0.

www.nationalarchives.gov.uk/doc/open-government-licence/version/3/

GRANGIS - UK PUBLISHING 2022.
Thank you for taking the time to leave us a review regarding this version

★★★★★

For further inquiries, contact us at:
www.grangis.com / contact@grangis.com

www.ingramcontent.com/pod-product-compliance
Lightning Source LLC
LaVergne TN
LVHW080545210926
848481LV00024B/2684
* 9 7 9 8 8 8 5 5 9 0 9 6 9 *